SECTARIAN POLITICS IN THE GULF

COLUMBIA STUDIES IN MIDDLE EAST POLITICS

COLUMBIA STUDIES IN MIDDLE EAST POLITICS

MARC LYNCH, SERIES EDITOR

Columbia Studies in Middle East Politics presents academically rigorous, well-written, relevant, and accessible books on the rapidly transforming politics of the Middle East for an interested academic and policy audience.

SECTARIAN POLITICS IN THE GULF

FROM THE IRAQ WAR TO THE ARAB UPRISINGS

FREDERIC M. WEHREY

COLUMBIA UNIVERSITY PRESS

NEW YORK

Columbia University Press
Publishers Since 1893
New York   Chichester, West Sussex
cup.columbia.edu
Copyright © 2014 Columbia University Press
Paperback edition, 2016

Library of Congress Cataloging-in-Publication Data
Wehrey, Frederic M.
Sectarian politics in the Gulf :
from the Iraq war to the Arab uprisings / Frederic M. Wehrey.
p.   cm. — (Columbia studies in Middle East politics)
Includes bibliographical references and index.
ISBN 978-0-231-16512-9 (cloth : alk. paper)—
ISBN 978-0-231-16513-6 (pbk. : alk. paper)—
ISBN 978-0-231-53610-3 (e-book)
1. Persian Gulf States—Politics and government—21st century. 2. Saudi
Arabia—Politics and government—21st century. 3. Shi'ah—Relations—
Sunnites. 4. Sunnites—Relations—Shi'ah. I. Title.
DS247.A138W44   2014
953.05'4—dc23
2013003977

Columbia University Press books are printed
on permanent and durable acid-free paper.
Printed in the United States of America

Cover Design: Thomas Beck Svan
Cover Image: Joseph Eid © Getty

CONTENTS

ACKNOWLEDGMENTS

M any people provided invaluable support throughout the process of researching and writing this book. At every stage, my parents offered much-needed guidance, love, and encouragement. At Oxford, my thesis supervisor, Philip Robins, was a tremendous mentor, coach, and critic. His thoughtful and frequently incisive comments on numerous drafts not only improved the final version but made me a better scholar. Marc Lynch, Toby Craig Jones, Christopher Davidson, Augustus Richard Norton, Edmund Herzig, Louise Fawcett, Matar Ebrahim Matar, Mona Kareem, Gregory Gause, Avi Shlaim, and Jaʿfar al-Shayeb provided helpful critiques of the manuscript at various stages. Samuel Blatteis, Joost Hiltermann, Nathan Brown, Michael Herb, Dafna Rand, Stéphane Lacroix, and ʿAli Al-Ahmed were extremely generous in passing along contacts in the region. As a scholar I have been blessed with a number of colleagues whom I also count as wonderful friends. Many of them provided wise counsel and general encouragement throughout this endeavor: Jerry Green, Michael Doran, Roham Alvandi, Dalia Dassa Kaye, Matteo Legrenzi, Theodore Karasik, and Larry Rubin. Alexandra Siegel, Paul Wulfsberg, Ilonka Oszvald, and Annie Barva deserve special thanks for their editorial assistance in the final stages of this book. Institutional support was crucial throughout the many stages of this book. In this area, I am especially grateful to Marwan

Muasher at the Carnegie Endowment for International Peace and Jim Thomson at the RAND Corporation. The analysis in this book owes much to the numerous interviews I conducted in the Persian Gulf from 2006 to 2012; I extend my deep appreciation to the officials, clerics, youth activists, politicians, scholars, journalists, and astute observers in the region who shared their insights with me.

INTRODUCTION

THE ENIGMA AND PERSISTENCE
OF SECTARIANISM

This study is an exploration of an important but frequently misunderstood source of tension and instability in the Persian Gulf Arab states—the divide between Shiʿa and Sunni adherents of Islam. It aims to offer an explanation for the conditions under which sectarian tensions became a prominent feature of Gulf political life, and it assesses the impact of sectarianism on the region's domestic politics.

The Shiʿa–Sunni split has long perplexed scholars and observers of the Middle East, particularly since 2006. During this momentous year, the civil war in Iraq had risen to a steady crescendo of violence, and it seemed, at least from the outside, that the warring protagonists were lining up neatly along Shiʿa and Sunni lines. Elsewhere in the region, the Lebanese Hizballah had electrified the Arab world with its battlefield performance against the vaunted Israeli army—a triumph that further sharpened Sunni Arab fears about an inexorable "rise of the Shiʿa" and the expanding influence of the Islamic Republic of Iran. In the Gulf, officials, commentators, and everyday citizens grew increasingly wary of the ripple effects of this regional turmoil on their own affairs, with some going so far as to warn that their normally tranquil corner of the Middle East was not immune from the calamity of sectarian strife. Virtually every institution in Manama, Riyadh, and Kuwait City appeared to be shaken by the seemingly tectonic shifts at work in the region: Shiʿa–Sunni discord buffeted the region's media, parliaments, schools, seminaries, and trade unions.

There has been no shortage of efforts in the Arab world to diagnose sectarianism's root causes. For Arab commentators and writers, the culprits range far and wide. Many see Sunni–Shiʿa tensions as the product of meddling by "foreign, extraregional parties"—most commonly, Iran.[1] According to this narrative, sectarianism is a relatively recent and largely artificial import to the region, the product of Iran's 1979 Islamic Revolution. "The arrival of Islamists to power in Iran is the spark that lit the fuse of sectarianism in the Arab world," argued a commentator for al-ʿArabiya television in mid-2012.[2] "Iran is working hard to pour oil on the fire of sectarian rivalries and to light discord between classes of our society," wrote another.[3] Aside from Iran, the United States appears frequently as an instigator, along with Israel. According to this narrative, the disastrous U.S. occupation of Iraq was the chief catalyst for sectarianism's spread across the region, part of a larger diabolical plot by Washington to pit the Arab world against itself.[4] Arab commentators, particularly in the Gulf, increasingly see Iran as working hand in hand with the United States on this plan, often with Israel.[5] More recently, President Bashar al-Asad of Syria and Prime Minister Nuri al-Maliki of Iraq have joined the list of culprits.

A smaller number of Arab writers attributes more local, domestic roots to sectarianism. These writers assign blame to the perfect storm of media (especially satellite TV and social media such as Twitter), domestic extremists (both Sunni and Shiʿa), and political marginalization.[6] Such conditions and their attendant effects on sectarian tensions are especially pronounced in societies emerging from authoritarian rule. An even smaller fringe sees sectarianism as a largely instrumental tool in the hands of authoritarian rulers, who mobilize religious leaders to spread a sectarian discourse with the aim of bolstering their control over society.[7]

In the West, policymakers, analysts, and academics have been similarly fixated on sectarianism. Many latched on to a reading of the Middle East map that lent primacy to sectarianism—an interpretation advanced and popularized by Vali Nasr's famous book *The Shiʿa Revival*.[8] The new Middle East, Nasr argued, would be marked by increasing Shiʿa politicization and assertiveness, which would in turn produce a Sunni countermobilization. There were corresponding discussions in U.S. policy circles that the newly empowered Arab Shiʿa—in particular the Shiʿa seminaries in Najaf, Iraq—might prove a useful counterweight to the Islamic Republic of Iran.[9] Others believed that an ascendant Shiʿa bloc might help America wean itself away from its frequently problematic alliance with Saudi Arabia.[10] The sectarian paradigm, regardless of its policy implications, has proved extremely appealing for policymakers grappling with a rapidly changing Middle East.[11]

And it has persisted, even in the face of other seismic shifts in the region. In the wake of the Arab uprisings, when it seemed that Shiʿa–Sunni tensions had been eclipsed by a potent blend of youthful rage, populism, and class dissent, the sectarian bogeyman lingered. In early 2011, with the fall of U.S.-allied Sunni regimes in Tunis and Cairo, Western policy analysts were arguing that the revolts had taken a decidedly sectarian turn and that Iran, as a patron and provocateur of the Shiʿa, was poised to reap the benefits.[12] By late 2012, though, it seemed the tables had turned. With the battering of the al-Asad regime in Syria, the rise of the Muslim Brotherhood (al-Ikhwan al-Muslimun) in post-Mubarak Egypt, Qatar's activism across the region, and the break between the Islamic Resistance Movement in Palestine (Harakat al-Muqawama al-Islamiyya, better known as HAMAS) and Iran, Western observers proclaimed that the balance of power had shifted in favor of the Sunnis.[13]

Underpinning all the commentary, both Arab and Western, a key question lingers: Why is sectarianism a recurring and much lamented fact of political life in the Middle East and, in particular, in the Gulf? Is it an inescapable historical and cultural reality of the region or the product of manipulation by political elites and the media? A nefarious foreign-policy tool of Iran, the United States, or Saudi Arabia? Or is it simply an artificial construct employed by Western academics to make sense of the region's complex politics?

This book aims to tackle these questions in the context of the Gulf states where the Sunni–Shiʿa divide matters the most: Bahrain, Saudi Arabia, and Kuwait. It aims to uncover why sectarianism has emerged as such a potent force in the political life of these countries by unpacking the interplay between regional turmoil and domestic developments. Starting with toppling of Saddam Husayn and ending with the Arab uprisings of 2011, the study analyzes how regional shocks to the Gulf system have affected sectarianism in each state, either as a political affiliation, a form of societal identification, or a regime strategy to blunt demands for democratic reform. It pays particular attention to the role of domestic institutions—parliaments, consultative councils, local assemblies, clerical establishments, and the media—in both tempering and exacerbating sectarianism.

In this context, sectarianism in the Gulf must ultimately be seen as the result of a damaged ruling bargain: the legitimacy deficit of Gulf rulers, feeble or dysfunctional participatory institutions, and uneven access to political and economic capital bear much of the blame for the prominence of Sunni–Shiʿa tensions in times of regional tumult. Added to these factors has been the dangerous policy of Gulf regimes—in particular Bahrain and Saudi Arabia—of stoking sectarianism to prevent the emergence of broad-based opposition movements. In practice, this has meant portraying Shiʿa activists as the local agents of Iran, Iraq, Hizballah, or Syria to divide them from reform-minded Sunni liberals and Islamists.

THE STRUCTURE OF THE STUDY

The narrative falls into four parts. Part I sets the stage by tracing the roots of sectarianism in the Gulf to the region's societal make-up and governing structures as well as the lingering memory of the Islamic Revolution in Iran. Chapter 1 explores how Shiʿa and Sunni identities have historically interacted with other forms of social and political affiliation in the Gulf. It also shows how the failure of top-down reforms, political exclusion, and the unequal distribution of economic resources sowed the seeds for the mobilization of sectarian identity. The next chapter discusses how these dynamics played out in the wake of the Iranian Revolution—a seismic event whose sectarian aftershocks in the Gulf are still felt today. In many respects, the revolution forms a prism through which Gulf regimes and some Sunni elites continue to view ideological challenges to their authority. Most important, the revolution set a template for sectarian countermobilization that has informed the policies of Gulf governments throughout the post-2003 era and, especially, in response to the contagion of the 2011 Arab uprisings.

The remainder of the book is divided into three parts, each focusing respectively on sectarianism in Bahrain, Saudi Arabia, and Kuwait from 2003 to 2012. For each country, the chapters explore how regional influences and domestic institutional factors combine to affect the attitudes, calculations, and strategies of Shiʿa political actors as well as the policies of Gulf regimes and Sunni elites. In each of these Gulf states, regimes brought to bear co-optive and repressive resources to manage demands for political change; whether by design or accident, these policies frequently ended up inflaming sectarian tensions.

In many respects, then, the protests that crashed over Bahrain and Saudi Arabia in early 2011 are the products of this failed sectarian strategy. The last chapter in each country section discusses these uprisings in depth, showing how Shiʿa actors initially framed their protests as nonsectarian demands for peaceful reform. Very quickly, however, this approach was undone by a combination of domestic and regional factors. These factors include generational and ideological divisions among the Shiʿa, a concerted media and political campaign by Gulf regimes and Sunni elites to tar the protests as sectarian inspired, and the ripple effects of yet another shock to the regional system—the civil war in Syria.

PUTTING SECTARIANISM IN CONTEXT: DOMESTIC AND REGIONAL FACTORS

Like any social and political identity, sectarian affiliation has coexisted alongside a number of other frequently competing attributes—class versus class, tribal versus nontribal, indigenous versus immigrant, settled versus nomadic, generation versus generation, and so on. The doctrinal split between the Sunni and Shiʿa is not itself an a priori determinant of conflict or tension. At various points in history, however, sectarian identity has assumed greater prominence. Political elites have instrumentalized it, and ordinary citizens have defined themselves by it to the exclusion of other affinities.

Contrary to many assumptions in the region, sectarian identity is not "activated" solely by foreign actors or events; its ultimate roots are found in the domestic context, although wars, revolutions, and foreign meddling certainly play a contributing role. The strength of transnational identities across the Arab world—such as sect, ethnic group, and tribe—along with authoritarian rule and weak identification with the state have meant that upheaval in one corner of the region reverberates strongly in another. The Shiʿa–Sunni split is often the lowest common denominator for interpreting these conflicts, and the resulting partisanship is often highly sectarian. The recent explosion of satellite television and social media has amplified this effect.

To fully understand sectarianism, therefore, it is necessary to shift the focus from religious and historical explanations to the complex interplay between domestic and regional factors. Two of these factors have long been the source of misunderstanding and deserve some initial clarification.

Shiʿa Transnationalism and Sectarianism

Of the factors influencing sectarianism in the Gulf, one of the most misunderstood is the nature of the Shiʿa and their transnational affinities. With the exception of Oman, all of the Gulf Cooperation Council states are ruled by Sunni monarchies, and three of them—Bahrain, Saudi Arabia, and Kuwait—contain significant Shiʿa populations that have been afflicted with varying levels of political marginalization, economic deprivation, and religious discrimination. Bereft of social capital and access to political power, the Shiʿa of these states have frequently looked outside the Gulf for empowering, revolutionary ideologies to challenge the monarchical status quo—at various times, these ideologies have included Nasserism, Baʿathism, communism, and revolutionary Islamism from Iran. Familial and clerical bonds that link the Gulf Shiʿa to their coreligionists in Lebanon, Iraq, and Iran have enabled this ideological diffusion. Since the 1990s, however, the majority of Gulf Shiʿa have pushed for their rights within the political framework of their respective states, advocating peacefully for greater reform and sometimes cooperating with Sunni

Islamists and liberals. Nevertheless, suspicion of them persists because of their transnational ties.

Among these ties, the most significant is the uniquely Shi'a religious institution of the *marja' al-taqlid* (literally, "source of emulation"; in practice, venerated senior Shi'a clerics whose edicts provide guidance over spiritual, social, juridical, and, in some cases, political matters). Because the authority of the *marja'* is theoretically not limited by national borders, the institution has proven problematic for Shi'a integration by fueling Sunni suspicions of Shi'a disloyalty to the state. At the core of this suspicion are the questions of whether the transnational authority of the *marja'* is directive or consultative and whether it extends beyond spiritual and social affairs to political matters. Some Shi'a writers have argued that for the Shi'a to truly integrate, they must first reform the institution of the *marja'iyya*, adapting it to the demands of the modern nation-state. This debate is still going on among the Shi'a themselves and has been profoundly affected by regional events.

Regional Shocks and Sectarianism

A second frequently misunderstood facet of sectarianism in the Gulf is the impact of regional upheaval. In the Gulf's modern political life, the most significant of these shocks are the 1979 Iranian Revolution, the Iraq War starting in 2003, the 2006 Lebanon War, and the Arab uprisings of 2011. Contrary to arguments in the Arab world and by some Western analysts, these seminal events contributed to sectarianism but did not cause it.

As noted, Arab commentators frequently blame the 1979 revolution in Iran as the historical wellspring of sectarianism. The Islamic Revolution undoubtedly cast Shi'a–Sunni divisions into sharper relief by injecting an activist, revolutionary sensibility into a Shi'a clerical discourse that had been historically quietist. Added to this, the new Iranian regime pursued an aggressive foreign policy that rejected the very legitimacy of the Gulf monarchs, while providing inspiration and material support for disenchanted Shi'a. But perhaps more important to the spread of sectarianism was the Sunni countermobilization. Faced with a revolutionary challenge from their Persian, Shiʿa-dominated neighbor, the Gulf Arab regimes, in particular Saudi Arabia, deployed Arabism and Salafism as part of a countermobilization strategy, both at home and abroad, to block the contagion of the Islamic Revolution. Although the local Shiʿa benefitted from institutional and economic improvements in the wake of the revolution, they were also subjected to mounting religious discrimination and were forced to demonstrate their nationalist bona fides. The 1990s tempered this pressure somewhat; Iran attempted to repair its relations with the Gulf. Gulf Shiʿa organizations, for their part, abandoned militancy in return for regime promises of political reform and economic improvements.

The 2003 invasion of Iraq and the toppling of Saddam Husayn effectively shattered this equilibrium and reinvigorated the sectarian divide as a feature of Gulf politics. From the Gulf perspective, the fall of the Iraqi dictator raised the specter of a Shiʿa-dominated Iraq that would form linkages with coreligionists in Iran and, more ominously, might inspire the Shiʿa in Saudi Arabia, Bahrain, and Kuwait toward greater agitation and even militancy. In conjunction, Iranian foreign policy took a sharply activist and nationalistic turn with the rise of the so-called new conservatives led by President Mahmud Ahmadinejad. Buoyed by windfall oil prices, Ahmadinejad adopted a strident, jingoistic tone toward the Gulf that stood in stark contrast to the previously more conciliatory approach of Presidents Muhammad Khatami and Hashemi Rafsanjani. Here again, Gulf regimes, lead by Saudi Arabia, mobilized along sectarian lines, deploying Salafism to counter the perceived spread of Iranian influence.

In 2006, the sectarian divide sharpened even more with the Hizballah–Israel war in Lebanon. Across the region, Arab publics applauded Hizballah's battlefield success against the vaunted Israeli military. For Gulf regimes that had historically prided themselves on backing the Palestinian cause, Hizballah's electrifying performance and its affiliation with the Gulf's historic rival, Iran, were tremendously unsettling. The Shiʿa across the region—and, by extension, Iran—appeared to be on the "winning side." Much of the alarm, however, was ultimately over the symbolic damage that the regional tide of events was inflicting on the legitimacy of Arab rulers. There was little danger that Iran or the Shiʿa posed a real *material* threat to the security of Arab regimes, particularly in the Gulf. Nevertheless, Gulf Arab governments became increasingly discomforted by what they saw as the appropriation of traditional pan-Arab virtues—upon which they had attempted to build their domestic legitimacy—by a rival Islamic sect and their Persian adversary.

The most recent and arguably most threatening shock has been the still unfolding uprisings that rocked the Arab world in early 2011. The winds of change were felt the strongest by the Shiʿa of Bahrain and Saudi Arabia but less so by those in Kuwait. The varying levels of protest in each country reflected the degree of Shiʿa integration in each and, more broadly, the distribution of political power and economic resources. In raising their voices, the Gulf Shiʿa were not goaded or inspired by an external Shiʿa patron (Iran, Hizballah, or clerical authorities in Najaf), despite the near-constant worries felt by Gulf regimes and Sunni actors. Rather, the contagion effect on Gulf Shiʿa embodied a markedly *nonsectarian* blend of youthful frustration, populism, and class. Put differently, the Shiʿa of Bahrain and Saudi Arabia rose up in solidarity with the crowds of Tunis and of Tahrir Square in Cairo rather than with their coreligionists in Najaf, Qom, and southern Beirut. That said, the Arab protests in the Gulf—particularly in Bahrain and Saudi Arabia—quickly acquired a sectarian gloss. The regimes and their supporters in these countries resorted to the timeworn tactic of portraying the protests as a bid for Shiʿa supremacy organized by Iran. Some radical voices in the Shiʿa opposition, for their part, found it useful to play up Shiʿa identity and at times to threaten to solicit Iran's support—an unwise attempt at leverage that played into the hands of Gulf regimes. In addition, the civil war in Syria has proven a godsend for Gulf regimes, providing a helpful bogeyman of sectarian strife and offering a useful distraction for their populations. This is especially so for Saudi Arabia, which has taken the most active policy role in Syria among the states under consideration. "The Syria war delayed the Arab Spring in Saudi Arabia by two years," quipped one Saudi reformist in early 2013.[14]

ABBREVIATIONS

AMAL	Lebanese Resistance Detachments (Afwaj al-Muqawama al-Lubnaniyya)
ARAMCO	Arabian American Oil Company; now Saudi ARAMCO
BCHR	Bahrain Center for Human Rights (Markaz al-Bahrayn li-Huquq al-Insan)
BDF	Bahrain Defense Forces
BFM	Bahrain Freedom Movement (Harakat Ahrar al-Bahrayn)
BICI	Bahraini Independent Commission of Inquiry (al-Lajna al-Bahrayniyya al-Mustaqila li-Taqassi al-Haqaʾiq)
BIFM	Bahrain Islamic Freedom Movement (Harakat Ahrar al-Bahrayn al-Islamiyya)
BTV	Bahrain Television
CPVPV	Committee for the Prevention of Vice and the Protection of Virtue (Saudi Arabia)
FJC	Freedom and Justice Coalition (Iʾtilaf al-Hurriyya wa al-ʿAdala) (Saudi Arabia)
GCC	Gulf Cooperation Council
HADAS	Islamic Constitutional Movement (al-Haraka al-Dusturiyya al-Islamiyya) (Kuwait)

HAMAS   Islamic Resistance Movement
        (Harakat al-Muqawama al-Islamiyya) (Palestine)
IAO   Islamic Action Organization
        (Munadhamat al-ʿAmal al-Islami) (Iraq)
IFLB   Islamic Front for the Liberation of Bahrain
        (al-Jabha al-Islamiyya li-Tahrir al-Bahrayn)
INA   Islamic National Alliance
        (al-Tahaluf al-Islami al-Watani) (Kuwait)
ISA   Islamic Salafi Alliance
        (al-Tahaluf al-Islami al-Salafi) (Kuwait)
MP   Member of Parliament
MVM   Movement of Vanguards' Missionaries
        (Harakat al-Risaliyyin al-Talaʾaʿ) (Saudi Arabia,
        Bahrain, Kuwait)
NUG   National Unity Gathering
        (Tajammuʿ al-Wahda al-Wataniya) (Bahrain)
OIC   Organization of the Islamic Conference
        (Munadhamat al-Muʾtamar al-Islami)
OIR   Organization for the Islamic Revolution on the Arabian
        Peninsula (Munadhamat al-Thawra al-Islamiyya fil-Jazira
        al-ʿArabiya) (Saudi Arabia)

SECTARIAN POLITICS IN THE GULF

PART I

THE ROOTS OF SECTARIANISM

ONE

GOVERNANCE, SOCIETY, AND IDENTITY IN THE GULF

Linked together by familial ties and dynastic structures, the rulers of Arab Gulf states constitute a sort of club that is highly conservative in outlook and has proven surprisingly resilient to the ideological forces, revolutions, and coups that have buffeted the rest of the Arab world. At the regional level, these states are part of a multilateral security structure, the Gulf Cooperation Council (GCC), that was formed in response to the 1979 Iranian Revolution. At the individual state level, security policies have typically followed a time-tested pattern: the dispersal of oil rents to placate potential opposition; the reliance on an external security guarantor, tribal patronage, and intermarriage; the construction of nationalist narratives that link the ruling families with the state; and, most recently, carefully calibrated political reforms.[1] Finally, the Gulf system is marked by a high degree of cross-border exchange: people, goods, and, most significantly for this study, ideas.

Aside from these linkages, the Gulf Arab states are united by a shared perception of threat and a shared discourse on security. For Gulf ruling elites, national security is frequently conflated with regime security, and the lines between external and internal security are similarly blurred.[2] F. Gregory Gause III has used Barry Buzan's concept of a "security complex" to argue that the Gulf states, as a whole, spend most of their energy and resources worrying about threats emanating from other states in the Gulf rather than from states outside the region.[3] Most important for this study, he argues that the Arab Gulf states are distinguished by the fact that transnational *ideological* threats—rather than conventional *military* ones—tend to define Gulf regime behavior. Throughout the modern history of the Gulf, these threats have included Nasserism, Ba'athism, communism, and revolutionary Shi'ism from Iran. Post-2003 fears of the so-called Shi'a crescent in the Gulf and the contagion of the 2011 Arab uprisings are only the latest variation of this trend.[4] However, as I describe in the next chapter, this threat is *not* a return to the revolutionary agitation that defined Iran's policy in the Gulf after the 1979 revolution. It nevertheless embodies many of the same features that proved so alarming to Gulf regimes in the 1980s: populism, rejectionism, and pluralism.[5]

A SECTARIAN TRIUMVERATE?

Because of their Shi'a populations, the regimes of Bahrain, Saudi Arabia, and Kuwait have been particularly concerned about the demonstration effect of post-2003 regional upheaval on sectarian tensions within their borders. The seismic events of 2011 only exacerbated these concerns. They thus form a sort of subset within the Gulf security system. In managing— and in some cases exploiting—this threat, these three regimes have frequently cooperated to suppress reform activism within their respective borders.

Much of this coordination over the Shi'a is rooted in fears of a contagion of political liberalization throughout the Gulf—the belief that parliamentary elections or constitutionalism in one state will inspire similar demands in another.[6] As discussed later in this chapter, in campaigning for their communal rights, Shi'a activists often push for political liberalization and frequently cooperate with like-minded reformists, whether secular, leftist, or even Sunni Islamist.[7] It is in the three regimes' interest, therefore, to emphasize the narrowly sectarian character of Shi'a political demands and to exaggerate their linkages to Iran. These tactics appear calculated to divide the Shi'a from other reform activists, to discredit their liberalizing agenda, and to alienate them from the general population.[8]

Below the regime level, there is a long history of political interactions among Shi'a activists and oppositionists in the three states, highlighting the potential diffusion effect of Shiʿa empowerment within the GCC. Much of this diffusion is not surprising, given the familial, tribal, and clerical linkages between the Shiʿa in each state. With regard to political activism, the Shiʿa in each state have long exchanged material and moral support for one another. In the aftermath of the Arab uprisings of 2011, this trend intensified with frequent expressions of mutual solidarity between Shiʿa protestors in Saudi Arabia and Bahrain. That said, there are sufficient differences in outlook and strategies, in addition to the distinctive histories and local context of each state, to undermine the notion of a *deliberately coordinated* Shiʿa movement in the Gulf. Shiʿa leaders themselves frequently acknowledge that each state's unique religious and sociopolitical context demands tailored approaches. For example, in commenting on Sunni–Shiʿa relations in Kuwait, Hassan al-Saffar, a key clerical figure in the Saudi Shiʿa movement, observes that the dominant *madhhab* (Islamic school of jurisprudence) in Kuwait is the Maliki school, which is doctrinally less hostile toward the Shiʿa than is the Hanbali *madhhab* in Saudi Arabia, which in his view creates more favorable conditions for Sunni–Shiʿa dialogue in Kuwait.[9] In other cases, Shiʿa activists are harshly critical of the missteps and mistakes of their coreligionists in other states. As a Saudi Shiʿa reformist noted in a 2007 interview, "The Bahraini Shiʿa made a huge mistake by siding with Iran. We are more mature than the Bahrainis; we have more discussions at the local level. In Bahrain, they are too busy with demonstrations to formulate a long-term agenda. The Saudi Shiʿa, on the other hand, have the 'Partners in One Nation' document."[10]

IDENTITY POLITICS IN THE GULF

Following the idea that Bahrain, Saudi Arabia, and Kuwait constitute a "system-within-a-system" due to their shared perceptions of threat and the ties among their respective Shiʿa communities, this section turns to exploring the politics of identity in the Gulf. Unpacking the overlapping and frequently competing forms of Gulf identity is important for understanding how states and nonstate actors responded to post-2003 events.

In terms of governance, identity can be a resource to be mobilized or exploited by rulers. But it is also a vulnerability—a fissure that is susceptible to external ideologies or regional shocks. For the Gulf states under examination, the key question is the extent to which Sunnism and Shiʿism have been meaningful categories of identity, at what level, and how they have been mobilized or exploited by various actors.[11] Similarly, what are the other competing forms of identity (nationalism, Arabism, or ecumenical notions of Islamic solidarity) that are either imposed from above or have emerged from below?

Degrees of Inclusion: Islam, Arabism, and Sunnism

Of the six GCC states, five are ruled over by Sunni families.[12] Despite this, sectarian primacy has generally not been one of the central ideological pillars of official governance in the GCC. As Michael Herb notes, the GCC regimes "do not stress Sunnism as the cornerstone of their identity. . . . [They] are not Sunni in the sense that the Turkish state is Turkish."[13] At the ideational level, therefore, the regimes of the Gulf have historically deployed ecumenical forms of Islam and Arabism to buttress their standing, both within individual states and within the broader inter-Arab and regional arena. The legitimacy of Gulf rulers is thus tied in part to how well their domestic governance and foreign policy reflects these norms, particularly in times of regional challenges on the Arab–Israeli front or from the Islamic Republic of Iran.

But in the post-2003 environment, the norms of Arabism and Islam in the Gulf became increasingly conflated with Sunnism by regimes and pro-regime voices. This conflation was largely a defensive reaction to the regional rise of Iran and its usurpation of causes that had traditionally been the sole purview of Sunni Arab powers. In the wake of the Arab uprisings of 2011, this dynamic intensified as Gulf regimes—in particular Bahrain and Saudi Arabia—used sectarianism to stave off the wave of populist contagion from Tunis and Tahrir Square.

National Identity and Sectarian Challenges

Several Gulf states have more recently undertaken ambitious projects for inculcating their respective publics with state-centric nationalism.[14] This nationalism is a relatively novel form of self-identification, given the long-standing importance of tribal ties and Islam as pillars of governance and the fact that the Gulf did not experience the wrenching process of violent decolonization that produced a more dialectical form of nationalism in other Arab states.[15] A number of postcolonial shifts in the regional and global environment has aided regimes in implementing these programs. As discussed in the next chapter, the external specter of the 1979 Iranian Revolution and its aftermath helped solidify nationalist sentiment in the Gulf, while at the same time bolstering the role of conservative Islam in political and public life.

This was particularly so in Saudi Arabia, which mounted a concerted attempt to "out-Islamicize" the Islamic Republic. In the case of Kuwait, the Iraqi occupation of 1990–1991 had a galvanizing effect on national self-identification—especially among the Shiʿa, who were able to parlay their role in the anti-Iraqi resistance into greater recognition by the state. In Saudi Arabia, the environment after September 11, 2001, with its attendant threat of American intervention and the rumored dismemberment of the kingdom, helped rally the Saudi populace behind the idea of national unity.[16] The U.S. invasion of Iraq and the resulting fear of Iranian power and sectarian strife also aided regime-sponsored nationalist projects in the Gulf. What becomes less clear is the impact of the Arab uprisings. In meeting the spillover of the uprisings, Gulf regimes have resorted to the timeworn strategies of providing subsidies and attempting to portray opposition movements as narrowly sectarian in character. But the long-term sustainability of this is uncertain.

Aside from being a more recent component of regimes' nationalist projects, sectarianism is present at the societal level. Historically, its manifestations are stronger during times of upheaval and distress, particularly among those denied access to political capital and economic resources. Yet it has also proven expedient and useful for actors who are closely affiliated with regimes. For example, for the Salafi clerical establishment in Saudi Arabia, sectarianism has very real, material benefits; it ensures their continued and exclusive access to political power. The formal recognition of Shiʿa identity—whether in the political, legal, or cultural sphere—would effectively undermine this primacy. In other cases, sectarianism can be a useful instrument for political elites, in particular candidates in elections or parliamentary members, to rally constituents or deflect criticism over their failings in office. And as mentioned previously, Gulf regimes themselves have at times found it useful to paint the reformist opposition as explicitly sectarian in character as a sort of divide-and-rule tactic or in order to deflect pressures for democratization. In other cases, self-awareness of sectarianism has increased in public space because of regional events. Commentators frequently blame this phenomenon on external manipulations—the product of a Saudi–Iranian proxy struggle or a U.S.-inspired plot to weaken and divide the Islamic *ummah* (community).[17]

At various points in history, however, sectarian identity has become "politicized" and a more prominent marker than other forms of affiliation. A common refrain in the Gulf is that the 1979 Iranian Revolution was responsible for this "activation" of Shi'a identity in the Gulf and that the process was repeated in the wake of the 2003 Iraq invasion and the subsequent rise of Iranian power.[18] Similarly, outside observers and Gulf regimes themselves frequently point to the uniquely Shi'a institution of the *marja'iyya* and its transnational authority as an obstacle to Shi'a integration and a recurring source of sectarian tensions.[19]

A more nuanced interpretation, acknowledges the contributing effect of these regional events and transnational influences but locates the causal roots of this politicization (the so-called Shi'a revival) in the *domestic* distribution of power in the Gulf states themselves—specifically, the exclusion of the Shi'a from governance and economic resources and the capacity (or incapacity) of the state's institutions.

GOVERNANCE, SOCIETY, AND THE SHI'A

Bahrain, Saudi Arabia, and Kuwait share both similarities and differences in their domestic structures and resources: bureaucracies, participatory institutions, and oil wealth. It is important to understand these variables both as tools for governance—the capacity to co-opt and coerce political opposition—but also as filters through which regimes mediate the impact of the regional environment.[20] In many respects, then, these institutions act as a sort of buffer between Gulf societies and transnational forces— that is, ideologies, ideas, and events. Their maturity and strength, this study argues, has played a determinant role in managing sectarianism in each state's domestic politics.

To set the stage for this analysis, the following sections offer a case-by-case overview of each state's political structures, societal divisions, and reform processes as well as their respective Shi'a communities. It is important to note here that the Shi'a communities in each state do not constitute a monolithic bloc. Shi'a politics are stratified by class, ideology, clan, and personality distinctions. That said, within the larger context of Gulf reform and threat perception, it is analytically useful to speak of Shi'ism as a form of identity.

BAHRAIN

Bahrain's domestic context is distinguished from that of the other GCC states by several factors relevant to this study. Bahrain is the Gulf's first postoil economy: unlike the other GCC states, it is largely bereft of petroleum reserves and depends on income from tourism, banking, heavy industry, and Saudi subsidies. The absence of rent has significantly impacted the regime's calculations and strategies toward domestic reform. Since 1999, it has used carefully calibrated liberalization and the provision of social services as a means to stave off domestic dissent, while also proving adept at playing societal and political groups against one another.[21]

To understand the nexus between external events and sectarianism in Bahrain, it is important to trace the legacy of the country's brief democratic experiment in the early 1970s. From 1961 through 1999, Bahrain's political landscape was effectively dominated by a partnership between the emir, 'Isa bin Salman, and his brother, the prime minister, Khalifa bin Salman. Under the two, a sort of division of labor emerged, with the emir enjoying greater popularity because of his accessibility and espousal of reform and the prime minister, who supervised much of kingdom's bureaucracy, budget, and security forces, acting the part of the authoritarian overseer.

In 1973, the emir oversaw the opening of a thirty-person elected Parliament with full legislative power, inaugurating a brief period of participatory politics in Bahrain.[22] But in 1975 the emir abruptly closed the

Parliament due to a burgeoning alliance between leftist and religious blocs that would have effectively overturned a repressive state security law. As Bahraini scholar Abdulhadi Khalaf has argued, the first Parliament was never a truly democratic body, but rather a form of institutionalized tribalism and sectarianism with certain rules of conduct; once those rules were breached by an emerging nationalist coalition that sought to erode the ruling Al Khalifa family's absolutism, the experiment was ended.[23] The Parliament thus served as a template for the way quasi-democratic structures are used by the Bahraini ruling family to manage and exploit sectarianism—a trend discussed at greater length in subsequent chapters.

Democratic reforms during the first half of the 1990s were mostly cosmetic. In 1993, the emir created an unelected Consultative Council (Majlis al-Shura), which possessed no legislative power and did not lead to any significant policy changes. The outbreak of major political violence in 1994 and extending through 1999 (whose roots are discussed in greater depth later) injected an economic urgency to the demands for more substantial political reforms. Aside from Saudi oil subsidies, Bahrain's economy is largely dependent on financial services, off-shore banking, tourism, and some heavy industry—all of which were threatened by anti-regime unrest.[24]

It was not until the 1999 accession of Crown Prince Hamad bin ʿIsa to the throne that more substantial reforms began to take shape. Here again, the driver appears to have been largely economic and preemptive—a tactic to reassert state control after nearly six years of unrest, but without fundamentally altering the relationship between ruler and ruled.[25] The new reforms, framed by the emir as "concessions," included the right to form political parties or "associations," the curtailment of state security laws, the release of 320 political prisoners—including a revered Shiʿa cleric who had been a major inspiration behind the dissent of 1994—the pardoning of dissidents abroad, and the creation of a forty-person elected Parliament.[26] The removal of the despised British chief of the Bahraini security services, Ian Henderson, and the disbandment of the security agency responsible for the mid-1990s crackdown were greeted with particular applause. In 2001, the emir introduced the National Action Charter, which called for the creation of a constitutional monarchy, a bicameral legislature for a National Assembly (Parliament) structure composed of an elected Council of Representatives (lower house) and an appointed Consultative Council (upper house), an independent judiciary, and women's political participation. It also gave all men and women older than twenty the right to vote. The document was widely endorsed in a national referendum in February 2001. The net effect of these initiatives was to create a state of near euphoria, particularly among lower-class Shiʿa.[27]

By 2002, however, these reforms had either stalled or evaporated, fueling new levels of cynicism and resentment, particularly among the Shiʿa. In October 2002, the emir, having now designated himself king and his son Salman the crown prince, issued restrictive press and publication laws that gave the regime widespread censorship power. More important, the king unilaterally revised the 1973 Constitution, subordinating the elected Parliament to an appointed Consultative Council and depriving the Parliament of the ability to formally introduce new legislation or exert financial oversight over government ministries.[28] The weakening of this elective body, along with electoral gerrymandering designed to ensure Sunni dominance, spurred a widespread Shiʿa boycott of the 2002 parliamentary elections. The result was a Parliament dominated disproportionately by Sunni Muslim groups.

The Bahraini Shiʿa

Alone among the other Gulf states, Bahrain has a majority Shiʿa population, estimated at 70 percent.[29] A strong narrative of disenfranchisement informs the Shiʿa's collective memory; historic Shiʿa control of Bahrain since 1500 was overturned in 1782 with the conquest of the island by the Al Khalifa family. A long period of feudal-like governance thus ensued, with the Al Khalifa relegating the Shiʿa to the status of tenant cultivators—a relationship that was buttressed by assistance provided to the ruling family by Sunni Arab peninsular tribes such as the al-Dawasir. In the Shiʿa collective memory, therefore, the Al Khalifa and their tribal allies are frequently described as usurpers and conquerors.

In recent years, the Shiʿa have enjoyed the freedom to express their religious identity through their own mosques and mourning houses, or maʾatim. For example, the government does not hinder the two-day Shiʿa celebration of Ashura, and the Bahraini Ministry of Information has provided full media coverage of this event. Yet Shiʿa continue to suffer politically and economically. They are underrepresented in key government ministries and are prohibited from serving in Bahrain's security forces.[30] In the economic sphere, the Shiʿa constitute a large portion of Bahrain's labor force, which is in part a legacy of their historically lower status as pearl divers, cultivators, and employees of Bahrain's oil company, the Bahrain Petroleum Company, before the decline of Bahrain's oil reserves in the 1970s and partly the result of continued government discrimination.[31] A strong sense of class-based resentment therefore fuels Shiʿa activism. Many of their grievances stem from the uneven distribution of resources, housing shortages, unemployment, corruption, and the ruling family's perceived nepotism—concerns they share with lower- and middle-class Sunnis.

Overlaying the class and political dimension, there are divisions along ethnic lines between baharna (sing. bahrani) and ʿajam Shiʿa that have important implications for understanding sectarian dynamics in the kingdom. The baharna are Shiʿa of Arab origins who migrated to Bahrain to escape political and religious persecution during the ʿAbbasid and ʿUmmayyad caliphates. The baharna are the principal proponents of the narrative of Shiʿa "authenticity," arguing that the archipelago was a Shiʿa Arab state before its conquest by the Sunni Al Khalifa and their allied tribes in 1782. There are strong familial linkages between the baharna Shiʿa and the Shiʿa of the Qatif and Ahsa oases in eastern Saudi Arabia. The baharna have typically filled Bahrain's working class as laborers, cultivators, pearl divers, and oil workers.

The ʿajam are ethnic Persians who came to Bahrain from Iran, many in the first part of the twentieth century, and currently occupy positions in the merchant class and intelligentsia. They historically have suffered the greatest repression from the Bahraini regime because of their ties to Iran; until 2000, they were denied full citizenship. That said, they have tended to avoid political activism, given their dependence on the regime. There has been little intermarriage or interaction between the ʿajam and the *baharna*. However, one by-product of the revolt stemming from the 2011 Arab uprisings (discussed at length in chapter 5) has been increased cooperation between the ʿajam and *baharna*.[32]

Shiʿa activism in Bahrain has been the most vocal and, at times, militant among the three cases under examination. As discussed in the next chapter, a strong legacy of distrust informing the regime's views of the Shiʿa stems from the 1980s and early 1990s, when Iranian-backed Shiʿa groups such as the Bahraini Hizballah and the Islamic Front for the Liberation of Bahrain (IFLB, al-Jabha al-Islamiyya li-Tahrir al-Bahrayn) called for the overthrow of the Al Khalifa. The decline of these groups was the result of changes in Iranian policy as well as the holding of parliamentary elections, which facilitated the ascendancy of Shiʿa moderates while marginalizing hardliners.[33]

Prior to the uprising of early 2011, the most serious episode of unrest in Bahrain was the 1994–1999 intifada.[34] A demand for a return to the 1973 Constitution provided the framing of the revolt and the arbitrary arrest of a young Shiʿa cleric, ʿAli Salman, lit the spark. The protests appear to have been also rooted in new economic and social policies that affected small shopkeepers, industrial workers, and Shiʿite women.[35] The shift from violent opposition tactics, such as bombings, to a more peaceful repertoire of mass demonstrations beginning in April 1998 was not directly the result of reforms, but because the regime allowed these expressions of dissent, while it simultaneously eroded popular support for the "fringe" by inflicting collective punishment on entire villages beginning in the fall of 1997.[36] The uprising's suppression via mass punishment coincided with the ascension of the new emir to the throne, raising expectations for a new era of change.

It is important to recognize the prominence of this uprising in the historical memory of Shiʿa activists today. On the eve of the 2006 parliamentary elections, several Shiʿa activists—one of whom was a major inspirational force behind the 1994 intifada—indicated that the cycle of cynicism had once again swung full circle, with youthful anger approximating the level of the early 1990s.[37] Yet as discussed more fully in chapter 3, this disenchantment produced splits in the Shiʿa movement between those willing to participate in the country's parliamentary elections and those espousing a more rejectionist stance.

SAUDI ARABIA

Among the case countries, Saudi Arabia is unique because of the magnitude of oil rent and the influence of its Salafi religious bureaucracy on domestic policies—particularly toward Shiʿa cultural and religious identity.[38]

The main contours of the kingdom's first push toward reform occurred in the aftermath of the 1991 Gulf War. It is important not to overstate these initiatives as truly democratic in character; as discussed later, the country has been consistently placed at the bottom of the Freedom House rankings and remains one of the most closed, authoritarian states in the world. These moves should instead be viewed as proto-democratic but significant in the Saudi context in the sense of opening channels of communication between ruler and ruled in a society where political quietism was both expected and largely embraced.

Ironically, some of the kingdom's initial steps in this direction were the result of pressure from decidedly undemocratic quarters—the loose current of Salafi clerics and activists inspired by Muslim Brotherhood ideology, who later came to be known as the Sahwa or "awakened" clerics.[39] Enraged by the Al Saʿud regime's decision to allow U.S. troops on Saudi soil and critical of the clerical establishment's sanctioning of this move, these figures became increasingly politicized, airing their grievances against the regime in public through popular TV programs and sermons and submitting a set of petitions in 1991 and 1992.[40] Although these petitions sought to bolster clerical primacy in the kingdom's social affairs, they also called for an end to corruption and nepotism, the appointment of a consultative council free from government influence, and increased freedom of expression.[41] This movement had a ripple effect on subsequent reform initiatives with a more universal focus. As Gwenn Okruhlik notes, "Islamists opened the floodgates of criticism in the kingdom by invoking the Islamically grounded right to advise the ruler."[42] At the same time, petitions emerged from Shiʿa clerics and activists that also endorsed a consultative council, but with more emphasis on ending sectarian discrimination.

These early petitions are significant for several reasons. First, the very act of submitting them marked the injection of "issues" into the public

realm, a radical departure from the closed nature of governance deliberations in the kingdom and the clerical practice of offering *nasiha* (advice
or exhortation) to the Al Saʿud *in private*.[43] Several activists, including a
Salafi reformist close to the Sahwa, noted that the establishment of public channels of communication with the ruler—whether through petitions, the series of National Dialogues begun in 2003, or the municipal
councils—has increased the legitimacy of the Al Saʿud and fostered a
normative shift with respect to dissenting opinions. Second, the clerical
nature of these early demands enabled the regime, via quasi-democratic
reforms, to co-opt and split the Sahwa clerics, some of whom were a major
ideological source for al-Qaʿida, in both its domestic and its international
manifestations.[44]

Responding to the petitions, in 1992 the king promulgated the Basic
Laws—a semiconstitutional document that set up the sixty-person[45] Consultative Council, whose membership is technocratic and geographically
diverse, and whose statutes include the right to question cabinet members
and review government social and economic policies before promulga-
tion. Although this body has fallen short of its original mandate, it provides an aspirational framework for democracy activists in the kingdom
today; in March 2007, reformists in Jeddah, Riyadh, and the Eastern Province listed direct elections to the Consultative Council as one of their top
reform priorities.[46]

The Saudi Shiʿa

In Saudi Arabia, the Shiʿa comprise an estimated 10 percent of the population and are concentrated in the eastern provinces of the country.[47] As
in Bahrain, they have been systematically excluded from major government ministries, the armed forces, and the security services. Also like in
Bahrain, Shiʿa–Sunni tensions are overlaid with center–periphery tensions and class differences. In 1913, the predominately Shiʿa areas of Ahsa
and Qatif were brought under the control of Ibn Saud and his tribal allies from the central Najd region and later incorporated into the modern
Saudi state in 1932. In the subsequent period of nation building, the eastern areas remained subordinated to the central Najd region—in economic

development, political power, and prominence in the state's official narratives. Authenticity and colonial subjugation are therefore key themes in Saudi Shiʿa discourse—Saudi Shiʿa activists, like the *baharna* in Bahrain, typically emphasize their indigenous roots with self-referential terms as *al-asala al-shiʿiya* (Shiʿa authenticity) and *abnaʾ al-mintaqa* (sons of the region). Government policies, in contrast, are denounced for their exclusive character with such neologisms as *al-ʿasabiyya al-madhhabiyya* (sectarian solidarity) and *tanjid* (literally, "to make something Najdi").[48]

This political and provincial marginalization has been compounded by religious discrimination that is largely a function of the symbiotic and pragmatic alliance between the ruling Al Saʿud and the Salafi religious establishment. In return for legitimating the family's rule, the Salafi establishment is allowed a prominent place in the kingdom's public and social discourse. Although the clerics are hardly uniform in their outlook toward the Shiʿa, they are generally united in the view that the Shiʿa are deviants from the Salafi view of Islamic orthodoxy and are consequently denigrated as *rawafidh* (rejectionists; singular, *rafidha*). Adding to this rhetorical exclusion, the Shiʿa have faced difficulty operating their own mosques, practicing the Jaʿfari code of jurisprudence, and maintaining mourning houses (*husayniyat*, the equivalent of Bahrain's *maʾatim*).[49]

Yet, as discussed in the next chapter, the Saudi Shiʿa have generally eschewed militancy or ties to Iran. In 1993, the militant Shiʿa leadership of the Organization for the Islamic Revolution on the Arabian Peninsula (OIR, Munadhamat al-Thawra al-Islamiyya fil-Jazira al-ʿArabiya) returned home from exile and, in return for promising to abandon violence, received assurances from the Saudi government regarding reform and a redress of Shiʿa grievances.[50] Saudi Shiʿa opposition activity since then has consisted largely of petitions, participation in municipal council elections, and cooperation with like-minded reformists among Saudi liberals and Sunni Islamists. In tandem, Saudi Shiʿa intellectuals and writers have offered counternarratives of state formation, deploying the vocabulary of authenticity and national belonging.[51] Some Shiʿa lay activists have gone further, arguing that reform *within* the Shiʿa community itself is a prerequisite for any national integration—specifically, a rethinking and reinterpretation of the institution of the *marjaʿiyya*.[52]

In contrast to these reform-minded activists and intellectuals, a few Saudi Shiʿa clerical figures continue to adopt a more rejectionist view, advocating a boycott of Saudi state institutions. In the wake of the 2011 uprisings, a new cadre of youth activists has emerged that has challenged the authority of the older clerical reformists by arguing that participation in state institutions and dialogue has produced few improvements.[53] Subsequent chapters explore how the balance of power between these currents in the Saudi Arabian Shiʿa community was affected by post-2003 changes in the regional environment and especially the 2011 Arab uprisings.

KUWAIT

Kuwait differs significantly from Bahrain and Saudi Arabia in a number of areas: the strength of its participatory institutions and the integration of its Shiʿa into political life, economic realm, and narrative of the state's formation. It is frequently held up as the success story among the three cases—a state where a strong constitution, an empowered parliament, a relatively independent press, and a civil society embodying the tribal precepts of *shura* (consultation) and *diwaniya* (discussion venues) have combined with plentiful oil reserves to bolster the ruling family's legitimacy and to mitigate social dissent. That said, a number of scholars have recently challenged this narrative, highlighting the salience of sectarianism as a political fissure and critiquing the shortcomings of the state's political institutions.[54] Kuwait, like the rest of the Gulf, has not been completely immune to transnational ideological threats with the potential to mobilize opposition to the ruling family and fray the country's social fabric.[55] In the post-2003 era, this has been especially apparent during the sectarian aftershocks of Lebanon's 2006 war and in the aftermath of the Arab uprisings of 2011.

Kuwait's progress on reform, although notable and significant in the Gulf context, has been far from even or linear. Many of the ruling family's initial steps toward liberalization were prompted by the perception of external threat and the need to solidify its constituents' loyalty.[56] The first Constituent Assembly (al-Majlis al-Taʾsisi) was elected in 1961, and a fifty-member National Assembly or Parliament was elected in 1963. Compared to the governmental bodies in the rest of the Gulf, the Kuwait Parliament is endowed with broad powers of accountability and oversight. Although it cannot issue a vote of no confidence for an entire cabinet, it can nevertheless declare that it will not cooperate with the cabinet or with the prime minister and can subject individual ministers to questioning or "interpellation" (*istijwab*).[57]

Despite this progress, limits exist. The ruling family maintains broad control over key ministry posts and can exercise ultimate control over the Parliament through the threat of suspension—a threat that technically violates the Constitution, but that the family has nevertheless implemented on two separate occasions when the emir believed the Parliament had grown too powerful (1976–1981 and 1986–1992). Yet the most glaring defects of Kuwait's reform process derive from within the Parliament itself. Specifically, a lack of coordination among deputies and the tendency for representatives to use the Parliament as a platform for parochial skirmishing rather than for legislating programs have limited its legislative and oversight ability. Moreover, as later chapters show, in times of regional conflict the Parliament has been buffeted by increased sectarian wrangling and grandstanding. Such fissures have important implications for Kuwait's democratic progress. As Michael Herb has argued, "Kuwait tends to make progress toward democracy only when the parliamentary opposition overcomes its internal differences and demands concessions from the ruling family."[58] In addition, the extent of parliamentary criticism is further circumscribed by the Al Sabah family's control of oil rents. Kuwaiti citizens know that their livelihood depends in large measure on this regime-controlled resource. Thus, oppositionists rarely overstep certain red lines in criticizing the ruling family.

In tandem with the formal institution of parliament, Kuwaiti politics is distinguished by a strong associational life and nascent civil society. Much of this openness dates back to eighteenth-century concepts of *shura* (consultation). In the 1990s and early 2000s, this informal participation was given structure in the practice of the *diwaniya*. In these semiprivate, salonlike venues, political matters, justice, the economy, and societal issues are aired, discussed, and debated. The *diwaniya* are therefore important accommodative resources for the Kuwaiti government. Though not completely egalitarian in nature, they serve an important function by fostering an informed citizenry and creating a sense of political community. Added to these precepts is Kuwait's historically open print media and television coverage. As Mary Ann Tétreault notes, "One of the strongest democratizing institutions in Kuwait is the space created by widespread consumption of news and opinion in the print press and at *diwaniya*."[59]

The Kuwaiti Shi'a

Kuwaiti Shi'a have historically enjoyed better access to Kuwaiti political institutions and economic resources than their counterparts in Bahrain and Saudi Arabia. Unlike in Bahrain and Saudi Arabia, no historical narratives of resistance to territorial usurpation inform the Kuwaiti Shi'a collective memory. Kuwaiti Shi'a make no claim to being the original inhabitants of Kuwait and in fact acknowledge their diasporic identity. That said, several societal divisions exist that have fractured the parliamentary opposition and enable the ruling family to employ divide-and-rule tactics. Most significant, the *hadhar–badu* divide is a key fissure that straddles sectarian boundaries. The *hadhar* are Kuwait's settled, merchant class centered in Kuwait City, whereas the *badu* are the rural, historically nomadic inhabitants in the districts lying outside the capital.[60] These identity categories have important implications for understanding political mobilization in Kuwait—the wealthier *hadhar* have formed the backbone of support for the Al Sabah, whereas the historically marginalized *badu* have frequently composed the opposition, often forming the core of Kuwait's Salafi movement. Kuwaiti Shi'a themselves are further divided between Arab Shi'a who hail from the Ahsa oasis in Saudi Arabia and Bahrain (the *hasawiyyin* [sing. *hasawi*] and the *baharna* [sing. *bahrani*], respectively) and the *'ajam*, or those of Iranian descent.

The Kuwaiti Shi'a possess relative freedoms in multiple areas. In the economic sphere, they occupy a different social strata than their counterparts in Bahrain and Saudi Arabia. They are largely middle class and constitute some of Kuwait's most important merchant families. In the religious realm, the Kuwaiti Shi'a enjoy freedom of worship and the ability to practice the Ja'fari creed in school. For its part, the Al Sabah has relied on the Shiʿa as counterweights to political challenges from Kuwaiti Sunni notables and, later, from Arab nationalists. As discussed in the next chapter, this contract endured from 1938 until the post-1979 period of political violence, when the Shiʿa community fell under the leadership of Iranian-inspired clerics and when Shiʿa deputies in Parliament began to challenge the Al Sabah openly. The relationship was later repaired through the ruling family's judicious use of reforms and liberalization following the Iraqi occupation of 1990–1991, but it was never fully restored.

Thus, in the run-up to the 2003 period, Kuwaiti Shiʿa had much more favorable perceptions of the Al Sabah's legitimacy than their counterparts in Bahrain and Saudi Arabia did of their ruling families. Shiʿa oppositionists have frequently attached themselves to the Kuwaiti reform movement, allying themselves with liberal Sunni Islamists.[61] Yet these bonds were frayed in the wake of the Iraq War and, especially in the aftermath of the Arab uprisings.

State–society relations in Bahrain, Saudi Arabia, and Kuwait provide the backdrop for understanding the new politics of sectarianism in the post-2003 era. Political institutions, reform processes, and the balance of power between different societal actors are crucial for assessing how and why sectarianism arises in the Gulf.

The three countries also constitute a unique security "subsystem" in the Gulf because of their regimes' shared perception of the Shiʿa threat, albeit at different levels. The rulers of each state have all used Arabism, Islam, and monarchical privilege as norms of governance and legitimacy. Sectarianism has presented a challenge to these norms, often as a result of external regional events and internal power disparities. But sectarianism has more frequently served as a useful instrument for regimes and their supporters to deflect pressures for reform, mobilizing their populations against an external challenge, and to divide the opposition. The template for this sectarian strategy, which continues today, was first applied in the aftermath of the 1979 revolution in Iran.

TWO

THE LONG SHADOW OF THE
IRANIAN REVOLUTION

To understand Shiʿa–Sunni relations in the post-2003 era, it is important first to examine the seminal impact of the Iranian Revolution on Gulf societies. A seismic event in Gulf political life, the Iranian Revolution and its aftermath continue to weigh heavily on sectarian relations today, acting as a lens through which domestic actors view regional events such as the Iraq War, the 2006 Lebanon War, and, less explicitly, the Arab uprisings of 2011. Gulf media, official statements, and Sunni websites draw frequent analogies between Iran's incitement of Gulf Shiʿa after 1979 and the contagion effect of Iran's expansion of power following the toppling of Saddam Husayn.[1] Frequent accusations against Gulf Shiʿa as Iranian fifth columns bear a striking resemblance to charges levied after the Iranian Revolution, with many anti-Shiʿa tracts and materials being recycled and redistributed. For their part, Shiʿa actors are careful to distance themselves from the revolutionary decade, asserting that both the domestic context in the Gulf and Iran's external policies have evolved significantly.

The postrevolutionary decade established a pattern of strategies by regimes and Gulf Shiʿa that continues to be relevant in the period under examination. Gulf regimes since 2003 have deployed tactics that bear a striking resemblance to those pursued in the aftermath of the revolution: preemptive reforms to mitigate Shiʿa discontent, "sectarian balancing" (co-opting Sunnis to balance the Shiʿa), and tacitly encouraging vitriolic anti-Shiʿa discourse by Sunni clerics, repression, and censorship. Most significant, however, the revolutionary decade highlighted the importance of domestic structures (political institutions and state resources) as buffers against external ideological influences and as determinants of regime threat perception.

GULF DOMESTIC CONDITIONS ON THE EVE OF REVOLUTION

Contemporary Arab commentators since 2003 have frequently assigned Iran a high degree of agency in inspiring Gulf Shiʿa on the basis of shared transnational linkages (clerical, sectarian, familial, and ideological). The appearance of Sunni–Shiʿa divisions as markers of identity, both in the post-1979 context and since 2003, is similarly often thought to be the result of a deliberate Iranian strategy.[2] Such assertions, however, discount the importance of the domestic structural context in determining Gulf Shiʿa receptivity to the revolution's message and model. In each country on the eve of the revolution, Shiʿa were faced with a combustible blend of rising expectations, poor living conditions, and limited avenues for political participation. But the degree to which these grievances were translated into militancy depended more on state resources and institutions than on Tehran's policies of incitement or religious ties between the Shiʿa of the Gulf and the Shiʿa of Iran.

Bahrain

In Bahrain, Shiʿa grievances on the eve of the revolution were fueled by rising birth rates, declining oil rents, and a widening gap between Sunni and Shiʿa living standards. Poor economic conditions were compounded by increased political repression, culminating in the declaration in 1974 of a state security law that gave the regime the right to arbitrarily arrest and imprison for three years anyone deemed a threat to the state.[3] The move provided the catalyst for a burgeoning alignment among liberal, leftist, and Islamist parliamentarians, which the ruling family attempted to split by offering inducements to the Islamist deputies.[4] After this tactic failed, the regime decreed the suspension of the Parliament in 1975.[5] According to several Bahraini interlocutors interviewed in 2006, the suspension of Parliament helped amplify the effects of the revolution, in particular Ayatollah Ruhollah Khomeini's rhetorical criticism of the Gulf's hereditary rulers.[6]

Saudi Arabia

In Saudi Arabia, the Shi'a proved receptive to the revolution's message due to the economic and social marginalization of the Eastern Province and, in particular, to disappointment that the region's oil wealth had not improved local conditions.[7] Added to these factors, the government's official discourse on modernization raised Eastern Province inhabitants' expectations and sharpened the contrast between the eastern periphery and the central Najd region.[8] In the political realm, Shi'a frequently complained about the lack of constitutional guarantees for freedom of speech and the press.[9] Increased discrimination in the cultural sphere (such as the banning of Ashura mourning processions in public) were further sources of resentment, stemming in part from the Al Sa'ud family's increased reliance on the Salafi clerical establishment to legitimate their rule—a trend that was accelerated by the ideological challenge posed by revolutionary Iran.[10]

Yet within the marginalized Eastern Province, economic, demographic, and doctrinal differences affected levels of Shi'a sympathy for the revolution, particularly between the two principal Shi'a hubs, the oases of Qatif and Ahsa. Qatif evinced the highest sympathy for the revolution and, as discussed later, served as the epicenter of the 1979 intifada because its inhabitants suffered the most from a lack of social services and infrastructure. Qatifis are both urban and rural dwellers, occupying a broad swathe of the social spectrum: Saudi Arabian American Oil Company (ARAMCO) workers, university students, and the middle classes, who had a long tradition of leftist and labor activism.[11] Qatifis also had a long tradition of cosmopolitanism and interaction with outside ideological forces, whether

Nasserism, Baʿathism, or Marxism. According to an early member of the OIR, "Qatif always interacted with the Arab world. In 1962, for example, we celebrated the liberation of Algeria and applauded Nasserism. Iranian influence was helped by organic factors—but it was certainly not greater than Cairo's influence. After all, our teachers in Qatif were all Egyptians."[12]

The inhabitants of Ahsa, for their part, were landless peasants and more inward looking. Their expectations were not raised by the regime's narrative of modernization, and they seemed ambivalent about openly protesting the regime.[13] Doctrinal religious distinctions further sharpened the differences in living standards between the two communities. Qatifis follow the Usuli school of Shiʿa thought, whose interpretation of jurisprudence mandates stricter obedience to Shiʿa *marajiʿ* (clerical sources of emulation); Hasawis follow the Akhbari school, which tends to rely more on the canonical Islamic texts—the Qurʾan and the hadith.[14] Finally, interviews with Shiʿa activists reveal an entrenched ambivalence and tension between the inhabitants of Ahsa and those of Qatif; according to one Qatifi activist, Ahsa is a "backwater" whose inhabitants were "always following us [Qatifis]."[15]

Kuwait

As noted in the previous chapter, Kuwait stands in marked contrast to Bahrain and Saudi Arabia in terms of its participatory institutions, civil society, and the favorable views of the ruling family among nearly all sectors of the citizenry. That said, as in Bahrain, in Kuwait shifting economic conditions and demographics during the mid- and late 1970s created receptive audiences to the Iranian Revolution's message. Declining oil revenues spurred a demand by traditional Shiʿa merchant families for a greater voice in politics. At the same time, an emerging Shiʿa middle class was challenging the wealthier Shiʿa merchant families, demanding greater political participation to compensate for their lack of financial resources.[16]

Added to these economic grievances, the Shiʿa suffered from a continuing lack of political access in Kuwait. The Kuwaiti Council of Ministers contained only one token Shiʿa, and Kuwaiti Shiʿa were forbidden from serving in sensitive posts in the military and oil industry.[17] More significant, the principal channel for the Shiʿa to influence regime decision making—the National Assembly (Parliament)—had been dissolved since 1976. As in the case of Bahrain, the absence of this participatory structure amplified the revolution's impact.[18]

In sum, the Shiʿa in all three cases possessed a strong revolutionary potential, rooted in frustrated expectations for economic improvement, political marginalization, and growing cultural discrimination. In addition, demographic fissures within each country's Shiʿa community—tensions between lay and clerical activists as well as between traditional elites (landed notables) and an emerging middle class—intensified the revolution's impact. The clerical and middle classes seized upon Iran's revolutionary rhetoric and ideology to challenge the old social hierarchy. As discussed in depth in the next section, the ultimate outcome of the revolution's contagion effect in each case was mediated and tempered by domestic structures and state capacity or by their absence.[19] To fully understand this interplay between external shock and domestic response (both among Shiʿa actors and the state), it is important to understand the Iranian regime's intent and policies toward the Gulf.

THE THREAT FROM IRAN: INCITEMENT AND CONTAGION

Even if the transnational affinities to Iran are not as great as commonly assumed, the Gulf Shiʿa are intensely cognizant that events, statements, and policies from Iran affect their domestic standing—by either heightening or dampening regime suspicions. Much of Iran's media overtures since 2003 have been decidedly nonsectarian, emphasizing the gap between ruler and ruled and trumpeting the Islamic Republic's continued steadfastness to pan-Arab causes such as Palestine. In the decade following the Iranian Revolution, however, Tehran adopted a more strident religious tone that, although appealing to both Sunnis and Shiʿa, was nonetheless interpreted by Gulf regimes as serving the narrow communal interests of the Shiʿa.[20]

Iran's policies toward the Gulf during and after the revolution exploited a number of channels and tactics, most significantly clerical networks, media, and the training and funding of Shiʿa militant cadres. Ayatollah Khomeini appointed Friday prayer leaders in Gulf countries who would later play a pivotal role in mobilizing Gulf Shiʿa via mosque sermons and *husayniyat*. In Bahrain, a key interlocutor was Hadi al-Mudarrisi, an Iranian cleric whom the shah had exiled to Bahrain. In 1978, Iranian media announced that he had been appointed as Khomeini's personal representative (*wakil*) in Bahrain. By early September, his activities were augmented by Ayatollah Sadiq Ruhani, who made explicit threats to overthrow the Bahraini regime if it did not adopt a more Islamic form of government. Ayatollah ʿAbbas al-Muhri, an Iranian-born cleric who held Kuwaiti citizenship, was appointed as Khomeini's representative in Kuwait.[21]

Tehran also pursued a policy of clandestine military support to Shiʿa networks in the Gulf—a role it repeatedly denied. In 1981, the Islamic Revolutionary Guards Corps established the Office of Liberation Movements, headed by Muhammad Montazeri and Mehdi Hashemi, who reportedly visited Kuwait and Bahrain on several occasions.[22] Gulf Shiʿa clerical figures and lay activists affiliated with the Movement for Vanguards' Missionaries (MVM, Harakat al-Talaʾiʿ al-Risaliyyin)—many of them followers of Ayatollah Muhammad al-Shirazi, the so-called Shiraziyyin current—had particularly close ties with this office and with the Revolutionary Guards more broadly; many were reported to have received military training in Iran.[23] These individuals later proved instrumental in setting up the IFLB and the OIR in Saudi Arabia as local branches of the MVM, with the goal of extending the Iranian Revolution.

Iran's dissatisfaction with its ability to control the OIR and shifting factional politics inside Tehran led it to establish a more pliant group in Saudi Arabia, the Hizballah al-Hijaz.[24] By the late 1980s, Iranian figures such as future supreme leader ʿAli Khamenei and then-president Hashemi Rafsanjani questioned the OIR and MVM's enthusiasm for exporting the revolution, resulting in strained ties and an eventual loss of patronage.[25] In Kuwait, Iran played a direct hand in sponsoring terrorist attacks by members of the Iraqi Daʿwa Party and Lebanese Hizballah (with marginal involvement by Kuwaiti Shiʿa) as a strategy to dissuade Kuwait from supporting Iraq during the Iran–Iraq War. In the media realm, Iranian-backed radio stations such as Radio Tehran and Radio Ahvaz and a number of monthly written periodicals in the Gulf provided a steady attack on the

Islamic legitimacy of Gulf royalty and the gap between ruler and ruled.[26] Many of the statements, as noted, were decidedly nonsectarian and universalist in their appeal—an effort by Tehran to break out of the narrow parochialism of the revolution's Shiʿa roots.

The Iran–Iraq War proved to be a powerful, if oft overlooked, determinant of Iran's policies toward the Gulf. Iraq's status and orientation have always been important factors in the Gulf geometry of power, especially for Riyadh and Tehran; a weak Iraq can arguably be said to increase rivalry between Saudi Arabia and Iran, whereas a strong Iraq can stabilize or moderate the tensions. Iran viewed the unprovoked attack by Saddam Husayn as having been undertaken partially in the service of Saudi interests to eradicate the revolution. Saudi Arabia supported Iraq as a buffer against Iran. Yet it was the war's impact on changes in the regional order that further strained relations. The war provided the context for the massive introduction of U.S. military aid and forces into the region, largely at Riyadh's invitation, which in Tehran's view fatally tipped the local balance of power to its disadvantage. The Iran–Iraq cease-fire in 1988 apparently vindicated the Saudi policy of using Iraq as a local buffer against Iran, and in Tehran the war's termination spawned an intense reformulation of Iranian Gulf policy toward a less antagonistic stance.

Taken in sum, the Iranian Revolution and Tehran's subsequent policies toward the Gulf during the Iran–Iraq War presented a direct threat to Gulf regimes and raised the specter of revolutionary contagion throughout the region. Yet in each case focused on here the revolution's impact and Tehran's policies were filtered and tempered by the local context—the distinctive histories and culture of each country's Shiʿa community, preexisting Shiʿa grievances and societal fissures, and the resources that their respective regimes brought to bear. These variables combined to affect how the Gulf Shiʿa interpreted and responded to the revolution.

SHIʿA MOBILIZATION AND REGIME RESPONSE

In each country, Shiʿa responses to the revolution spanned a broad continuum: from peaceful demands for reform and political activism to boycott and riots to calculated acts of violence and terrorism against the state.

Characterization of these activities varies widely among scholars. Some have portrayed them as being initially spurred by the revolution but following a logic and pattern that were entirely dictated by local conditions. Others have framed them as an "emulative" process, in which the Gulf Shiʿa saw the revolution as a model and their own activism as a sort of re-enactment. A small minority of scholars and observers sees the Gulf Shiʿa as a veritable extension of Iranian policy.[27] Although elements of each view are present, it is more accurate to describe the revolution as providing the framework for social mobilization—an empowering vocabulary of political action that proved highly appealing to segments of the Shiʿa polity. Contemporary observers recall that the revolution emboldened the Shiʿa to assert their communal identity against a long history of marginalization—for the first time, the Gulf Shiʿa were "proud" of their sectarian pedigree.

It is difficult, however, to assign direct causality to the revolution—in many cases, the roots of Shiʿa politicization in the Gulf began much earlier, as witnessed by the activities of the Shiraziyyin prior to the 1979 revolution. Several preexisting Shiʿa networks in the Gulf aligned themselves with the revolution in the hopes of bolstering their appeal and legitimacy among their constituents.

Bahrain

In Bahrain, the Iranian Revolution spurred spontaneous demonstrations and organized resistance, but it also exposed fissures among the Shiʿa community over ideology, strategy, and goals. The more violent, radical strain of Shiʿa activism that sought to replicate the Iranian Revolution in Bahrain failed to attract a significant following and was significantly weakened after its thwarted coup attempt in 1981. Yet the regime's ability to fully placate Shiʿa dissent was limited by demographic reality and its fear that incremental reforms would eventually lead to the unseating of the royal family.

Before the revolution, most Shiʿa in Bahrain had lobbied for their rights as part of a broad-based, largely nonsectarian movement led by leftists, Baʿathists, and Nasserists. In the late 1960s and early 1970s, a new generation of clerical leaders began to emerge, encouraged by the formation of like-minded Shiʿa groups in Lebanon (Lebanese Resistance Detachments [Afwaj al-Muqawama al-Lubnaniyya]), Saudi Arabia (the OIR), and Iraq (the Islamic Action Organization [IAO, Munadhamat al-ʿAmal al-Islami]).[28] In 1968, a young Bahraini cleric, ʿIsa al-Qasim, helped found the Islamic Enlightenment Society (Jamʿiyyat al-Tawʿiyya al-Islamiyya), which attracted a large following of judges, doctors, and engineers and secured a parliamentary voice as part of the Religious Bloc (al-Kutla al-Diniyya). These figures and their networks were aided in their efforts to mobilize Bahraini Shiʿa by longstanding Shiʿa cultural institutions, such as the *maʾatim* (mourning houses), and the establishment of Shiʿa cultural journals such as *al-Mawqif*. In the run-up to the revolution, members of the Enlightenment Society began their first correspondence with Ayatollah Khomeini during his residence in Najaf and later sent congratulatory telegrams to the postrevolutionary government. The first distinctively Shiʿa protests in Bahrain occurred after the arrest of a Bahraini Shiʿa leader, Muhammad ʿAli al-Ekri, followed by similar unrest after the Saddam regime's execution of Ayatollah Muhammad Baqir al-Sadr in Iraq.[29]

After the revolution, the secular opposition effectively disappeared, and activism among the Bahraini Shiʿa was marked by competition between two opposing Shiʿa religious currents that disagreed on goals and tactics of opposition and that drew their support from different demographic segments of Bahraini society. The first, the Bahrain Islamic Freedom Movement (BIFM, Harakat Ahrar al-Bahrayn al-Islamiyya), was formed by Bahraini students studying in London. The BIFM was effectively an extension of the Enlightenment Society, comprised overwhelmingly of Bahraini Shiʿa of Arab origin (*baharna*).[30] It pushed for peaceable reform within the framework of existing political structures, calling for a restoration of the Parliament.

The second current was the IFLB, formed in late 1979 under the leadership of Hadi al-Mudarrisi. The IFLB drew its membership from Bahrainis of Iranian origin and followers of Grand Ayatollah al-Shirazi.[31] Backed by Iran, it explicitly called for the overthrow of the Bahraini government and its replacement with an Islamic republic.[32] The IFLB also expressed solidarity with other Shiʿa Islamist movements in the Gulf, holding Ashura processions that coincided with the intifada of the Eastern Province in Saudi Arabia. After May 1980, the IFLB shifted its tactics from protests to clandestine violence, concluding after the Bahraini security forces had killed a number of protesters and expelled the IFLB leadership (Ruhani and Mudarrisi) that protests would not be sufficient to bring down the regime. In 1981, the Bahraini regime announced it had thwarted a coup attempt by the IFLB, arresting more than three hundred suspects and later charging a core cadre of seventy-three with receiving arms, funding, and training from Iran. Although the majority of the group consisted of Bahrainis, it also included Saudis, a Kuwaiti, and an Omani.[33] The coup attempt had a number of important implications for the course of Shiʿa–state relations through the 1980s and 1990s. The arrest, trial, and deportation of the IFLB's key leaders marked the start of a steady decline for the militant organization.[34] The BIFM in its turn saw its fortunes rise as the sole remaining opposition umbrella.

The Bahraini government's response to the revolution's effect blended coercion, punishment, and inducement. Its goals were fivefold: to weaken or destroy the radical, Iranian-inspired opposition; to co-opt and placate the moderates; to build legitimacy for the ruling family; to increase the size of the middle class and bureaucracy; and to reduce the demands on the welfare state by increasing other modes of production.[35] It offered a number of concessions and improvements to Shiʿa living standards and political participation—tactics that were designed to win over the moderates by demonstrating a modicum of progress on reform while further marginalizing the hard-liners.

At the same time, the government portrayed all Shiʿa activists as fifth columnists for Iran, thus splitting them from their secular and liberal allies.[36] Much of this approach followed a timeworn pattern of inflating the external influences on domestic opposition movements, depending on whatever ideology was ascendant at the time. As a senior member of one Bahraini Shiʿa Islamist group noted to the author, "The regime has played the Iran card against the Shiʿa since 1979, but in the 1920s it was the Communists; in the 1950s it was the Nasserists."[37]

In many cases, evolving regional events, in particular the Iran–Iraq War, influenced the regime's strategy. When Iran had the upper hand, Bahraini authorities made a number of conciliatory gestures to the Shiʿa; when Iraq gained ground, there were further restrictions. Another important effect was Saddam Husayn's closure of Najaf as a seat of Shiʿa learning. Bahraini seminary students increasingly went to Qom, Iran, in the 1980s for study, but the Bahraini regime banned them from returning—a move that further weakened the opposition's leadership and organizational structure. In the early 1990s, these clerics returned under a general amnesty decree, providing mobilizing guidance for the uprisings of the mid-1990s.[38]

Many of the regime's efforts proved insufficient to fully placate the underlying power inequalities that fueled Shiʿa activism. By the early 1990s, the absence of participatory structures had stimulated a broad-based constitutional movement, whose demands included a restoration of the 1973 Constitution and the Parliament, the freeing of political prisoners, and further improvements in Shiʿa living conditions. Once again, the regime responded with a mix of cosmetic concessions, such as the creation of the thirty-person Consultative Council (Majlis al-Shura), which had no real legislative powers, representing both Sunnis and Shiʿa. Importantly, the Shiʿa on the council were drawn from wealthy merchant families rather than from the middle and lower classes that constituted the bulk of the opposition.[39] These measures thus did little to alleviate the Shiʿa's class-based grievances, which fueled the uprising of 1994–1999.

Saudi Arabia

In Saudi Arabia, the Iranian Revolution presented the Shiʿa with similar choices between peaceful activism and militancy. Reactions to the revolution were varied: spontaneous demonstrations, clandestine opposition activity, and demands for political reform. The Saudi Shiʿa failed to develop a coherent, organized movement of resistance for several reasons: intra-Shiʿa divisions based on locale, clerical pedigree, and family; the absence of a charismatic unifying leader; and differing levels of grievances among the Eastern Province's towns and villages, which impacted Shiʿa calculations about activism.[40]

For the Saudi Shiʿa, the 1979 Iranian Revolution spurred a shift from quietism to activism. The catalyzing event in Shiʿa activism, which continues to dominate the Saudi Shiʿa historical memory, was the seven-day clash of November 1979, known among the Shiʿa as the Intifada of Muharram 1400. The protests began after leaders of the Shirazi-inspired

MVM—Hassan al-Saffar and Tawfiq al-Sayf—organized public Ashura processions in Qatif in direct violation of a ban that had been in place since 1913.[41] The revolt quickly spread to nearby villages, and the regime's repressive response—via the Saudi National Guard—was swift. At least two dozen Shi'a protesters ultimately perished. By December, the MVM leaders of the uprising had formally declared the OIR.[42]

Although in part inspired by the Iranian Revolution, many of the protestors' mobilizing grievances were domestic and in some cases nonsectarian. The late 1970s saw growing disappointment among the Shi'a at the government's failure to deliver on its promises of modernization to the Eastern Province, where living conditions contrasted sharply with the growing opulence of Saudi elites in the central Najd region. In a manifesto of seven statements released in December 1979, the OIR listed three reasons for the uprising: marginal living conditions in the Eastern Province; lack of freedom of expression; and the Saudi regime's hostility toward the Islamic Revolution in Iran. Water shortages in Shi'a villages and towns were a particularly onerous grievance, especially when compared to the abundance at the nearby Sunni enclaves of Dammam and Khobar.

Participants in the demonstrations were diverse, reflecting the broad, nonsectarian nature of these economic grievances. Oil workers from Saudi ARAMCO and university students constituted a large majority of the protestors.[43] Many of their demands reveal a generational conflict exacerbated by the revolution—the younger generation of protest organizers questioned the accommodating stance of Shi'a notables, landowners, and merchants.[44]

The aftermath of the uprising had important implications for the Saudi Shi'a. The Shirazi leadership of the OIR left Saudi Arabia, establishing themselves in Iran, Syria, the United States, and Europe. In Iran, the Office of Liberation Movements repeatedly pressured the OIR to resume militant activity in Saudi Arabia, but the remaining leadership considered further violence as futile in the wake of the postintifada crackdown.[45] The OIR saw its fortunes further decline as the balance of power in Iran's factional struggle shifted away from its principal patron, Montazeri, and toward the current supreme leader, 'Ali Khamenei.[46] By the mid-1980s, it grew increasingly estranged from the new centers of power in Iran and began focusing its media and propaganda attacks on the Saudi regime. The death of

Khomeini, the warming of Saudi–Iranian relations, and the 1991 Gulf War were further drivers of an ideological shift among the OIR's leadership. "When Khomeini died, the idea of *velayet-e faqih* [literally, "guardianship of the Islamic jurist," the ideological foundation for the Islamic Republic of Iran] died with him," noted a senior Shiʿa cleric in the Kingdom.[47]

By the early 1990s, the OIR was increasingly framing the struggle for Shiʿa rights as part of a nationwide campaign to develop the peripheral provinces and recognize the diversity of the kingdom's local identities. In 1993, the exiled OIR leadership in London and the Saudi regime began a series of talks, resulting in a general amnesty offer by the regime and a promise by the OIR to cease publications critical of the regime and to reject any fealty to Iran.[48] The regime released a number of Shiʿa political prisoners, rehired sacked Shiʿa employees of ARAMCO, and promised to undertake reforms that would remove discrimination against the Shiʿa in the political and cultural realm. That said, the numbers of Shiʿa employed by ARAMCO steadily dwindled as new hires came from Sunni-dominated parts of the country.[49]

Another consequence of the OIR's shift in strategy and distancing of itself from Iran was the establishment of Hizballah al-Hijaz, a smaller, cell-like organization that explicitly advocated the establishment of an Islamic republic on the Arabian Peninsula through violent means.[50] A key catalyst for the formation of the group and its sponsorship by the Iranian regime was the death of more than four hundred Iranian pilgrims during a 1987 hajj riot—an event that led to a precipitous decline in Saudi–Iranian relations. For the next decade, Hizballah al-Hijaz remained the most militant Shiʿa movement in Saudi Arabia, opposing the OIR's reconciliation with the regime and carrying out a series of attacks on Saudi soil, which culminated in the 1996 bombing of the U.S. Air Force barracks at Khobar Towers in Dharan. It also conducted an extensive propaganda campaign against the regime with the publication of a monthly journal, *Risalat al-Haramayn*, from 1989 to 1995.[51] Following the 1996 Khobar bombings, the arrest of several high-ranking members, and the warming of Saudi–Iranian relations, Hizballah al-Hijaz focused increasingly on propaganda (via the Internet) and social activism.[52] Former leaders Hassan al-Nimr and ʿAbd al-Karim al-Hubayl coalesced into the so-called current of the Khat al-Imam (Imam's Line) among Eastern Province Shiʿa; they remain unapologetic defenders of *velayet-e faqih* as a governing principle and of Iran as a patron.[53]

The Saudi regime's response to the domestic effects of the revolution was diverse, incorporating both coercive and conciliatory measures. Importantly, it focused most of its efforts in alleviating the material hardships of the Eastern Province Shiʿa. It announced new development projects on the eve of Ashura in 1980, and it pardoned several prisoners.[54] Roads and schools proliferated, although the region's first hospital was not opened until 1987. In 1985, King Fahd replaced the notoriously harsh governor of the Eastern Province, Abd al-Muhsin bin Abdallah Al Jiluwi, with Muhammad bin Fahd. It allowed greater openness in the public display of Shiʿa rituals, allowing the Shiʿa call to prayer with its unique mention of ʿAli.[55]

Yet there were limits to the regime's recognition of Shiʿa identity because of the royal family's partnership with the Salafi clerical establishment, whose interpretation of Islam is doctrinally hostile toward Shiʿism. One collateral result of the revolution was the royal family's gradual empowerment of the clergy to burnish their Islamic credentials in the face of the Iranian challenge and to insulate themselves from domestic criticism of their "impiety." Tacitly encouraging the proliferation of anti-Shiʿa fatwas (formal clerical pronouncements or edicts) was a way for the ruling family to close ranks with Sunni opposition clerics, and it served the additional purpose of countering the ideological challenge from Iran. The regime formally sponsored the publication of a number of influential anti-Shiʿa tracts, which achieved wide circulation after the revolution and, as discussed later, were reprinted and redistributed in the post-2003 period.[56]

Kuwait

The Kuwaiti case differs from Bahrain and Saudi Arabia in a number of respects. As noted in the previous chapter, Kuwaiti Shiʿa enjoyed greater levels of integration in the state's political life, economic prosperity, and narrative of nation formation. In turn, the ruling family enjoyed a greater degree of legitimacy among Kuwaiti Shiʿa than did its counterparts in Bahrain and Saudi Arabia. In addition, Kuwait's tradition of *diwaniya* (discussion forums) and Parliament provided the citizenry with access to decision making.[57] Taken in sum, these structural factors helped temper the impact of the revolution and informed the strategies of the Shiʿa in Kuwait.

Two broad political trends emerged among the Shiʿa in Kuwait, reflecting the demographic split between indigenous Kuwaiti Shiʿa and Iranian-born Shiʿa. Each group's strategy and tactics differed significantly, with the indigenous Shiʿa preferring to use peaceful means to press for political reforms—namely, the restoration of the suspended Parliament—but the Iranian Shiʿa, along with Shiʿa from Iraq, forming the core of those who were involved in terrorist attacks and strikes. Yet, as discussed at length later in this section, a broad government crackdown against the Shiʿa beginning in 1983 spurred the Kuwaiti-born Shiʿa to become increasingly involved in acts of terrorism.[58]

The central mobilizing figures in the Kuwaiti Shiʿa response to the 1979 revolution were ʿAbbas al-Muhri and Muhammad al-Shirazi—both Iranian-born clerics. Al-Muhri served as a clerical leader for the Kuwaiti ʿajam (Persian born), and al-Shirazi enjoyed greater support among the indigenous Arab Shiʿa. Al-Muhri's activism began in August 1979 with a series of conferences and sermons focused on advancing political reform in Kuwait and restoring the Parliament rather than on Shiʿa communal rights. His audience reportedly included a broad swathe of Kuwaiti Shiʿa, from both the Daʿwa and the Shiraziyyin currents, as well as Sunnis.[59] For his part, al-Shirazi pursued a somewhat bifurcated role. Among Kuwaitis, he focused principally on religious and humanitarian affairs, setting up the country's first hawza (seminary) and establishing an important charitable institution that survives to this day.[60] In tandem with these steps, however, he used Kuwait as a base to inspire and instigate Shiʿa movements elsewhere on the peninsula, such as the OIR in Saudi Arabia and the IFLB in Bahrain.[61]

The month of November 1979 proved to be a catalyzing moment for the Shiʿa in Kuwait, with important ramifications for the future course of Shiʿa activism. On November 16, several hundred Iranian Shiʿa demonstrated in front of the U.S. embassy in Kuwait in solidarity with the Iranian seizure of the U.S. embassy in Tehran. Fifteen days later the U.S. embassy was again besieged, this time by more than a thousand Kuwaiti and Iranian Shiʿa, who broke through the embassy's walls, only to be repulsed by Kuwaiti security forces. The protest coincided with the intifada in the Eastern Province of Saudi Arabia, demonstrating the importance of cross-border solidarity among the Gulf Shiʿa in the wake of the revolution. A key instigator of the protest was Muhammad al-Shirazi, who delivered a sermon exhorting his listeners to besiege the embassy.[62]

From the regime's perspective, al-Shirazi's involvement demonstrated the potentially dangerous mobilizing capacity of clerics and, more broadly, of Iranian Shiʿa on Kuwait's indigenous Shiʿa populace. One of its key objectives, therefore, was to split the two groups to prevent collaboration and to channel Shiʿa demands toward more narrowly communal aims in place of broad-based political reforms.[63] It pursued these objectives through a widespread policy of "criminalizing" the Iranian Shiʿa—publicizing the seizure of Iranian arms caches and explosives, enacting laws that forbade the ownership of Kuwaiti land by non-Kuwaitis, and, most important, by deporting Iranian Shiʿa starting in the fall of 1979.[64] In September, the regime stripped ʿAbbas al-Muhri of his citizenship and deported his entire family to Iran. This action reportedly came on the heels of a government effort to persuade him to redirect his activism toward more parochial Shiʿa demands—that is, the construction of mosques and *husayniyat* (mourning houses). Muhammad al-Shirazi was deported shortly thereafter in 1980.[65]

In tandem with these actions, the regime undertook a number of structural reforms intended to solidify the loyalty of the indigenous Shiʿa merchants, to marginalize the Iranian clerics, and to unify the Kuwaiti polity as a whole. The intent, according to many interlocutors, was to create a pressure release for deliberation and debate that would undercut the Iranian agitators' propaganda appeals. In addition, the regime hoped that a National Assembly would provide it a window into the public's emerging issues of concern before antagonism was fueled against the government.[66] Restrictions on the press were also loosened—a measure that was calculated both as a pressure release and as a means for the ruling family to be cognizant of the issues being debated and circulated.[67]

The spate of terrorist attacks and bombings that afflicted Kuwait in the early and mid-1980s have often been ascribed to the impact of the Iranian Revolution on Kuwaiti Shiʿa. More accurately, however, the first attacks—conducted overwhelmingly by Iraqi Daʿwa cadres living in Kuwait, the IAO directed by Muhammad Taqi al-Mudarrisi, Muhammad Hussayn Naʾini, and Hizballah in Lebanon—should be seen as the playing out of the Iran–Iraq War on Kuwaiti soil rather than as an expression of Kuwaiti Shiʿa sympathy with the Iranian Revolution.[68] The goal of these attacks was to effect a change in Kuwait's foreign policy—a curtailment of its support to Iraq during the Iran–Iraq War—rather than to provoke improvements in domestic governance. The most damaging of these attacks—in terms of repercussions for the Shiʿa in Kuwait—were the bombings of seven sites on December 12, 1983, including the U.S. embassy and Kuwait's airport. The campaign culminated with an attempt on the life of the Kuwaiti emir by Lebanese Hizballah member ʿImad Mughniyah in 1985.

The consequences for Shiʿa activism were profound. The period from 1983 to 1986 saw a further decline in the fortunes of the Kuwaiti Shiʿa as the regime stepped up its deportations to include not just Iranian-, Iraqi-, and Lebanese-born Shiʿa, but also those born in Kuwait, purged Shiʿa from sensitive positions, and arrested peaceful dissenters in a broad dragnet. The Kuwaiti press contributed to a growing climate of hysteria and fear regarding Iranian fifth columns and the Shiʿa more broadly. The period from 1986 to 1988 saw a marked increase in the number of Kuwaiti Shiʿa citizens involved in terrorist attacks, many of them unplanned or undirected by the Daʿwa cadres. These so-called citizen bombers were drawn from prosperous merchant families who would not otherwise have grievances against the regime. One possible explanation is that the repressive and expansive regime response—specifically by the Ministry of Interior—to the Mughniyah attack turned sectors of the Kuwaiti Shiʿa populace against the regime, making them more responsive to appeals for violence.[69] The post-Mughniyah period was marked by increased surveillance of Shiʿa *husayniyat*; purges of Shiʿa from military, security, and education posts; and mass firings from oil refineries—all of which contributed to a growing sense of Shiʿa estrangement.[70]

The Iranian Revolution and its aftermath continue to exert a powerful influence on the historical memory of Gulf regimes and Shiʿa actors. It provides a lens through which the external shocks of the Iraq War and even the Arab uprisings of 2011 are filtered. It offered lessons in political strategies for both Shiʿa actors and regimes that informed post-2003 policies and actions. For governments in the Gulf, it demonstrated the utility of a divide-and-rule approach to the Shiʿa opposition and the benefits of mitigating dissent through political and economic reform.

Domestic political structures and state resources rather than ideological affinity with Iran or specific actions by Iran played a determinant role in framing Shiʿa responses and strategies. The absence of pluralistic institutions and poor living conditions were among the principal grievances of the Shiʿa who responded to the revolution. Shiʿa strategies were subsequently informed by the presence or absence of institutions that offered channels to redress grievances.

In Bahrain, the availability of a parliament and a constitution (albeit in a suspended form) produced a bloc of Shiʿa opposition that was willing to use peaceful means in contrast to a more violent trend that aimed for the overthrow of the ruling family. The regime made limited progress on mitigating these grievances—a shortcoming that eventually helped fuel the uprising of the mid-1990s.

In Saudi Arabia, the absence of any sort of participatory structure that could act as a pressure release combined with the economic marginalization of the Eastern Province to spark the Intifada of Muharram 1400. The regime's subsequent efforts to improve living conditions in the Eastern Province, along with promises of political reform and an end to cultural discrimination, helped fracture the Shiʿa opposition between the OIR and the more militant Hizballah al-Hijaz.

In Kuwait, the Parliament and the *diwaniya* helped temper the impact of the revolution and exposed a split between the peaceful strategies of the Kuwait-born Shiʿa and the militancy of those hailing from Iran. The regime tried to co-opt the nonviolent trend through calibrated reforms, while pursuing a harder line of arrest and deportation toward the militant strain. Yet the inclusion of Kuwait-born Shiʿa in a repressive dragnet against terrorism suspects in 1986 proved to be a major error by the regime that radicalized a segment of the citizenry. From 1986 onward, Kuwaiti Shiʿa participated in violent acts that previously had been conducted almost entirely by Iraqi, Iranian, and Lebanese Shiʿa.

PART II

BAHRAIN

THREE

DEBATING PARTICIPATION

The Bahraini Shiʿa and Regional Influences

Of the three countries under examination, none was more affected by
the regional upheaval of the Iraq War than Bahrain. The collapse of
the Saddam regime in Iraq and the political empowerment of Iraq Shiʿa
left Bahrain the only country in the Arab world where a Sunni minority
rules over a Shiʿa majority. The ensuing civil war in Iraq exacerbated the
island's longstanding sectarian tensions, sharpened the opposition's critique of the regime, and put strains on Bahraini participatory institutions
such as the Parliament. The dramatic, unfolding narrative in Iraq—the
reemergence of Najaf as a center of Shiʿa religious authority, the 2005 National Assembly (Parliament) elections, the sieges of Najaf and Fallujah,
and the sectarian strife that followed the early 2006 bombing of the Shiʿa
al-ʿAskari Mosque[1]—became a filter through which Bahrainis interpreted
their own contentious politics. Put differently, the Iraq War was a form of
political theater that compelled Bahraini elites and ordinary citizens not
simply to observe, but to participate and "reenact" in a highly partisan
manner.

This participation took a number of forms and was frequently accompanied by fierce debate. For a sizeable bloc of the Shiʿa, elections in Iraq
provided the impetus to end their previous boycott of Bahrain's Parliament. The reemergence of Grand Ayatollah ʿAli al-Sistani as a respected

spiritual and increasingly political figure with transnational influence among the Shi'a spurred a debate about the scope and role of clerical authority in Bahrain. Among Sunnis, there were frequent and vocal expressions of solidarity with embattled Sunnis in Fallujah and a rising sense of alarm at Shi'a triumphalism, particularly after the bloody campaign against Iraqi Sunnis carried out by Shi'a paramilitaries affiliated with the Sadrist movement and the Maliki government.

Closely related, the rise of Iranian power injected a new dynamic into identity politics and political liberalization in Bahrain. It gave regime supporters and hard-line Sunnis a useful bogeyman to discredit Shi'a oppositionists as puppets controlled by Iran. For some Shi'a political actors, it provided leverage against the regime; if reforms stalled, they warned, the Shi'a would have no choice but to turn to Iran. Most important, however, Iran's growing assertiveness in the region decreased the willingness of the Bahraini government's principal patron, Saudi Arabia, to support liberalization on the island. Riyadh saw any loosening of political control in Bahrain and, in particular, the holding of elections as a net gain for its strategic rival.

SHI'A POLITICAL ACTORS

To understand the degree to which regional events outside Bahrain influenced the Shi'a, it is first necessary to canvass the various Shi'a political societies, their leaders, and their platforms. As noted, Bahraini Shi'a society is marked by ethnic, theological, and class differences, to say nothing of disagreements over political strategies. The Shi'a of Bahrain have long enjoyed a rich tradition of association and civil society, of which formal political parties (known as "societies" under Bahraini law) are only one part.[2] The formalization of Shi'a politics first occurred as a result of the sweeping changes brought by the accession of the new emir (later king) Hamad bin 'Isa in 1999. On February 5, 2001, a broad-ranging amnesty allowed the return of 108 dissidents abroad, many of them Shi'a clerics and lay figures who would later form the core of the Shi'a political leadership.[3] Under the National Action Charter in 2001, the king allowed for civil "societies" to register as de facto political parties, although the law that governed their funding and scope was not formalized until 2005.[4] Municipal council elections were then announced for May 9 and parliamentary elections for October 24, 2002—both of which proved to be crucial testing grounds for the newly formed Shi'a blocs.

There are more than twenty-four such political societies in Bahrain, but the most active and influential Shi'a Islamist groups in the post-2003 period are the National Islamic Accord (Jama'iyyat al-Wifaq al-Watani al-Islamiyya, or al-Wifaq for short) and Islamic Action Movement (Harakat al-'Amal al-Islamiyya, or al-'Amal).[5] The period 2003–2010 saw the Shi'a political field marked by intense fissures and debates regarding participation or boycott (first in 2002 and then in 2005) as well as the role of clerical authority in shaping strategy. Most significant, al-Wifaq was confronted with defections in 2005–6 by its senior leadership, resulting in the formation of the Movement for Liberties and Democracy (Harakat Haq al-Hurriya wa al-Dimuqratiyya, or al-Haq), which rejected electoral participation and called for a continued boycott on the basis that the 2002 Constitution was illegal. Both movements grappled with how to balance the imperative of national loyalty with transnational ties outside Bahrain.

Al-Wifaq

With a reported sixty-five to seventy thousand active members, al-Wifaq is Bahrain's largest Shi'a Islamist political society.[6] It was formed around the exiled leadership of the Islamic Enlightenment Society and the BIFM—which later became the Bahrain Freedom Movement (BFM, Harakat Ahrar al-Bahrayn)—and draws its base of support from clerics and laypersons among Bahrain's middle and lower classes.[7]

Ideologically, al-Wifaq's membership incorporates Bahrain's al-Da'wa current and adherents of various *maraji'*. Many of its members, in particular the leaders, are drawn from the *baharna* Shi'a; a strong narrative of nativism thus informs its discourse.[8] In addition, there has been long-standing tension between leftist leaders of the 1990s who were integrated into its ranks and the clerical leadership, which quickly assumed dominance.[9] Perhaps to assuage these tensions, the society has emphasized that

its goals are largely secular—political and economic reform—although its
identity is firmly Islamic.

At the center of the movement is its charismatic young leader, ʿAli
Salman, born into a poor Shiʿa family, who studied on a fellowship at
King Saud University in Riyadh and then had theological training in Qom,
Iran. This cleric has long exerted a powerful magnetism on Bahraini Shiʿa
politics and popular mobilization. It was his detention on December 5,
1994, that helped spark the five-year intifada in Bahrain.[10] Yet his grip is
not all-encompassing. Al-Wifaq is governed by an eleven-member board
and receives spiritual and sometimes political guidance from Bahrain's senior Shiʿa clerical body, the Islamic Scholars Council (Majlis al-ʿUlamaʾ),
whose chairman is ʿIsa al-Qasim.[11] ʿAli Salman is thus forced into a position of building consensus. As discussed at length later in this chapter,
he reportedly opposed a boycott of the 2002 parliamentary elections (a
position that ʿIsa al-Qasim shared) but was forced into recanting this position because of the weight of popular opinion in al-Wifaq.[12] Since its inception, al-Wifaq's key demands have included a contractual constitution
that would permit the elected Parliament to have a greater range of legislative and oversight powers. Specifically, al-Wifaq has opposed the 2002
amended Constitution's expansion of powers to the royalty, especially the
king.[13] A strong class-based agenda informs its platform—it has pushed
for the alleviation of unemployment, which it sees as stemming from excessive corruption and discrimination. It relatedly seeks transparency in
government budgeting and increased hiring of Shiʿa in key ministries and
in the armed forces. It has also sought to enact a law on political societies
that would make state funding mandatory and permit foreign funding.[14]

Al-ʿAmal

Aside from al-Wifaq, the other significant Shiʿa grouping that participated
in the 2002 boycott and later competed against al-Wifaq in the 2006 elections is al-ʿAmal. This society was formed in 2001 from remnants of the
IFLB in the wake of the general amnesty that accompanied King Hamad's
reforms. Its adherents follow the Shiraziyyin current, represented by Aya-

tollah Sadiq al-Shirazi in Qom and Grand Ayatollah Muhammad Taqi al-Mudarrisi in Karbala. Despite its militant history and ties to Iran, al-ʿAmal has generally the same goals as al-Wifaq.

Although continually viewed with suspicion by Bahraini Sunnis, al-ʿAmal has largely abandoned its radical agenda since the 1990s, has participated in elections, and has pushed for political reform via peaceful channels. In arguing for participation in democratic structures, an ʿAmal leader noted in a 2006 interview, "We are working within the system because if you have a system, you can make corrections. The problem is when that system becomes dominated by a family."[15] Al-ʿAmal's shift from militant activism in the 1980s and 1990s is therefore instructive for what it reveals about the co-optive capability of Bahraini political reform.

Once al-Wifaq had consented to participating in the elections, competition and tension arose between the two Shiʿa societies. In the run-up to the 2006 elections, al-ʿAmal charged that ʿIsa al-Qasim and the Islamic Scholars Council had unfairly endorsed al-Wifaq, arguing that it was not appropriate for clerics to be politically partisan.[16]

THE PARTICIPATION DEBATE AND THE FRACTURING OF AL-WIFAQ

The decision of whether to participate in Parliament created significant fissures among the Shiʿa. The first litmus test occurred in the October 2002 elections. Having secured a majority of council seats in Shiʿa-dominated areas in the May 2002 municipal council elections, al-Wifaq seemed assured of a second victory in the October 2002 parliamentary elections. But the municipal voter turnout was only 47 percent. Al-Wifaq's leadership cadre was faced with the prospect of an even lower turnout in the upcoming parliamentary elections, given mounting opposition to the king's recent edicts to circumscribe the Parliament's legislative and oversight powers. This was particularly evident within al-Wifaq itself, where a hard-line current led by the deputy chairman Hassan Mushayma and the revered intifada leader ʿAbd al-Wahhab Husayn was challenging ʿAli Salman's more conciliatory approach.

To manage these tensions, al-Wifaq formed a formal alliance with four other societies to boycott the 2002 elections. The coalition, known as the Four-Way Alliance (al-Tahaluf al-Rubaʿi) was composed of al-Wifaq; al-ʿAmal; the National Democratic Action Society (al-ʿAmal al-Watani al-Dimuqrati, al-Waʿd), a leftist and liberal/secular society that had taken on this name in 2005; and the National Democratic Coalition (al-Tajammuʿ al-Qawmi al-Dimuqrati), a Baʿathist group. As noted earlier, there was reportedly opposition to this move to a coalition by senior clerics such as ʿIsa al-Qasim and even ʿAli Salman himself, both of whom were forced to switch their position in the face of popular opposition to participation in the election.[17] From this point until the 2006 elections, the alliance sought to exert pressure on the regime through petitions as a way to convey its opposition to the 2002 Constitution. In April 2004, for instance, the coalition submitted a petition to the king, reportedly signed by seventy thousand people, objecting to the amended constitution and calling for exclusive legislative power for the elected Parliament rather than for the appointed Consultative Council. Yet the government's repeated response was that the time for petitions had ended with the formation of the Parliament. In addition, it arrested scores of activists from al-Wifaq.[18]

In the face of this deadlock, there emerged growing splits within al-Wifaq between pro-participation currents and those favoring a continued boycott. In 2004, the moderate wing of the al-Wifaq's leadership—comprising Nizar al-Baharinah, ʿAbd al-Nabi al-Darrazi, and Khalil al-Marzuq—resigned from the society's board of directors in protest of the ongoing boycott. Al-Baharinah announced his intention to form a separate political society that would participate in the upcoming 2006 elections.[19] Later that year, Hassan Mushayma issued a scathing attack on "separatists" within al-Wifaq's ranks, arguing that this dissension would dilute the Shiʿa position and bolster the regime's by enabling it to dispense "crumbs" to the newly formed society.[20]

By the fall of 2005, however, al-Wifaq and its allies had apparently shifted its tactic toward participation, with ʿAli Salman making a number of speeches in Friday sermons and local *majalis* (councils) about the need to field candidates in elections.[21] The impetus that prompted the change was the belief that nearly four years of boycotting had yielded little in the way of material improvement for the Shiʿa. Another motive was the 2005 enactment of a new law that would criminalize existing societies, including al-Wifaq, unless they registered as "official" political societies.[22] Critics considered the law a thinly guised attempt to force the opposition into the system and secure their de facto endorsement of the 2002 Constitution.[23]

AL-WIFAQ'S ALLIANCE WITH AL-WAʿD

One important result of al-Wifaq's decision to participate in elections was the formalization of its longstanding ties with the leftist-nationalist al-Waʿd society. The partnership proved mutually beneficial to both sides. An al-Waʿd official described the relationship as stemming from three common goals: an end to discrimination of all forms, a strong constitution, and better distribution of wealth.[24] An unstated goal of the alliance was to deflect any moves by the government that al-Wifaq was challenging the government out of parochial sectarian motives—the presence of its al-Waʿd allies added an important secularist and nationalist dimension to its activism. In addition, al-Waʿd had hoped that a presence in Parliament would keep the legislature focused on holding the regime accountable and improving the lives of its constituents rather than on sectarian wrangling. "Al-Waʿd has a healing power in Parliament; it stands in the middle between the Shiʿa and the Sunnis," noted an al-Waʿd official.[25] Yet, as discussed at length in the next chapter, this attempt at neutral mediation in a climate of sectarian polarization led Sunni Islamists and some regime actors to view al-Waʿd as a "traitor" to the Sunni cause.

THE IMPACT OF AL-SISTANI ON BAHRAINI SHIʿA POLITICAL STRATEGIES

An important development that spurred the shift toward participation was the December 2005 parliamentary elections in Iraq, which secured the Iraqi Shiʿa a large majority. In speeches and articles, al-Wifaq and its supporters set about trying to draw parallels between the Bahraini and Iraqi contexts, citing the hazards of boycotting by pointing to Iraq's Sunnis while applauding the "political maturity" of the Iraqi Shiʿa.[26] According to an editorial in the newspaper *al-Wasat*, "Participation does not mean accepting the political outcome to which the U.S. occupation has led. However, it is a sign of willingness to join the struggle and to take part—from a legislative position—in resolving the many crises and the other expected repercussions in Mesopotamia. . . . [P]articipation is not the final act of the political scene. Instead, it is the first."[27]

The society also began a concerted effort to seek an endorsement of its position from Grand Ayatollah al-Sistani. Al-Sistani's role is a matter of much debate and speculation. Many Shiʿa interviewed in November 2006 widely believed that he issued a fatwa, or edict, endorsing participation in the elections. Yet this assumption obscures the nature of his authority and, as noted previously, his reticence to intervene explicitly in the political affairs of other states. The pattern of local actors' attempting to appropriate his consent and authority for local leverage is not unique to Bahrain. Rather, it is found throughout the region—so much so that al-Sistani's office has issued several statements decrying the use of the grand ayatollah's imprimatur for local political agendas.

What is clear is that al-Sistani's newfound maneuverability and profile in Iraq enabled Bahraini actors to harness his transnational authority in the service of local agendas. A critical test of his authority came in February 2006 in the aftermath of the bombing of the al-ʿAskari Mosque in Samarra, Iraq—one of Shiʿism's most revered sites in Iraq. Al-Sistani issued a call for demonstrations across the Middle East, which was heeded in Bahrain when more than one hundred thousand protestors took to the streets the Friday following the attack.[28]

In Bahrain, the first attempt to solicit his backing was made by the Islamic Scholars Council, led by ʿIsa al-Qasim, through al-Sistani's son.[29] At the same time, another Bahraini cleric, Husayn Najati, who is al-Sistani's formal representative in Bahrain, claimed to have received guidance from al-Sistani to endorse the elections. But he was completely excluded from the Islamic Scholars Council's attempt to gain al-Sistani's endorsement because he is a rival of ʿIsa al-Qasim and a recent arrival to the Bahraini clerical scene.[30] The dispute shows that the local context—clerical rivalries and institutions—was a key factor in mediating transnational influences.

This was also the case regarding the Haq movement, al-Wifaq's principal rival for Shiʿa support, which also sought to leverage clerical authority and external influences as part of a local political struggle.

THE RISE OF THE REJECTIONISTS: HAQ AND ITS ALLIES

In the midst of this initiative, longstanding splits among the Shiʿa reemerged, and a more hard-line faction, led by Hassan Mushayma, split from al-Wifaq. He was joined by other intifada luminaries such as Saʿid Shehabi, ʿAbd al-Wahhab Husayn, and ʿAbd al-Hadi al-Khawaja. Mushayma subsequently formed the Haq movement, which from 2006 on mounted a serious challenge to al-Wifaq's strategy of peaceful engagement.[31]

Haq announced its creation in November 2005 with the argument that al-Wifaq's participation in the elections made it a compromised society. As noted, well before 2005 tensions were brewing in al-Wifaq's ranks, between clerics and seasoned lay activists of the intifada. It is likely that the decision to form Haq was as much a result of these cleric–lay tensions as it was a dispute over political strategy and the merits of boycotting or participating. In the context of the Iraq War and al-Wifaq's solicitation of al-Sistani's backing, these tensions would only worsen.[32]

Broadly speaking, Haq's strategy and goals include an abolition of the 2002 Constitution, which it considers to be illegal, and a return to the 1973 one. Given its constituency of lower-class Shiʿa in marginalized suburbs such as Sitra, Jid Hafs, Muharraq, and Sanabis, it has also made housing improvements one of its key priorities.[33]

According to Haq leaders, a key obstacle to reform has been Prime Minister Khalifa bin Salman al-Khalifa, whom Haq perceives as spearheading Shiʿa repression and being exceptionally hard-line on matters of reform, particularly when compared to the more progressive and open-minded crown prince. Another key goal was the removal of the minister for cabinet affairs, whom the so-called Bandar Report in September 2006 alleged to be the architect of a secret plot to tip Bahrain's sectarian balance in the favor of the Sunnis (to be discussed at length in chapter 4, on the Sunni countermobilization in Bahrain).[34]

Haq's tactics have included a variety of public-disobedience measures: street protests, barricades, destruction of traffic lights, boycotts, and marches, which have earned its followers the appellation "Trotskyites" from its detractors and rivals. Its confrontations are deliberately provocative in an attempt to elicit a crackdown by the security forces, thus drawing more Bahrainis into its ranks. At key junctures, Haq has appeared to escalate the level of violence of these tactics to include Molotov cocktails and firebombs—possibly as a means to subvert initiatives from its rival, al-Wifaq, or to exert increased pressure on the government. In tandem, it has mounted a skillful public-relations campaign with Western governments that has focused on publicizing Bahrain's official discrimination toward the Shi'a and human rights abuses. In August 2006, this campaign culminated in a petition to the United Nations calling for a referendum on the 2002 Constitution.[35] Much of this outreach was coordinated with two other rejectionist groups—the Bahrain Center for Human Rights (BCHR, Markaz al-Bahrayn li-Huquq al-Insan) and the BFM.

Haq's Ambivalent Relationship with Clerical Power

An important dimension of Bahraini Shi'a politics in the post-2003 era is a struggle between Haq and al-Wifaq to win clerical endorsement for their respective political strategies. In numerous interviews in late 2006, Haq's leaders bemoaned al-Wifaq's ability to secure the backing of senior clerics and in some cases denigrated the political maturity of Bahraini Shi'a for falling under the sway of clerical influence.[36] In particular, al-Wifaq's attempts to solicit the endorsement of Grand Ayatollah 'Ali al-Sistani created significant challenges for Haq to mobilize Shi'a sentiment in favor of its boycotting strategy. According to an Haq official, "Haq's job is difficult after al-Sistani's ruling. We don't want to move in the direction of provocation. In principle, we are not in favor of elections, but we don't want to be seen as opposed to clerical rulings. We know religion plays a big part in 'popular' movements, but in some cases this religious aspect is demeaning."[37]

Haq tried to circumvent clerical power through a number of tactics. First, it attempted to portray its movement as nonsectarian, thus attracting more lower-class Sunnis who would be immune to the appeals of *maraji'* such as al-Qasim. This attempt was reportedly aided by the fact that Haq's informal leadership includes a number of Sunni leftists, such as the esteemed intifada activist 'Ali Rabi'a.[38] Second, Haq appears to have orchestrated a whisper campaign suggesting that the regime had reached a quid pro quo with prominent Shi'a clerics such as 'Isa al-Qasim to secure their support in rallying the Shi'a to participate in elections. In return for the clerics' pro-participation stance, this narrative went, the government agreed to drop the controversial Family Law that would erode clerical power over Shi'a social affairs.[39]

Third, Haq leaders noted in interviews that they were playing a waiting game, simply letting al-Wifaq's parliamentary experiment run its course. When the latter society failed to deliver meaningful improvements to the lives of its constituents, the weight of Shi'a support would shift back to Haq's camp. To further erode public confidence in al-Wifaq, Haq sought to portray al-Wifaq—in leaflets, sit-ins, and Internet material—as conspiring with conservative Sunni Islamists in Parliament to enact restrictive social codes on divorce, inheritance, and other social matters, while ignoring the promises about economic and political change that had secured its electoral victory in the first place.

Importantly, the growing prominence of the Lebanese Hizballah movement gave the Haq movement a model of steadfastness and resistance that it used to critique al-Wifaq's pro-participation stance.[40] This development came at a time when Bahraini youths became increasingly enamored of Hizballah's battlefield performance against Israel in 2006 and when Hizballah CDs, posters, billboards, and other memorabilia appeared widely in Bahraini Shi'a suburbs such as Sitra, Sanabis, and Jid Hafs. Haq's leadership went so far as to warn that the "Hizballah model" might take root in Bahrain if the regime did not enact substantial reforms.[41]

Finally, Haq sought to deploy its own cleric to counter al-Wifaq's clerical support. Some Haq supporters regard a Qom-trained cleric, Muhammad,

as their *marja*ʿ. Sanad hails from a prominent family in Manama and follows the Shiraziyyin and al-Mudarrisi currents, but he enjoys far less clout
in Bahrain than does al-Qasim or ʿAbdallah al-Ghurayfi or al-Sistani's intermediary, Husayn Najati. He spends only two months out of the year in
Bahrain, thus limiting his domestic appeal. That said, he has nonetheless
lent Haq a degree of clerical credibility, particularly after he affixed his
name to the list of signatories on the Haq-sponsored petition to the United
Nations demanding a referendum on the 2002 Constitution and an inquiry
into the illegal granting of Bahraini citizenship to Sunni Arabs from Yemen, Saudi Arabia, Pakistan, and other states.[42]

In December 2005, shortly after Haq's formation, Sanad was arrested at
the Manama airport after returning from a trip abroad. The incident provided Haq a ready-made opportunity to mobilize in the street; the movement organized a sit-in and demonstration in Muharraq, near the airport
where he was detained. Violence quickly broke out, leading to several arrests. Shiʿa protestors descended on Bahrain's main shopping mall and the
Formula One racetrack, leading to further arrests and violence. Weekly
sit-ins were subsequently held for both the imprisoned cleric and for the
arrested protestors.[43] The entire aftermath of Sanad's arrest proved to be a
boon for both the stature of the previously obscure cleric and Haq's campaign against al-Wifaq. In the words of one observer, an activist with al-
Waʿd, the Sanad affair provided "clerical top cover" for Haq as a counterweight to al-Sistani's endorsement of al-Wifaq.[44]

The BCHR and the BFM

Aside from Haq, the other grassroots Shiʿa movements that continued
to boycott the Parliament were the BCHR and the BFM. The BCHR was
founded in 2001 by ʿAbd al-Hadi al-Khawaja, an activist affiliated with the
IFLB who had been exiled to Denmark after the mid-1990s intifada and returned to Bahrain in 2001 as part of the general amnesty. The society was
initially registered with the government as a nongovernmental organization in 2001, but this license was revoked after al-Khawaja gave a speech
in 2004 criticizing the prime minister's economic policies. Al-Khawaja's
subsequent imprisonment sparked weeks of rioting. Although the society

has included a number of leftists and liberals in its ranks, its goals reflect a Shiʿa Islamist agenda close to that of al-Wifaq. Yet there are also several important distinctions. In contrast to al-Wifaq's decidedly nonsectarian approach, the BCHR frequently used Shiʿa symbology in its banners and propaganda, including visual depictions of ʿAli and the Battle of Karbala. In addition, the organization has focused almost exclusively on drawing attention to the government's human rights abuses and on occasionally calling for the removal of the royal family.[45]

The BFM was founded by former al-Wifaq luminary Saʿid Shehabi, who resigned in 2005 and rejected the government's amnesty offer to return to Bahrain, preferring instead to stay in London. The organization continues to be based in London, where its media organ, the Voice of Bahrain (Sawt al-Bahrayn), draws public attention to human rights abuses and calls for a return to the 1973 Constitution.[46]

REGIONAL UPHEAVAL AND SHIʿA MOBILIZATION: HOW MUCH CONTAGION?

As noted in the previous chapter, the stigma of foreign—and specifically Iranian—influence has long bedeviled Gulf Shiʿa actors. In the post-2003 regional environment, this dynamic in Bahrain was exacerbated by the escalation of sectarian strife in Iraq, tensions over Iran's nuclear program, and Iran's gains in Lebanon following the 2006 Hizbollah-Israel war.

Regime actors and their Sunni allies in Bahrain frequently accused the Shiʿa societies of being guided by the hand of Iran, Grand Ayatollah al-Sistani, the Lebanese Hizballah, or Bahraini clerics loyal to Iranian Supreme Leader ʿAli Khamenei.[47] As one Salafi cleric and regime supporter noted in 2006, "Shiʿa policies in Bahrain depend on who is ruling in Iran and in Najaf. Most of their decisions are made outside the country. This is our main problem with them—the *marjaʿiyya*. We say to them, 'If you are Bahrainis, then make decisions as Bahrainis.'"[48] Echoing this view, a Sunni hard-line member of the National Islamic Platform Society (Jamaʿiyyat al-Minbar al-Watani al-Islami, or just al-Minbar), Muhammad Khalid Ibrahim, noted that the Sunnis are "outgunned" by the *marajiʿ*. Multiple Sunni interlocutors described ʿIsa al-Qasim as the "most powerful man in

Bahrain" or Bahrain's "third branch of government," who sought to black-mail the government by threatening to mobilize al-Wifaq's supporters in protest.[49] According to this narrative, al-Qasim opposed the government's attempts to pass the Family Law, which included a provision for Ja'fari legal code, because it would undercut his influence over Bahraini Shi'a social matters. "He wants to be the godfather of the Shi'a," noted a promi-nent Sunni newspaper editor.[50] When al-Qasim attempted in 2008 to press the government to release prisoners, an outspoken independent Salafi member of Parliament (MP), Jasim al-Sa'idi, attacked his nationalist bona fides, saying in Parliament: "Had you been in Iran, which you love and defend, you would not have dared—even one in a million—to criticize its government or attack its leaders or interfere in what does not concern you. Had you dared and done this, your head would have rolled or you would have disappeared in the jails of anger."[51]

The Limits of Foreign Clerical Influence

Yet al-Wifaq's close ties to 'Isa al-Qasim and its relations with *maraji'* out-side the country are tempered by several factors. First, there are limits to clerical power over the political choices of Bahraini Shi'a and specifically al-Wifaq. In the society's early days, previously dominant clerics of the al-Da'wa current such as 'Isa al-Qasim, 'Abdallah al-Ghurayfi, and 'Abd al-Amir al-Jamri lacked the legitimacy that many lay activists and younger clerics had earned during the 1990s intifada. They therefore assumed a secondary role in the society's formal leadership structure.[52] More impor-tant, however, the Shi'a constituencies of these *maraji'* are not unthinking supplicants who will blindly follow their political edicts—many interlocu-tors have stated that clerics should stick to matters of *fiqh* (Islamic ju-risprudence) and spirituality. On political matters, they have frequently deferred to seasoned lay activists and younger clerics who have on-the-ground experience.[53]

Added to this, senior *maraji'* outside Bahrain, in particular the politi-cally quietist Grand Ayatollah al-Sistani, are careful to avoid issuing ex-plicit guidance on political matters in countries outside their own. A se-nior official in al-Wifaq noted as much in a 2006 interview, saying, "The *marjaʿiyya* doesn't interfere in affairs outside their countries of origin."[54] Local clerics will frequently inflate their relationship with external *marajiʿ* to bolster their own prestige—a tactic that inadvertently fuels Sunni suspicions about Shiʿa loyalty. For example, in the run-up to the 2006 parliamentary elections, ʿIsa al-Qasim's website displayed statements from foreign *marajiʿ* such as Muhammad Husayn Fadlallah, al-Sistani, and Khamenei enjoining Bahrainis to vote. In fact, these directives were issued to the Shiʿa as a whole throughout the region and were not directed to Bahrain specifically and certainly not to al-Qasim personally.[55]

Another key example is ʿIsa al-Qasim's opposition to the government's Family Law. According to diplomatic reporting, the al-Wifaq parliamentary bloc opposed the government's attempts to pass the Family Law under instruction from ʿIsa al-Qasim, who argued that al-Sistani had not approved its provisions. Yet when the Wifaq parliamentarians met with al-Sistani personally in 2009, he argued that it was not his place to interfere and that Qasim himself was qualified to decide the matter. In other instances, clerics will also wait to gauge the winds of public sentiment and then issue an edict or endorsement to make it appear as if their influence is greater than it actually is.

ʿAli Salman's pragmatic, nationalist political outlook means that al-Wifaq is sensitive to how public opinion perceives the society's linkages to actors and entities outside the country. He has sought to balance expressions of support for external clerics (which can be used to bolster the society's credibility among its constituency) with the need to avoid antagonizing both the regime and potential Sunni partners. For example, in the run-up to the invasion of Iraq, he was careful to emphasize that al-Wifaq supported a secular, democratic Iraq.[56] At the same time, he has organized popular demonstrations of solidarity for Grand Ayatollah al-Sistani, such as a sit-in to support the cleric's mediation efforts in Najaf. On the issue of Iranian support, he has been adamant about the society's independence and autonomous decision making. In a May 2007 interview, he stated: "I have been involved in political activity since 1992 as a leader of the opposition. I can swear by God's book that from that time until now, we have not received a single dinar from Iran. If Iran supported Hizballah with money and weapons, it has no foothold in Bahrain and has no influence on the Shiʿite position. We are extremely clear in Bahrain. Iran is a neighboring Muslim country, but it is a country, and we are a country. We are independent in our decisions and do not allow anyone to interfere in our internal affairs."[57]

Finally, Salman has been similarly guarded and cautious toward the Lebanese Hizballah. "We respect Hizballah's organizational skills, but we are not emulating them," he said in 2006. "In fact, they can learn from us."[58] Much of al-Wifaq's respect for Hizballah was for the same reasons Hizballah was adored at one time by Arabs across the Middle East—for its battlefield successes against Israel rather than as a Shi'a organization with ties to Iran. The same logic applies to the Bahraini Shi'a's embrace of the Palestinian intifada of Gaza—the dramatic images frequently inspired protests, graffiti, and other demonstrations of solidarity. For example, in December 2008, Bahraini Shi'a staged protests in support of Palestinians in Gaza, prompting the Bahraini minister of interior to ask the Parliament to enact legislation making street protests subject to harsher penalties.[59]

These expressions of support illustrate an important point about the impact of the regional environment on Bahraini Shi'a sensitivities and in particular the limits of foreign influence on Shi'a activism. In some cases, events that are unconnected to the rise of Iran or the ascendancy of Shi'a power in Iraq had an equally strong effect on Shi'a sensitivities. Protests in Sitra and Manama in March and May 2005 were inspired more by Lebanon's Cedar Revolution and Ukraine's Orange Revolution than by any incitement from Iran or exhortation from Najaf-based Shi'a authorities. In particular, these national-based demonstrations appear to have resulted in a "rebranding" of Shi'a protest symbols, discarding Iranian and Hizballah flags in favor of the Bahraini flag emblazoned with the slogan "Constitutional Reform First."[60] And of course, as will be discussed in chapter 5, it was a decidedly nonsectarian and populist event that inspired the Pearl Roundabout Uprising of February 2011.

The post-2003 regional environment impacted Shi'a goals and strategies in Bahrain—but in subtle and discrete ways that are not commonly acknowledged. Al-Wifaq's calculations about ending its four-year boycott were partially legitimated by the emergence of independent Shiʿa religious authorities in al-Najaf. It is inaccurate, however, to say that Grand Ayatollah al-Sistani directly influenced the society's decision making. The Iraqi cleric, as well as his local Bahraini interlocutors—ʿIsa al-Qasim and Husayn Najati—continually emphasized that it was not the place for foreign-based *marajai'* to interfere in local politics. He nonetheless played a pivotal role in providing the post facto justification for al-Wifaq's parliamentary participation.

The decision to participate in Parliament provoked deep fissures within the Bahraini Shiʿa political movement. Haq's emergence signified the continued appeal of a radical, rejectionist posture for many disenchanted Shiʿa, particularly youth in long-marginalized villages. The rising profile of the Lebanese Hizballah and its war with Israel provided a useful model for Haq to legitimate its own decision to boycott the elections and to contrast its "steadfastness" with al-Wifaq's more accommodating stance. Despite these influences, regional events related to the rise of Iran and the Shiʿa were not the principle mobilizing force behind dissent in Bahrain.

Nevertheless, the stigma of foreign affinities has continually dogged the Bahraini Shiʿa and formed an important part of the regime's countermobilization, to be discussed in the next chapter. To overcome this stigma, al-Wifaq has been careful to frame itself as a loyal opposition, using nationalist symbols such as the Bahraini flag. In addition, the society allied itself with the secular, leftist group al-Waʿd in an attempt to deflect the regime's timeworn accusation that it was acting out of parochial sectarian motives. As the next chapter will discuss, the presence of al-Waʿd did play a role in mediating between al-Wifaq and Sunni Islamists. Yet the interplay between rising regional tensions and regime repression undermined this cross-sectarian strategy, resulting in a Parliament that became increasingly polarized along sectarian lines to the detriment of legislation that would hold the regime accountable or improve the lives of Bahraini citizens.

FOUR

SECTARIAN BALANCING

The Bahraini Sunnis and a Polarized Parliament

In the midst of the Iraq War, the ruling Al Khalifa family in Bahrain tried to institutionalize the Shiʿa opposition and blunt the appeal of more rejectionist elements. At the same time, it pursued a strategy of countering Shiʿa activism by sponsoring the formation of a united Sunni Islamist bloc, naturalizing foreign-born Sunnis to offset the Shiʿa's growing demographic weight, and blocking any legislation that could upset the existing balance of power. It was a dangerous sectarian strategy that ultimately weakened the social fabric of the country and fed into growing discontent—not just among Shiʿa but lower-class Sunnis.

A contested institution, Bahraini's Parliament stood at the center of the post-Iraq sectarian and geopolitical turbulence. Parliamentary politics became steadily polarized in the wake of Iraq's escalating strife and post-2003 regional tensions. MPs used parliamentary sessions to make increasingly strident expressions of solidarity with Iraq's warring factions, which in turn triggered gestures of support by their sectarian counterparts and occasionally walkouts. The al-Wifaq bloc's inability to deliver real reforms created a climate of mounting cynicism and frustration among a more youthful generation of activists that would eventually spark the revolts of early 2011.

FROM LOYAL OPPOSITION TO REGIME BULWARKS: THE SUNNI ISLAMISTS

Bahrain's two Sunni Islamist societies—the National Islamic Platform Society (al-Minbar), an organization that follows the ideology and strategy of the Egyptian Muslim Brotherhood, and the Islamic Authenticity Society (Jamaʿiyyat al-Asala al-Islamiyya, or just al-Asala), a Salafi organization—proved to be critical bulwarks for the regime in both managing and exploiting the sectarian aftershocks of the Iraq War. The Sunni societies themselves were both animated and in some cases radicalized by the effects of the Iraq War and the regional rise of Iran that played out in Bahrain—in particular, the perception of Shiʿa ascendancy after the 2005 elections in Iraq, the rise of the Sadrists, Bahrain's worsening bilateral relations with Iran, and the corresponding sense of Sunni decline that was manifested in the U.S. siege of Fallujah.

Al-Minbar

Al-Minbar is the political wing of the al-Islah society formed in 1984 under the patronage of ʿIsa bin Muhammad Al-Khalifa, a former labor and social affairs minister and one of the king's uncles.[1] As a Muslim Brotherhood entity, al-Minbar has strong linkages to other Brotherhood groups, particularly in Kuwait (the al-Islah society) and, to a less degree, in Egypt. Its members are quick to point out the divergence between the Brotherhood's program in Egypt and its own platform in Bahrain, which reflects the island's more liberal social mores, cosmopolitanism, and unique political culture.[2] Al-Minbar counts among its members a number of Sunni *hawala* (Sunni Arabs who migrated to western Iran and then returned to Bahrain) and has a largely middle-class constituency (teachers, professionals, and reportedly a high number of police officers). Its platform includes programs for social welfare, education, justice, the arts, women's rights, and market liberalization.

On political matters, it adheres squarely to the royal line. Indeed, its secretary-general, Salah ʿAli, stated repeatedly that the appointed Consultative Council, Parliament's upper house, is a necessary interim step in the process of educating Bahrain's citizenry. "The problem is a lack of parliamentary education in the ranks of the ordinary people," he noted in a 2006 interview. "People don't understand the role of parliament; they think it is always about 'services.'"[3] Although this lament refers principally to the Shiʿa's demand for an empowered Parliament, many al-Minbar interlocutors also pointed to political apathy among Bahrain's Sunnis, noting that they are politically "outgunned" by the Shiʿa. "The Shiʿa are focused on politics; the Sunnis are focused on their cell phones," quipped a Minbar MP in 2006.[4]

Despite hewing to the royal line on politics and reform, al-Minbar has emphasized its conciliatory approach to the Shiʿa. In 2002, for example, al-Minbar's parent entity, al-Islah, held a meeting chaired by ʿIsa bin Muhammad Al-Khalifa, which included the revered Shiʿa cleric ʿAbd al-Amir al-Jamri as one of its attendees. After the 2006 elections, al-Minbar began cooperating with al-Wifaq on social issues and women's rights.

That said, the society also has hard-line adherents who adopted an increasingly vociferous stance against the Shiʿa in the midst of the ongoing turmoil in Iraq. Among them, an MP affiliated with al-Minbar, Muhammad Khalid Ibrahim, was vocal about linking the spread of sectarianism in the Bahraini Parliament to Iraq's sectarian strife. Democracy, he has argued, has exacerbated sectarianism in Bahrain rather than dampened it—and much of the blame is due to the Shiʿa, who have adopted maximalist demands under inspiration from Iran. Yet Ibrahim himself has hardly been a neutral bystander. In 2004, he submitted a motion for a resolution in support of Iraq's besieged Sunnis in Fallujah, which triggered a swift Shiʿa rejection by the al-Wifaq bloc.[5] He has also repeatedly called for increased collusion against the Shiʿa between the al-Minbar bloc and Bahrain's other Sunni Islamist society, al-Asala, which is a Salafi society.[6]

Al-Asala

Al-Asala is the political wing of the Islamic Education Society (Jamaʿiyyat al-Tarbiya al-Islamiyya), Bahrain's main Salafi organization.[7] Founded in

2002, al-Asala draws its support from lower-class Sunnis, principally in Muharraq and Riffa. As is typical with Salafi groups, al-Asala members adopt a more doctrinaire interpretation of Islam that is reflected in dress, social mores, and political practice.[8] Indeed, many have arrived at Salafism after a long journey through other Islamic trends and organizations, which they found unsatisfying or insufficiently rigorous.[9] The al-Asala bloc has historically been more apolitical and at the same time more critical of the ruling family than al-Minbar has because the Salafis have less vested economically and less to lose by challenging the status quo.[10] One important effect of the subsequent perception of Shiʿa ascendancy was the reversal of both these trends: Bahrain's Salafis became more supportive of the ruling family and more political, fielding candidates. Indeed, one independent, nonaligned MP noted in 2006 that the royalty "made politicians out of the Salafis in order to counter the Shiʿa."[11]

There is a strong Saudi influence on al-Asala's outlook that includes moral support and reportedly funding. ʿAdil al-Maʿawada, a key figure in the society who up until 2005 served as its secretary-general, has looked to the grand mufti of Saudi Arabia for guidance on jurisprudence and social matters. During the siege of Fallujah, a local Bahraini reportedly asked al-Maʿawada for guidance about whether it was theologically permissible to attack Westerners in Bahrain in solidarity with Iraq's Sunnis. Al-Maʿawada, citing the Saudi grand mufti, replied in the negative; as nonbelievers residing in an Islamic land, Westerners were a protected category under the Islamic juridical concept of ʿahd (covenant).[12]

The post-2003 environment and the growing fear of Shiʿa ascendency, both in Bahrain and throughout the region, had a polarizing effect on al-Asala, creating a climate where more moderate voices were drowned out by hard-liners evincing a more doctrinaire and hostile attitude toward the Shiʿa. Two notable examples occurred in 2004 and 2005. When in 2004 a prominent Salafi figure and member of the al-Asala board of governors, Salah al-Jawdar, invited the al-Wifaq leader ʿAli Salman to his home, he was subsequently removed from the board. In 2005, when al-Maʿawada, the al-Asala secretary-general, visited the home of the Speaker of the Parliament, ʿAbd al-Hadi al-Marhun—affiliated with the leftist, secular society al-Waʿd—and gave a speech referring to the Bahraini Shiʿa as "Muslims" rather than by the more dogmatic and derogatory term *rawafidh* (rejectionists), he, too, was subsequently forced out by al-Asala's board of governors.[13]

As discussed later in this chapter, more hard-line politicians came to represent the voice of Bahraini Salafis, particularly in Parliament, which they used as a forum to attack the Shiʿa. These politicians included the MP Jasim al-Saidi, an independent Salafi, whose denigration of ʿIsa al-Qasim in June 2008 sparked weeks of rioting by the Shiʿa, and Muhammad Khalid Ibrahim, an MP who was technically aligned with the al-Minbar bloc but whose anti-Shiʿa views caused several Shiʿa to view him as the "Salafi" wing of the Bahraini Muslim Brotherhood.[14]

COOPERATION BETWEEN THE SUNNI ISLAMISTS

One important by-product of the Sunni sense of siege was increased cooperation between the normally antagonistic al-Minbar and al-Asala societies. During the 2002 elections, relations between the two blocs were marked by antagonism, with the key points of divergence being doctrinal views about loyalty to the Bahraini state and Constitution. Salafi parliamentarians, in contrast to those from al-Minbar, refused to swear allegiance to the Bahraini Constitution based on their doctrinal view of the inviolability of the Qurʾan as the only legitimate source of law.[15] Al-Minbar members have chided al-Asala for this doctrinaire practice. "The Salafis demand total obedience to the ruler and the principle of *takfir* [excommunication]; they alternate between extremes. Al-Minbar doesn't have extremes," noted one al-Minbar activist and middle-class engineer.[16] For its part, al-Asala criticizes al-Minbar as too opportunistic. "Al-Minbar needs the Salafis; but quite frankly they will be friends with you only if they need you," noted a prominent al-Asala figure.[17]

Aside from doctrinal differences, the two societies represent different socioeconomic sectors of Bahrain, with al-Minbar appealing to a middle-class constituency drawn from the *hawala* and al-Asala being more lower class and tribal.[18] In the 2002 elections, several interlocutors noted that the al-Asala bloc had effectively outmaneuvered the al-Minbar society through the provision of social services during the preelection campaign. According to some observers, al-Asala was further aided by the perception that al-Minbar was penetrated by the Bahraini security services.[19]

But in the run-up to the 2006 elections, the two societies appeared to have shelved their differences to avoid splitting the Sunni Islamist vote and to counter an emerging coalition between the Shi'a al-Wifaq society and the leftist al-Wa'd. Shi'a activists and their leftist allies allege that this cooperation was deliberately fostered by the Al Khalifa as a sort of sectarian balancing strategy. Those Sunnis who tried to remain independent or engaged in outreach to the Shi'a were increasingly criticized. For example, al-Asala criticized 'Aziz Abul, an independent Sunni candidate in a largely Shi'a district, for running on an al-Wifaq ticket and thus "betraying" the Sunnis.[20]

ENGINEERING DEMOGRAPHY? THE ALLEGATIONS OF THE BANDAR REPORT

In September 2006, a Sudanese-born adviser to the Bahraini Cabinet Affairs Ministry, Salah al-Bandar, released a 240-page report alleging a secret plot by members of the royal family to exploit the island's sectarian fissures and marginalize the Shi'a in advance of the parliamentary elections. The report accused the minister of state for cabinet affairs and member of the royal family, Ahmed bin Atiyatallah Al-Khalifa, of orchestrating the payment of more than six million U.S. dollars for operatives to establish a secret spying cell on the Shi'a, the creation of official nongovernment organizations, the sponsorship of a proselytization campaign of converting Shi'a to Sunnism, and the creation of Internet forums and text messages intended to spread sectarian strife.[21]

The report was a watershed event in Bahraini politics that profoundly impacted the climate of sectarian relations. For many Shi'a oppositionists, it confirmed longstanding fears about the regime's intent and the growing menace from Sunni mobilization. "The Bandar report brought to the surface what many people already suspected; what is new is the documentation," noted a longtime activist.[22] The report's disclosures also proved to be a boon to Haq and its efforts to undermine al-Wifaq's pro-participation stance.

Among the report's most damning revelations was confirmation of a long-standing trend by the government of recruiting foreign Sunnis from the tribal areas of Pakistan, Yemen, Syria, and Saudi Arabia into the Bahraini security services and then granting them citizenship.[23] From Shi'a oppositionists' perspective, this practice was a dangerous escalation of sectarianism and potentially a Faustian bargain with the regime, for three reasons. First, granting citizenship rights to these soldiers was seen as part of the larger strategy to tip the island's demographic balance and make the Shi'a a minority. Second, several oppositionists pointed out that, given the soldiers' origins in the tribal areas of Pakistan, Yemen, and Syria, the recruitment practice could inadvertently be creating a backdoor for the importation of al-Qa'ida's ideology.[24] And last, it was further illustration of the divide between rulers and ruled, creating what one activist called a "*cordon sanitaire*" for the regime.[25]

SECTARIAN POLITICS IN PARLIAMENT

Parliamentary politics in Bahrain from 2002 to 2010 were a critical test of the state's ability to manage the shocks of the post-2003 regional upheaval. In some respects, they created a climate of hope for positive change that acted as a pressure release. Groups that otherwise might have been inspired toward radicalism by the unfolding events in Iraq and the rise of Iran were effectively "nationalized" and developed vested stakes in the Bahraini political project. The unelected Consultative Council continued to exist as the principal obstacle to real reform; oppositionists frequently pointed to the unicameral legislature of 1973–1975 as the starting point for any reform.

In the years following the 2006 elections, parliamentary life became increasingly polarized and rife with sectarian wrangling. Deputies spent excessive time trying to mark their identity rather than responding to their constituents' needs. The Salafi groups sponsored by hard-line elements in the royalty became more entrenched and publicly hostile toward the Shi'a.[26]

The Parliamentary "Reprieve," 2002–2006

The aftermath of the 2002 elections and the escalation of conflict in Iraq had several important effects on parliamentary dynamics. The boycott of the elections by the Shiʿa meant that the Parliament was stacked with pro-regime supporters whose legislation alienated the Shiʿa. The inclusion of the Salafi and Muslim Brotherhood–affiliated blocs helped solidify the Sunni Islamist alliance with the regime that would become even more important in the run-up to the 2006 elections.

From the regime's perspective, the years from 2002 to 2006 were a sort of grace period that allowed the government to foster greater collusion between the Sunni Islamist societies and to encourage their participation. According to an official in the Ministry of Foreign Affairs, "The [Shiʿa] boycott was good. It gave breathing space for the government and allowed it to brush up on its performance. The 2002 elections were a good trial run. Nobody else had the guts to do anything like this in the region."[27]

Interlocutors describe the postelectoral mood in 2003 as calmer and more optimistic. Yet doubts remained, and suspicions mounted about the government's commitment to real reform. The widely despised prime minister, Khalifa bin Salman, retained control of important government portfolios. Senior positions were reserved for the royalty, and the issue of corruption had not been touched. Moreover, there was no opposition bloc in Parliament; the ten Shiʿa who did hold seats were loyalists.[28]

During this period, the appointed Consultative Council emerged as a lightening rod for debates about the pace and scope of reforms. Under the 2002 Constitution, the Consultative Council vets all legislation submitted by the Parliament. Oppositionists frequently charge that there are "too many safety valves" for the regime—the government can submit its own proposals, which take precedence over those submitted by the Parliament. Even if a measure passes the Consultative Council, the king can veto it. The entire process can take up to two years. "The elongation of the process equals veto power," noted a prominent activist.[29]

Many oppositionists spoke admiringly of the Kuwaiti Parliament, arguing that this institution and the traditional *diwaniya* helped defuse sectarianism and promote "real democracy."[30] For its part, the Bahraini government maintained that the bicameral parliamentary structure, in particular the appointed Consultative Council, was necessary to prevent the Parliament's excessive religiosity, political immaturity, and sectarian passions from destabilizing the country. Regime supporters argued that the more liberal-leaning members of the Consultative Council were a necessary check against the Islamist-dominated Parliament.[31]

In the wake of the Bandar report, popular seething against the regime reached levels not seen since the mid-1990s intifada. In April 2006, the newly formed Haq began a campaign of bombings and organized riots to demonstrate its capacity as a spoiler. In leaflets distributed in mosques, it stated that the violence would continue until the Bahraini Shi'a were better represented in a parliament that was fully endowed with legislative power. In several interviews, leaders of Haq stated that the Bahraini Shi'a would endure roughly one year of no movement from the new Parliament before Shi'a public opinion would once again swing back toward Haq's confrontational militancy.[32] Many respondents warned that the expiration of the "grace period" of al-Wifaq's parliamentary tenure without any tangible benefits could push many Shi'a into the ranks of Haq and toward more violent expressions of dissent.[33]

The regime made several attempts to regulate sectarian tensions. Just prior to the 2006 elections, the regime convened a series of multisociety debate forums, the Muntadayat, on topics related to economic reform, civil liberties, and media freedom. According to the forum's organizer, these sessions were designed to implement the regime's "incremental" approach to "change management"—equipping parliamentary candidates and voters in the skills of consensus building, debate, and tolerance for opposing viewpoints.[34] Yet there was a conspicuous absence among the debate participants at these sessions—the two key Sunni Islamist societies, al-Asala and al-Minbar. Subsequent interviews with Bahraini analysts and a Muslim Brotherhood member indicated that this lack of attendance was because they did not have well-developed campaign platforms to address the forum's issues.[35] This absence inevitably fueled the perception among the Shi'a and other oppositionists that the Muntadayat, although appearing on the surface to promote the norms of civil debate and pluralism, were simply a regime ploy to allow liberals and Shi'a to blow off steam.

Deadlock and Disenchantment, 2007–2010

The run-up to the 2006 elections was marred by widespread charges of gerrymandering, "floating" voting stations, and voting by recently naturalized Sunnis. Nevertheless, al-Wifaq secured seventeen out of forty seats—a significant gain, but one that was still short of the majority necessary to enact legislation. Al-Wifaq's liberal allies in al-Waʿd failed to gain a seat, thus depriving the Parliament of a potential secular mediator—the role that al-Waʿd politician ʿAbd al-Hadi al-Marhun had played in the previous Parliament. Sunni Islamists from al-Asala and al-Minbar gained eight and seven seats, respectively. Independent Sunni Islamists secured another eight seats.[36] The final electoral results were an even split between Sunni and Shiʿa, suggesting a Parliament that would grow increasingly polarized. Al-Wifaq thus emerged facing two challenges: Sunni Islamists in Parliament and the activism of Haq and the BCHR/BFM, which threatened to siphon away Shiʿa support as disenchantment grew.

In al-Wifaq's first year in Parliament, there were signs that it was softening its advocacy of "Shiʿa issues" and trying to reach consensus with Sunni parliamentarians.[37] Much of this cooperation may have stemmed from ʿAli Salman's belief that Bahraini's Sunni Islamists were dominated by moderates who could be engaged with a view toward marginalizing the hard-liners. In a 2006 interview, a senior al-Wifaq official noted: "The *takfiri* strand of the Salafis is a minority; we have moderate Salafis here. There won't be a clash in Bahrain—we can weather the storm, despite the war in Iraq."[38]

Regardless of intent, al-Wifaq faced increasing criticism from within the society and without that its parliamentary "experiment" was failing to yield concrete results. From December 2006 to April 2007, there were nearly weekly protests, tire burnings, and barricades in Shiʿa villages—events that al-Wifaq routinely denounced. In addition, al-Wifaq frequently mobilized its own countermarches, usually numbering twenty thousand to forty thousand people.[39] Inside Parliament, al-Wifaq increasingly resorted to walk-outs to register its displeasure and frustration.[40]

Faced with mounting accusations of collusion with the government, al-Wifaq launched a concerted campaign to challenge the government's naturalization policy. In March 2008, ʿAli Salman submitted a motion to compel the minister of state for cabinet affairs, Ahmed bin Atiyatallah Al-Khalifa, to appear before the Parliament for questioning about his role in the activities exposed in the Bandar report's allegations. The measure marked the first time the Parliament had sought to question a government figure—a potential watershed for opposition politics in the country.

In response, the Sunni Speaker of the Parliament submitted a counter-motion for deliberation, arguing that calling ministers before the Parliament was unconstitutional. The Sunni loyalists rallied behind the government, defeated the measure, and submitted their own proposal to summon the Shiʿa minister for municipalities and agriculture, Mansour bin Rajab, on charges of corruption. The resulting deadlock paralyzed the Parliament for six weeks. In the end, ʿAli Salman reportedly reached a deal with the government to withdraw its summons of Atiyatallah if it could submit questions about the government's naturalization policy. In return, al-Wifaq would not oppose the questioning of bin Rajab.

Al-Wifaq subsequently joined forces with al-ʿAmal to form the National Committee to Combat Political Naturalization (al-Hamla al-Wataniyya li-Munahadat al-Tajnis al-Siyasi), culminating in the submission of a series of recommendations on naturalization to the Parliament on October 15, 2008.[41] They included forming a regulatory body to monitor officials and departments involved in the naturalization process and enforcing greater transparency in the granting of citizenship.[42] By late 2009, al-Wifaq had shifted tactics once again. Its representatives began negotiations with regime supporters in Parliament, including Sunni Islamists from al-Asala and al-Minbar to enact constitutional amendments, in an effort to show increasingly frustrated constituents that it was keeping its preelection promises.[43]

REGIONAL SHOCKS ON PARLIAMENTARY LIFE

In each period of Bahrain's parliament, the regional crises—Iraq's strife, Iran's rise, and the 2006 Lebanon War—reverberated across the country's political spectrum. As noted, the crescendo of violence in Iraq became a sort of prism through which the Bahraini Shiʿa and Sunnis viewed their politics.[44] Marches and rallies in support of the protagonists in Iraq polarized the already tense political field in Bahrain. As one member of the al-Wifaq bloc in Parliament noted, "In every multi-sect society, sometimes incidents occur that can be construed as a kind of sectarian feud . . . and that is due to the transnational cultures that occur in the region, similar to the sectarian conflict that is taking place in Iraq or Afghanistan. Naturally there are those that sympathize with this or that sect."[45]

The initial invasion of Iraq in March 2003, the U.S. assault on Najaf in May 2004, the November 2004 battle of Fallujah, and the February 2006 bombing of the Shiʿa al-Askari Mosque in Samarra served as catalysts for demonstrations in Bahrain that exacerbated local power inequalities.[46] The battle of Fallujah in particular provoked fierce parliamentary skirmishes. Deputies from al-Minbar argued that the fighting against U.S. troops was "legitimate resistance," whereas Bahraini Shiʿa deputies labeled the city's defenders as "terrorists." By late 2004, ʿAbd al-Hadi al-Marhun, a member of the liberal Waʿd society, noted that the Parliament had become excessively focused on partisan expressions of solidarity with Iraq's Sunni and Shiʿa protagonists. Al-Marhun subsequently proposed a "code of honor" that would eschew expressions of sectarian solidarity and would "put Bahrain first."[47] The code and al-Marhun's mediation role highlight the important functions that al-Waʿd played in the first Bahraini Parliament—as a sort of interlocutor and intermediary between Sunni and Shiʿa deputies.

The July 2006 Lebanon War injected a further destabilizing dynamic into Bahraini politics. The charismatic figure of Hassan Nasrallah and Hizballah's battlefield performance against Israel proved to be a powerful inspiration to Shiʿa who opposed participation in the elections. The presence of Hizballah banners and posters throughout the Shiʿa areas in Bahrain, particularly at al-Wifaq headquarters and Haq leader Hassan Mushayma's home, further stirred the regime's suspicions and played into the hands of those accusing the Shiʿa of being foreign proxies. This tension was exacerbated in mid-2008 with Hizballah's May 8 move into West Beirut against the Future Movement (Tayyar al-Mustaqbal), a predominantly

Sunni movement. In Bahrain, this assault was widely interpreted as a blow to Sunnis everywhere and further evidence of Shiʿa ascendancy. An editorial in the pro-government newspaper *al-Watan* argued that the Bahraini Shiʿa were emulating Hizballah's strategy of "continually raising the ceiling of demands and creating crises."[48]

Yet there was little concrete evidence of Hizballah's involvement in the Bahraini political scene, either rhetorically or materially. If Hizballah did intervene, it was only to emphasize that Bahraini politics was the autonomous preserve of the Bahrainis themselves and not for a Lebanese national entity to influence or determine. In 2004, for example, a Bahraini activist reportedly asked Hizballah for assistance in hospital administration and charitable work, but Hizballah refused, citing the need to preserve Bahraini sovereignty.[49] Later, on the eve of the 2006 elections, Haq secretary-general Hassan Mushayma reportedly met with the deputy secretary-general of Hizballah, Naʿim Qasim, while on the hajj to solicit his views on how to approach the upcoming elections. Qasim declined to comment, however, stating that the matter was for Haq to decide as a Bahraini entity.[50]

The longstanding accusation that Bahraini Shiʿa were acting as agents of Iran intensified in the context of rising regional tensions with the Islamic Republic. In some cases, tactical errors by the Bahraini Shiʿa fed regime paranoia and empowered hard-line voices. In late 2008, for example, the local Shiʿa group called the Renewal Cultural Association (Jamʿiyyat at-Tajdid al-Thaqafiyya al-Ijtimaʿiyya) contacted the Iranian and Iraqi embassies in Bahrain to seek the advice of Qom- and Najaf-based Shiʿa *marajiʿ* about violations of the Bahraini Constitution. Bahrain's Sunnis predictably responded that the Shiʿa were loyal to Iran, and the head of the Bahraini National Security Agency, Khalifa bin Abdullah bin Muhammad Al-Khalifa, warned of banning the group if it persisted in its foreign outreach.[51] In another instance in 2008, the founding president of the BCHR, Nabil Rajab, warned that the Bahraini Shiʿa might turn to Iran if their demands were not met. "There is no guarantee," he warned, "that future frustration will not force people to adopt extremist views and seek help from foreign powers not liked by Bahrain, such as Iran."[52]

The escalating tensions in North Yemen between Zaydi Shiʿa insurgents (which Saudi Arabia and the government of Yemen allege are backed by

Iran) and the Yemen government injected yet more tension into the Bahraini Parliament. In late 2009, the hard-line Salafi MP Jasim al-Saidi accused al-Wifaq of having met with ʿAbd al-Malik al-Huthi, the field commander of the Zaydi insurgency.[53] Bahrain's Parliament later introduced a motion to issue a statement expressing solidarity with Saudi Arabia in its struggle against the Zaydis. Al-Wifaq's representatives abstained, arguing that Bahrain's foreign policy should avoid interference in other countries' affairs—a move that created even more suspicion about the nationalist bona fides of the Shiʿa.[54]

That said, there were also instances where the inclusion of al-Wifaq in the Parliament also provided an opportunity for the society to demonstrate its nationalist bona fides. In July 2007, Husayn Shariatmadari, editor of the Iranian newspaper *Kayhan* and a confidante of the Iranian supreme leader, argued that Bahrain was rightfully a province of the Islamic Republic. More than five hundred Bahrainis, including al-Wifaq lawmakers, gathered outside the Iranian embassy in Bahrain to protest the statement.[55] In February 2009, al-Wifaq MPs responded harshly to a statement by Iranian MP Darioush Ghanbari that if there were a referendum, Bahrainis would vote overwhelmingly in favor of union with Iran.[56]

In response to these regional challenges, some Bahraini officials, led by the crown prince, appeared to believe that economic reform rather than lasting political changes to Bahrain's participatory institutions would be the surest way to insulate the Shiʿa against potential mobilization and incitement by foreign influences. If political reform was mentioned at all, it was as a process rather than a desired end state. A high-ranking member of the Ministry of Foreign Affairs noted in 2006: "There is no doubt that Iran, Iraq, and Hizballah are playing a role in instigating something we've never seen before. But we can absorb it with economic reform. Most people are focused on their personal standard of living, not on sectarian issues. It is easy to convince unemployed youth if religious scholars preach that the Shiʿa are being targeted. But people believe in Bahrain more than Shiʿism or al-Qaʿida. Reform has given them hope."[57]

Pro-regime voices not only tolerated this fractiousness but appeared to deliberately encourage it to bolster the role of the Al Khalifa as "indispensable" mediators for an immature citizenry and buffers against Iranian encroachment. "There are two ways," argued a member of al-Minbar.

"Saddam's way or the Al Khalifa's way. The Al Khalifa are mediators; without them, Bahrain would go the way of Lebanon or Iraq."[58]

During this period, the role of Saudi Arabia became increasingly important for the Al Khalifa—as a counterweight to Shiʿa activism and the perceived threat of Iranian encroachment. Many interlocutors in Bahrain pointed to Saudi influence as playing a determinant role in preventing the Al Khalifa from accommodating the Bahraini Shiʿa or liberalizing the political system. According to a senior member of Haq, "The Saudi perception is that the liberalization of Bahrain equals the 'Iranization' of Bahrain."[59] Echoing this sentiment, a senior Saudi diplomat in Manama noted on the eve of the 2006 Bahraini parliamentary elections that "we are watching the elections very carefully. The Iranian hand is very strong. We don't want the country handed over to Iran."[60] In the run-up to the 2006 elections, a video reportedly surfaced showing members of the al-Dawasir tribe in Saudi Arabia signing up to vote in the Bahraini parliamentary elections—an effort to tip the sectarian scales by soliciting Saudi support.[61] Other interviewees suspected that the Al Khalifa frequently used Saudi opposition to reform as a pretext to defer making any changes toward democratization. According to one activist in Bahrain, "The Al Khalifa tell us, 'Our hands are tied because of our Saudi patrons.' This is complete rubbish. The Saudis have tolerated liberalization in nearby Qatar and Kuwait."[62]

Yet the actual boundaries of Saudi tolerance would become devastatingly clear in early 2011, when the country was shaken to its core by a popular uprising born of mounting frustration with stalled reforms, parliamentary gridlock, and the Al Khalifa's policy of sectarian divide-and-rule.

FIVE

INTO THE ABYSS

The Pearl Roundabout Uprising and Its Aftermath

Sparked by revolts in Tunis and Cairo, the 2011 uprising in Bahrain was a watershed in the country's political life, a major breach in the country's already frayed social fabric. The unrest, originally cross-sectarian and populist, as well as the government's response to it pitched the country deeper into sectarian polarization. This polarization resulted in part from deliberate government policies and in part from fissures and schisms in the opposition. As the Pearl Roundabout revolt unfolded, the regime skillfully played up sectarian tensions and the bogeyman of Iran. The protestors, despite their best efforts at trying to convey solidarity with protests in Cairo's Tahrir Square and in Tunis, were increasingly tarred as protégés and proxies of Iran and the Lebanese Hizballah.

The tipping point in the revolt, however, was the March 14 Saudi, Emirati, and Kuwaiti intervention in Bahrain, which undermined the mainstream opposition, polarized Bahraini society along sectarian lines, and effectively "regionalized" the popular protests. In tandem, new levels of sectarianism seeped into every corner of Bahraini society. Whatever civility and unity remained were battered by the perfect storm of hard-liner support to Sunni Islamists, a vitriolic media campaign against the licensed opposition societies, and growing radicalization among Shi'a youth.

Underpinning all of this tumult was the erosion of real participatory institutions and forums for dialogue.

THE DOMESTIC ROOTS OF MOBILIZATION

The fact that the Arab uprisings arrived with such force on the tiny archipelago can be explained in part by the mounting frustration among many sectors of the Shiʿa populace with the mainstream Shiʿa opposition bloc, al-Wifaq. Throughout its parliamentary tenure from 2006 to 2010, the society had accomplished little in the way of material improvements for its constituents or substantial political reforms.

One of the few areas where it could claim success was anticorruption, and even here it faced considerable obduracy from the regime, which culminated in a fierce crackdown in late 2010. Starting in August, the regime mounted a dragnet arrest campaign of Shiʿa oppositionists. Most of those detained were members of the outlawed Haq movement, including its spokesperson ʿAbd al-Jalil al-Sinqays. But the government also stripped the pro-Sistani cleric Husayn Najati of his citizenship and arrested a Shiʿa minister for allegedly funneling money to Iran's Islamic Revolutionary Guards Corps (IRGC).

A likely driver behind the crackdown was the burgeoning cross-sectarian cooperation that had appeared in recent months. Sunni and Shiʿa legislators from al-Minbar, al-Asala, and al-Wifaq temporarily shelved their differences to collaborate on an investigation into the appropriation of public land by the royal family.[1] As discussed earlier, such coordination has long been a red line for the royal family. The government reportedly blocked the parliamentary committee from examining records from the registry land—a move that is forbidden according to the Constitution. "We were in the middle of a war," recalled a former al-Wifaq MP. "It was eight months of siege. The government was trying to break the back of the committee."[2]

Despite this crackdown and despite popular disappointment with its performance in Parliament since 2006, al-Wifaq won all of the eighteen seats it had contested, a one-seat gain from the 2006 elections. In many respects, its success was borne of a realization that, despite its failings, it was still the only viable option. "People were angry with al-Wifaq, but they voted out of protest," noted one observer. "And it had won some applause for its recent anticorruption investigation, which was its only real success."[3]

In the wake of its electoral success, al-Wifaq it saw its main media outlet, the newspaper *al-Wasat*, shuttered by the government. A broad media crackdown ensued: several popular blogs were shut down, as was the Facebook site of the revered mid-1990s intifada leader ʿAbd al-Wahhab al-Husayn. Blackberry service—a longtime instrument for al-Wifaq to reach its constituents—was effectively shuttered, stopped by the Bahraini security services.[4] In late December 2010, the prime minister made public calls for greater regional cooperation on combatting "cyber terror." "The use of cutting-edge technology to undermine international relations is a dangerous phenomenon," he stated in a press interview.[5] The net effect was that control of the Shiʿa information sphere gradually fell under the de facto control of a younger cadre of unlicensed, informal activists who had grown impatient with the older and increasingly cautious current of Shiʿa clerics represented by al-Wifaq secretary-general ʿAli Salman. Most importantly, however, the younger, unaffiliated networks were savvier in the use of Facebook and Twitter, which connected them to activists in Tunisia, Egypt, and, to a lesser extent, Libya.[6]

CONTAGION FROM TUNIS AND TAHRIR SQUARE

Despite the longstanding fears of Sunni actors and regimes in the Gulf, it was not the fatwas of Shiʿa *marajiʿ* in Najaf or Qom or the exhortations of Iran's satellite TV that ultimately mobilized the Shiʿa. In the end, it was a populist, nonsectarian contagion from North Africa that ultimately sparked the revolt.

"In the early days of the revolt at Tahrir Square, a lot of us wanted to help Egypt and Tunis," noted one young activist. "The reason many of us got on Twitter in the first place was to follow what was happening in Egypt."[7] An al-Wifaq spokesperson acknowledged this dynamic during a surprisingly frank interview with *al-Sharq al-Awsat* in March 2011: "The demonstrations that took place were an extension of what happened in

Tunisia and Egypt. We admit openly that the political societies did not anticipate the magnitude of the events, just as the governments did not anticipate the magnitude of the existing moves. The incident erupted on February 14 at the personal initiative of young Facebook activists. The political societies quite humbly admit that they were not the primary political mover of the incidents."[8]

Of course, al-Wifaq would have an interest in portraying the revolt as a surge of populism from the street—a wave of discontent that it was riding rather than instigating. But inside accounts of al-Wifaq's internal deliberations corroborate this interpretation, painting the picture of an institutionalized opposition bloc that was utterly taken aback by the scale of popular seething that was largely beyond its control. "I remember being at a meeting with Shaykh ʿAli Salman, trying to decide how we would respond," recalled one senior member of the organization. "We couldn't decide. We thought nothing would happen."[9]

Shortly after the revolts in Tunisia and Egypt, groups of young, loosely organized youths established Facebook pages exhorting followers to mobilize against the regime on February 14, 2011. It is important to note that the calls for demonstrations were largely nonsectarian in outlook; most demanded peaceful reforms and refrained from directly criticizing King Hamad or calling for the overthrow of the Al Khalifa. A few pages did, however, call for "revolution" and the "fall of the regime" (isqat al-nidham). The date of the planned protests were laden with symbolism— February 14 marked exactly ten years since the vote for King Hamad's National Action Charter had transformed the kingdom into a constitutional monarchy. To commemorate the day, the regime had festooned the streets of Manama in banners lauding the kingdom's progress toward democracy. The planned protests, however, represented an entirely different counternarrative—and a brazen critique of the government's failure to carry through with its promised reforms.[10]

In the run-up to the protests, secret negotiations between the royalty and the opposition began. The king summoned al-Wifaq's secretary-general, ʿAli Salman, for talks, exhorting him to call off the planned demonstrations. For his part, ʿAli Salman pressed the king for a formal announcement of reform that would stipulate that the prime minister would be elected from outside the royal family. Implicit in this demand was the dismissal of the current prime minister, Khalifa bin Salman Al-Khalifa, in office since 1971 and a longtime foe of the Shiʿa and political liberals. Deploying a longstanding argument, the king stated that the GCC states—Saudi Arabia in particular—would not countenance the removal of the prime minister.

February 14 arrived with no announcement from the king, and so demonstrations began. Al-Wifaq initially did not publicly sanction the demonstrations, but neither did it prevent its own members from joining them.[11] On February 16, it joined with other Shiʿa Islamist societies and leftist groups in forming an alliance that called for increased support for the youth activists. At the same time that al-Wifaq was confronted with this surge from the street, ʿAli Salman and the moderate cadre of the society's leadership entered into intense negotiations with the crown prince's office. According to one interlocutor present at the meetings, the crown prince had stated that he had "extracted authority" to enter into negotiations.[12] But to what end? Some observers argued that his mandate all along was to simply end the protests, not to negotiate real structural reforms or make concessions. Others asserted that he was in fact initially handed real authority by the king but was gradually overtaken by hard-liners. Regardless of which version is accurate, the longer the impasse persisted, the more that hard-liners within both the opposition and the ruling family gained the upper hand.

In the predawn hours of February 17, 2011, the Bahraini government tried to clear the thousands of protestors who had gathered at Pearl Roundabout, the central traffic circle near the financial district that would later become the iconic symbol of the uprising. With tear gas, rubber bullets, and birdshot, the security forces descended on the unsuspecting sleeping demonstrators. Four were killed immediately, and hundreds of others were injured in a crackdown that came to be known as "Bloody Thursday." It was the beginning of many violent excesses by the regime; all told, at least eighteen civilian deaths were documented by an independent commission for the February–March timeframe, attributable to torture or excessive use of force.[13] Arbitrary imprisonment, denial of medical care, and the prosecution of medical professionals for providing care to protestors were other abuses.[14]

In justifying the move into the Roundabout, the foreign minister invoked the specter of a "sectarian abyss." In fact, the regime incursion hastened a Sunni–Shiʿa split in what had originally been a populist, cross-sectarian protest.[15] In response, al-Wifaq pulled its eighteen members out of the Bahraini Parliament. The licensed Shiʿa societies adopted increasingly maximalist positions. Slogans circulating on the street gradually shifted from advocating "reform" to calling for "toppling" the regime. On March 8, the unlicensed Shiʿa Islamist societies—Haq, the Islamic Loyalty Society (al-Wafaʾ al-Islami), and the BFM—formed the Alliance for a Republic (al-Tahaluf min ʿajl Jumhuriya), which called for the ouster of the Al Khalifa and the creation of a democratic republic.[16] Importantly, the alliance lent its support to the networks of youth activist that had coalesced under the broad title of the February 14 Youth Coalition (Iʾtilaf Shabab Thawrat ʿArbaʿat ʿAshr Fibrayir) rather than to the licensed Shiʿa societies, which it viewed as compromised.[17]

Al-Wifaq was thus increasingly forced to go on the defense, to explain to its constituents and to its interlocutors within the royal family—namely, the crown prince—that the rejection of dialogue was confined to a small fringe of the opposition. At the same time, it was forced to adopt a more unyielding line in negotiations to keep the increasingly impatient youth groups on board and to prevent them from drifting into the camp of the Alliance for the Republic.[18] Regime hard-liners, for their part, worsened the prospects for a negotiated settlement by apparently sanctioning the deployment of paramilitaries into Shiʿa areas and at Pearl Roundabout on March 11. In response, supporters of the Alliance for a Republic marched on the royal court in al-Rifah and the al-Safriya Palace (the king's residence) in Sadad.[19]

Al-Wifaq had warned against the move, arguing—correctly—that it would enflame tensions and play into the hands of royal hard-liners led by the prime minister.[20] In an attempt to distance itself from the protests in front of the royal palace and perhaps assuage the crown prince's concerns, ʿAli Salman rallied his followers to keep the roads open and tried to confine the protests to Pearl Roundabout. But the following day he launched his own counterprotests in front of the prime minister's residence—undoubtedly the result of pressure on al-Wifaq from the increasingly restive youth. "ʿAli Salman's mistakes were threefold," noted one Bahraini activist almost a year later, in late February 2012. "He dithered, he raised slogans to tame the radicals, and he felt compelled to launch his own counterdemonstrations."[21]

At the same time this was happening, the crown prince—under pressure from U.S. officials—extended an offer to discuss most of the opposition's demands in a public dialogue and to put the outcome of these talks before a popular referendum. On March 13, 2011, he put forward his "seven principles" to guide future dialogue, including a parliament with full authority and fair voting districts—measures that tracked closely with al-Wifaq's demands. But al-Wifaq never formally responded to this offer, arguing that before any dialogue could proceed, the current government had to resign, and elections had to be scheduled for the Constituent Assembly.[22] Here again, divisions within the Shiʿa opposition came into play. Al-Wifaq's maximalist demand sprung from the need to build consensus with more rejectionist Shiʿa voices and to keep the support of the Pearl Roundabout demonstrations. Anything less and the society feared it would lose control.

On March 13, just after the crown prince issued his "seven principles," protestors aligned with the Alliance for a Republic blockaded Manama's financial district—a watershed move that placed al-Wifaq in a fatally untenable position. For the prime minister, regime hard-liners, and their supporters in Riyadh, this provocation—combined with al-Wifaq's prevarication on dialogue—was a bridge too far. It buttressed the case for the intervention of Saudi and GCC forces into Bahrain on March 14. And perhaps more worrisome, it pushed the emerging Sunni opposition deeper into the regime's arms.

ENTER THE SUNNI OPPOSITION

An important dimension of the Arab uprisings' impact in Bahrain was the formation of new Sunni opposition groups, comprising actors outside the historically pro-regime societies al-Asala and al-Minbar. Among these new organizations, the most prominent was the umbrella group National Unity Gathering (NUG, Tajammuʿ al-Wahda al-Wataniya) led by ʿAbd al-Latif al-Mahmud, a Sunni cleric. The coalition included two Sunni Islamist parliamentary groups—the Muslim Brotherhood–affiliated al-Minbar society and the Salafi al-Asala society, as well as one nonparliamentary group, the Shura Islamic Society (Jamʿiyyat al-Shura al-Islamiyya).

The NUG has long been the subject of controversy and confusion, with many observers—especially oppositionists—alleging that it is simply a government-sponsored counterweight to the Shiʿa, an "opposition to the opposition." But such accusations obscure the NUG's very real roots in growing Sunni disenchantment with the government. Certainly, it frames itself as a loyal opposition; unlike the more radical elements of the Shiʿa opposition, it never called for the downfall of the monarchy. Yet it also embodied the frustrations of lower-class Sunnis, particularly in the mixed-Sunni–Shiʿa suburb of Muharraq, with corruption, housing shortages, and cuts in subsidies.[23]

In many respects, these issues also formed the grist of al-Wifaq's program; a senior al-Wifaq official noted as much in a September 2012 interview, saying that "the [National Unity] Gathering shares 85 percent of our program."[24] But unlike al-Wifaq, the NUG never called for fundamental structural and political changes to bring about economic and lifestyle improvements.[25] Whenever it veered toward more systemic criticism of the regime, it quickly retreated or offered retractions.[26] As noted by one liberal Sunni oppositionist who frequently served as a mediator between the Shiʿa opposition and the NUG, "I wish the NUG would call for a full, elected Parliament that does not share power with the Consultative Council. They allude to this, but they never call for it."[27]

In the early stages of the uprising, the NUG pursued a dual-track strategy of holding its own demonstrations and entering into dialogue with al-Wifaq. On February 20, 2011, it organized a rally of 300,000 people in front of Bahrain's largest Sunni mosque, al-Fatih (a later report lists a more modest figure of 120,000). On March 2, it held another large gathering, claiming 200,000.[28] Importantly, the NUG was buttressed by the addition of the institutionalized Sunni Islamist opposition (al-Asala and al-Minbar), who joined the outpouring of Sunni populism as a way to compensate for their poor performance in Parliament.[29]

A key initial demand in NUG's counterdemonstration was that the largely Shiʿa-sponsored protests be stopped from escalating into further violence. According to this narrative, NUG's supporters "joined from schools, workplaces, hospitals out of fear of Shiʿa violence."[30] The NUG held three meetings with al-Wifaq: on February 27, March 6, and March 13.

"We think the problem is the Shiʿa opposition—they want a new state, so they reject dialogue," commented ʿAbd al-Latif al-Mahmud later in a September 2012 interview. "Bahrain discovered them."[31] And in an interview with al-Sharq al-Awsat during the uprising, al-Mahmud elaborated on his views that the protests were simply cover for al-Wifaq to implement a sectarian agenda: "The schemes of the Shiʿa sect were not supposed to be carried out this year. They were planned to be implemented in the upcoming years. However, the two revolutions in Tunisia and Egypt have encouraged some leaders of the Shiʿa sect to carry out their schemes. Their demands exceeded the legitimate demands of the Sunni opposition; they have gone beyond this to a higher ceiling of constitutional and political demands."[32]

THE GCC PENINSULA SHIELD INTERVENTION: REGIONALIZING THE CRISIS

On March 14, 2011, Saudi tanks and troops, joined by a small contingent of Emirati soldiers, rolled across the King Fahd Causeway into Manama under the authority of the GCC's Peninsula Shield force. The ostensible aim of the GCC intervention was to shore up the Bahraini regime against an insurgency that was allegedly being incited and directed from Tehran. Evidence of Iranian support, however, has been slim to nonexistent. As discussed in previous chapters, Bahraini Shiʿa actors, from both the parliamentary al-Wifaq bloc and the rejectionist Haq movement, have from time to time threatened to seek Iranian patronage if their demands for reform are not met. But such warnings are mostly bluster, intended as leverage over the Al Khalifa. Moreover, in the months that followed the outbreak of the protests in 2011, al-Wifaq was assiduous in publicly urging Iran not to meddle in Bahraini affairs.[33] That said, on February 28, 2011, Haq leader Hassan Mushayma, in an interview with the Lebanese newspaper al-Akhbar, threatened to seek Iranian assistance if Saudi Arabia intervened.[34]

Whether Iran was actually involved in encouraging or stoking the revolt is beside the point. The Saudi government saw its intervention in

Bahrain—a neighbor often described as its Cuba or Puerto Rico—as a strategic imperative to a restore the kingdom's prestige in the wake of regionwide setbacks to Iran in Lebanon and Iraq. The move was also calculated as a shot across the U.S. bow in the wake of the overthrow of Hosni Mubarak, Riyadh's ally against Iran, whom King ʿAbdallah had accused the United States of casually discarding. The intervention was less explicitly intended as a visible show of monarchical solidarity in the midst of regional tumult. And discussed at length later in this chapter, a third audience may have been Saudi Arabia's own Shiʿa population and, more broadly, domestic opposition.[35]

Across the region, the Saudi intervention into sectarian relations in Bahrain sent ripple effects, enraging Shiʿa populations in the Gulf, Lebanon, and Iraq and prompting a war of words between Sunni and Shiʿa clerical authorities. Unsurprisingly, Iran's response to the crisis was particularly harsh. Iranian foreign minister ʿAli Akbar Salehi verbally condemned the intervention and launched a concerted diplomatic campaign to persuade the United Nations, the Organization of the Islamic Conference (OIC, Munadhamat al-Muʾtamar al-Islami), the Arab League, and even Turkey to halt the crackdown.[36] Supreme Leader ʿAli Khamenei and President Mahmud Ahmadinejad quickly joined in the chorus of Iranian condemnation.[37] Pro-regime clerics from Qom and senior Revolutionary Guards officials demanded a firmer response by Iran, and the paramilitary vigilante group Supporters of the Party of God (Ansar-e Hezbollah) predictably announced plans for a jihad in Bahrain.[38] Importantly, Iranian voices sought to characterize the uprising as largely nonsectarian and populist in nature.[39]

The counter-response from Bahrain and Saudi Arabia to Iran's provocations was immediate. Saudi editorialists and officials were insistent that it was Iran that was playing the sectarian game and that the Saudi intervention was simply acting in the interests of GCC fraternity and common security.[40] For example, Tariq al-Humayd, the editor in chief of *al-Sharq al-Awsat*, took the Iranian foreign minister's statement that "Iran will not stand with its hands tied" as "clear evidence of Iran's sectarian orientation." He went on to argue that "[t]he [Peninsula Shield Force] did not go to Manama to support a particular sect, but rather it went in response to an official request from Bahrain."[41]

Elsewhere in the region, the intervention triggered similar expressions of partisanship. From Lebanon, Hassan Nasrallah condemned the deployment—a statement that would later fuel Bahraini regime accusations of material support to the Bahraini protestors by the Lebanese Hizballah. From the Sunni side, the popular, Qatar-based cleric Yusuf al-Qaradawi framed the uprising as a sectarian bid for power by Iran, thus implicitly endorsing the Saudi incursion.[42]

Yet it was in Iraq where the ripple effects were the strongest. From Najaf, Grand Ayatollah ʿAli al-Sistani—the most popular *marjaʿ* for Bahraini Shiʿa—took the unusual step of actively endorsing the protests, arguing that Bahrainis have an unassailable right to peaceful protest.[43] The firebrand Shiʿa cleric Muqtada al-Sadr went further, urging his followers in Iraq to mobilize in support of the protestors.[44] In the southern, predominately Shiʿa city of Basra and elsewhere in Iraq, the call appears to have been heeded: for three days, approximately twenty thousand protestors marched to condemn GCC's intervention, shouting slogans and burning effigies of the Al Khalifa and the Al Saʿud.[45] Joining the chorus, Shiʿa politician Ahmed Chalabi formed a committee of solidarity with Bahrainis.[46] Throughout the Iraqi Shiʿa media, comparisons were rife between the 1991 intifada in Iraq against Saddam Husayn and the current travails of Bahraini Shiʿa.[47]

At the domestic level, the Saudi intervention created an even starker polarization of Bahraini politics. It placed al-Wifaq in an untenable position toward its constituents, undermining its legitimacy. Those Sunnis who had joined the protests were frightened by the specter of Iran's involvement and al-Wifaq's withdrawal from politics—and the Bahraini government was able to exploit these fears to divide the opposition.

THE REGIME RESPONDS: DELEGITIMIZING AL-WIFAQ

In tandem with the mobilization of Sunni Islamists under the NUG, the government relied on other societal groups to fracture the opposition and divide al-Wifaq from any allies. First, it attempted to create the impression of a split between al-Wifaq and its liberal allies—namely, al-Wa'd. In an April 2011 press campaign, the regime noted that al-Wa'd—along with two other liberal societies that had allied themselves with al-Wifaq—broke from al-Wifaq over its explicitly sectarian stance.[48] In fact, al-Wa'd never broke with al-Wifaq—its tactics and announcements during the revolt roughly paralleled al-Wifaq's up to and including the pullout from the National Dialogue in July 2011.[49] In tandem with this move, the Bahraini judiciary sought to dissolve al-Wifaq on the grounds that it was breaching the Constitution. The move was averted only through the direct intercession of senior U.S. State Department officials, but the government would raise the issue of criminalizing the society again in June and September 2012.[50]

Royal hard-liners gave a platform to a vocal Shi'a critic of al-Wifaq, a young cleric named Muhsin al-Asfur. In the summer of 2011, al-Asfur issued a number of provocative statements aimed at undercutting al-Wifaq. He cast doubt on the Pearl Roundabout protests as truly popular in character, arguing that they had nothing in common with the movements in Tunis and Cairo but were rather the handiwork of a small group of provocateurs led by al-Wifaq. He announced the formation of a rival Shi'a organization to al-Wifaq, a political society composed of "loyal professionals" that aimed to fill the eighteen parliamentary seats left vacant by the al-Wifaq deputies. In perhaps his most pointed attack on al-Wifaq, he cast doubts on the clerical bona fides of 'Ali Salman, stating in an interview that "[Salman] went to Qom for seven years and worked as an office boy. He was regarded as a joke there."[51]

As 2011 unfolded, the regime resorted to the timeworn tactic of tarring al-Wifaq as a pawn of foreign powers—Iran, Iraq, the Lebanese Hizballah, the United Nations, and even America. In May, the *Gulf Daily News* reported on Wikileaks disclosures that al-Wifaq had requested U.S. pressure on the Bahraini royal family and that its cadre had received training from the U.S.-based National Democratic Institute in "how to avoid the demands of its voters."[52] The report also alleged that the cables proved that al-Wifaq and Haq were actually two sides of the same coin. "We will not hesitate to join the Shi'a on the streets if they decide to stand behind Mushayma," stated an al-Wifaq member in a cable cited in the report.[53] Also in May, the government sharpened its critique of al-Wifaq's foreign dealings, accusing its municipal council members of meeting with the United Nations in Manama and requesting greater assistance.[54]

Most significant, the Bahraini government leveled multiple accusations that Lebanese Hizballah was actively training Bahraini protestors, especially those from Haq and al-Wifaq. In March 2011, for example, the Bahraini foreign minister alleged extensive support between the Lebanese militant group and Bahraini Shi'a, going so far as to assert that the very problem of sectarianism itself had been imported to the archipelago by Hizballah and Iran.[55] In late April, the Bahraini government sent to the United Nations secretary-general a confidential report detailing extensive evidence of Hizballah's material support.[56] A widespread press campaign followed via op-eds and news stories in the state-sponsored press. In one illustrative example, an opinion writer in the pro-regime daily *al-Watan* exhorted her readers: "Let us stop calling Hizballah an opposition. We need to remind them that their real name is Hizballah and not al-Wifaq, so that the whole world knows with whom it is dealing."[57]

Yet evidence of actual material support was slim. An independent commission's report (to be discussed more fully later) conveyed no evidence, nor did official U.S. statements.[58] According to some sources, a major basis for the accusation was that al-Wifaq's movement of protestors from Pearl Roundabout to strategic points throughout the city paralleled similar tactics employed by Lebanese Hizballah during its May 2008 incursion into West Beirut.[59]

REGIME COUNTERMOBILIZATION IN THE MEDIA

In tandem with this strategy of trying to discredit al-Wifaq as an Iranian proxy, the Bahraini regime conducted an extensive media campaign against the protests, designed to isolate the movement from outside sympathizers and portray it in a negative, sectarian light. This effort took shape in two key areas: traditional news outlets and social media.

First, traditional news outlets such as satellite TV and newspaper coverage were suppressed or minimized. Al-Jazeera and al-'Arabiya, the two major pan-Arab television outlets, covered the protests and the crackdown only sparingly—most of their news was focused on Libya. The result was that domestic coverage of the revolt was dominated by the official state television channel, Bahrain TV (BTV), which predictably characterized the protestors as being Shiʿa in composition and taking their cues from Tehran. Iran's Press TV and the Iranian-controlled Arabic satellite television station al-ʿAlam devoted equal time to both Libya and Bahrain, covering the latter with increasingly critical and strident language. Hizballah's television network al-Manar was another important, foreign source of news on the crisis.[60] Since BTV and the Sunni-controlled satellite TV stations did not host Bahraini Shiʿa figures, those protest leaders who wanted a platform for their views appeared on al-Manar, al-ʿAlam, or Iraqi Shiʿa channels, which provided further grist to the Bahraini government's accusations that the protest movement was being directed from Iran.[61]

In the realm of print media, restrictions were similarly draconian. On April 2, 2011, the Bahraini Ministry of Interior suspended the country's only independent, opposition newspaper, al-Wasat, whose editor in chief, Mansur al-Jamri, had been a longtime critic of the regime. The reason given by the government was the allegation, aired on BTV, that the paper had published articles on the unrest that had been copied from reports published at an earlier date in other countries. Al-Jamri admitted the mistake but argued that the newspaper had been the victim of a sting operation carried out by the government because its editorial slant was sympathetic to the protests. Publication was resumed only after most of its senior editors, including al-Jamri, were replaced.[62] Although al-Jamri was subsequently reinstated, the newspaper's board was increasingly polarized, with many Sunnis boycotting it. A number of outside observers, including Human Rights Watch, noted that the paper's coverage of arrests, detentions, and deaths in custody was "considerably reduced." The Human Rights Watch report went on to note that al-Wasat's coverage of events in Bahrain had become virtually indistinguishable from that of official Bahraini outlets.[63]

Despite these measures, the suppression of traditional media pales in comparison to the broad crackdown on social media during the unrest. The Bahraini government was undoubtedly aware of social media's dangerous potential for mobilizing and coordinating street protests. As noted, it instituted an Internet-filtering policy and shut down the websites of popular opposition leaders such as ʿAbd al-Wahhab al-Husayn. It also ordered that a Blackberry service provider shut down its service.[64] In the wake of the February 17, 2011, demonstrations, this suppression intensified.

A key theme informing the government's policy was that sectarian extremists had effectively hijacked social media—in particular Twitter, YouTube, and Facebook—to use these outlets to weaken Bahrain's social fabric and unity. It was incumbent upon all Bahrainis, the regime urged, either to actively demonstrate in opposition to these voices or to stop using social media altogether in order to deny the extremists an audience.[65] The regime ironically used these same social media to send out its message. On February 20, for example, a Facebook page with the title "Silent Peace—Bahrain" appeared on the Internet, exhorting Bahraini citizens to refrain from using Facebook and Twitter from the hours of 10:00 A.M. to 10:00 P.M. daily. The stated reason was to begin the process of national reconciliation and healing. "Enough hurtful things have been said online," the page read. "But that is the cost of having the beautifully diverse population that we have."[66] In April, the official Bahrain News Agency published an interview with a Bahraini Internet user underscoring the government's ambivalent view of social media as a double-edged sword: "I believe that 70 percent of the Bahrain situation was segregated [sic] through the sectarian rumors and broadcast messages. Therefore, I am against them all. Unfortunately, the negative impact of Facebook and Twitter outweighed their positive ones in recent events, since people were misusing them instead of trying to fix things."[67]

At the same time, pro-regime and pro-unity Facebook sites began springing up, as a counter to the protestors' "Day of Rage" sites. According to their founders, these Facebook sites, like the appeal to stop using Facebook altogether, were intended to combat the dangerous sectarianism and extremism that was polarizing the state. For example, on June 22, 2011, Bahrain's National Dialogue Media Center established a presence on YouTube, Twitter, and Facebook.[68] The Bahrain News Agency announced an expanded presence on social media sites, with the aim of publicizing the "achievements . . . of the royal reform project."[69] Foreign Minister Khalid al-Khalifa became a regular presence on Twitter, with many of his tweets reposted on Bahrain's traditional media sites.[70]

FAILED ATTEMPTS AT DIALOGUE

It is important to note that the government's response was not wholly confined to repression and countermobilization. As discussed earlier, the opposition found in the crown prince's office what appeared to be a committed interlocutor and partner. But the faltering dialogue between the two sides was undone by both al-Wifaq's increasingly hard-line position—itself a reflection of youth dynamics beyond its control—and the strength of hard-liners in the royal court, led by the prime minister and backed by Saudi Arabia.[71]

In late May 2011, however, the king himself unilaterally announced a National Dialogue between the government and the opposition. Unlike the informal talks between the crown prince and al-Wifaq, the new outreach was rooted in a fundamental asymmetry. The dialogue took place after the government, backed by Saudi and Emirati troops, had mounted a broad-based campaign of arrest, detentions, and alleged torture, effectively degrading the scale and strength of the protests. Moreover, the royal family dictated the terms of the dialogue with Saudi guidance but little input from the opposition. The topics ranged from governance to the electoral system to women's and children's rights. There was also no mention of a popular referendum, and any recommendations resulting from the deliberations would have to be approved by the king.[72]

From the opposition's perspective, the most onerous aspect of the dialogue was the regime's screening and vetting of its participants. More than 320 individuals took part, but only 25 of them represented the opposition societies. Each society was asked to send five representatives—al-Wifaq ultimately sent only four because its fifth nominee was imprisoned.

Al-Wifaq's participation startled many observers—a possible explanation was last-minute pressure from the United States and the belief that participation—and then a theatrical, public withdrawal—would help strengthen its bona fides with the increasingly impatient Shiʿa street.[73] Al-Wifaq's ally al-Waʿd also participated, to the surprise of many, despite the fact that its license had been revoked in March and its chairman, Ibrahim Sharif, had been arrested and sentenced to five years in prison.[74] "The arrest of Ibrahim was a signal to the Sunnis," noted one activist later. "They are saying to everyone: 'Nobody is safe. We will go after you. You have to pick your sides.' "[75]

An especially contentious issue regarding the dialogue was the presence of many "oppositionists" who were in fact government loyalists. These loyalists included the NUG, led by ʿAbd al-Latif al-Mahmud, and representatives from the major Sunni Islamist groups al-Asala and al-Minbar.[76] Most onerously from the Shiʿa perspective, the pro-government delegation included ʿAdil Flayfil, a former Bahraini intelligence officer accused of playing a prominent role in suppressing the mid-1990s intifada. In the run-up to the dialogue, Flayfil threw a number of provocative taunts at al-Wifaq that ran counter to the dialogue's spirit of national reconciliation: "I would love to sit at the table with Shaykh ʿAli Salman from al-Wifaq and other opposition groups for the National Dialogue. But there is an Iranian agenda in this dialogue that will be promoted and I am afraid it will cause the collapse of the entire talks. I demand [al-Wifaq and Haq] to put down their weapons and stop guerrilla training in Iraq, Iran, Lebanon and Syria."[77]

On July 17, 2011, less than three weeks after the dialogue commenced, al-Wifaq pulled out. In a letter to the chairman of the dialogue, al-Wifaq's delegates cited the government's nonnegotiable preconditions and the regime's unwillingness to hold "fair" and "transparent" elections. According to a source present at the meetings, the trigger for the walkout was a highly inflammatory reference to the Shiʿa as *rawafidh* (rejectionists) by the Salafi MP Jasim al-Saʿidi.[78] In a subsequent interview with al-Jazeera, ʿAli Salman elaborated on the deeper roots of al-Wifaq's rejection of the dialogue. The society's representation in the sessions was limited to 1.6 percent of the participants, yet al-Wifaq, he claimed, represented 60 percent of the Bahraini population.[79]

Al-Wifaq's withdrawal quickly triggered a cascade of similar walkouts by its like-minded allies. Three of the leading liberal opposition groups—the National Democratic Assembly (al-Tajammuʿ al-Watani al-Dimuqrati), al-Waʿd, and the Progressive Democratic Tribune Association (Jamʿiyyat al-Minbar al-Dimuqrati al-Taqaddumi)—launched similar critiques of the sessions and announced their withdrawal on July 18.[80] Throughout 2012, the same complaints would resurface continually. One senior official in al-Wifaq commented in a 2012 interview, "The government is trying to dilute the dialogue. It is not serious. It brings everyone to the table. The NUG is 'remote control' for the regime. We tell them, if you are going to bring the NUG, then bring Mushayma and 'Abd al-Wahhab Husayn—they are the people. If they are not part of the dialogue, you will have a problem. But in our view both sides are too extreme: Wahhab cannot call for a republic, and the NUG cannot say the prime minister must be appointed."[81]

When the dialogue finally concluded in late July, the government had agreed to expand the Parliament's legislative and oversight powers, according to a statement by the official Bahrain News Agency. Yet al-Wifaq was unconvinced, and its delegates to the dialogue subsequently lambasted the outcome as fraudulent because the sessions had been stacked with government loyalists or phony "oppositionists." "The dialogue is clearly theater, the goal of which was to market a particular dish," noted al-Wifaq official Hadi al-Musawi in a news conference on July 24. "What came out of the official media on the dialogue exposes lies and deceit."[82]

The government's Sunni supporters predictably seized on these withdrawals and al-Wifaq's rejection of the results as evidence of the opposition's intransigence and, even more ominously, its deference to foreign powers—namely, Iran. The Salafi society al-Asala was especially vocal on this point. Its spokesman claimed that the Shi'a Islamist group had taken orders directly from Iran, citing the fact that al-Wifaq pulled out of the dialogue two days after the head of Iran's powerful Guardian Council, Ayatollah Ahmad Jannati, had stated in his Friday sermon that dialogue was pointless and had called for an "Islamic occupation of Bahrain."[83] Other Sunni actors were similarly critical. In an interview with al-'Arabiya, NUG leader 'Abd al-Latif al-Mahmud condemned al-Wifaq for trying to "exacerbate the crisis" for self-serving ends.[84]

Although al-Wifaq had rejected the king's offer of dialogue as inherently flawed and stage managed, it had tried to leverage external support in mediating the crisis as it was happening. Specifically, in late March 2011 'Ali Salman solicited mediation from Kuwait's Speaker of the Parliament Jasim al-Khurafi.[85] The ultimate goal, however, was to secure intercession from the Kuwaiti emir himself. On March 27, al-Wifaq told foreign news sources that it had accepted Kuwaiti mediation and that an al-Wifaq delegation had traveled to Kuwait City for preliminary discussions with a range of officials and nonofficial interlocutors. On the next day, however, the Bahraini Foreign Ministry issued a vehement denial of Kuwait's role.[86] Jasim al-Khurafi was careful to tell a Kuwaiti newspaper that he had yet to receive any formal invitation from the Bahraini authorities. "If I receive an invitation," he said on March 26, "I will welcome it because it is from my dear brothers, but I will not accept or reject it until I have consulted the competent authorities in Kuwait."[87]

In October 12, 2011, al-Wifaq issued its Manama Document, which specified its vision for a Parliament with legislative and oversight powers, an independent judiciary, the drawing of equitable voting districts, and an end to discrimination against the Shiʿa. The document would later become a reference point for al-Wifaq's subsequent negotiations, but pro-government commentators saw it as evidence of al-Wifaq's perfidy against the state. The tone of attacks against al-Wifaq became increasingly more strident and violent. Even the crown prince, previously a voice of moderation and deliberation toward al-Wifaq, became increasingly rigid, arguing in television interviews that he would no longer tolerate any calls for boycott.[88] In the midst of these attacks, an independent fact-finding body commissioned by the king to investigate the violence of February and March 2011 released its highly-anticipated report.

THE BASSIOUNI REPORT AND ITS AFTERMATH

In November 2011, the Bahrain Independent Commission of Inquiry (BICI, al-Lajna al-Bahrayniyya al-Mustaqila li-Taqassi al-Haqaʾiq, also known as the "Bassiouni Commission" after its head, the Egyptian war crimes expert M. Cherif Bassiouni) released a highly critical report on the government's conduct during the unrest. Citing the "use of unnecessary and excessive force, terror-inspiring behavior, and unnecessary damage to property," the report went on to criticize the government's systematic policy of arbitrary detentions, denial of medical care, and torture.[89] It found no evidence of a link between Iran and the protestors, nor did it attribute any abuses to the Saudi and GCC troops present in the country. The BICI's report, along with other critics of the Al Khalifa, argued that the continued marginalization of the Bahraini Shiʿa and the stalling of political reform were radicalizing larger segments of the Shiʿa populace. At the same time, however, it

criticized the opposition for failing to respond to the crown prince's offer of dialogue.[90] Importantly, the commission's recommendations were
intended to prevent further abuses and bring to justice those who were
implicated in the crackdown. But it never addressed the need for broader
structural reforms, which had fueled the unrest in the first place.[91]

The government took some measures to implement the recommendations, but both opposition and outside parties such as the United States
criticized many of these measures as hollow and token.[92] Trials of security
officials involved in abuses were confined to the lower ranks, and oversight bodies that the BICI had recommended lacked real authority. "The
regime has created the shells of institutions and reforms recommended by
BICI, but it needs to breathe life into them," noted one Western diplomat.[93]

Meanwhile, there was mounting evidence that sectarianism was seep-
ing deeper into Bahraini society—in some cases with regime hard-liners'
tacit encouragement. In December, the mixed Sunni–Shi'a neighborhood
of Muharraq was wracked by rioting after Sunni citizens assaulted a Shi'a
Ashura procession whose participants were allegedly shouting political
slogans. In the wake of the chaos, hard-line Sunni voices voiced support
for the assault, and both the royal court minister and the prime minister
criticized the Shi'a for being deliberately provocative. The minister of interior, however, appeared to take a more evenhanded view; in the aftermath of the rioting, he called for an investigation into the Sunni assault
on the procession.[94]

In early and mid-2012, there were signs that the hard-line faction was
ascendant, claiming a new "normalcy" in Bahrain's domestic affairs. Bahrain's successful hosting of the Formula One Grand Prix no doubt buoyed
this sentiment—the car race and its attendant throngs of foreign specta-
tors were long anticipated as a litmus test for Bahrain's recovery from the
2011 unrest. The release of a halted U.S. arms delivery was another boost.
In the fall of 2011, concerns about the government's abuses had prompted
a U.S. Congress resolution to delay the planned sale of $53 million worth
of arms, including forty-four Humvees and several hundred missiles. A
U.S. State Department press release on January 27, 2012, indicated that a
portion of the sale was in fact proceeding, using a clause that allowed military equipment totaling less than one million dollars to be sold without
congressional approval. In the release, the State Department cited "ini-

tial steps" by the Bahraini government in implementing the BICI's recommendations and stated that the equipment—comprising nonlethal spare parts—was being used to "reinforce reforms in Bahrain."[95] Not included in the release, the State Department emphasized, were Humvees and munitions, such as tear gas canisters and stun grenades, that the Ministry of Interior used for crowd control.[96]

The arms sales was ostensibly intended to shore up the more moderate, pro-reform crown prince against the hard-liners—the State Department announced the approval during a visit by the crown prince to Washington in May 2012. Yet the crown prince had been steadily stripped of significant authority and diplomatic support since the Saudi intervention in Bahrain. Moreover, the conservative royal faction—which include the Bahrain Defense Forces (BDF) commander—interpreted the transfer as a "win" and a sign of normalcy in U.S.–Bahrain relations.[97] For the opposition, specifically al-Wifaq, the arms release was a disheartening blow, confirming that Washington, in the words of one activist, "carries a large carrot and a small stick" in its dealings with the regime.[98] It also undercut al-Wifaq's strategy of engaging with the regime, lending further credence to more militant voices from the rejectionist camp and empowering the February 14 Youth Coalition.[99]

Encouraged by these developments, regime hard-liners took a number of steps to further consolidate control. In late April, the royal government appointed Samira Rajab, a former Consultative Council member and Baʿathist sympathizer whose partisan support for Saddam Husayn and attacks on Grand Ayatollah Sistani had long exacerbated sectarian tensions in Bahrain.[100] The regime concurrently arrested human rights activist Zaynab al-Khawaja for staging a protest to demand the release from prison of her father, the BCHR founder ʿAbd al-Hadi al-Khawaja; she was later sentenced to a month in prison. On May 5, the government detained another popular dissident, Nabil Rajab, for his tweets.

There were additional restrictions in the media and legislative realm. Many of these restrictions increasingly took aim at cleric authority. The Bahraini Parliament passed legislation on May 9 that increased the punishment for assaults on security forces and issued a number of threats against the Shiʿa cleric ʿIsa al-Qasim. In July, Bahraini courts ruled in favor of a government petition to dissolve al-ʿAmal (Islamic Action Movement), citing its adherence to the teachings of "a religious scholar who bla-tantly calls for violence and instigates hatred"—a reference to Muham-mad Taqi al-Mudarrisi and, more obliquely, 'Isa al-Qasim.[101] In the media realm, state television renewed its attacks on Bahrain's only independent newspaper, *al-Wasat*. On the streets, opposition sources and outside non-governmental organizations cited increasingly forceful tactics by security forces, such as the use of bird pellet shotgun shells at close range, the forc-ible breaching of homes, and tear gas fired directly at protestors.[102]

PRESSURES ON AL-WIFAQ FROM BELOW

As a result of this crackdown and the resulting stalemate on reform, the institutionalized Shi'a opposition represented by al-Wifaq lost ground to the more radical February 14 Youth Movement. Intra-Shi'a tension on the island was historically framed through the lens of conflict between the Shiraziyyin and Da'wa currents of the Shi'a community. But since the Pearl Roundabout uprising, clerical lineage or ethnic distinctions seem to mat-ter less; class and generational differences are now the main fissures af-fecting Shi'a activism. The Shi'a opposition has increasingly been infused with a more populist, youthful orientation, one that rejects participation in government-sponsored dialogue and the Parliament and dismisses the authority of al-Wifaq's spiritual and political referent, 'Isa al-Qasim.

The Rise of the February 14 Youth Coalition

This new trend is embodied in the February 14 Youth Coalition. Forged in the early days of the uprising, the coalition is a leaderless network of youth activists formed along neighborhood lines and adept at using social media for coordinating protests. The movement has shown a strong affin-ity toward the imprisoned leaders of Haq, al-Wafa', the BCHR, and the BFM. That said, it is not monolithic in either its geographic roots or its sources of political inspiration. Some elements look to the exiled leader-ship of the BCHR, whereas others have ties to the Najaf-based Bahraini opposition.[103] In addition, the movement's street demonstrations and assaults on police stations are conducted by highly autonomous, secretive networks usually organized by neighborhood, town, or village.[104] What binds them together are a generational cohesion—they tend to be in their teens and twenties—and their demand for an abolition of the monarchy and the creation of a democratic republic.

The movement frames itself as an "internal counterrevolution" aimed at the paralyzed and aging leadership of al-Wifaq and its disappointing engagement with the regime, which since the 2006 parliamentary elections has yielded little in the way of tangible improvements for Bahrain's Shiʿa.[105] In interviews, activists spoke of ʿAli Salman as having forfeited the revolutionary credentials he won during his role as a leader of the mid-1990s intifada and through his subsequent imprisonment. "Al-Wifaq has become 'the domesticated opposition' [al-muʿarada al-muddajna]," a youth activist lamented.[106] The leader of al-Wifaq himself seemed to acknowledge this characterization in September 2012, noting that "on February 14, 2002, the king changed the National Action Charter; the youth were ready to rise. We told them, 'Give us a chance with dialogue.' In the 2006 parliamentary elections, we participated; in 2010, the youth said, 'See, you achieved nothing.' Now we can't say we are on the right track."[107]

Of course, the intransigence of the February 14 Youth Coalition may have certain benefits for al-Wifaq in its dealings with the regime—creating a useful "good cop, bad cop" dynamic. "We tell the regime, 'Deal with us,'" noted Salman. "We are the ones calling for peaceful reform and a constitutional monarchy, while the youth and the Alliance [for a Republic] are calling for the downfall of the [royal] family."[108]

The Youth Coalition's tactics on the streets have also become more and more brazen, moving away from Molotov cocktails and toward crude improvised explosive devices. "Before, we used to see the youth throw Molotov cocktails and run. Now they throw them and stand their ground," observed one Western diplomat in September 2012.[109] A strong theme of anti-Americanism increasingly informs the movement's discourse and actions. Shortly after the announcement of the release of U.S. arms to Bahrain in May 2012, the movement declared a "Week of Resisting American Arms Sales" on its Facebook page, an announcement emblazoned with blood-drenched shotgun shells stamped "U.S.A." In tandem, the movement sent dozens of protesters toward the U.S. Navy's Fifth Fleet headquarters in Juffair. Another important attribute of the February 14 Youth Coalition is its strong affinity with Shiʿa activists in neighboring Saudi Arabia. Shiʿa protests in Saudi Arabia's Eastern Province, sparked by the arrest of the popular Saudi Shiʿa cleric Nimr al-Nimr, have elicited demonstrations of solidarity by the February 14 Youth Coalition and vice versa.[110]

Contestation of Shiʿa Clerical Authority

In press statements and speeches, the Bahraini regime has increasingly targeted Shiʿa clerics such as ʿIsa al-Qasim for inciting street protests by Bahraini youth. But this exclusive focus on clerical authority as a determinant and driver of Shiʿa activism, often mirrored in some outside analyses, is misplaced.[111] New forces in the Shiʿa political scene are increasingly challenging the traditional authority of clerics, who are thus being forced to adapt their positions to prevailing popular sentiment. As discussed previously, clerics may attempt to take credit for protests and decisions when in fact they provided only post facto endorsement or legitimation. This trend is not new; Shiʿa clerical authority in Bahrain has always been subject to a give-and-take process of debate and consensus building between lay activists, the political elite of al-Wifaq, and Shiʿa constituents.

But since the Pearl Roundabout uprising, the "street"—embodied by the February 14 Youth Coalition—has acquired greater authority and prominence through the use of social networking technology. Specifically, many in the coalition downplay ʿIsa al-Qasim's political authority, deferring instead to imprisoned Shiʿa leaders such as Hassan Mushayma (Haq), ʿAbd al-Wahhab Husayn (al-Wafa), and ʿAbd al-Hadi al-Khawaja (BCHR). According to one activist in the February 14 Youth Coalition, "I don't like the clerics; they belittle the February 14 movement as just kids. These clerics say that 'we [the clerics] own the streets.' But actually the February 14 movement does."[112]

In tandem with this challenge from the street, internal shifts are under way within al-Wifaq that weaken the clerics' role. Al-Wifaq's second-tier leadership is increasingly drawn from secular lay activists, as is its parlia-

mentary representation. In 2006, for example, there were five Shi'a clerics in the Bahraini Parliament; in 2010, there were only two (Hassan 'Isa
and Hassan Sultan). Similarly, the most likely candidates to succeed 'Ali
Salman as the Wifaq secretary-general—Khalil al-Marzuq or 'Abd al-Jalil
Khalil—are not clerics.[113]

Taken in sum, these developments further erode the role of 'Isa al-
Qasim, whose influence over al-Wifaq stems in large measure from his
personal relationship with 'Ali Salman. But there are growing signs of
divergence between the two. For example, in February 2012 al-Qasim
exhorted the Shi'a to "smash the mercenaries [security forces] wherever
you find them," whereas 'Ali Salman was simultaneously trying to adopt a
more conciliatory, peaceful tone.[114]

This dissonance undermined al-Wifaq's negotiating strategy while playing into the hands of regime hard-liners, who have attempted to portray
al-Qasim as the mouthpiece for al-Wifaq. As a result, some within al-Wifaq
have been trying to restrict the public profile of clerics in the society's
activities. According to one al-Wifaq official, interviewed in March 2012,
"We are trying to minimize the role of clerics in the schedule of micro-
phones [agenda at rallies]. We preferred that clerics not be involved."[115]

FRACTURING AND ENTRENCHMENT
OF THE SUNNI OPPOSITION

A similar dynamic is at work among the mainstream Sunni opposition
groups.[116] As noted, in NUG's vocal demands for better jobs, government
subsidies, and salaries, the group stood in marked contrast to the more
quietist Sunni current represented by al-Minbar and al-Asala.[117] That said,
the NUG never addressed the broader question of political reform and
participation, leading many observers to question whether it was simply
a regime-sponsored counterweight to the mostly Shi'a-led protests.[118] Regardless, the NUG's position produced a number of important fissures and
defections starting in late 2011.

The most significant of these splits has been the Awakening of al-Fatih
(Sahwat al-Fatih, "al-Fatih" referring to the mosque in Manama where the

group holds rallies), a youth-oriented Islamist current that broke off from the NUG in late 2011.[119] Its leadership comprises conservative, former parliamentarians from al-Minbar—Muhammad Khalid Ibrahim and Nasser Fadala. Some have characterized the Awakening as the youth wing of al-Minbar, but interviews conducted in September 2012 suggest that this composition does not translate into control by al-Minbar over the group's strategies and tactics. In its manifestos and protests, the Awakening criticizes the NUG's leadership for being too cautious, too close to the regime, and too friendly to the opposition.[120]

Like the February 14 Youth Coalition, the Awakening has taken to the streets, advocating a form of vigilantism to confront and counter Shi'a protests. In its rhetoric and Internet presence, it is also highly critical of U.S. policy in Bahrain, believing that Washington is conspiring with Tehran to hand over the kingdom to al-Wifaq. The group has also reached out to like-minded Sunni figures and groups across the Gulf; it hosted the radical Kuwaiti professor and al-Qa'ida sympathizer 'Abdallah al-Nafisi to speak at a rally at the al-Fatih Mosque on the anniversary of the February 14 uprising.[121]

Regional events also played a role in hardening Sunni opinion in Bahrain and isolating more moderate elements. Hard-line Salafis increasingly used the Syrian conflict to galvanize their Sunni constituents. On August 5, social media in Bahrain was abuzz with news that Salafi politicians from the al-Asala society had visited the Free Syrian Army to deliver humanitarian aid to hospitals and shelters.[122] Citing the "calls of religion and pan-Arabism," the Salafis' visit was widely publicized with photos.[123] In the ensuing weeks, however, the visit stoked acrimony, with Shi'a oppositionists arguing that it had violated Bahraini laws on supporting terror groups and money laundering, but pro-government voices defending it as a private, humanitarian mission. Shi'a commentators found the visit especially ironic because the government in usual circumstances heavily scrutinized and regulated the transfer of Shi'a charitable donations (khums) outside Bahrain.

Although the Foreign Ministry distanced itself from the visit and urged Bahrainis to avoid traveling to conflict zones, pro-government commentators lambasted the Shi'a's criticism of the visit as yet another sign of their perfidy, "sectarian bigotry," and support for the Asad regime.[124] Like the

Iraq War, the 2006 Lebanon War, and the Huthi rebellion in North Yemen, the Syria conflict pushed the Bahraini Shi'a to defend their nationalist legitimacy against accusations of outside loyalty. For many Bahraini Sunnis—officials and opposition—the Shi'a uprising in Bahrain was a sort of retaliation by Iran for the Gulf Arab support for the anti-Asad uprising. "You pinch me here, I'll pinch you there," noted one senior official in the Bahraini Foreign Ministry.[125] On August 25, al-Wifaq issued a lengthy refutation of this accusation, arguing that the Bahraini protests were autonomous and homegrown and that they predated the Syrian opposition.[126]

Some outside observers and Bahraini actors have attributed the fracturing of the Sunni Islamist camp to deliberate regime policies—an attempt to prevent the NUG from growing too strong by inducing defections within its ranks. According to this narrative, the prime minister and the royal court minister subsidized the NUG as a means to counterbalance the Shi'a. When the NUG began to act more independently, like a "real opposition," however, regime hard-liners induced the creation of the Awakening as an offshoot that would be more pliable to their aims. Given the shadowy nature of royal politics, this claim is unlikely to be definitively substantiated. At first glance, it seems to impart too much omnipotence to the regime over the country's Sunni political field. That said, it is likely that hard-line regime elements attempted to co-opt Sunni rage, harnessing the resulting rancor toward the Shi'a. This possibility is even more likely in light of emerging divisions in the royal family.

ROYAL FACTIONALISM: THE RISE OF THE AL KHAWALID

As noted in previous chapters, analysts have long divided the Al Khalifa between a moderate, pro-reform camp led by the crown prince and a reactionary faction led by the prime minister, with the king falling somewhere in between. However, this rather simplistic dichotomy has been complicated by the rise of a more conservative faction that wields even greater power than the prime minister, led by Royal Court Minister Khalid bin Ahmed Al-Khalifa and the BDF commander Khalifa bin Ahmed Al-Khalifa. Sharing blood ties (the two are brothers, part of the so-called Al Khawalid branch of the Al Khalifa) and a common ideological outlook, the two figures have advocated an uncompromising line toward Shiʿa-led dissent.

At its core, the division reflects a difference of approaches in how to address the country's crisis, with one side preferring to see it through a security lens, but the other recognizing the need for dialogue and graduated, calibrated reforms. For the former faction, led by the Al Khawalid branch, sectarianism has been an especially useful tactic; it delegitimizes the institutionalized Shiʿa opposition while forestalling the emergence of a truly broad-based, grassroots movement. In this tactic, they are aided by their close association with Muslim Brotherhood and Salafi figures as well as by their oversight of the state's principal tools of political and social control. The royal court minister bankrolls the main state-owned daily, *al-Watan*, which gives him a powerful platform to denigrate al-Wifaq as a proxy of Hizballah and Iran. His brother, Khalifa, heads the country's armed forces, which, although doctrinally assigned the role of external defense, have an important auxiliary role in keeping public order at home (the BDF was implicated in the deaths of two protestors in February and March 2011).[127] In recent interviews, Khalifa has been among the most strident voices accusing al-Wifaq of receiving Iranian (and U.S.) funding and calling for the government to confront this society with an iron fist.[128]

In tandem with the rise of the Al Khawalid, the crown prince saw his influence steadily decline starting in mid-2011, epitomized by the dismantling of many of his economic projects that were intended to liberalize the Bahraini market and attract investment. The king has been similarly overshadowed; he announced an amendment to the Constitution that failed to substantively address the BICI's recommendations and that was quickly dismissed by al-Wifaq.[129] In early 2012, these divisions were thrown into even sharper relief by renewed discussions of a political and military union between Bahrain and Saudi Arabia.

THE POLARIZING DEBATE OVER GULF UNITY

A political and military merger of the Gulf Arab states, beyond the parameters of the GCC, was first mentioned by King ʿAbdallah during the thirty-second GCC summit on December 19, 2011. Starting in early 2012, the idea of union—specifically between Bahrain and Saudi Arabia—reverberated across the Bahraini political field, animating the Sunni Islamists, disheartening the Shiʿa opposition, and exposing subtle rifts within the royal family.

The scheme predictably stirred expressions of support from outspoken Sunni critics of the Shiʿa. At al-Fatih Mosque—long the epicenter of Sunni activism—there were weekly gatherings in support of union. Among regime voices, the Al Khawalid were among the greatest supporters of the scheme. "Unity is the lifeline for us all, not only officials. It will serve us all," noted the BDF commander Field Marshal Khalifa bin Ahmed Al-Khalifa.[130] Importantly, the king and crown prince were more circumspect and muted, highlighting their sensitivity to union's detrimental effect on dialogue and calibrated reforms as a means of dealing with the opposition.

The February 14 Youth Coalition unsurprisingly (to the Shiʿa) denounced the move as the "GCC falsity union." Al-Wifaq and ʿIsa al-Qasim argued that any decision on union should be decided through a popular referendum, citing the precedent of the vote on the country's independence.[131] Other critics of union argued that it would not only marginalize the Shiʿa as a demographic group but also provide regime hard-liners a useful pretext for avoiding reforms. "They [the hard-liners] could just say, 'Sorry, it is out of our hands now; the Saudis are calling the shots,'" noted one Bahraini academic.[132] The irony of Sunni Islamist support for union with Saudi Arabia was not lost on the Shiʿa, whom these same Sunnis had long accused of jeopardizing Bahraini sovereignty because of their alleged ties to Iran.[133] Finally, it is important to note that union exposed a further rift between al-Wifaq and its longtime allies from the kingdom's Sunni liberal community, the al-Waʿd society.[134] Long infused with the pan-Arab ideology of its Nasserist and Baʿathist pedigree, al-Waʿd welcomed the Gulf union proposal as, in the words of one interlocutor, the "first step toward Arab unity."[135]

At its core, the debate over union with Saudi Arabia embodied two very different interpretations about sectarianism, ideological contagion, and the threat from Iran. For regime hard-liners, union aligned closely with their broader approach to the "Shiʿa issue" as a regional security threat rather than a political and social problem with roots in the state's institutional deficiencies.[136] The very real potential for opposition mobilization—whether from incitement by Iran or by the contagion of the Arab uprisings—necessitated a repressive response at home and a stronger regional alliance with fellow Sunnis. By contrast, reformists and activists saw good governance and reform as the best barriers against regional turmoil buffeting the tiny kingdom. "What protects Bahrain from the regional environment is a regime based on citizenship," noted one al-Wifaq official. "But unfortunately the regime is using trouble in the region to undermine people and strengthen its power."[137]

PART III

SAUDI ARABIA

SIX

LOYALTIES UNDER FIRE

The Saudi Shiʿa in the Shadow of Iraq

Shiʿa–state relations in Saudi Arabia are distinguished from those in Bahrain by demographics, economic resources, regime type, and strategic geography. First, the Shiʿa of Saudi Arabia constitute only 10 to 15 percent of the total population, meaning that political reforms do not carry the implicit threat of a Shiʿa takeover, as they do in Bahrain.[1] As noted in chapter 1, the Saudi Shiʿa enjoy more economic advantages and a higher standard of living than their Bahraini counterparts but suffer from greater religious discrimination stemming from the monarchy's alliance with the Salafi clerical establishment. Unlike Bahrain and Kuwait, there are limited venues for political participation, resulting in Shiʿa strategies that are focused more on intellectual activism and securing cultural rights. Regional tensions with Iran have also impacted Shiʿa–state relations in Saudi Arabia to a greater degree than the other cases. The Saudi monarchy is acutely sensitive to how its rivalry with Iran impacts its legitimacy at home and abroad, and this vulnerability has obstructed reform progress on the Shiʿa issue. Finally, most of the Twelver Shiʿa in Saudi Arabia are a relatively compact minority residing in the Eastern Province. A strong sense of provincial marginalization thus informs the outlook of many Shiʿa activists.

The Iraq War had a profound impact on the strategies of the Saudi Shiʿa, the balance of power between different ideological currents, and Shiʿa relations with other reformists across the kingdom. Faced with initial suspicion that they would seek to mimic the newly empowered Shiʿa of Iraq, Shiʿa activists went to great lengths to demonstrate their continued loyalty to the Saudi state and reemphasize that their push for reforms would respect the territorial integrity of the Saudi state and the sovereignty of the House of Saud. Shiʿa figures from the Islahiyyin pursued a four-pronged approach: using the longstanding practice of the petition to voice their demands; attempting to situate the institution of the *marjaʿiyya* in a local context, while distancing the community from Iran; building bridges with other sects and reform currents; and participating in the National Dialogue and the municipal council elections.

Yet this conciliatory approach was ultimately thwarted by the regime and, in particular, by hard-line members of the Salafi establishment, whose anti-Shiʿa views and sense of siege became more pronounced as a result of the conflicts in Iraq and Lebanon. In the face of this opposition, a younger generation of Shiʿa activists grew increasingly disenchanted with the conciliatory approach of the more pragmatic currents of the Islahiyyin. A heavy-handed response by the regime to disturbances in 2008 and 2009 ensured that the balance of power would shift even further toward more rejectionist voices. As in Bahrain, the interplay between regional tensions and domestic stalemate created a combustible mix of youthful frustration and intra-Shiʿa fissures—forces that made the Eastern Province highly susceptible to the aftershocks of the uprisings in Tunisia and Egypt.

INITIAL SAUDI SHIʿA REACTIONS
TO THE IRAQ WAR

In many respects, the run-up to the 2003 Iraq War proved to be a boon to the Shiʿa reform movement in Saudi Arabia. As noted in chapter 1, much of the Shiʿa reconciliation with the Saudi regime had taken place in the 1990s as a result of an improvement in Saudi–Iranian bilateral relations, the chilling of relations between the OIR and its supporters in Iran, and the Saudi regime's amnesty offer to exiled Shiʿa oppositionists.

The rapprochement can also be attributed to the growing Sunni Islamist threat—specifically, the so-called Sahwa movement (see chapter 1)—

faced by the Saudi regime and the regime's desire to contain the Sahwa and avoid a "two-front war" with the Sahwa and the Shiʿa.[2] As Stéphane Lacroix argues, the Saudi regime "played the card of the Shirazi Shiʿite opposition" to manage the Sahwa challenge. The first goal was to relieve pressure on the Saudi regime, but also to prevent the Sahwa from developing contacts with the Shirazi opposition in exile.[3] The Shiʿa, for their part, grew closer with moderate, liberal Sunni Islamists who felt threatened by the growing trend of jihadi extremism. The latter figures included notable reformers such as Hassan al-Maliki, ʿAbd al-Aziz al-Qasim, ʿAbdallah al-Hamid, and Matruk al-Falah.[4] Like the Shiʿa, these so-called Islamo-liberals believed that political reforms within the framework of the monarchy represented the best countermeasure to radicalism.[5]

Aside from these burgeoning contacts, the invasion of Iraq accelerated the regime's desire for rapprochement and reform by raising the specter of Shiʿa agitation or even secession inspired by the ascendency of Shiʿa in Iraq.[6] Saudi Shiʿa leaders and activists, however, were careful to situate their demands in the local context and to downplay any notions of triumph in Iraq. The leading Shiʿa cleric of the Islahiyyin, Hassan al-Saffar, emphasized in repeated interviews, sermons, and writings that what was happening in Iraq was not so much the empowerment of the Shiʿa, but a redressing of a previous power imbalance. In 2004, he lauded the ability of Shiʿa and Sunni in Iraq to bridge their differences and avoid sectarian strife, particularly in the wake of the assassination of revered Iraqi Shiʿa cleric ʿAbd al-Aziz al-Hakim.[7]

At the same time, an opposing school saw in the regime's growing fears an opportunity for leverage—a way to remind the Al Saʿud that although the Shiʿa were loyal for now, this loyalty should not be taken for granted, particularly in the context of rapidly escalating regional tensions.[8] Writing on al-Jazeera's website in 2004, Hamza al-Hassan, a longtime ideologue with the OIR who would later break with al-Saffar, wrote that the Saudi Shiʿa's propensity to look outside the kingdom for guidance, inspiration, and support would continue as long as the community faced discrimination: "In light of the continuation of the policy of discrimination on a denominational basis, the Shiʿa exterior, whether it is in Iran, Iraq, Lebanon, or Bahrain, will play a role in the manifestation of the Saudi Shiʿa personality psychologically, politically, and religiously. In the absence of domestic inclusion in the national crucible, eyes look outward to seek assistance, ideas, and positions."[9]

THE SHIʿA PETITION CAMPAIGN

Despite these scattered warnings that the Shiʿa in Saudi Arabia might look outside the kingdom for patronage, the main thrust of the Shiʿa reform initiative by the Islahiyyin was to lobby peaceably for change, demonstrating continued Shiʿa fealty to the kingdom. The principal vehicles for accomplishing this change immediately following the 2003 invasion were petitions to the royal family—a traditional and uniquely Saudi venue for communicating with the monarchy. In 2003, the crown prince received a total of five petitions from clerics and activists across the sectarian and political spectrum that called for a range of reforms: a constitutional monarchy, a loosening of media restrictions, judicial reform, economic liberalization, and greater respect for the kingdom's sectarian, tribal, and regional diversity. The first petition, "Ruʾiya li-hadir al-watan wa mustaqbalihi" (A Vision for the Present and the Future of the Nation), was the product of more than five months of debate and discussion by Sunni, Shiʿa, and liberal intellectuals, clerics, and community leaders.[10] Importantly, sensitive issues such as women's rights and school curricula reform were dropped from the petition in order to preserve consensus between the clerical and liberal wings of the petition drafters. A total of twenty Shiʿa activists signed the petition, representing a circle of intellectuals who had long pushed for sectarian dialogue: Muhammad Mahfouz, Jaʿfar al-Shayeb, Najib al-Khunayzi, and Zaki al-Milad.[11] According to several Shiʿa activists in the Eastern Province, the document remains the cornerstone for reform.[12]

In April 2003, the Shiʿa submitted their own petition, "Al-shurakaʾ fi al-watan al-wahid" ("Partners in One Nation"), signed by 450 clerics, intellectuals, notables, and community leaders.[13] The document is remarkable as an unprecedented assertion of Shiʿa identity in a state that eschews recognition of sectarian diversity. The document went beyond the traditional Shiʿa demands for religious recognition and demanded political representation and power sharing. At the same time, it pledged unconditional loyalty to the ruling family and tried to deflect any accusations of Saudi Shiʿa susceptibility to foreign influence. It was also notable that it included signatories from diverse and doctrinally distinct Shiʿa communities in the kingdom—the oases of Ahsa and Qatif and the miniscule Shiʿa community in the western city of Medina.[14]

The response from the regime helped stir Shiʿa expectations. For the first time, the ten-day Ashura commemoration was allowed in public; political prisoners were released; and Shiʿa publishing flourished, albeit in an incremental manner.[15] Reflecting on these gains, Hassan al-Saffar proclaimed in 2007 that the Saudi government was "much more focused now on delivering rights than ever before."[16] Yet he was also careful to emphasize that these successes were not the result of the rise of the Shiʿa in Iraq but were rather a "correction of the situation"—that is, a granting of legitimacy that had previously been denied.[17]

Fewer restrictions emboldened some Shiʿa activists and their Sunni allies to assert their demands with even more force. The campaign culminated with the December 2003 submission of a petition demanding a constitutional monarchy. This appeal proved to be a red line for the royal family—the regime's response was delayed but harsh. Liberal activists and three Shiʿa were arrested and imprisoned in March 2004.[18] The crackdown and then–crown prince ʿAbdallah's subsequent silence over the detentions served as a visible reminder to the Shiʿa of the limits of reform and stirred considerable suspicions about ʿAbdallah's motives. According to the Shiʿa activist and author Fouad Ibrahim, "The sudden campaign of detentions of March 15, 2004, ended any expectations of supposed reforms by Crown Prince ʿAbdallah. The deal was broken after that man [ʿAbdallah] resorted to silence over the arbitrary detentions of the symbols of the reform trend. . . . [T]he word *reform* has since been replaced by the word *development*."[19]

SHIʿA EFFORTS AT SECTARIAN DIALOGUE AND COOPERATION

Aside from petitions, Shiʿa activists pursued a second strategy aimed at building bridges with Sunni liberals and moderate Islamists. This strategy

served the twofold purpose of strengthening the push for reform and isolating more radical Salafi voices opposed to liberal reforms. In interviews
and in published works, many leading Shiʿa and their Sunni counterparts believed that sectarian identity was itself not an important fissure
or marker among the general populace. The recurring problem, they argued, was extremists on both sides, whose vociferous posturing tended to
drown out voices of reconciliation. According to a noted Sunni reformist
and interlocutor with the Eastern Province Shiʿa, "Sectarian dialogue in
the kingdom has progressed thanks to the maturity among the 'center' on
both sides. The key problem is that the moderates are forced to retract
under pressure from extremists."[20]

The Shiʿa initially pursued this dialogue in the context of official, regime-sanctioned channels. Starting in 2003, then crown prince ʿAbdallah
held a series of well-publicized and high-level National Dialogue sessions
that focused on discussing socioeconomic issues and bridging the gap
between Sufis, Salafis, Shiʿa, and other sects. Much of the initial impetus was framed as a counterterrorism measure. In a speech accompany-
ing the opening of the first National Dialogue Center in Riyadh in 2003,
ʿAbdallah argued that the dialogues were intended to "provide an atmosphere where . . . new ideas that reject terrorism and extremist thought
can emerge."[21] In subsequent sessions, discussions focused on women's
rights, youth, and regional and tribal identity.[22]

In tandem with these domestic forums, ʿAbdallah sought to broker sectarian dialogue outside the kingdom. Under the auspices of the OIC, Saudi
Arabia convened a 2005 conference in Mecca that passed a resolution recognizing the four Sunni *madhahib* (Hanbali, Shafiʿi, Maliki, and Hanafi)
plus two Shiʿa schools (the Zaydi and Jaʿfari) as legitimate and sacrosanct
expressions of Islam. Given the kingdom's long history of religious exclusivity, this resolution was a remarkable step toward reform. The former
leadership of the OIR (al-Saffar, al-Shayeb, and others) participated in the
conference, as did some former members of the Hizballah al-Hijaz.[23] A
similar conference was held in Mecca on June 4–6, 2008, with the intent
of preparing for dialogue with non-Muslims. Yet King ʿAbdallah used the
opportunity to also explore greater rapprochement with the Shiʿa. Three
Shiʿa attended, including Hassan al-Saffar and Iran's Expediency Council
chairman, ʿAli Akbar Hashemi Rafsanjani. Both were photographed with

the king in highly publicized meetings.[24] Yet the dialogue sessions had no effect on the Saudi Salafi establishment's exclusionary views. Many of the figures in this group grew increasingly anti-Shi'a in their outlook due to the perception of Sunni losses in Iraq and Lebanon as well as to rumors of regionwide conversions from Sunnism to Shi'ism, particularly after the 2006 Lebanon War.[25]

By 2007, there was growing Shi'a disenchantment with the National Dialogue sessions, with one reformer denigrating the meetings as "hollow debating societies" and another stating that they were designed to keep the Shi'a "talking rather than acting."[26] Still other figures believed that the government had effectively "stolen" the idea of sectarian dialogue from the Shi'a and their Sunni allies, with the intent of regulating and controlling it to prevent coordinated opposition activity.[27] These critics pointed out that in many cases the dialogue sessions, in particular the fifth one in 2006, were focused on respecting the *external* "other" rather than on promoting *domestic* dialogue among Saudi Arabia's various sects.[28] And, as discussed at length in the next chapter, the dialogues came under increasing attack from hard-liners within the Salafi clerical establishment. For example, on May 30, 2008, five days before the start of the Mecca Conference, a group of twenty-two Salafi clerics issued a statement denouncing Shi'a Islam as "the most evil sect" of the nation.[29]

To counter these official obstacles, moderates such as Hassan al-Saffar, Ja'far al-Shayeb, and Muhammad Mahfouz adopted a more informal strategy starting in 2006 that focused on circumventing the regime-sanctioned channels and building cross-sectarian ties. The ultimate goal, according to al-Saffar, was to create "space for the moderate middle" and to diminish the standing of Shi'a and Sunni radicals. A key foundation of this initiative was the practice of holding weekly "salons"—informal gatherings for discussion of intellectual, social, and political topics, not unlike the *diwaniya* in Kuwait and the more formal *ma'atims* of Bahrain. Al-Shayeb's salon, known as the "Tuesday Salon" (Salon al-Thulatha), acquired particular prominence among the Shi'a and later among Sunni liberals outside the Eastern Province.[30] Topics ranged from organizing Shi'a cultural festivals to social issues such as women's rights, intersectarian dialogue, and youth. Toward the end of 2010, the forums increasingly focused on Shi'a rights in neighboring Bahrain and Kuwait.[31]

In addition to these meetings, the Eastern Province Shiʿa traveled to liberal Sunni salons. The earliest of these initiatives occurred in 2001 with a visit by Hassan al-Saffar to a weekly salon in Riyadh organized by the Sunni reformist ʿAbdallah al-Hamid.[32] In subsequent years, al-Saffar and other Shiʿa activists conducted numerous other dialogue sessions, which culminated in al-Saffar's unprecedented visit to the Salafi strongholds of al-ʿUnayza and al-Qasim in 2007. Even Khat al-Imam figures such as Hassan al-Nimr joined in the dialogue.[33]

At the intellectual level, a major figure in the push for reconciliation was the Shiʿa writer Muhammad Mahfouz, who published a series of works on doctrinal understanding among the kingdom's diverse Islamic sects. A key example is a 2007 book entitled *Al-hiwar al-Madhhabi fi al-Mamlaka al-ʿArabiyya al-Saʿudiyya* (Sectarian Dialogue in the Kingdom of Saudi Arabia), which includes contributions from Sunni and Shiʿa scholars across the country—Malikis, Hanbalis, Shafiʿis, Hanafis, Zaydis, Ismaʿilis, and Twelver Shiʿa.[34] Yet, as discussed more fully in the next chapter, this effort at dialogue was undermined by the worsening conflict in Iraq and the 2006 war in Lebanon, both of which stirred suspicion between Sunni liberals and their Shiʿa allies. It was also torpedoed by a regime-sanctioned policy that sought to prevent the formation of a united, Sunni–Shiʿa opposition. As a noted Sunni reformist had lamented earlier, "Sunni–Shiʿa dialogue has collapsed. The liberals accuse the Shiʿa of not criticizing [Iraqi Shiʿa cleric Muqtada] al-Sadr enough; the Shiʿa accuse the liberals of being closet Wahhabis."[35]

SHIʿA EFFORTS TO CONTEXTUALIZE THE *MARJAʿIYYA*

As noted in the previous chapters on Bahrain, the issue of the *marajiʿ al-taqlid* (literally, "sources of emulation"—venerated senior clerics who exert influence over Shiʿa religious, social, cultural, and, in the case of Iran, political affairs) has been a powerful lightening rod for Sunni criticism of Shiʿa national loyalty. Many of the Shiʿa reform movement's efforts, therefore, were aimed at placing the institution in a local context and assuaging Sunni fears about the political influence of foreign—and specifically Iranian—*maraji*.

Interviews in the Eastern Province indicate that the most popular *marja* by far is Grand Ayatollah 'Ali al-Sistani, based in Najaf, Iraq. According to some interlocutors, 70 to 80 percent of Saudi Shi'a follow his guidance. Much of this support stems from the fact that Hassan al-Saffar, the leading local cleric, chose al-Sistani as his *marja* after the death of Ayatollah Muhammad al-Shirazi in 2001. In a 2007 interview, al-Saffar stated that he had weighed choosing Shirazi's younger brother and successor, Sadeq, as his *marja*. But al-Saffar said that he found Sadeq's views incompatible with the current realities that the Eastern Province currently confronted.

In writings and statements, al-Saffar went to great lengths to distance himself from *maraji* outside the country. In an early 2007 interview, he downplayed al-Sistani's role in Saudi affairs, saying, "I never receive formal guidance from al-Sistani."[36] A February 2007 newspaper article further explicated the views he had expressed in heated correspondence with the Salafi cleric Sa'd al-Burayk, who had accused al-Sistani of labeling Sunnis as infidels and of interfering in Saudi domestic affairs.[37] Al-Saffar mounted a lengthy rebuttal, citing al-Sistani's own writings on the limited spiritual role of the *marja* in the affairs of other countries.[38] In an interview on al-'Arabiya television a few years earlier, al-Saffar had argued that Sunni Islamists themselves look to external sources of religious authority: "[I]n all religions and sects scholarly and religious links are not limited by geography and political borders. There are Sunnis throughout the world who follow the fatwas of [Saudi] shaykh 'Abd al-Aziz bin Baz. Does that disturb their national affiliation and loyalty? Another example is that many Muslims outside Egypt follow the opinions and fatwas of al-Azhar University, and this does not contradict their patriotism."[39]

Aside from al-Saffar, even the staunchest Shi'a defenders of *velayet-e faqih* (Islamic government), which accords significant political power to the *marja*, argued for a more nationalist interpretation of the concept, which would allay Sunni anxieties in the kingdom. For example, the former Hizballah al-Hijaz cleric and fervent Khamenei supporter Hassan al-Nimr argued in a 2007 interview that the institution of the *marja'iyya* by nature precludes clerics from commenting on the affairs of other states.

Al-Nimr cited the example of Ayatollah Khomeini, who even when he was residing in Iraq before the Iranian Revolution refused to discuss domestic Iraqi affairs.[40]

Other reform activists asserted that the very process of engaging in dialogue with the monarchy and formulating a "road map" of desired improvements helped build confidence with the regime and removed the external *marja'* as a source of suspicion.[41] Several activists contrasted this process with the case of Bahrain, where, as discussed in the previous chapter, local Shi'a actors tried to solicit a formal endorsement by al-Sistani to legitimate their political strategy. As the Saudi Shi'a intellectual Muhammad Mahfouz noted, "We are more mature than Bahrain—there is more local discussion about the local agenda. [Unlike in Bahrain,] nobody here expects a statement from al-Sistani because he himself knows that Saudis will do what they need to do."[42]

Seeking to bolster their nationalist bona fides even further, some Shi'a intellectuals pushed for a Saudi-based *hawza* (seminary) for training Shi'a clerics—to create an indigenous, Saudi-born *marja'*.[43] In their view, this institution would remove any basis for accusing the Saudi Shi'a of loyalty to foreign authority. "The government says we are loyal to Iran and Iraq, and this would undercut their argument," noted a key proponent of this school of thought, Muhammad Mahfouz.[44] Mahfouz and others argue that the Al Sa'ud and their Salafi allies set a precedent for using indigenous religious training as a counterweight to foreign ideological interference. In the 1970s, for example, the regime's establishment of Imam Ibn Saud University to train Saudi Salafi scholars was meant to end the longstanding influence of the Egyptian Muslim Brotherhood over religious affairs inside the kingdom.

It should be noted, however, that the *hawza* initiative did not enjoy universal support among Shi'a activists. First, several Shi'a interlocutors argued that the relevance of the *marja'* in Saudi Shi'a social and political affairs was declining; most ordinary Shi'a are simply not versed in the minutiae of Shi'a jurisprudence to discern the differences among various *maraji'*. The idea of "emulation," they argued, is largely a symbolic function. More important, much of al-Sistani's prestige among the Saudi Shi'a is rooted less in his mastery of jurisprudence and more in his political role as an Iraqi statesman and defender of the Iraqi Shi'a (despite the fact that al-Sistani himself vigorously denies this role). Moreover, secular, leftist figures argue that reducing the profile of the *marjaʿiyya* should itself be a first step in reforming the sect of Shiʿism before any national integration can be accomplished.

DISTANCING THE COMMUNITY FROM IRAN

Closely related to this effort, Saudi Shiʿa figures have tried to distance themselves from Iranian influence—a difficult task given the Saudi regime's enduring memory of the 1979 intifada in the Eastern Province. As mentioned in chapter 2, the main pro-Iranian group in Saudi Arabia, the Hizballah al-Hijaz, was effectively decimated after the Khobar Tower bombings and the warming of Saudi–Iranian relations in the late 1990s. The remnants of the organization have focused mostly on charitable and religious activities as well as on Internet activism. Several key individuals have reportedly attained positions in the Saudi educational and judicial realm without abandoning their allegiance to Supreme Leader ʿAli Khamenei as their *marjaʿ*. These individuals include Dr. ʿAbd al-Hadi al-Fadli, who became the head of the Arabic language department at King ʿAbd al-Aziz University in Jeddah, and Ghalib al-Hamad, who was temporarily appointed as a Shiʿa judge in Qatif in 2005.[45] Despite their inclusion in the regime's educational bureaucracy and legal sphere, these individuals remain unapologetic supporters of Khamenei, Iran, and *velayet-e faqih*.

As regional tensions between Saudi Arabia and Iran rose—particularly after the 2006 Lebanon War—this allegiance provided the pretext for Salafi attacks on the nationalist loyalty of the Shiʿa, prompting a countercampaign by the main current of the Shiʿa reform movement, led by the Islahiyyin. On the issue of *velayet-e faqih*, Hassan al-Saffar in particular has gone to great lengths to emphasize that the idea belongs solely in the Iranian context and has no applicability in Saudi Arabia. The concept, he argued in a 2007 interview, was inextricably linked to Ayatollah Khomeini. "When he died," al-Saffar stated, "the idea died with him."[46] In a separate press interview, al-Saffar reminded readers that although the OIR enjoyed a safe haven in Iran after the 1979 intifada, Iranian authorities gradually restricted his activities because of his ambivalence over *velayet-e faqih*, which culminated in the expulsion from Iran of the OIR leadership in 1988.[47]

Al-Saffar's criticism of *velayet-e faqih* was echoed by the noted intellectual and OIR ideologue Tawfiq al-Sayf. Al-Sayf's major work on Shiʿa political thought, *Nadhariyat al-Sulta fi al-Fiqh al-Shiʿi* (Theories of Political Power in Shiʿa Jurisprudence) criticizes the excessive politicization of the Shiʿa clergy, singling out Iran's *velayet-e faqih* for special attention.[48] In a 2007 interview with al-Hurra TV, al-Sayf noted that the authority of a *marjaʿ* transcends modern state boundaries but does not extend into political affairs. Many of the Sunni accusations against the Shiʿa, he argued, stem from conflating the Shiʿa's affinity for religious authorities with loyalty to the states where they reside.[49] Al-Sayf also played a major role in translating the works of Iranian clerics opposed to *velayet-e faqih* into Arabic and disseminating their ideas to Saudi audiences. A key example is his translations of the work of Muhammad Hussayn Naʾini (1860–1936), who exerted a strong influence on the intellectual lineage of Grand Ayatollah al-Sistani. Naʾini was a major advocate of Islamic constitutionalism and devoted particular attention to the rights of minorities in Islamic societies. His book *Tanbih al-ummah wa-tanzih al-milla* (Warning the Community of Believers and Cleansing the Sect) demolishes the Shiʿa idea of waiting for the Hidden Imam, which underpins the legitimacy of clerical rule in Iran.[50] Al-Sayf believed it has also hindered Shiʿa efforts at national integration in Saudi Arabia.

For its part, Iran has taken care to avoid the appearance of deliberately inciting the Saudi Shiʿa toward confrontation with the Saudi regime or Sunni citizens. For example, in 2007 the Qom-based ayatollah Nasir Makarim al-Shirazi issued a statement exhorting the Saudi Shiʿa to avoid provoking Sunnis. He implied that Iran was sensitive to the Saudi Shiʿa's delicate balance between national loyalty and sectarian identity: "We are observing your conditions carefully and cautiously because of the exceptional situation you are living."[51] As discussed in the next chapter, however, Iran did not exhibit a similar discretion toward the Saudi regime and the Salafi establishment, which it accused of distorting Islam and exacerbating regional tensions with support for Sunni jihadists in Iraq.

The effort to delink the Saudi Shiʿa from Iran suffered a serious setback during the 2006 war in Lebanon. Hizballah's battlefield performance against Israel spurred widespread Saudi Shiʿa demonstrations of solidarity and support. Yet these protests and outpourings of support had less to do with sectarian solidarity or endorsement of Iran and more with Hizballah's (and particularly its leader Hassan Nasrallah's) populist and rejectionist appeal.[52] Shiʿa across the spectrum expressed adulation for the Lebanese militant group and its war with Israel, which contrasted sharply with the Salafi establishment's antagonistic stance. Even moderates such as al-Saffar evinced unqualified support for Hizballah; in a sermon in August 2006, he exhorted Muslims everywhere to support the Lebanese resistance.[53]

Yet, as discussed in the next chapter, the most significant impact of the Lebanon War was not on the Shiʿa, but rather on the regime and the Salafi establishment, who unleashed a torrent of anti-Shiʿa invective in the wake of the war. This outpouring, in turn, triggered a series of articles, speeches, and web commentary by the moderates reiterating their loyalty to the Al Saʿud and arguing that it was the Salafis' fatwas, rather than any Shiʿa actions, that were eroding the country's unity. These growing tensions also inspired an emerging Shiʿa radical faction, which saw in the rise of Hizballah an opportunity to pressure the Al Saʿud and to undermine the conciliatory approach of Shiʿa moderates.

THE SHIʿA REJECTIONIST CHALLENGE

As noted in chapter 1, the Saudi Shiʿa community initially contained strong links to revolutionary Iran, given the influence of Ayatollah Muhammad al-Shirazi, who remained a defender of *velayet-e faqih* until his death in 2001, and Ayatollah Muhammad Taqi al-Mudarrisi, the head of the IAO in Iraq. Yet with the warming of relations between the Eastern Province Shiʿa and the Saudi regime in the mid-1990s and the general sense of hope that accompanied the accession of Crown Prince ʿAbdallah to the throne, this current became marginalized. By 2008, the pendulum had begun to swing in the opposite direction: when it became apparent that al-Saffar's and the Islahiyyin's moderate, conciliatory approach had failed to deliver, more activist, rejectionist voices secured an ever-increasing constituency.

The Rise of Nimr al-Nimr

The key figure of this more activist current was the cleric Nimr al-Nimr, based in the village of al-ʿAwamiya near Qatif.[54] Hailing from a clerical family with a long pedigree of antiregime activity, al-Nimr studied under Ayatollah Muhammad Taqi al-Mudarrisi in Tehran and then in Damascus before returning to Saudi Arabia in 1999. Al-Nimr followed the guidance of Ayatollah Muhammad al-Shirazi as his *marjaʿ* until al-Shirazi's death in 2001.[55] When al-Shirazi died, al-Nimr reportedly asked al-Mudarrisi whether he should consider him as his new source of emulation. Al-Mudarrisi, who had also taken al-Shirazi as his *marjaʿ*, advised al-Nimr that he should continue to regard al-Shirazi as his *marjaʿ* but refer to al-Mudarrisi on matters that al-Shirazi could not resolve.[56]

In the early 1990s, when al-Saffar and the Islahiyyin started their dialogue with the Saudi regime and emphasizing Shiʿa loyalty to the Saudi government, al-Nimr deployed Khomeini's concept of *taghut* (tyrannical rule) to provide juridical support of Shiʿa rejection of the Al Saʿud—which al-Saffar had also referenced.[57] In the context of the post-2003 stagnation of reforms and increased anti-Shiʿa vitriol from the Salafi establishment, al-Nimr's rhetoric grew even more brazen. In January 2008, he called for the formation of a new "Righteous Opposition Front" (Jabhat al-Muʿarada al-Rashida), which would constitute a sort of umbrella group for Shiʿa clerics and lay activists to attack the corruption of the Saudi state and counter the rhetoric of the Salafis.[58]

In July of that year, he delivered a sermon declaring support for Iran's nuclear program and its right to retaliate against America and destroy Israel, arguing that Saudi Shiʿa should stand with Iran "heart and soul" in the event of a conflict.[59] Later that same month, in an interview with IslamOnline, al-Nimr warned that if Saudi Shiʿa demands were not met, they would have no other choice but to turn to a foreign power for support—presumably Iran.[60] In subsequent statements, however, al-Nimr denied making these provocations, while at the same time reaffirming his longstanding demands for sweeping reforms: an end to sectarian discrimination, a release of political prisoners, greater representation, and economic development of al-ʿAwamiyya.[61]

Above all else, though, it was this appeal to greater dignity that reso-nated most strongly among al-ʿAwamiya's despondent inhabitants. "Nimr speaks to what we are feeling in hearts," noted one young activist in the town to the author in early 2013.[62] Yet for a regime bedeviled by mount-ing tensions with its Persian rival and growing agitation from the Salafi establishment, al-Nimr's outspokenness was a bridge too far. In August, Saudi authorities moved to arrest the fiery cleric. He was released only twenty-four hours later—under the condition that he promise not to lead Friday prayers in al-ʿAwamiya.[63] His absence was short-lived.

The Medina Clashes and Their Aftermath: Mounting Pressures on the Islahiyyin

On February 20, 2009, clashes broke out between Shiʿa pilgrims visiting the graves of revered Shiʿa imams in Medina and members of the Commit-tee for the Prevention of Vice and the Protection of Virtue (CPVPV)—the regime's so-called morality police. Although accounts differ, the trigger for the unrest was the CPVPV's reported videotaping of female Shiʿa pil-grims. The security forces moved into the Shiʿa neighborhoods of Medina, beating and arresting their residents.[64] Dozens were injured. From the Shiʿa's perspective, the regime's response to the crackdown was ambiv-alent, suggesting that the CPVPV's provocation had been partially con-doned at official levels. The newly appointed second-in-line, Prince Nayif, equivocated in his condemnation of the incident, further incensing the Shiʿa.[65] In a subsequent press interview with the Saudi newspaper *Ukaz*, Nayif appeared to justify the heavy-handed response, stating that Saudi Arabia follows "the doctrine of Sunnis" and that although some citizens "follow other schools of thought . . . the intelligent among them must re-spect this doctrine."[66]

For Shiʿa in the Eastern Province, the disturbances proved to be a cata-lyzing event. The regime's ambivalent response seemed to confirm the growing suspicion of a halt or reversal to the royal family's fifteen-year outreach to the Shiʿa. Demonstrations quickly broke out in Qatif, al-ʿAwamiya, and Safwa, marking the most serious outbreak of Shiʿa dissent since the 1979 intifada. In a Friday sermon, Hassan al-Saffar blamed the conservative religious establishment for the events and warned that the country risked sliding down a path of sectarian chaos like Iraq.[67] In March, al-Saffar and a Shi'a delegation traveled to Riyadh to secure the release of the detainees from King 'Abdallah—an apparent move to demonstrate their clout with the government to an increasingly disenchanted youth cohort.[68] Although the prisoners were released, Shi'a rage against the riots had spread far beyond the borders of the kingdom. In London, Shi'a of different nationalities protested in front of the Saudi embassy, while in Kuwait the radical Shi'a cleric Yasir al-Habib called for the creation of a "Greater Bahrain" that would encompass the Eastern Province, Bahrain, Kuwait, and Basra.[69]

From al-'Awamiya, Nimr al-Nimr used the disturbances to break his ban on preaching. In a Friday sermon on March 13, 2009, he lambasted the regime and warned of secession as the only remaining option. It was a fiery performance that attracting unprecedented numbers of frustrated young men and quickly gained widespread fame on the Internet as the "dignity speech."[70] In its brazenness and unsparing rejection of dialogue, it also proved deeply unsettling to the more pragmatic figures in the Islahiyyin.[71]

Unsurprisingly, the speech's call for secession aroused the ire of the regime, which acted swiftly, arresting al-Nimr and a number of his supporters and imposing a curfew on al-'Awamiya. Far from stifling dissent, the arrests sparked widespread calls for solidarity with al-Nimr, ironically increasing the very influence the regime had hoped to contain. Activists across the Eastern Province organized sit-ins to release the al-'Awamiya protestors.[72] In April, a group of sixty Shi'a personalities, including eighteen noted clerics, issued a statement expressing solidarity with the village's inhabitants and demanding an end to sectarian discrimination, while at the same time distancing themselves from the calls for secession.[73]

Yet the most significant impact of the Medina riots and the ensuing crackdown in al-'Awamiya was the sharpening of debates within the Shi'a community about the pace and scope of reform. In early March, Hamza al-Hassan, one of the OIR's early ideologues who now resides in London, announced the formation of the Salvation Movement on the Arabian Peninsula (Harakat Khalas fi al-Jazira al-'Arabiyya). Citing the sluggish pace of reform as the key driver behind its formation, the group explicitly re-

jected the gradualist and participatory approach of the Islahiyyin, arguing that "self-determination" was a "legitimate right" for any persecuted
group.[74]

The events of early 2009 would not be the last time that the regime's
repressive response to al-ʿAwamiya inflamed popular sentiment in the
East—and put pressure on the more cautious elements of the Islahiyyin.
By late 2010, a younger, more activist cohort of Saudi Shiʿa was increasingly seeing the older cadre of Islahiyyin as having been co-opted by the
royalty and having failed to deliver any meaningful improvements. It was
a growing divide that would eventually reach its apogee in the wake of the
uprisings in Tunis and Cairo. For its part, the Saudi regime contributed to
this growing frustration by pursuing a explicitly sectarian strategy in the
Eastern Province: cultivating Salafi alarmism over the rise of the Shiʿa,
enacting carefully calibrated reforms that never fully addressed the roots
of provincial marginalization, and attempting to split the Shiʿa away from
their Sunni reformist allies.

SEVEN

UNDER SIEGE

The Salafi and Regime Countermobilization

From 2003 onward, the Saudi regime's strategy toward domestic Shiʿa activism was influenced by a convergence of domestic vulnerabilities and regional threats: the ruling family's symbiotic relationship with the Salafi establishment, which was doctrinally opposed to Shiʿism, and the kingdom's geostrategy rivalry with Iran. These influences were apparent in two areas.

First, the initial invasion of Iraq raised the specter of Shiʿa mobilization in Saudi Arabia to a degree that was not found in Bahrain and Kuwait. The Saudi Shiʿa are concentrated in the oil-rich Eastern Province, so in the run-up to the war there was growing fear in Saudi officialdom that, inspired by Shiʿa empowerment in Iraq or encouraged by Iran (or even the United States), the Eastern Province Shiʿa might move toward secession. The Saudi regime launched a number of preemptive reform measures designed to placate Shiʿa unrest.

Second, the period 2003–2010 witnessed the stalling or reversal of many reforms instituted after September 11, 2001, as a result of the sense of siege engendered by the Iraq War and perceptions of Iran's ascendency. The Iraq War, the 2006 Lebanon War, and even the Zaydi rebellion in neighboring Yemen created a domestic backlash among the Salafi clerical establishment. Many of these figures, holding powerful positions in education, censorship, and social affairs, were doctrinally opposed to Shiʿism and saw any formalization of Shiʿa rights as a threat to their power and privileged access to the royal family. Popular Salafi clerics and nongovernmental religious organizations agitated for a greater Saudi role in defending Iraq's Sunnis from Iranian-backed Shiʿa militias. To close ranks with these figures, the monarchy tacitly permitted the proliferation of anti-Shiʿa tracts, sermons, and web statements, many of them recycled from the kingdom's ideological counteroffensive against the Iranian Revolution of 1979.

THE SPECTER OF IRAN AND ITS IMPACT ON DOMESTIC THREAT PERCEPTION

In assessing the regime's strategy toward its Shiʿa population, it is important to characterize Saudi Arabia's strategic threat perception of Iran since 2003 and the way this perception influenced its domestic policies toward its Shiʿa population. For the Al Saʿud, Iran has long represented a strategic and ideological rival that threatened the ruling family's legitimacy on the domestic and regional stage. The removal of Saddam Husayn in 2003 upset a traditional equilibrium of power in the region that, although largely psychological, was nonetheless significant. According to this narrative, Iraq has served as a gateway for Iran to project its influence across the region, upstaging Arab governments on traditional pan-Arab concerns such as Palestine and Lebanon and allegedly meddling in newer, more peripheral conflicts such as the Zaydi rebellion in Yemen.[1] In these areas, Iran has pursued what can best be described as an aggressively nonsectarian, "Arab street" strategy that appeals to Arab publics by emphasizing Iran's commitment to the Palestinian cause and its resistance to U.S. pressure on the nuclear issue.[2] This activism contrasted sharply with the posture of Arab rulers, in particular the Al Saʿud, and thus formed an indirect critique of their legitimacy.

On the domestic front, sectarian strife in the region forced King ʿAbdallah into a tenuous balancing act between the Shiʾa and elements of the Salafi establishment. During the Iraq War, more radical Sunni clerics pressured the monarchy to take a more partisan stand in assisting Iraq's Sunnis while avoiding any concessions to the Shiʿa at home. As Iraq descended into internecine strife, these pressures on the Saudi monarchy grew in intensity, and Sunni–Shiʿa distinctions became more of a marker of political and social identity.[3]

SALAFI REACTIONS TO SHIʿA "ASCENDANCY"

In managing Shiʿa mobilization after 2003, the Saudi regime's policies were both constrained and enabled by the Al Saʿud's symbiotic relationship with the Salafi establishment, many of whom were implacably opposed to any formalization of Shiʿa identity in the kingdom.[4] Despite their animosity toward the Shiʿa, the Saudi clerical field is hardly a monolithic bloc. Indeed, the clerical landscape can be divided into three broad currents that reflect their proximity to and dependence on the monarchy: the establishment clerics, the Sahwa, and the *takfiri* clerics.

The establishment clerics are the official *ulema* (Islamic clerics) occupying key positions in the government's religious bureaucracy. As such, they exert substantial control over censorship and social and cultural affairs. Given their dependence on the royal family for their financial livelihood, these figures are generally responsive to regime interests and requests. At the same time, the regime relies upon these figures for the imprimatur of religious legitimacy.

As mentioned in chapter 1, the Sahwa are Salafi clerics and activists who, inspired by Muslim Brotherhood ideology, emerged in the late 1980s as opponents of the Al Saʿud's close relationship with the West and critics of the royal family's excesses and corruption. The Sahwa have traditionally occupied the lower strata of the clerical bureaucracy or been excluded altogether, but they have enjoyed greater legitimacy than the establishment clerics because of their personal charisma. Many hail from less prominent families in regions outside the Najd. Two of their main proponents, Safar bin ʿAbd al-Rahman al-Hawali and Salman al-ʿAwda, were imprisoned (with the backing of a fatwa from establishment clerics) in the mid-1990s due to their belligerence against the Saudi regime and their support for al-Qaʿida. Upon their release, however, al-Hawali and al-ʿAwda—together with other Sahwa clerics—drew increasingly closer

to the regime's orbit. Many were used by the Ministry of Interior as interlocutors with al-Qaʿida fugitives.

The *takfiri* clerics are so named for their embrace of the Islamic precept of *takfir*—to repudiate a person or social entity as un-Islamic and
therefore liable to a range of sanctions from estrangement from the rest
of the Islamic community to death. Many of these figures were former
Sahwa clerics who were imprisoned in the mid-1990s and subsequently
radicalized. Indeed, the so-called "*takfiri* troika"—Nasir al-Fahd, ʿAli bin
Khudayr al-Khudayr, and Ahmed al-Khalidi—appear to have coalesced in
the notorious al-Haʿir prison south of Riyadh.[5] They have been the most
vitriolic opponents of any concessions to the Shiʿa and, in some cases,
have called for their death. They have also provided exhortations for jihad
in Iraq and attacks on Americans. In response to the 2003 residential com-
pound attacks, the Saudi regime arrested a number of *takfiri* clerics. The
movement was further weakened by the public recantation of violence by
al-Khudayr, al-Fahd, and al-Khalidi in 2003. In appearances on Saudi television in November and December of 2003, al-Khudayr argued that *takfir*
must be applied carefully and with restriction. All three clerics have subsequently professed opinions on *takfir* that are much more closely aligned
with those of the establishment clerics. Critics and reformists argue that
this school continues to influence Saudi youth via sermons and websites.[6]

In many instances, these groupings reflect geographic origin—the
establishment clerics are drawn primarily from the province of Riyadh,
whereas many of the Sahwa and *takfiri* clerics hail from Qasim, Asir, and
the Hijaz. Institutional affiliation (whether university, mosque, or prison)
is an additional factor in their alignment, as is tribe.

As discussed later, it is important to note that Salafi positions on Iraq,
the Lebanese Hizballah, and the Shiʿa frequently reflect a clerical jockeying for power—between the "center" (the Najdi–Riyadh establishment)
and the "periphery" (Sahwa clerics from the Hijaz, Asir, and Qasim). In
this struggle, sparring factions use anti-Shiʿism as a normative weapon
against their clerical rivals and against the al-Saud. As in the case of Bahrain, Salafi alarm over Shiʿa mobilization in Saudi Arabia was ultimately
rooted more in domestic power rivalries—in particular, the fractured
nature of Saudi clerical politics—than in any shift in strategy by the Shiʿa
themselves.

The regime's role in managing, suppressing, or encouraging Salafi clerical discourse on the Shiʿa has been the subject of some debate. Some see
ʿAbdallah as well meaning in his intentions toward reform but hamstrung
by hard-line elements in the religious bureaucracy and nongovernmental
organizations. Others take a more cynical view, interpreting anti-Shiʿism
as a useful political weapon for the monarchy itself—a means to close
ranks with the potential critics in the Salafi establishment, deflect popular
sentiment away from the regime's failings and toward an internal "other,"
and to secure the cooperation of the Shiʿa themselves by portraying the
monarchy as a "buffer" against the Salafis.[7]

What is likely is that the ambivalent relationship between the royalty
and the Salafi establishment, in particular the so-called Sahwa clerics, is
a product of the government's longstanding practice of co-option and divide and rule toward the kingdom's diverse religious currents. As noted in
the previous chapter, the government in the early 1990s tacitly sanctioned
the emergence of Shirazi Shiʿa activism as a counterweight to the Sahwa
movement. The goal was not so much to enlist the Shiʿa in inducing defections from the Sahwa's ranks, but to relieve pressure on the regime so
it could focus on addressing the more pressing threat from the Sahwa.
A similar dynamic was at work with the regime's loosening of strictures
on Sufi movements in the Hijaz.[8] By the early 2000s, however, the regime faced a concerted threat from al-Qaʿida, and both establishment and
Sahwa clerics became useful interlocutors and allies in the ideological
struggle to turn young Saudis away from al-Qaʿida. It can be argued that
the "price" of this cooperation was increased tolerance for the Salafi clerics' anti-Shiʿa outlook. And, at any rate, this outlook itself became a useful
tool in the Saudi balancing strategy against Iran, particularly after the U.S.
invasion of Iraq.

Salafi Alarm Over Iraq's Civil War

Salafi alarmism toward the escalating violence in Iraq and the rise of the
Shiʿa began shortly after the invasion. In 2004, a group of Saudi Salafi cler-
ics, many drawn from the Sahwa camp, issued a fatwa on the eve of the
U.S. assault on Fallujah, tacitly endorsing jihad against American forces.

Importantly, the document called for Sunni–Shiʿa cooperation against the occupying U.S. forces.[9] Yet after the Sunni boycott of elections in Iraq and mounting sectarian tensions, Saudi Salafi figures increasingly conflated Shiʿism with U.S. imperialism—resurrecting a longstanding trope of the Shiʿa as internal traitors to Islam. In particular, one Salafi website carried a picture of Iraqi Shiʿi national guardsmen holding pictures of Grand Ayatollah ʿAli al-Sistani together with photographs of U.S. tanks in Baghdad that had rosaries hanging from their barrels.[10]

The bombing of the Shiʿa al-ʿAskari Mosque in Samarra on February 22, 2006, and Iraq's subsequent descent into internal strife brought new exhortations by Saudi Salafi clerics for Saudi volunteers to rush to the aid of their embattled coreligionists in Iraq. In December 2006, Saudi clerics joined Iraqi clerics in signing a statement that denounced the killing of Iraqi Sunnis at the hands of Shiʿa. "We should openly side with our Sunni brothers in Iraq," the document stated, "and lend them all appropriate forms of support." The signatories included noted Sahwa clerics Safar bin ʿAbd al-Rahman al-Hawali and Nasir al-ʿUmar.[11] Other clerics soon followed suit, including moderate Sahwa clerics who had previously been known for their outreach to the Shiʿa, such as Salman al-ʿAwda.[12] On January 21, 2007, the cleric ʿAbd al-Rahman bin Jibrin posted another exhortation for jihadi volunteers to Iraq, accusing the Iraqi Shiʿa of mounting atrocities against the Sunnis and lambasting the Shiʿa as un-Islamic.[13] All of this occurred in a more generalized climate of anti-Shiʿa and anti-Iranian seething that followed the execution of Saddam Husayn at the hands of the Shiʿa-dominated government in Iraq, which created further pressures on the Saudi Shiʿa.[14]

From early 2006 through 2008, popular Salafi clerics and their supporters were issuing a flurry of anti-Shiʿa, anti-Iranian fatwas, tracts, sermons, and Internet postings, calling for violence against the Shiʿa in Iraq and sectarian repression at home. From the Shiʿa point of view, the Saudi government appeared to be complicit in this vitriol—much of it bore a strong resemblance to the kingdom's ideological offensive against the Iranian Revolution in the 1980s. Indeed, many of the same anti-Shiʿa texts and tracts deployed in that campaign enjoyed new currency in the context of the increasingly polarized sectarian climate of the Iraq War. Of critical importance, both Salafi and Shiʿa interlocutors in Saudi Arabia

highlighted the ideological impact of a key Salafi figure in the 1970s, Muhammad Surur Zayn al-ʿAbidin, whose anti-Shiʿa, anti-Iranian writings
acquired new currency within Saudi Arabia.[15] Another important marker
in the rising preeminence of anti-Shiʿism as a feature of modern Salafi discourse was the proliferation, beginning roughly in 2005, of Salafi websites
explicitly devoted to anti-Shiʿism. Many frequently cited anti-Shiʿa rhetoric drawn from the pantheon of Salafi ideologues, including Muhammad
Ibn ʿAbd al-Wahhab, Ibn Taymiya, ʿAbd al-Aziz bin Baz, and Abu Muhammad al-Maqdisi.[16]

Salafi Fears Over the Rise of Lebanese Hizballah — and Debate

Adding to the alarm over Iraq, the 2006 Lebanon War provoked further
vitriol by the Salafi establishment, which accused the Saudi Shiʿa of being proxies for Hizballah. As noted in chapter 6, sporadic demonstrations
were held in Shiʿa communities in the Eastern Province in solidarity with
Hizballah and indirectly with Iran.[17] Yet they were likely motivated by
the same sentiment that spawned similar street demonstrations in Cairo,
Amman, and elsewhere — applause for Hizballah's brazen challenge to the
status quo rather than any expressions of sectarian affinity.

Regardless of motive, Shiʿa in the Eastern Province of Saudi Arabia during this period were subjected to growing pressures from hard-line Salafi
clerics, who launched a barrage of anti-Shiʿa invective to counter the mobilizing appeal of Hizballah's battlefield victory.

Yet the Lebanon War also opened up significant debate within the
Salafi establishment, revealing longstanding class and ideological fissures
and demonstrating that anti-Shiʿism was a useful political weapon in a
struggle for privilege and access to power. It is critical to emphasize that
the 2006 Lebanon War, like the 1979 Iranian Revolution, was interpreted
by Salafi factions in Saudi Arabia through different lenses depending on
their proximity to the Al Saʿud. Those with a vested interest in the monarchy — the so-called establishment clerics — decried Hizballah for provoking an Israeli attack, sowing *fitna* (chaos), and pursuing narrowly sec-

tarian goals.[18] Those farther outside the circle of power tacitly endorsed Hizballah's brazen victory to highlight the Saudi regime's immobility, impiety, and illegitimacy.[19]

Much of Salafi clerical debate and discourse on the Shi'a centered around a fatwa banning Sunni support for Hizballah issued by 'Abdallah bin 'Abd al-Rahman bin Jibrin, a respected member of the Senior Ulema Council (Hay'at Kibar al-'Ulama') who in 1991 had issued an edict authorizing the killing of Shi'a.[20] Bin Jibrin's fatwa on Hizballah had originally been issued in April 20, 2002, and reposted to Salafi web forums in July 2006.[21] By early August, bin Jibrin had reversed his position, possibly under pressure from the Al Sa'ud.

Despite this volte face, the fatwa and the issue of support for Hizballah became a lightning rod for a wrenching intra-Sunni debate about sectarianism and tolerance of Shi'ism inside the kingdom. Within the Sahwa camp, ultraconservative clerics issued similar fatwas, decrying Hizballah as a blasphemous organization and, by extension, denigrating the Saudi Shi'a as *rawafidh* (rejectionists) and disloyal citizens. The prominent Sahwa cleric Safar al-Hawali, who had boycotted King 'Abdallah's 2003 National Dialogue because of Shi'a participation, condemned Hizballah as the "Party of Satan" (Hizb ash-Shaytan).[22] On his website, Nasir al-'Umar asserted that Hizballah's war had diluted and distracted attention from the Sunni resistance against the forces of oppression and aggression.[23] More moderate clerics such as 'Awadh al-Qarni, Salman al-'Awda, and Muhsin al-'Awaji took a more tempered view, framing Hizballah as a legitimate "resistance movement" and arguing that doctrinal differences between Sunni and Shi'a should be temporarily shelved. According to Salman al-'Awda, "We have our differences with Hizballah; they are substantive and deeply rooted like the rest of our differences with the Shi'a. However, this is not the time to play out our differences and be divided. . . . [O]ur main enemy is the Jews and criminal Zionists."[24]

For their part, establishment clerics such as Rabi bin Hadi al-Madkhali and 'Abd al-Muhsin al-'Ubaykan supported the original bin Jibrin fatwa as a means to insulate the monarchy from the mobilizing appeal of Hizballah's battlefield success.[25] In particular, the judiciary cleric al-'Ubaykan challenged Hizballah's authority to call for jihad, citing the well-trod Islamic precept that only the *wali al-amr* (commander of the faithful) can call for jihad.[26]

In the Eastern Province, the Shiʿa perceived the entire debate over the bin Jibrin fatwa as a critical litmus test of the regime's commitment to reform. In opinion pieces and interviews, Shiʿa clerics and activists pointed to the regime's silence on bin Jibrin's fatwa and on those issued by his anti-Shiʿa supporters Nasir al-ʿUmar and Safar al-Hawali as a telltale sign that the monarchy either was powerless to confront these Salafi voices or, more ominously, saw a utility in not censuring them. A vocal Shiʿa journalist, Husayn ʿAllaq, published an article attacking the bin Jibrin fatwa, arguing that sectarian discrimination was harmful to the nation's unity.[27] For its part, the Saudi organization Hizballah al-Hijaz carried a statement on its website, al-Hramain, stating that the bin Jibrin fatwa was an affront to the entire nation of Islam.[28] The website of the more moderate news service al-Rasid carried an editorial attacking the Saudi media's apparent endorsement of the bin Jibrin fatwa: "No matter how hard the Saudi media tries to justify this strange position, it cannot hide the truth that this position will only serve Israel's interests and its aggression."[29]

Anti-Shiʿism engendered by the Lebanese conflict, as in the case of Iraq, proved to be a disastrous setback to the Saudi Shiʿa's efforts to delink themselves from the regional environment and the timeworn accusations of loyalty to Iran. This dynamic resurfaced again in 2009 with the Zaydi rebellion in neighboring North Yemen.

Salafi Vitriol Toward the Zaydi Rebellion in Yemen

The long-running conflict in neighboring Yemen between Zaydi Shiʿa insurgents in the northern Saʿada Province and the regime in Sanaʿa reverberated strongly inside Saudi Arabia. Although the Zaydi Shiʿa are doctrinally distinct from the Twelver Shiʿa that predominate in eastern Saudi Arabia, Bahrain, Kuwait, and Iran, many in the Saudi Salafi establishment nevertheless interpreted the conflict through a Sunni–Shiʿa lens.[30] This was particularly so in light of the Saudi government's repeated charge that Iran was providing financial and lethal aid to Yemeni insurgents, know as

"Huthis" after the prominent Zaydi leader Husayn al-Huthi (d. September 2004). Media accusations of Iranian involvement intensified after Saudi Arabia's unilateral military intervention in North Yemen on November 5, 2009.[31] Even more reformist newspapers such as *al-Watan* condemned the Huthis as "agents of Iranian sectarian expansionism."[32] Like the Lebanon War, the Huthi conflict provoked a flurry of anti-Shiʿa invective from hard-line Salafi clerics that placed further pressure on the Saudi Shiʿa. In November 2009, for example, the conservative Salafi cleric Nasir al-ʿUmar published a lengthy anti-Huthi and anti-Shiʿa tract entitled "The Declaration of the Ulema Regarding the Aggression of the Huthi Rejectionists" on his website al-Muslim.[33] The tract was signed by forty other Salafi clerics.

In response to this attack and others, the Saudi Shiʿa launched a stream of editorials and statements to demonstrate their nationalist bona fides and delink themselves from any association with the Zaydi Shiʿa. The al-Rasid website published a lengthy rejoinder to al-ʿUmar's treatise, and prominent clerics and activists such as Hassan al-Saffar, Tawfiq al-Sayf, and Najib al-Khunayzi argued in other forums that the Saudi Shiʿa position on the Huthis was indistinguishable from that of the Saudi regime. "We all are partners in this country," wrote al-Saffar in early November 2009, "and we must close ranks with our leadership to prevent any attack."[34] At the same time, these Shiʿa figures opposed Saudi Arabia's military invention into North Yemen, both al-Sayf and al-Saffar arguing that the conflict should be solved by Yemenis themselves. This caveat predictably incurred further suspicion from their Salafi detractors.

Aside from the Shiʿa response, a number of liberal Sunni writers used the Huthi conflict to obliquely argue for a reexamination of the kingdom's discriminatory policies toward its own Shiʿa population. For example, the liberal writer Turki al-Hamad argued that the reason the Huthis in Yemen had turned to Iran for support was not sectarian affinity, but rather a lack of political participation and economic opportunity. This phenomenon, he noted, would replicate itself in any Arab state where tribalism and sectarianism had displaced civil society.[35] Echoing this view, an editorial in the daily *al-Elaph* offered a rebuttal to al-ʿUmar's tract, asserting that continued marginalization of the Shiʿa would further entice Iran to meddle in the affairs of both Yemen and Saudi Arabia.[36]

SALAFI OPPOSITION TO ʿABDALLAH'S REFORM INITIATIVES — AT HOME AND ABROAD

An important effect of these regional tensions was a hardening of Salafi views toward domestic reform.[37] As noted in chapter 6, one of the most important avenues for Shiʿa mobilization was participation in King ʿAbdallah's National Dialogue sessions. Yet the monarchy's ability to accommodate Shiʿa demands was hampered by opposition from the powerful Salafi establishment, whose influence was felt not just on domestic religious affairs, but on the kingdom's legitimacy and standing abroad.

On May 30, 2008, five days before the start of King ʿAbdallah's conference on sectarian dialogue in Mecca in early June, a group of twenty-two hard-line Salafi clerics issued a statement on the Internet denouncing Shiʿism as "the most evil sect of the nation, and the most hostile and scheming against the Sunnis and Muslims collectively."[38] In response, the Shiʿa al-Tawafuq website carried a lengthy counterpetition signed by 85 clerics and activists, which attacked the Sunnis as suffering "psychological complexes."[39] Al-Saffar later called on the Saudi government to enact the necessary legislation to criminalize sectarian hatred and incitement to violence. He also exhorted moderate Sunnis to confront *takfiri* statements.[40]

In May 2009, King ʿAbdallah's outreach to the Shiʿa suffered a further blow when the newly appointed imam of the Grand Mosque, ʿAdil al-Kalbani, labeled the Shiʿa as infidels during an interview with the BBC. As the first Grand Mosque imam of African descent, al-Kalbani was widely thought to signify ʿAbdallah's commitment to greater tolerance and pluralism in the kingdom (he had been nicknamed the "Saudi Obama"). The comments elicited a mild to nonexistent response from the mainstream Saudi media — a nonresponse that only confirmed Shiʿa suspicions about the regime's ambivalence toward Salafi vitriol.[41]

THE FACE OF JANUS: REGIME POLICIES TOWARD THE SAUDI SHIʿA

Bedeviled by opposition to the Shiʿa by the Salafi establishment, the Al Saʿud grappled with the double-edged nature of political reform. On the one hand, moderate elements of the ruling family recognized that calibrated and managed reforms could serve to bolster the regime's legitimacy at a time of mounting regional tensions and in the face of a serious domestic challenge from al-Qaʿida. On the other hand, the monarchy recognized that Shiʿa activists frequently allied themselves with liberal Sunni reformers to demand political changes that the ruling family perceived as a threat to their survival—namely, constitutionalism. What resulted from this dilemma was an inconsistent and Janus-faced approach toward the Shiʿa after 2003 that ended up fueling increased dissent, particularly among the younger generation.

Preemptive Reform: The Municipal Council Elections

On March 3, 2005, Saudi Arabia held elections for local municipal councils—the first elections held on a nationwide basis in more than four decades. Unlike in Bahrain, in Saudi Arabia the issue of participation in elections did not spur significant debate among the Shiʿa. The stakes were relatively low—the municipal councils oversaw basic services, and in the Eastern Province half of the seats were appointed by the government. Participating did not carry political costs for the moderate branch. Even former radicals such as Hassan al-Nimr, a former leader in the Hizballah al-Hijaz, participated in the elections, while at the same time remaining an adherent of *velayet-e faqih* and embracing Khamenei as his *marjaʿ*.[42] The Shiʿa enthusiasm for participation was rooted in part in the euphoria and inspiration that accompanied the Shiʿa electoral victory in neighboring Iraq. "There was the sense that 'we'll do it like the Iraqis,'" noted a Saudi Shiʿa activist.[43]

In many respects, the Saudi Shiʿa saw the elections as the culmination of promises made during the initial dialogue with then crown prince ʿAbdallah. Many of the moderates saw political participation as a way to demonstrate to their constituency their ability to deliver services and other material benefits. Even if the scope of the councils was limited, they were still seen as a way to educate the citizenry in the skills of grassroots democracy. "Municipal elections play a limited role," noted Jaʿfar al-Shayeb, the mayor of Qatif, "but at least it allows people to speak up."[44] A Shiʿa member of the appointed Consultative Council (Majlis al-Shura) echoed this view, arguing that the councils were designed to give the citizenry rudimentary practice in democracy: "The municipal council elections are in effect a socioeconomic reform—some people view it as a political reform, but this is stretching it. The municipal councils start us on the learning curve. To effectively delegate power, the regime must know that people are accountable."[45]

In the final tally, voting in the Eastern Province fell along sectarian lines, with Shi'a securing all five municipal council seats in Qatif and five out of six in Ahsa.[46] In the predominately Sunni municipality of Dammam, Sunni businessman swept the elections.[47] Unlike in Bahrain, in Saudi Arabia there was little evidence of gerrymandering by the regime to preserve Sunni dominance. Rather, the opposite occurred—districts were reshaped to guarantee the Shi'a a voting majority in Shi'a areas. A key gesture by the regime before the elections was the separation of the predominantly Shi'a city Qatif from the mixed city Dammam as a separate municipality by the minister for municipal affairs, Mita'ab bin 'Abd al-Aziz. Given Qatif's importance as the epicenter of the 1979 intifada, the government's willingness to recognize and formalize a Shi'a role in local governance is significant. Similarly, the municipality of Ahsa is a sensitive area for the government—it covers the sprawling Ghawar oilfield.[48]

In interviews, major Shi'a leaders in the East appeared pleased with the results, asserting that the elections were the natural continuation of a process that included the National Dialogue and the National Society for Human Rights (Jam'iyya al-Wataniya li-Huquq al-Insan). At the same time, there was caution about excessive expectation of change and that Saudi policy was "always a deliberate, gradual process."[49] Shi'a commentators argued that because the municipal councils received their budgets from the Ministry of Municipalities, they were hamstrung in their ability to affect meaningful reforms and alleviation of the Eastern Province's material grievances. Their role was ultimately consultative—to submit recommendations to the ministry rather than to enact legislation.[50]

Gatekeeping Cross-Sectarian Dialogue— or the Policy of Divide and Rule

As noted, one result of the escalating regional tensions in Iraq and Lebanon was a fraying of cooperation between Sunni reformists and their

Shiʿa allies. Even moderate Saudi Sunnis who had been previously aligned with Shiʿa reformists interpreted Saudi Shiʿa expressions of solidarity for Muqtada al-Sadr and Hizballah as a worrisome form of triumphalism— what one interlocutor called "a winner-take-all mentality."[51] For their part, Shiʿa activists grew increasingly suspicious that their erstwhile allies in the Sunni reform camp were, in the words of one activist, "closet Wahhabis."[52] As noted by a Sunni liberal writer on the Shiʿa al-Rasid news service website, "It is very clear that the consequences of the recent war [the 2006 Lebanon War] have caused an unexpected fissure in the invisible alliance between Saudi Shiʿa and the Sunnis who are categorized as liberal or secular."[53]

In the wake of the Lebanon War, it appeared that the Saudi government was encouraging these splits, harnessing regional tensions to fracture the opposition. In November 2006, for example, the regime disbanded a burgeoning attempt by Shiʿa religious scholars to coordinate with the national astronomical society to formulate a common, cross-sectarian method for forecasting the arrival of the new moon. Although the issue was a seemingly esoteric one, from the regime's point of view it would have marked the breaching of a major conceptual barrier that had kept the two sects divided.[54] "The government doesn't want cooperation among the sects; it tries to be the doorway through which all dialogue must pass," noted a prominent Shiʿa intellectual in Qatif.[55] "There will never be reform as long as the regime enforces a policy of *tasnif* [segregation]," argued another prominent activist in Ahsa.[56]

Another illustrative example occurred when a number of Sunni and Shiʿa moderates tried to dampen the inflammatory effects of the Salafi establishment's anti-Hizballah and anti-Shiʿa fatwas. Most notably, the Sunni activist Mikhlif bin-Dahham al-Shammari conducted joint Sunni–Shiʿa prayers at a Shiʿa mosque in the Eastern Province. The Shiʿa al-Rasid website reported that al-Shammari was physically harassed by "Salafi extremists" and that the prayers were cancelled indefinitely. Later, in February 2007, the Saudi security services arrested al-Shammari for having visited Hassan al-Saffar. Ostracized by his own tribe (which received substantial patronage from the Saudi government) and frequently in prison, al-Shammari has since become an icon of sympathy and support among the Saudi Shiʿa; the al-Rasid website frequently reports on his predicament and prominently displays his photo.

Aside from these instances, some Shiʿa activists wondered whether tacitly promoting sectarianism might have a certain utility for ʿAbdallah—to deflect potential criticism by Salafi clerical constituents and to undercut the mobilizing appeal of Iran's anti-Western rhetoric on the Arab street. This argument holds that Salafis are the "stick" wielded by the Al Saʿud to secure Shiʿa cooperation, with the royals portraying themselves as benevolent protectors against the Salafi extremists.[57] There is also a political and economic utility to this approach. According to a former member of the Saudi Ministry of Interior's General Investigation Directorate—the principal regime organ for the collection of intelligence on domestic opposition—the security services are widely spread throughout the country, with the majority, roughly one thousand officers, focused on the Qasim region alone. In contrast, there are only one hundred officers assigned to the East.[58]

Regardless of how many forces the regime was committing to the East, by 2010 its policy in the East had devolved to a Janus-faced blend of co-option and delegitimation. It had used the 2005 municipal council elections as a preemptive and co-optive mechanism, pitting Sunni and Shiʿa reformists against one another to prevent the emergence of a united opposition and tacitly permitting sectarian vitriol from the Salafi establishment. It was a time-tested strategy and one that would be applied to even greater effect in the wake of the 2011 Arab uprisings.

EIGHT

WAVING ʿUTHMAN'S SHIRT

Saudi Arabia's Sectarian Spring

In October 2011, an editorial appeared in the Saudi daily *al-Hayat* that invoked the specter of Iranian meddling to argue, in unusually strident language, for harsher measures against Shiʿa protests in the Eastern Province: "It is time to admit that there are fighting groups in Qatif that have been trained in Iran, Syria, and Lebanon, and to start liquidating and purging them from the country rather than listening to the deceit of those who raise slogans such as 'rejecting sectarianism' in the same way as ' ʿUthman's Shirt' to violate the country's security."[1]

As Muslims and students of Islamic history know, " ʿUthman's Shirt" is an emotive reference to the early struggles for succession in Islam: ʿUthman Ibn Affan was the third caliph whose murder at the hands of a mutiny paved the way for the nomination of ʿAli as his successor. In the ensuing civil war, ʿUthman's nephew Muawiyah (also the first caliph) rallied popular support against ʿAli by waving ʿUthman's bloodied shirt that was retrieved from the site of his assassination. Arguably the first instance of sectarian incitement, the waving of ʿUthman's Shirt is used by the author of this *al-Hayat* article to accuse the Saudi Shiʿa of trying to dissimulate about their real objectives—in other words, using calls for democracy and political reform as a smokescreen for narrowly sectarian goals.

Ironically, though, the analogy is more accurately applied to the policies of hard-liners in the Saudi regime and their allies in the Salafi clerical establishment. The Saudi regime has long deployed a sectarian narrative to isolate the Shiʿa and split them from like-minded Sunni reformists. The strategy was used to great effect in the aftermath of the Arab uprisings, when protests in the Eastern Province were initially coordinated with demonstrations elsewhere but fell apart due to mutual distrust among Sunni and Shiʿa.

Among the disaffected Shiʿa of the Eastern Province, the uprisings of Tunis and Tahrir Square were greeted with exuberance and elation. A younger generation of activists seized on the revolts to mount a challenge against the older Shiʿa leadership. Long-dormant linkages between the Shiʿa and Sunni oppositionists elsewhere in the kingdom and abroad were rekindled. Yet the planned "Day of Rage" did not materialize as expected. Protests were confined to scattered, isolated demonstrations in Qatif that were quickly and quietly dispersed. In part because of a concerted regime strategy to "sectarianize" the Day of Rage, Sunni protestors in the Najd and Hijaz and the uncommitted who were still testing the political winds never showed up.

In the weeks and months that followed, the regime managed dissent through a three-pronged strategy: using an intensified crackdown on protest instigators, bloggers, clerics, and lay activists; attempting to preemptively silence any future dissent through a package of subsidies and economic aid; and by working with certain Shiʿa clerics to dampen the protests.

Despite this strategy, the long-marginalized pockets of dissent in the East—al-ʿAwamiya and, to a lesser extent, Qatif—would not be cowed. Starting in the fall of 2011, an increasingly harsh security response resulted in protestor deaths, which in turn spawned even more protests. A turning point in this sectarian strategy was the July 9, 2012, shooting and imprisonment of the firebrand cleric Nimr al-Nimr, whom the regime had long accused of siding with Iran and calling for secession of the Eastern Province. From this point onward, the older clerics and activists' control over youthful street rage eroded. Attempts at cross-sectarian dialogue by both older activists and a younger generation using social media stalled due in part to regime politics and to the spillover of regional tensions from the Syrian civil war and the impasse in Bahrain.

DISSENT IN THE EASTERN PROVINCE: LOCAL VERSUS NATIONAL AGENDAS

In many respects, the Arab uprisings' arrival at the Eastern Province represents the culmination of several trends that had been coalescing in the area since 2009. The riots in Medina and the ensuing crackdown laid bare the failed promises of reform that had begun with the National Dialogue. The Shiʿa attempt at unofficial coordination with Sunni reformists had also foundered. The older cadre of the Islahiyyin leadership under Hassan al-Saffar and Jaʿfar al-Shayeb found itself facing increased pressure by youthful activists who had grown disillusioned with dialogue and petitions.[2]

In the wake of Mubarak's fall in Egypt and the momentous changes sweeping the region, members of Islahiyyin once again deployed the petition strategy, cooperating with Sunni Islamists and liberals to sign a letter demanding a constitutional monarchy. The letter was titled *Ilan watani lil-islah* (The Declaration of National Reform), and its 119 signatories included Sunni reformists such as ʿAbd al-Aziz al-Qasim, Turki al-Hamad, and Khalid al-Dakhil, as well as Shiʿa activists such as Tawfiq al-Sayf, Jaʿfar al-Shayeb, and Najib al-Khunayzi. It urged a broad array of political and civil reforms, including an elected National Assembly, the protection of human rights, and, importantly, a federal system that would give greater authority to provincial governments.[3] The latter was especially important as a grievance that united both Sunnis and Shiʿa. Echoing Shiʿa frustration in the East, Sunni activists in the western Saudi Arabia grew increasingly angry at the central government's maladroit handling of flooding in Jeddah in 2009 and again in early 2011 that left hundreds dead. But for the youthful activists in the eastern part of the country, inspired by the crowds of Tunis, Tahrir Square, Benghazi, and Pearl Roundabout, the petition was emblematic of a timeworn approach that had failed to bring results.

It is important to note that the Shiʿa youth in the East had initially planned their protests as part of a broader, national movement for demonstrations on March 11, 2011—heralded variously as a "Day of Rage," a "Day of Longing," and, increasingly, the "Hunayn Revolution"—a historical reference to the Battle of Hunayn fought between the Prophet Muhammad and his followers, on one side, and a Bedouin tribe, on the other, near Ta'if in 630 C.E.[4] It is unclear who started the pages that first began appearing on the Internet in late February. Many observers attributed them to dissidents based overseas, most notably the London-based Movement for Islamic Reform in Arabia.[5] Others feared that they were a deliberate ploy by the Saudi regime to entrap dissidents.

On March 1, many of the Saudi youth groups appeared to have coalesced under an umbrella movement called the "Free Youth Coalition" (I'tilaf al-Shabab al-Ahrar), which issued a lengthy, twenty-four-point set of demands, including the release of political prisoners, an end to corruption, the cancellation of all "unjustified debts and taxes," an elected Consultative Council, and an independent judiciary.[6] Importantly, the planned demonstrations were billed as expressions of solidarity with the protestors in Tunis, Tahrir Square, and Benghazi.

As March 11 approached, however, websites and Facebook pages appeared that advanced uniquely Shi'a demands and reforms specific to the Eastern Province. This development later proved a watershed in the fracturing of the opposition and, arguably, the demise of the Arab uprising in Saudi Arabia. The branching of the Day of Rage into a Shi'a-specific protest stoked significant online debate among the web-based activists in the Saudi opposition movement. Critics—many of them self-identified Sunnis—lambasted the Shi'a organizers for pursuing a narrowly "sectarian" agenda that diluted the overall movement and played into the regime's hands. Even worse, they attacked the Shi'a for scheduling their protests three days before the planned Day of Rage protests on March 11—an accelerated timeline that they perceived as a brazen act of one-upmanship.

The first Facebook pages that focused specifically on the Eastern Province appeared around March 3. Around the same period, a larger page was launched, "The Eastern Region Revolution," which is still active and includes links to video clips and publications.[7]

The organizers of the page made clear that their agenda was distinct from the larger Hunayn Revolution. The site listed as its core demand the release of nine "forgotten" Shi'a prisoners who had been detained for sixteen years without a trial because of their alleged involvement in the 1996 bombing of U.S. Air Force housing at Khobar Towers as well as the release of Tawfiq al-'Amir, a cleric from al-Ahsa who had been arrested on February 27 for calling for a constitutional monarchy.[8] The page also called for sit-ins on March 9 in Qatif—at least two days before the Day of Rage planned throughout the kingdom. In setting this date, the organizers argued that the case of the forgotten prisoners would be drowned out "among all the other slogans shouted on [March 11]." "Our Revolution," the Free Youth Coalition asserted, "is a condemnation of the hideous crimes committed by [the governor of the Eastern Region Province] Muhammad bin Fahd."[9]

The reaction from other voices of the opposition was swift and loud. An online commentator named Salma al-Shihab demanded that the name "Eastern Region Revolution" be changed "because it reflects a regionalist tendency which is something that the creators of this page have complained about . . . that the Hunayn Revolution is sectarian based. Indirectly, you have fallen into the same trap."[10] Other Internet voices claimed to represent the sponsors of the main Day of Rage, arguing that it was founded and led by Sunnis and that the Shiʿa's own Day of Rage risked polarizing and spitting the movement. "[Our] movement will never agree to support a sectarian or a factional plan or a suspicious one, and will not risk backing a controversial plan," the poster noted.[11]

SHIʿA PROTESTS ERUPT . . . AND CLERICS TRY TO STEM THE TIDE

The first Shiʿa protests occurred nearly eight days before the planned Day of Rage protests, on March 3, 2011, when roughly one hundred protests in al-ʿAwamiya and Qatif marched in solidarity with the forgotten protestors.[12] Similar protests occurred the following day after Friday prayers in Qatif, al-Ahsa, al-Safwa, and al-ʿAwamiya. Facebook pages listed the release of Tawfiq al-ʿAmir as a core demand of the demonstrations.[13] The regime responded with the arrest of twenty-four protesters on the street in Qatif.[14] Several were reportedly injured.[15] On March 8, Saudi authorities released al-ʿAmir, along with the twenty-four other detained protestors, in an apparent gesture of conciliation.[16] Al-ʿAmir reportedly met with the governor of the Eastern Province, Prince Muhammad bin Fahd, who agreed to form an investigatory committee to look into Shiʿa grievances.

These concessions, however, did not stem subsequent protests on March 9 and 10. Approximately six hundred to eight hundred protestors demonstrated in Qatif, again citing the forgotten prisoners as their rallying cry. The police responded with percussion grenades and rubber bullets, sparking condemnations from local clerics—most vociferously, Hassan al-Nimr.[17] By March 11, the police presence on the streets of Qatif was described as "massive," and the demonstrations had spread to al-Ahsa, al-ʿAwamiya, Safwa, and Dammam. Importantly, the Islahiyyin-affiliated website of the al-Rasid news service tried to distance these protests from the broader Hunayn Revolution—perhaps to avoid antagonizing Sunni reformist allies and provoking a greater regime crackdown.[18] Sporadic protests continued through the week but took a more dramatic turn with the intervention of Saudi forces in Bahrain on March 17. Rally slogans and chants increasingly focused on the withdrawal of Saudi forces and expressions of solidarity with Bahrain's protestors.[19] "One people, not two," a placard in Qatif read, referring to the unity of Bahraini and Saudi Shiʿa.[20] Al-Saffar himself issued a statement condemning the Saudi incursion into Bahrain.[21]

As in Bahrain, the older clerical cadre struggled to contain the youthful rage bubbling beneath them. Much of this took place in behind-the-scenes negotiations with the Eastern Province governor Prince Muhammad bin Fahd and in dialogue with youth. Clerics from across the ideological spectrum took part: luminaries from the Shirazi current, such as Hassan al-Saffar, but also leaders of the Khat al-Imam (Hassan al-Nimr and ʿAbd al-Karim Hubayl), followers of Mudarrisi (Muhammad Hassan Habib), and conservatives/traditionalists (Munir al-Khabbaz, Mansur al-Jishi, and ʿAbdallah al-Khunayzi).[22] On March 9, a fifteen-member youth delegation from Qatif met the governor of Eastern Province for the release of nine "forgotten" prisoners accused of the 1996 Khobar Towers bombing, as well as imprisoned writers such as Husayn Allaq. At the same time, Khunayzi led a delegation to Riyadh.[23] On March 30, another clerical delegation consisting principally of the Khat al-Imam clerics (Hubayl and Hassan al-Nimr) and the traditionalists (Khunayzi and Jishi) visited the Eastern Province deputy governor Jiluwi bin Abd al-Aziz bin Musʾad al-Saud.[24] On April 21, a group of thirty-five Shiʿa clerics from diverse ideological currents and family backgrounds issued a statement calling for an end to the protests. The statement, posted to the al-Rasid news service website and communicated widely through mosques and *husayniyat* exhorted Shiʿa youth to withdraw from the streets in order to give the Saudi authorities time to implement reforms.[25]

In many instances, however, these outreach efforts toward the regime put the clerics in direct conflict with the youth. Nowhere was the criticism more intense than toward two clerical figures "conservatives" or traditionalists, Mansur al-Jishi and ʿAbdallah al-Khunayzi, who had endeavored to facilitate the release of political prisoners but were derided by youth activists as collaborators. In commentary on Twitter and YouTube as well as in the press, activists scoffed at them for acting as "intelligence agents," conspiring with the regime's *baltijiya* (thugs), or simply displaying a "lack of experience and self-awareness."[26]

In response to clerical efforts, there was slim to little evidence of any concessions by the government. Even worse, the government began what appeared to be a concerted crackdown. At the same time the negotiations were under way, the regime was detaining 120 protestors and maintaining a near constant presence of security forces, helicopters, and armored vehicles on the streets of Qatif. On August 3, 2011, Tawfiq al-ʿAmir was once again arrested, sparking further demonstrations, particularly among his supporters in al-Ahsa, and prompting expressions of solidarity on the Facebook page "The Eastern Region Revolution."

On October 3, 2011, protests took their most violent turn yet when security forces clashed with armed protestors in al-ʿAwamiya, which resulted in the wounding of eleven police officers and three civilians.[27] Video posted on Facebook showed masked youth assaulting a police station. The confrontation was reportedly sparked after Saudi police attempted to arrest a sixty-year-old man in an effort to force the surrender of his son, who had been taking part in pro-Bahrain protests.[28]

Across the Saudi blogosphere and media landscape, the al-ʿAwamiya clashes sparked debate and reflection about the underlying roots of sectarianism. The Saudi Ministry of Interior predictably blamed the disturbances on "foreign parties" and threatened to meet the dissent with an "iron fist."[29] The official Saudi press largely echoed this line, with the popular columnist Mshari al-Dhaydi arguing that it was Iran's hand, not sectarian inequality, that was driving the violence.[30]

From the other side, Shi'a and pro-reform voices lambasted the regime's heavy-handed response as an unmasking of its true character. Some compared the al-'Awamiya disturbances to the Syrian protests, arguing ominously that they were a harbinger of even worse violence throughout the kingdom.

THE REGIME'S MEDIA COUNTERMOBILIZATION

In response to the appearance of Facebook pages calling for a Day of Rage, the Saudi regime launched a campaign to discredit and undermine the protestors, deploying a wide range of themes: emphasizing the destructive nature of the protests, delegitimizing them on the basis of Islamic law, and, importantly, framing them as serving Shi'a parochial interests. A wide range of outlets conveyed these messages, using both traditional and social media: the Interior Ministry, the Senior Ulema Council, conservative and reformist newspapers (such as al-Madina and al-Watan, respectively), and Facebook pages that emphasized solidarity with the regime.

On March 5, the Ministry of Interior issued a forceful statement reiterating that protests were illegal and that those participating would be subject to prosecution.[31] This missive was further buttressed by a fatwa issued by the Senior Ulema Council that prohibited protests by citing Islamic legal precepts against the spreading of fitna (chaos).[32] A succession of other fatwas soon followed that served simultaneously to delegitimize the protests and to "remind" the royal family that the support of the Salafi establishment was a critical buffer against popular protests. The popular conservative cleric Muhammad al-Habadan went so far on his website, Nur al-Islam, as to argue that support from the Salafi clerics was the only reason the royals had not gone the way of Mubarak in Cairo.[33]

Elsewhere on the Internet, the regime sponsored—albeit indirectly—the creation of Facebook pages that attempted to discredit and isolate the Day of Rage organizers. The most notable was "Together Against the Hunayn Revolution" and "May Allah Blacken Their Faces." On both pages, as in a plethora of YouTube videos, there were frequent references to the Shi'a and Iran as the hidden instigators behind the Day of Rage protests.[34] The charges were sufficient to force the Free Youth Coalition to issue a statement on

March 7, 2011, on its Facebook page that "all the organizers [of the Day of Rage] are Sunnis."[35] At least some observers believe that this partially explains the dismal showing of public support for the protests, particularly among Sunnis. "The Sunnis are afraid—they are caught between Sa'ad al-Faqih and the Eastern Province," noted one longtime Saudi dissident.[36]

Aside from this countermobilization, the regime undertook more repressive measures in the media realm. In February, it enacted a new law that requires online newspapers to be licensed by the Interior Ministry. Activists complained that the law was sufficiently vague to encapsulate many forms of online discourse, such as video messaging and mobile phone texting.[37] Even after the Day of Rage fizzled, there were calls for the organizers to be prosecuted.[38]

In late 2011, the regime took additional measures to monitor and suppress online activism in the Eastern Province. It reportedly banned You-Tube channels that posted videos of Eastern Province protests.[39] Given the popularity of Facebook and Twitter, a Saudi Ministry of Interior spokesman announced on November 2 that police in the Eastern Province would set up a Facebook presence and would assign a special team to monitor social media in the region. The goal of the Facebook page, according to the source, was to encourage tips and information from anonymous sources regarding "outlawed" activity in the region.[40] Nearly simultaneously, the regime blocked a number of Eastern Province pages; the most significant of them was "Steadfastness for the Borders of Qatif," which rallied opposition to government moves to shrink the administrative boundaries of Qatif.[41]

PREEMPTIVE SUBSIDIES AND REFORM

The regime launched a massive campaign of economic and social aid to dampen dissent. It also undertook limited, calibrated political reform of municipal council elections. On February 23, 2011, following a three-month absence abroad for medical treatment, King 'Abdallah announced a benefits package totaling 130 billion dollars. Subsequent press releases detailed the program as alleviating the impact of inflation, introducing an unemployment benefit (an especially salient concession for the Eastern Province Shi'a), providing a state scholarship program for Saudis studying abroad, constructing affordable housing, and maintaining an "inflation allowance" for Saudi state employees.[42]

Later, on March 22, the government's Ministry of Municipal and Rural Affairs announced that the first stage of elections for the kingdom's 219 municipal councils would be held on September 22, 2011. Originally scheduled for October 2009, the elections had been repeatedly postponed, and the sudden acceleration of the timeline was seen as a preemptive concession by the regime to the burgeoning demands for reform.[43] That said, a key reform demand—the participation of women in the voting—was not included in the initial announcement, although King ʿAbdallah later announced that women would indeed be allowed to participate, albeit in the next elections.[44] Taken in sum, the announcement of the accelerated electoral timeline and the granting of suffrage to women must be seen as preemptive efforts by the regime to placate the opposition—at the expense of the more specific Shiʿa demands.

The Saudi regime used the failure of the protests as a validation of the Al Saʿud family's benevolence and legitimacy. "Everybody was surprised when this day of rage turned into a silent *bayaʿ* [oath of loyalty] that saw the Saudi public wordlessly express their support of the leadership," noted the editor-in-chief of *al-Sharq al-Awsat*, Tariq al-Humayd.[45] In a postmortem on why the protests fizzled, the Free Youth Coalition blamed the regime's attempts to impugn the organizers as foreign based, secular, or Shiʿa.[46] From the Shiʿa side, the failure of the revolts was attributed to Sunni apathy and the historic aversion of the Najdi heartland to mounting any sort of dissent against the status quo. According to one dissident, "Sunnis were afraid to come out—and this was not the first time they failed to protest. In 2004, Saʿad al-Faqih asked people to demonstrate, but only two hundred people showed up in Riyadh. Najdi culture simply doesn't have the protest gene. It is shameful to protest."[47]

RENEWED ESCALATION AND VIOLENCE

Yet the fizzling of the Day of Rage did not quiet the restive East—quite the opposite. It deepened the despair of a younger generation of Shiʿa activists, particularly in long-marginalized al-'Awamiya and, to a lesser extent, Qatif. If a single incident can be pinpointed that galvanized the youth to take to the streets, it was the weekend of November 19, 2011, when nineteen-year-old Nasser al-Mhayshi was shot dead at a checkpoint near Qatif. His body was reportedly left on the ground for three or four hours because the government refused to let his family collect it, sparking protests across the city. A second man, 'Ali al-Felfel, was then killed by police. By the end of the week, five people, including a nine-year-old girl, had been killed, and six others were wounded by police bullets. In a statement, the Interior Ministry reported its version of events, linking the protests to Iranian meddling: "A number of security checkpoints and vehicles has since Monday been increasingly coming under gunfire attacks in the Qatif region by assailants motivated by foreign orders."[48]

From this point on, tire burnings, drive-by shootings, street marches, and police raids became near nightly occurrences. Outside media access to al-'Awamiya all but ceased; the city had become a veritable war zone with ubiquitous checkpoints and armored vehicles. Government attempts to disperse the protests were heavy-handed, with frequent reports of live fire into armed crowds. At the same time, there *were* instances of armed assaults by Shi'a youth on police vehicles—an unsurprising outcome given the plethora of small arms in al-'Awamiya. Protestor deaths and imprisonments spawned an endless cycle of mourning and follow-up protests.

The weekend of February 10, 2012, offers an illustrative glimpse of how this escalation unfolded. On Friday afternoon, Nimr al-Nimr, the outspoken prayer leader of al-'Awamiya, delivered a fiery sermon demanding the end of the monarchy. Protestors then made their way across the city shouting demands for reform and the release of prisoners. A protestor threw an effigy of the interior minister at a row of armored antiriot vehicles. Shots may or may not have been fired at security forces. In the ensuing clashes, police shot twenty-one-year-old Zuhayr al-Sa'id in the stomach; he later died in the hospital. Then, according to the official ministry narrative of events, "while security men were following up on an illegal gathering in the town of al-'Awamiya in [the province of] Qatif on Friday [February 10], they were attacked by gunfire. They dealt with the situation by firing back, which resulted with the death of one."[49] By late

2012, more than sixteen young men had been killed by security forces in the Eastern Province, the majority of them from al-ʿAwamiya.

New Youth Activism . . . and Response from the Old Elite

Aside from the deleterious effects on conditions in the East, the violence had a broader political effect on the Shiʿa movement: it placed increasing pressure on the conciliatory, pro-dialogue approach of Hassan al-Saffar and the Islahiyyin. As noted previously, this trend of disenchantment was not new and had its roots in the 2008 Baqiʿ riots in Medina. But the post–Arab uprising violence clearly accelerated it.

As in Bahrain, much of the intra-Shiʿa friction was rooted in generational differences. The young dissenters of al-ʿAwamiya and Qatif had grown weary and impatient with the failure of the Islahiyyin to deliver tangible improvements in living conditions, jobs, and an end to pervasive discrimination.[50] There was the sense, particularly in al-ʿAwamiya, that Hassan al-Saffar and his cadre, like ʿAli Salman and al-Wifaq in Bahrain, had become institutionalized and effectively co-opted by the regime. "We have no relationship with al-Saffar. We don't consult with him. He never came out against us, so he must support us," noted one Shiʿa youth activist from al-ʿAwamiya.[51] In a 2012 sermon, al-Saffar acknowledged this same difference, warning that "although previous generations tolerated and adapted to problems, the current generation is different."[52]

In many respects, the youth groups' goals were similar to the Islahiyyin's—the release of political prisoners and a constitutional monarchy. Differences, however, arose over time frame and tactics. Inspired by the electrifying drama in Tunis, Cairo, and Benghazi, the youth groups seemed to have little tolerance for their elders' failed promises. "Where the shaykhs and the youth differ," noted one longtime youth activist in late 2012, "is their amount of patience [sabr]."[53] Toward local clerics, these young men held respectful but not overly deferential views. Certainly, any attempts by the regime to imprison or censor the clerics would provide a rallying cry for demonstrations. But this galvanizing effect was far from actual control or authority over the timing, scope, and tactics of youth-driven protests. "The clerics' role is limited to that of 'advisers,'" noted one activist. Echoing this point, another noted that "clerics such as Shaykh Munir [al-Khabbaz] or Shaykh Tawfiq [al-'Amir] tried to play a leadership role in the streets but couldn't. The youth respect Shaykh Tawfiq and want his release, but they don't consider him a leader."[54]

In interviews, these new youth activists described themselves as "post-ideological" and nonsectarian in their demands. Many youth generally eschew the arcane juridical debates among the various Shi'a maraji'; some went so far as to argue that the old divisions between the Khat al-Imam, the Shiraziyyin, and so forth were largely meaningless among younger activists. In conversations, several regarded Grand Ayatollah 'Ali al-Sistani as their preferred marja' precisely because he *stayed out* of their political affairs; one went so far as to characterize him as a "secular marja'" (marja' 'ilmani).[55]

In terms of organization, the youth activists have formed networks of cellular, leaderless groups such as the Free Youth Coalition,[56] Missionary Youth Movement (Shabab al-Harak al-Risali),[57] Solidarity Group (Majmu'at al-Tadamun),[58] Free Men of Sayhat (Ahrar Sayhat),[59] Free Men of Tarut (Ahrar Tarut),[60] Supporters of Qatif (Qatifiyyun),[61] and an all-women group, Women Supporters of the Zaynab School in Qatif (Zaynibiyat Qatifiyyat).[62] By far the most popular of these groups, at least in its web presence, is the Eastern Region Revolution (Thawrat al-Mantiqa al-Sharqiya), which has been active since March 2011 and has had more than sixteen thousand "likes" on Facebook and ten million YouTube views as of early 2013.[63] Like their youthful counterparts in Bahrain, these groups make skillful use of social media to coordinate street protests, to network with like-minded activists, and to disseminate criticism of the regime.[64] In their statements, many show a clear deference to the teachings of Nimr al-Nimr: a rejection of violence, sectarianism, and secession, accompanied by demands for sweeping political and social reforms.

In March 2012, several of these networks merged into the Freedom and Justice Coalition (FJC, I'tilaf al-Hurriyya wa al-'Adala).[65] The FJC plays a prominent role in organizing demonstrations across the region; in marches in Qatif and al-'Awamiya, its clenched-fist logo figures prominently on banners and placards. Although it maintains a robust Facebook presence, it has historically had little mention in the open media and has refused to divulge details about its size, membership, and leadership for fear of retribution by the authorities. In September 2012, however, the FJC disclosed that one of its founders, the longtime activist Hamza Alawi al-Shakhuri, had fled the country.[66]

For their part, older Shiʿa activists and intellectuals admire the youth groups' zeal and enthusiasm but criticize their naïveté in thinking that localized dissent by a sectarian minority can spark a Tahrir-style movement. "We are a minority, we are a province, we can't spark a revolution," noted one.[67] Others critique their lack of a program and organization, arguing that the FJC has fallen short of being a coherent umbrella structure and that the plethora of Facebook pages for other groups belies a degree of coherence and capability that does not actually exist on the ground.[68]

Regardless of these shortcomings, youth activism has had an impact in a number of areas. Most significant, it has forced statements and rhetoric by the Islahiyyin, in particular Hassan al-Saffar, to become increasingly more strident and critical of the regime. Long a supporter of the ten-year National Dialogue project, al-Saffar has never condoned or incited violence. But the escalating violence starting in late 2011 forced him to adopt a more unyielding position. For example, in his Friday prayer sermon on October 7, 2011, he directly attacked the Interior Ministry for its heavy-handed response to al-ʿAwamiya rioting in October, arguing that the regime's official language facilitated an atmosphere of sectarianism.[69] On February 10, 2012, he delivered a sermon obliquely highlighting the hypocrisy of the Al Saʿud in criticizing the bloodletting in Syria while simultaneously causing the civilian deaths in the Eastern Province—and refusing to apologize for it.[70] These statements, in turn, provoked an even sharper escalation in the press from Sunni and pro-regime voices. In an official statement, the Saudi Press Agency pounced on al-Saffar's "politically motivated" sermon—the government's most direct attack on the Shiʿa cleric.[71] Other press reaction was similarly vociferous.[72]

The consequences of this hard-line approach for the royal family were profound. By refusing any substantive concessions and continuing to address dissent as a security problem, the regime diminished the power and influence of its principal interlocutors in the Eastern Province. A turning point in this trend was the July 8, 2012, shooting and subsequent arrest of the increasingly popular cleric Nimr al-Nimr. This event shook the region to its core, prompting a stream of protests and violent clashes that has yet to fully abate.

Crossing the Red Line: The Shooting and Detention of Nimr al-Nimr

As noted previously, by 2011 Nimr al-Nimr was steadily gaining in popularity, not just in his hometown of al-'Awamiya, but among the Eastern Province's youth, who had grown frustrated with the cautious leadership of the Islahiyyin current. Yet in summer 2012, his firebrand rhetoric crossed a red line. In late June, al-Nimr delivered a rousing tirade against the ruling family, rejoicing in the recent death of the much-feared Prince Nayif, and imploring God to take the lives of the "entire Al Sa'ud, Khalifa, and Asad dynasties."[73] On July 8, Saudi security forces attempted to arrest him; according to regime sources, a car chase and firefight ensued. Nimr was wounded in the thigh, arrested, and taken into custody.

It is likely that intra-royal jockeying and the transition of power in the Interior Ministry contributed to the arrest; the newly appointed interior minister, Ahmed bin 'Abd al-Aziz, probably felt compelled to start his tenure with a firm hand. Following the arrest, he issued a scathing statement deriding al-Nimr as a marginal, mentally ill figure guilty of sedition.[74]

Another contributing factor to the arrest may have been the regime's crackdown on Sunni clerics and activists throughout 2012.[75] Specifically, the arrest of Yusuf al-Ahmed, a controversial figure who opposed some of King 'Abdallah's reforms on gender equality, became a rallying cry on Twitter. Added to this, the Al Sa'ud muzzled a number of hard-line clerics who tried to solicit donations for Syria; some of these clerics, such as Nasir al-'Umar, are among the kingdom's most vociferous opponents of the Shi'a. In the wake of this campaign, the ruling family may have felt compelled to take similar action against the Shi'a, to preempt potential criticism of the monarchy from hard-line Salafis. Why, the latter figures must have wondered, should the wrath of the regime be reserved for the Sunnis when Shiʿa transgressions—epitomized by al-Nimr's insulting sermons— went unpunished?[76] A pro-regime editorial appeared to reflect this attempt at "sectarian balancing," drawing a false equivalency between Shiʿa protests and the al-Qaʿida threat that plagued the kingdom in the early and mid-2000s. "Security forces confronted 'al-Qaʿida' with the same resolve," the author noted, "[that] they now employ when confronting those who incite sedition in Qatif."[77]

Opening a Volcano: Protests Spread Beyond al-ʿAwamiya

Far from quelling Shiʿa dissent, the arrest of Nimr al-Nimr galvanized the Eastern Province toward further protests. Ironically, many Shiʿa disagreed with al-Nimr's highly personalized attack on Prince Nayif following his death. But the regime's seemingly heavy-handed response—made even worse by graphic photographs of al-Nimr lying bloodied from a gunshot wound and sprawled in the back of a car—turned the outspoken cleric into a heroic icon for youth across the region. "Al-ʿAwamiya is just the opening of the volcano," noted one cleric. "And you don't judge the size of the volcano by its opening."[78]

Soon after al-Nimr was shot, the Facebook page "The Eastern Region Revolution" called for protests against the Al Saʿud across the country.[79] On July 12, 2012, the Saudi oppositionist website al-Jazira al-ʿArabiya posted a statement from a hitherto unknown opposition group called the "Youth of Qatif Revolution," which threatened "to assault police stations and blow up oil wells" if al-Nimr was not released.[80] Hundreds of Shiʿa protesters took to the streets, and clashes with security forces became an almost nightly occurrence.[81] The regime response shifted from arresting protestors themselves to targeting the infrastructure that sustained the dissent: mosques and their preachers. On September 16, Saudi security forces razed the ʿAyn Imam Husayn Mosque in al-ʿAwamiya, the mosque where Nimr al-Nimr had led daily prayers prior to his detention.[82] Ten days later, Saudi security forces arrested the Shiʿa cleric Husayn Radhi at his home in the eastern town of al-ʿUmran; the ostensible charge was organizing a protest against the notorious anti-Islam film *The Innocence of Muslims*, which had sparked deadly protests throughout the Arab and Islamic world.[83]

As before, the escalating violence placed further strains on the older activists' conciliatory approach. On July 14, a diverse group of thirty-seven Shi'a clerics from across the ideological spectrum signed a statement imploring Shi'a youth to remain steadfast, to cease all violence, and to avoid playing into the hands of the regime's "sectarian incitement."[84] A similar missive appeared later, on August 19, issued by seven, equally diverse Shi'a clerics: "We ask the people of this town to stand firmly against violence in all shapes and forms, and to condemn transgressions against lives and property." The document also called on residents to verify news before circulating them on social media websites to avoid "strife and chaos"— the clearest illustration yet of social media's electrifying effect on street dynamics in the East.[85]

Many younger activists saw these statements as a regime-sponsored ploy to stifle protests of any sort. "Their statement was just like the government's line—'Stop protesting, you are causing *fitna*,'" noted one young activist in an interview.[86] Many clerics who signed the statements were subjected to fierce criticism by Shi'a youth. Nowhere was this more apparent than in the case of 'Abd al-Karim al-Hubayl, the Khat al-Imam cleric and cofounder of Hizballah al-Hijaz, whom some contacts describe as the second most popular cleric among Saudi Shi'a youth, after al-Nimr. In the wake of signing the statement, al-Hubayl was subjected to withering criticism by Eastern Province youth on Twitter and in web forums.[87] "The youth lost confidence in him; he has one leg here and one leg there," noted one activist.[88] "Al-Hubayl flip-flops," noted another.[89]

Nor did al-Nimr's arrest placate Sunnis or stem the tide of Sunni demonstrations. The summer and fall of 2012 were marked by sustained protests in front of prisons in al-Qassim—a longtime stronghold of conservative Salafism.[90] Aside from rancor over prisoners, Sunni anger was directed at economic mismanagement and corruption, especially in the kingdom's non-Najdi periphery. Nowhere was this more evident than in the West, where torrential flooding that had wreaked havoc on Jeddah became a rallying cry for Sunni disenchantment. Young Shi'a activists argue that these Sunni demonstrators, whether they acknowledge it or not, were inspired by the outspokenness and protest culture of the East.

EFFORTS AT CROSS-SECTARIAN DIALOGUE

Attempting to tap into this current of activism, Eastern Province reformists launched a renewed effort at cross-sectarian dialogue with Sunnis across the country. As in the past, much of the dialogue took place beyond the purview of the regime's officially sanctioned "dialogue" forums, which many activists perceived as a means to regulate and circumscribe any sort of coordination on actual reform. A younger generation of activists have continued to use social media for outreach efforts. For example, in early 2013 a group of Shiʿa youth launched a Twitter campaign to invite Sunnis from Jeddah to a celebration on the night of the Prophet's birth. A similar outreach, known as the "Qatif Outreach" (Tawasul Qatif), has been ongoing for nearly four years.[91] "They all thought we spoke Persian here," joked one of the program's organizers.[92]

Despite these efforts, outreach has stalled, partly because of the entrenched sectarianism in Saudi society and government policy.[93] Many Salafi reformists remain tepid about associating too closely with Shiʿa. With no one is this more apparent than the immensely popular and provocative Salafi cleric Salman al-ʿAwda, who, although he has publicly hinted at democratic reforms, largely abandoned sectarian discourse, and received Shiʿa delegations,[94] has stopped short of an effective collaboration for fear of alienating his Sunni base. "The growing respect between Sunnis and Shiʿa has not translated into collective action," acknowledged one activist in Qatif. "We've done all we can; it is up to the Sunni reformists now."[95]

The reverberations of events in Syria on Saudi society further strained reform coordination. As Salafi clerics frame the civil war in sectarian terms—demonizing the Alawis—the Shiʿa of the Eastern Province have likewise come under increased pressure. Many are believed to sympathize with the Assad regime, despite the fact that Nimr al-Nimr, the most outspoken of the Shiʿa clerics, has called for the downfall of Bashar al-Assad. Statements by Syrian and Iranian officials have not helped matters; these governments typically speak about the affairs of the Eastern Province to advance their respective regional agendas. For example, in March 2012 the Syrian delegate to the United Nations proposed sending Syrian troops to protect the population of Qatif after the Saudi delegate suggested Saudi troops should be sent to Syria to stop the massacres against the Syrian people.[96]

In March 2013, as Saudi Arabia crossed the two-year anniversary of the 2011 Arab uprisings, the Eastern Province was caught between glimmers of hope and perennial disappointments. On the one hand, the government took some token steps to dampen sectarianism and "protect national unity"—including shutting down some TV channels that spouted anti-Shiʿa rhetoric, appointing an additional Shiʿa MP to the nonelected Consultative Council, and building an interfaith dialogue center in late November 2012 (in Vienna, Austria, an indication of the limits of dialogue inside Saudi Arabia).[97] Most important, however, the longtime governor of the Eastern Province, Prince Muhammad bin Fahd, was removed from his post, which he had held since 1985. He was derided among Eastern Province Shiʿa as "Mr. 50/50" for his alleged personal cut of local contracts, so his removal was greeted with loud applause. But many activists remained pessimistic about real change, noting that Eastern Province policy is centrally directed from Riyadh—from the Ministry of Interior, in particular—rather than at the governorate level.[98]

Many in the East point approvingly to a sweeping investigation into the disturbances of the East commissioned in 2012 by the King Faisal Center for Research and Islamic Studies and obtained by an opposition website. Based on extensive interviews in the province, the 125-page document is remarkable for its objectivity and detail in identifying the roots of eastern dissent as an entrenched social, economic, and political problem rather than giving the usual explanations of criminality or Iranian-assisted subversion. Its recommendations to the Saudi government are sweeping: stop the anti-Shia sectarian media campaign; get the Peninsula Shield Force out of Bahrain; release political prisoners, especially the "forgotten nine";

investigate the Ministry of Interior's actions in the Eastern Province; investigate and reform the practices of the local police station in al-ʿAwamiya; and provide comprehensive infrastructure and social development in al-ʿAwamiya.[99] "It is Saudi Arabia's own Bassiouni report," noted one Shiʿa activist in Safwa, referring to the Bahrain Independent Commission of Inquiry (see chapter 5).[100] Sadly, though, the document appears to have suffered a fate similar to that of its Bahraini counterpart. Given the entrenched institutional, political, and social forces driving sectarianism in the Kingdom, it seems unlikely that its recommendations will be fully implemented.

PART IV

KUWAIT

NINE

RENEGOTIATING A RULING BARGAIN

The Kuwaiti Shiʿa

As in the case of Saudi Arabia, Kuwaiti Shiʿa have frequently been subjected to pressure and hostility from hard-line Sunni Islamists, in particular the Salafi figures who came to dominate the political opposition starting in 2008. Regional events such as the Iraq War, Hizballah's rise in Lebanon, and growing fears over Iran exacerbated this tension in Kuwait, stirring Sunni alarm over Shiʿa ascendency. In the post-2003 era, the greatest threat to Kuwaiti stability and a major enabler of sectarianism came not from Shiʿa political or economic marginalization, but from Sunni tribes and Salafis, who felt excluded from the urban "center" and grew increasingly resentful of the alliance between the Al Sahah and the Shiʿa merchant class.

Like their counterparts in Saudi Arabia, the Kuwaiti Shiʿa used the invasion of Iraq as an opening to demand greater concessions in the cultural and religious sphere, while at the same time taking care to highlight their continued loyalty to the monarchy. At the same time, the post-2003 period witnessed increased factionalism among them. Encouraged by the reemergence of Grand Ayatollah ʿAli al-Sistani in Najaf, the Shiraziyyin in Kuwait attempted to marginalize their Shiʿa rivals in the pro-Iranian Islamic National Alliance (INA, al-Tahaluf al-Islami al-Watani).

Kuwait's quasi-democratic structures and media freedom proved to be a mixed blessing in the midst of this tension. On the one hand, they provided a pressure release for sectarian passions and a buffer against the external chaos of the Iraq War and growing alarm over Iran. At the same time, they seemed to encourage and harden sectarian identities in the emirate. This was particularly so after the parliamentary victory in 2008 of a tribal Salafi bloc, which launched a concerted campaign to bring down the government of the prime minister, whom it accused of neglecting the emirate's rural constituencies. In this struggle, the tribal Salafis frequently stirred up sectarianism and accused the prime minister of a pro-Shi'a, pro-Iran bias. The ongoing conflict in Iraq and growing fears over Iran fed into this strategy, polarizing the Parliament along sectarian lines and making it increasingly dysfunctional. For its part, the government was forced into a rearguard action, curtailing many of the reforms it had granted the Shi'a and, more worrisome, undoing many of Kuwait's much-vaunted political freedoms.

THE INITIAL PUSH FOR GREATER RIGHTS—WITH MIXED RESULTS

In the immediate aftermath of the 2003 invasion, Shi'a activists in Kuwait sensed a window of opportunity for advancing their rights. The immediate impact of the regional environment was manifested in a concerted Shi'a push for greater religious, cultural, and legal rights. In tandem, with the holding of parliamentary elections, the Shi'a community was marked by increased fracturing and factionalism between the pro-Iranian INA and the more moderate, nationalist faction of the Shiraziyyin.

As noted in the introduction, the Kuwaiti Shi'a were among the most vociferous opponents of the Saddam regime, given their role in the Kuwaiti resistance to the 1990–1991 occupation. Added to this, many had demonstrated their opposition to the Iraqi dictator much earlier, during the Iran–Iraq War, at a time when it was unpopular to do so. Several Shi'a personalities paid for this stance with prison time and other punishments. With the fall of Saddam, these activists attempted to parlay their long-standing opposition to Saddam into greater political and cultural rights.

The most vocal figure in this group was the cleric Muhammad Baqir al-Muhri, the scion of a prominent Shi'a family with ties in both Iran and

Iraq. Based in Iraq during the 1970s, al-Muhri came to Kuwait in the 1980s where he was a vigorous opponent of Saddam. He rose to prominence after the 1991 invasion and since 2003 has acted as Grand Ayatollah al-Sistani's representative in Kuwait.[1] To impart greater cohesion and authority to Kuwait's clerics, he formed the Association of Shiʿa Clerics (Tajammuʿ al-ʿUlamaʾ al-Shiʿa) in 2005. Much of the group's initial activism focused on securing concessions to Shiʿa identity in the public and media realm, such as the televised and unfettered observance of the Ashura celebration.[2] It also sought the establishment of a separate Shiʿa department in the Ministry for Religious Endowments, and a special Shiʿa court of appeal.[3]

Yet these goals met with stiff opposition from Sunni Islamists.[4] In particular, the Salafi MP Walid al-Tabtabaʾi—who would emerge in later years as the most vociferous opponent of Shiʿa rights—criticized the government for excessive deference to Shiʿa demands, citing in particular the public commemoration of Ashura. In mid-2004, al-Tabtabaʾi launched a concerted campaign to remove the Shiʿa minister of information, Muhammad ʿAbd al-Hassan, who had spearheaded the policy of greater media freedom and was the principal culprit behind Shiʿa empowerment in Kuwait. Despite an attempt at mediation by the prime minister, the minister of information submitted his resignation in December 2004, leaving the government bereft of a Shiʿa minister for the first time since the 1970s. The emir refused to appoint another Shiʿa in his place, a move that some Shiʿa observers interpreted as an effort to placate the Sunni tribal opposition and a subtle signal that they had perhaps grown too bold in their demands for reform in the wake of the U.S. invasion of Iraq.[5]

As late as 2010, there was growing resentment among lay and clerical Shiʿa figures that reforms had stalled or had been curtailed because of Salafi pressure. A key unmet demand was that the Shiʿa department be completely independent from the Ministry for Religious Endowments.[6] Education was another target for reform. Middle and high school textbooks continued to teach derogatory views of Shiʿism; Shiʿa critics singled out the use of the dogmatic and discriminatory terms *rawafidh* and *takfir* as particularly damaging.[7] According to a Shiʿa MP, "If you talk about Islam [in textbooks], talk about it in general terms. But the textbooks talk about Shiʿa/Sunni differences: 'This is *halal* [religiously permissible], this isn't,' and so on."[8]

At the university level, Shiʿa clerics such as those in al-Muhri's Association of Shiʿa Clerics issued appeals for Shiʿa teachers at the College of Islamic Studies at the University of Kuwait.[9] Shiʿa reformists likewise frequently complained about the lack of indigenous seminaries for the training of Shiʿa judges in Kuwait. Importantly, the establishment of such seminaries was framed as means to bolster the national integration of the Kuwaiti Shiʿa and allay Sunni suspicions—in the absence of Kuwait-based schools, aspiring Shiʿa judges were forced to travel to Iran or Iraq.[10]

Kuwaiti Shiʿa also voiced criticism of continuing discrimination by police. Even the smallest infractions tended to escalate in Parliament as opposing MPs seized upon the issue to undermine their rivals. In 2005, there was also a push by Kuwait's Ministry of Islamic Affairs to monitor mosques—both Sunni and Shiʿa. Because the ministry was dominated by Salafis, Shiʿa figures, in particular al-Muhri, interpreted the move as explicitly sectarian in nature.[11] In April 2010, for instance, Kuwaiti customs officials detained a group of Kuwaiti Shiʿa pilgrims returning from Najaf and seized several of their religious books. The minister of finance (whose portfolio included the Customs Department) subsequently intervened, but three Shiʿa MPs—ʿAdnan al-Mutawaʿ, Faysal al-Duwaysan, and Saleh ʿAshur—quickly criticized the affront.[12] Sunni MPs, however, argued that the Shiʿa's pressure on the government represented an unwarranted attempt to circumvent the law.

Sectarian Partisanship After the Iraq Invasion

As the Iraq War unfolded, sectarian relations in Kuwait grew increasingly strained.[13] Much of the partisanship for events in Iraq was instigated by Sunni Islamists. The U.S. siege of Fallujah, in particular, provoked strong expressions of outrage by Salafi deputies in Parliament, who demanded the government take a more explicit stance in favor of Iraq's Sunnis. "We will apply all forms of pressure on the Kuwaiti Parliament and groups in Kuwait in order to stand by our brothers in religion, language, and nationality," a spokesman for the Kuwaiti Salafi movement told al-Jazeera in 2004. Hinting at the royals' apparent pro-Shiʿa bias, he went on to exhort the regime to "show the same solidarity toward the defenders of Fallujah that it had shown toward the Shiʿa in al-Najaf and Karbala."[14]

As discussed in the next chapter, this tactic may have been in part calculated by the tribal (*badu*) Salafis to win the Sunni *hadhar* and merchants (many of them part of the Kuwaiti Muslim Brotherhood affiliate) over to their side.[15] The most expeditious way to do this was by pointing to the threat of Shiʿa ascendancy to enforce a sort of sectarian solidarity. As noted by the head of a nongovernmental organization in Kuwait City and a longtime observer of Kuwaiti politics, "The Sunni *hadhar* in Kuwait are afraid that the *badu* will overwhelm them eventually. The *badu* for their part, are telling the *hadhar* to watch out for the Shiʿa. The Shiʿa are telling the *hadhar*: 'We have to watch the *badu*.' "[16]

By early 2005, the holding of Iraqi parliamentary elections and the Sunni boycott stoked further alarm among Kuwait's Sunnis about Shiʿa ascendancy in the region. For their part, Kuwaiti Shiʿa leaders—like their counterparts in Saudi Arabia and Bahrain—were careful to avoid excessive applause for Shiʿa victories in Iraq lest they create suspicion about where their loyalties lay. For example, the Shiʿa cleric Muhammad Baqir al-Muhri stated: "We look to the Iraqi polls as a democratic process to elect a legitimate government. It will not be a sectarian Shiʿa government, but rather a national Iraqi government in which Sunnis and Kurds will take part."[17]

At the same time, al-Muhri and other figures tried to leverage Iraq developments to push for political reforms and greater concessions to Shiʿa identity. Al-Muhri, as noted, made increasingly frequent references to the edicts of Grand Ayatollah ʿAli al-Sistani—an effort that other Shiʿa regarded as ill timed and designed solely to bolster his own modest clerical credentials.[18] In 2004, he called for the inclusion of Shiʿa (Jaʿfari) jurisprudence into the school curriculum, citing political change in Iraq and the growing U.S. concern for Shiʿa rights in Kuwait: "Political change in Iraq and the international community's call for the governments of the region to guarantee religious freedoms have now given Shiʿa in Kuwait an incentive to achieve some of their old demands."[19]

Other politicians were even more explicit about drawing linkages between the shifting balance of power in Iraq and the necessity of similar changes in Kuwait. The Shiʿa politician and businessman ʿAli al-Matruk noted that "regional and international changes have taken place, and these should be taken into consideration. I believe boosting Shiʿa rights is overdue."[20]

The Shiʿa's ill-conceived analogies to Iraq unsurprisingly seemed to confirm the worst Sunni fears that the balance of power was shifting to their disadvantage. Salafi figures, citing al-Muhri's solicitation of U.S. support, accused the Shiʿa of attracting unwanted external interference in the domestic affairs of Kuwait.[21] Salafi deputy Walid al-Tabtabaʾi argued that forcing 85 percent of the student body (the Sunnis) to study Shiʿa jurisprudence would only promote "sectarian sedition" and would represent a capitulation to a "bullying superpower."[22] The emir himself eventually weighed in on the side of the Salafis (and prudence), warning that, given the chaos of Iraq, now was not the time to stir up sectarian passions.[23]

In October 2005, Sunni recriminations against the Shiʿa shifted from rhetoric to violence. A group of about fifty youths from the predominantly Sunni district of al-Jahra attempted to set fire to the Muhammad bin Abi Bakr Mosque in the district, pelting worshippers with stones and shouting anti-Shiʿa slogans that denigrated the Shiʿa as collaborators with the U.S. occupation of Iraq.[24] The minister of interior subsequently visited the mosque and assured Shiʿa deputies in the ministry at the time that the incident was "a childish action that had no sectarian implications."[25] Yet parliamentarians from both sides—Shiʿa and Sunni—interpreted the event as a watershed escalation between the two groups. The Shiʿa deputy Saleh al-ʿAshur criticized the protest as a "major infraction" that demanded a swift government response. From the Sunni side, a Salafi deputy, ʿAwwad Barad, demanded that the attackers be released immediately from custody.[26] Partly in response to Barad's demand, a group of thirty Shiʿa scholars and clerics—among them al-Muhri—issued a statement denouncing the event as an "alarm bell," condemning the government of failing to protect the mosque, and warning against the growth of increased intolerance among the "*takfiri*" strand of Kuwait's Salafis.[27]

As discussed at length in the next chapter, the government's policy for responding to such incidents was initially balanced, but by 2010 it had increasingly yielded to pressure from Salafi tribal parliamentarians. At times, it permitted displays of sectarian partisanship, and in other instances it cracked down on them. For example, in 2007 it refused to grant permission to a group of hard-line Sunni Islamists to stage a demonstration in support of what they called "the plight of Sunnis in Iraq." Concurrently, however, the government demurred on permitting the public celebrations of Ashura by the Shiʿa for fear it would provoke a Sunni backlash.[28] The regime's attempts to maintain sectarian harmony became increasingly difficult in the face of an escalating media war between Kuwait's Sunnis and Shiʿas.[29]

The Escalating Media War

As noted earlier, in the polarized climate of regional sectarian tensions Kuwait's media freedom proved to be a double-edged sword. On the one hand, it acted as a pressure release. On the other hand, it increased the fever pitch of sectarian partisanship for regional conflicts, particularly in Lebanon and Iraq. As noted by a Shiʿa MP, "In the 1950s, 1960s, and 1970s, people didn't talk about Shiʿa or sectarian rights. What has changed? Transparency and the spread of media. Today, if something happens in Bahrain, everyone knows about it."[30]

In the years that followed, Shiʿa media power effectively outgunned that of the Sunnis, prompting the Salafi tribal opposition to attack the government for failing to crack down on "divisive" media. In the period 2004–2009, a number of new, explicitly Shiʿa TV stations flourished. Among the most prominent was al-Anwar, founded in 2004 and owned by Saleh al-ʿAshur, an MP from the Shiraziyyin current.[31] The station advances the views of Ayatollah Sadiq al-Shirazi (the younger brother of Muhammad al-Shirazi) on religious matters but steers clear of political issues. Another key station affiliated with the Shiraziyyin is al-Zahra, established by the Kuwaiti cleric Habib al-Kazmi.[32] Like al-Anwar, al-Zahra has programming focused on the themes of Sunni persecution and Shiʿa victimization in Iraq. In 2006, for instance, al-Zahra referred to the February bombing of the Shiʿa al-ʿAskari Mosque in Samarra as the "Karbala of our times."[33]

Such stations, in turn, provoked the formation of anti-Shiʿa channels. One of the most prominent was the al-Safa network, which broadcast out of Egypt. An unnamed official from the channel told al-Jazeera in 2010 that it "adopts a Sunni line that opposes attempts to disseminate Shiʿite ideology to the Arab region." In October 2010, Nilesat, the Egyptian satellite communications company, had suspended the network, along with eleven other networks, for promoting sectarian violence. Officials at the network denied the suspension, arguing instead that they themselves had shut down the station because of repeated jamming by a foreign country "with wide influence" in the region—that is, Iran.[34]

Even nonsectarian, mainstream Kuwaiti TV frequently carried anti-Shiʿa programming. A particular source of resentment among Kuwaiti Shiʿa was the planned airing of a thirty-episode miniseries during Ramadan that revolved around the Shiʿa practice of *mutʿa*, or temporary marriage. Shiʿa in Kuwait, Bahrain, and Saudi Arabia widely interpreted the plot as a direct attack on a legitimate religious precept, and a number of Shiʿa clerics and parliamentarians issued statements against the transmission of the series.[35]

The Debate Over National Loyalty

As in the case of Bahrain and Saudi Arabia, the moderate Shiraziyyin endeavored to assert their nationalist bona fides in the face of attacks about their loyalty to Iran. As discussed in the next section, this effort was hampered by the presence of a parliamentary bloc that explicitly and unapologetically affiliated itself with Supreme Leader ʿAli Khamenei. Among the Shiraziyyin and Daʿwa currents, however, there was more circumspection and a concerted attempt to distinguish between the religious and spiritual appeal of the Islamic Republic and its political manifestations. This effort reflected the previous efforts of *marajiʿ* such as Muhammad al-Shirazi and Muhammad Taqi al-Mudarrisi to distance themselves from the pro-regime clerics of the Islamic Republic. The problem was that an increasingly polarized regional environment lent credence to more radical voices and forced the moderates (from both the Sunni and Shiʿa camps) into a corner.

As in the case of Bahrain and Saudi Arabia, Kuwaiti Shiʿa clerics publicized and inflated their access to foreign *marajiʿ* to boost their authority and popularity. These pronouncements provided fodder for political opponents—particularly from the more conservative Salafi currents—who accused the Shiʿa of being disloyal to the state. A key example is al-Muhri, whom many interlocutors accused of trying to inflate his stature as al-Sistani's *wakil* (representative or emissary).[36] In January 2007, al-Muhri sparked another uproar when he appeared to implicitly endorse the wave of bombings and assassination attempts that wracked Kuwait in the late 1980s. He told *al-Seyassah* that "[w]hat happened in the past was patriotic because the Shiʿa were aware that Saddam Husayn was a criminal and that he was going to invade Kuwait." Muhri's office later argued that he had been misquoted, and it issued a clarification in *al-Watan*.[37]

Another lightening rod was the Shiʿa cleric Yasser al-Habib. A young cleric (he was only twenty-one when he first attracted public attention), al-Habib issued a series of vitriolic, anti-Sunni statements that over the course of the next six years would place Shiʿa moderates under pressure, provoke the vitriol of Sunni extremists, and force the government to take the role of referee and arbiter. In November 2003, al-Habib was arrested and sentenced to ten years for an audiotaped sermon (in a private gathering) that allegedly slandered the first two Muslim caliphs (whom Sunnis regard as sacrosanct). In February 2004, he was pardoned by the Kuwaiti emir but was then rearrested and fled to London before he could be sentenced.[38]

From London, he formed the Servants of the Mahdi (Khaddam al-Mahdi) organization and continued to mount a series of attacks on the royal family, Shiʿa persecution, and the very creed of the Sunnis—all of which stirred Kuwaiti sectarian tensions.[39] In 2009, for example, he made several speeches exhorting the Shiʿa of the Eastern Province in Saudi Arabia to declare their independence and merge with Kuwait and Bahrain as part of a "Greater Bahrain."[40] In September 2010, he launched an exclusively Shiʿa satellite TV network, al-Fadak, with the banner "The Middle East Witnesses a Shiʿa Media Revolution" emblazoned on its website home page.[41] He also owns two websites and a newsletter for British Shiʿa Muslims, both of which disseminate his religious teachings and carry provocative statements, such as calling for "revolutionary change on the occasion of Ashura" and a "Shiʿa intifada."[42] As discussed at length in the next chapter, al-Habib's brazen statements contributed to the 2010 government crackdown and the curtailment of the emirate's relatively liberal media freedom.

THE IRAQ WAR AND THE FRACTURING
OF THE SHIʿA COMMUNITY

From 2003 onward, the Kuwaiti Shiʿa political field became increasingly factionalized due in part to the regional upheaval of the Iraq War. Unlike in Bahrain and Saudi Arabia, these splits were not the result of a disagreement about tactics or the efficacy of participating in the political process. All Kuwaiti Shiʿa groups were dedicated to affecting change peacefully through the institutions of the *diwaniya* and the Parliament. Even the most radical of the pro-Iranian figures accepted the legitimacy of the Al Sabah ruling family, the Parliament, and the *diwaniya*.[43] A key catalyst for the fracturing of these currents was the reemergence of Shiʿa clerical authorities in Iraq, such as Grand Ayatollah al-Sistani and, to a lesser extent, the Hakim family. The growing power of these figures provided inspiration in Kuwait for a brewing mutiny against the old Shiʿa merchant class (who had traditionally followed Iranian *marajiʿ*) by a newer generation of Shiʿa activists.[44]

Defections from the Pro-Iranian Current

One of the first instances of the fracturing of the Shiʿa polity was a three-way split between the Khat al-Imam (literally Line of Imam, those who identified Iranian Supreme Leader ʿAli Khamenei as their *marjaʿ* and embraced the political philosophy of *velayet-e faqih*), the Shiraziyyin, and the Daʿwa currents. In 1998, prominent lay activists of the Khat al-Imam, ʿAdnan ʿAbd al-Samad and ʿAbd al-Muhsin Jamal, as well as younger clerics such as Husayn al-Maʿtuk, founded the INA. Following the death of Ayatollah Ruhollah Khomeini, the group regarded Khamenei as their *marjaʿ*, but its members also took guidance from other Iran-born *marjaʿ* such as al-Sistani, Mirza Jawad Tabrizi, and Muhammad Taqi Bahjit.[45] The INA/Khat al-Imam was the first Shiʿa society to field parliamentary representatives after the first elections in 1981.

Yet in 2003 fissures began to emerge, specifically over the alliance's continued fidelity to *velayet-e faqih*. The 2003 Kuwaiti parliamentary elections dealt a further blow to Khat al-Imam. Despite its strength, it won only one of the five Shiʿa seats; the other four winners hailed from the *baharna*, Daʿwa, Shirazi, and nonaffiliated Shiʿa merchant currents.[46] Several observers have interpreted the society's loss and diminishing support as at least in part a function of the rise of Grand Ayatollah ʿAli al-Sistani in Iraq, which emboldened the Shiraziyyin and Daʿwa supporters who had previously toed the INA line to break away from the society, forge a partnership, and chart an independent course.[47]

Among the first groups to split from the INA/Khat al-Imam was a faction led by an eminent Shiʿa businessman, former minister of commerce ʿAbd al-Wahhab al-Wazzan.[48] Taking inspiration from the burgeoning reform movement under way in Iran under then-president Muhammad Khatami, al-Wazzan formed the Islamic National Accord (al-Tawafuq al-Islami al-Watani) in 2003.[49] In its organization and mission, the society was self-consciously modeled after Muhammad Khatami's Combatant Clerics Association (Majmaʿ-e Rowhaniyun-e Mobarez) in Iran. That same year the Shiraziyyin formed the Assembly for Justice and Peace (Tajammuʿ al-ʿAdala wa al-Salam) as a counterweight to the INA/Khat al-Imam. The assembly counted 110 active members, of whom more than 30 were women. The grouping was able to leverage the Shirazi current's vast and longstanding network of charitable foundations and cultural centers that had been set up in Kuwait in the 1970s. One of the society's principal aims was to advance Ayatollah al-Shirazi's more quietist interpretation of *velayet-e faqih* as an alternative to the INA's pro-Khomeini platform.[50]

A third society splitting from the INA, the National Pact Assembly (Tajammuʿ al-Mithaq al-Watani), was formed in July 2003 under the aegis of the Daʿwa current. From its inception, the society was under continual suspicion by critics inside the regime and among the Sunni Islamist currents because of its historic links with the Iraq-based Daʿwa current, which had fomented bombings in Kuwait in the 1980s.[51] When asked about the society's affiliation with Daʿwa's violent past, its secretary-general, ʿAbd al-Hadi al-Salah, prevaricated: "If the intent of Daʿwa was to fight Saddam, then we are honored to be affiliated with it. However, if the intent is to say that Daʿwa was behind the campaign of assassinations and bombings, then no, I beg your pardon, we are not part of it."[52]

The Shiraziyyin Versus the INA/Khat al-Imam

In 2004, the Shiraziyyin became increasingly assertive against their rivals in the Khat al-Imam and pushed for the establishment of several umbrella groups that were explicitly framed in the press as "anti-Hizballah"—that is, against the INA/Khat al-Imam. The first of these groups was formed in 2005 as the Front for Justice and Peace (Jabha lil-Adala wa al-Salam).[53] It was subsequently disavowed, however, by prominent cleric Muhammad Baqir al-Muhri and other personalities. In 2005, on the eve of the parliamentary elections, the Shiraziyyin made another attempt to isolate their rivals in the INA/Khat al-Imam current with the formation of the National Coalition of Assemblies (I'tilaf al-Tajamuʿat al-Watani). The coalition was modeled on the al-Sistani-backed Shiʿa bloc that had dominated the 2008 Iraqi parliamentary elections. It included the Daʿwa and Khatami factions as well as Muhammad Baqir al-Muhri's clerical association.[54] Table 9.1 depicts the major Shiʿa currents in Kuwait discussed this far, along with their ideological orientation and key members.

The Shiraziyyin were able to strike an important blow against the INA with a leak to the press about the INA's meetings with representatives of Supreme Leader ʿAli Khamenei at the Iranian embassy in Kuwait City in May 2004.[55] The entire incident tarnished the INA's legitimacy, provoking the ire of both the Salafi opposition and the government. The Kuwaiti Foreign Ministry later summoned the Iranian chargé d'affaires to lodge a protest about the meetings.[56] The issue of fidelity to Iran thus emerged as one of the central fault lines within the Shiʿa community—a fissure that widened with the escalation of regional tensions, particularly after the 2006 Lebanon War.

The run-up to the 2006 parliamentary elections proved to be a further dividing line between the currents. Specifically, a debate emerged over the reduction of electoral districts, with a group of twenty-nine parliamentarians submitting a motion to reduce the number of districts from twenty-five to five on the grounds that doing so would reduce tribal clientalism, vote buying, and government interference, while encouraging the growth of larger, more organized, and more disciplined political societies.[57] The motion was buttressed by a broad-based youth campaign, the

TABLE 9.1

KUWAITI SHIʿA POLITICAL ORGANIZATIONS, POST-2003

PARTY NAME	FOUNDING DATE	IDEOLOGICAL CURRENT	MARJAʿ	KEY MEMBERS
The Islamic National Alliance (INA, al-Tahaluf al-Islami al-Watani)	1998	*Khat al-Imam* (pro-Khamenei); also derisively known as the "Kuwaiti Hizballah"	ʿAli Khamenei, to lesser, extent, ʿAli Sistani, and Mirza Jawad Tabrizi	ʿAdnan ʿAbd al-Samad, Husayn Maʿtuk, Hassan ʿAbdallah Jawhar, and ʿAbd al-Muhsin Jamal
National Islamic Accord (*Jamaʿiyyat al-Wifaq al-Watani al-Islamiyya*)	2003	Reformist, pro-Khatami	ʿAli al-Sistani, Mirza Jawad Tabrizi, Sadiq al-Shirazi	ʿAbd al-Wahhab al-Wazzan
Assembly for Justice and Peace (*Tajammuʿ al-ʿAdala wa al-Salam*)	2004	Shirazi	Muhammad Sadiq al-Shirazi, ʿAli al-Sistani	Saleh ʿAshur, Rajib ʿAli, ʿAbd al-Husayn Sultan
National Pact Assembly (*Tajammuʿ al-Mithaq al-Watani*)	2005	Daʿwa	Muhammad Husayn Fadlallah	ʿAbd al-Hadi al-Salah, Yusuf al-Zilzila
National Coalition of Assemblies (*Iʾtilaf al-Tajamuʿat al-Watani*)	2005	Shirazi-led, anti-INA	Sadiq al-Shirazi, ʿAli al-Sistani	ʿAbd al-Husayn Sultan, Saleh al-ʿAshur, ʿAli al-Baghli, ʿAbd al-Wahhab al-Wazzan

Source: Salah al-Ghazali, *Al-jamaʿat al-siyastyya al-Kuwaytiyya fi qurn* (Political Parties in Kuwait Throughout the Century) (Kuwait City: Jamiʿyyat al-Haquq Mahfudha, 2007), 381–407; Laurence Louër, *Transnational Shiʿa Politics: Religious and Political Networks in the Gulf* (London: Hurst, 2008), 217–219, 253–255; author's interviews, Kuwait City, Kuwait, November 2010.

so-called Orange Movement (al-Haraka al-Burtuqaliyya al-Kuwaytiyya), that relied extensively on text messaging and innovative social media— a precursor to the Arab uprisings of 2011.[58] Importantly, Shiʿa deputies from the Shiraziyyin, such as Saleh al-ʿAshur and Yusuf al-Zilzila, opposed the measure, believing that the existing district structure allowed them to form alliances with moderate Sunnis against their rivals in the INA. For its part, the INA joined with the opposition in supporting the measure. The redistricting measure ultimately passed. The figure below shows this post-2006 district division in Kuwait City, with demographic traits overlaid.

Ironically, the new system backfired. The next Parliament, elected on May 17, 2008, was even more fractious, tribal, and sectarian. Sunni Islamist and tribal deputies won twenty-four of the Parliament's fifty seats. Moreover, the Shiraziyyin failed in their bid to weaken the INA in the 2006 Parliament—of the four Shiʿa deputies elected to Parliament, three were from the INA and one (Saleh al-ʿAshur) was from the Shiraziyyin.[59] Nevertheless, the result was a highly polarized Parliament, in which Sunni deputies latched on to the Shiʿa's pro-Iranian orientation as a means to

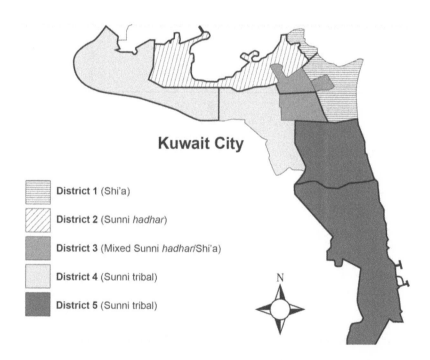

Kuwait City

District 1 (Shi'a)

District 2 (Sunni *hadhar*)

District 3 (Mixed Sunni *hadhar*/Shi'a)

District 4 (Sunni tribal)

District 5 (Sunni tribal)

N

discredit the Shiʿa bloc as a whole and to pressure the government into greater concessions for the Sunni tribes.

The Kuwaiti Shiʿa saw the Iraq War as an opportunity to push for increased cultural and religious rights, while at the same time emphasizing their nationalist bona fides and attempting to assuage regime and Sunni concerns about their loyalty. In tandem, the Iraq War produced increased factionalism among the Shiʿa societies in Kuwait. Emboldened by the rise of Grand Ayatollah ʿAli al-Sistani in Najaf, the Shiraziyyin attempted to marginalize their rivals in the INA. Much of this was facilitated by the policy of increased media freedom implemented by the Kuwaiti government in the U.S. invasion of Iraq.

Yet this openness also contributed to growing sectarianism in the emirate and the widespread Sunni perception that the Kuwaiti regime was decidedly pro-Shiʿa in its orientation. Parliamentary stability was undermined in part by Sunni alarm over the local impact of the 2006 Lebanon War, the 2008 assassination of Hizballah commander ʿImad Mughniyah, and the approach of the U.S. withdrawal from Iraq in 2009. These regional shocks made participatory politics in the emirate increasingly contentious and dysfunctional, prompting the government in 2010 to curtail media freedoms and civil liberties. Amidst this turbulence and rising Sunni vitriol, many observers—inside the country and throughout the Gulf—wondered if Kuwait's fragile democracy had fallen prey to regional tensions and sectarian passions. As one Kuwaiti commentator lamented in 2008, "You love the freedom that enables you to express your opinion freely and frankly, [but] you are afraid of it because it allows a person to raise the six-meter picture of Khamenei."[60]

TEN

TILTING TOWARD REPRESSION

The Sunni Opposition and the Kuwaiti Regime

The Kuwaiti regime's response to Shiʿa activism followed a pattern employed elsewhere in the Gulf—using calibrated reforms to placate Shiʿa dissent, while at the same time trying to avoid provoking Sunni Islamist sensibilities. In Kuwait, this game of sectarian balancing had higher stakes, particularly since elements of the royal family were confronted with a more concerted opposition from tribal Sunnis, starting in 2005. During this period, the Sunni tribes effectively withdrew from their previous alliance with the royalty, supplanting the liberals as the Al Sabah's main adversary. For these oppositionists—many of them *badu* drawn from the environs outside Kuwait City—anti-Shiʿism and sectarianism became a "card" to discredit the royalty, specifically the more liberal-leaning prime minister, and a tactic to win over the *hadhar* Sunnis.[1]

The regime was thus forced into the delicate role of mediating between this current and the Shiʿa, whom it increasingly came to rely upon as allies. Mounting regional tensions over Iran, Iraq, and Hizballah provided ample grist for the Sunni Islamists in their attacks on the government. Specifically, there were recurring charges by the Sunni tribal opposition that the Kuwaiti government was not doing enough to assist Sunnis in Iraq, was too close to the United States, and was being too partial to Iran's interests. Ironically, the position of the Sunnis in opposition represented a role reversal with the Shiʿa, particularly regarding Kuwait's policies in Iraq.[2]

Three incidents in particular highlight the way in which sectarianism became highly politicized in the tribe-versus-regime struggle. In February 2008, Shiʿa parliamentarians from the pro-Iranian INA attended a eulogy for the recently slain Hizballah commander ʿImad Mughniyah and made a number of laudatory remarks. The statements stirred uproar in Kuwait, given Mughniyah's alleged involvement in the spate of terrorist attacks that had afflicted Kuwait in the 1980s, including an attempt on the emir's life. The event quickly escalated into a sectarian confrontation, as the Shiʿa deputies attempted to qualify their remarks, while their Sunni opponents demanded their expulsion from Parliament. In November, amidst this increasingly polarized climate, the Kuwaiti cabinet tendered its resignation after three Sunni Islamist deputies filed a motion to interpellate the prime minister over his decision to allow the visit of an Iranian cleric who was perceived to be anti-Sunni. And in September 2010, the specter of Yasser al-Habib emerged again. The controversial Shiʿa cleric had made a disparaging remark about the Prophet Muhammad's wife Aisha—a revered figure among Sunnis, but one who is frequently denigrated by Shiʿa. Among Kuwait's Sunni Islamists, the insult quickly acquired the status of a cause célèbre. Salafi parliamentarians demanded al-Habib's immediate arrest and the revocation of his citizenship. The tension reached such intensity that Sunni opposition demanded the government rein in Shiʿa media. By late 2010, the Kuwaiti government had barred public gatherings and drastically curtailed media freedom—restrictions that were in part due to the worsening sectarian gridlock.

THE SUNNI ISLAMISTS: FROM REGIME BULWARKS TO OPPOSITION

To understand the Sunni and regime reaction to Shiʿism in Kuwait, it is first necessary to examine the government's longstanding practices of co-option and divide and rule. Specifically, it is important to understand how Sunni Islamist groups—the Muslim Brotherhood–inspired Islamic Constitutional Movement (al-Haraka al-Dusturiyya al-Islamiyya, HADAS) and the Islamic Salafi Alliance (ISA, al-Tahaluf al-Islami al-Salafi)—were transformed from loyal bulwarks of the ruling family into its main opposition.

HADAS: The Kuwaiti Muslim Brotherhood

Inspired by the Egyptian Muslim Brotherhood, HADAS has traditionally been the best organized of Kuwait's political societies. It has typically drawn its membership from the Sunni merchant and *hadhar* class and formally coalesced in the aftermath of the liberation of Kuwait in 1991, when the country's political field opened to formal "associations."[3]

One of the frequent charges by the Salafi opposition against HADAS was its coziness with Iran and the Shi'a. This accusations stems in large part from the historic animosity between the Salafis—drawn primarily since the 1980s from the ranks of Kuwait's *badu* population—and the wealthier *hadhar*, who constituted the bulk of HADAS. But beginning in 2003, HADAS did adopt a more nuanced and accommodative view toward the Shi'a in Kuwait. Unlike the Salafis, HADAS figures distinguished between the Shi'a minority who embraced Iranian ideology and the more nationalist Shiraziyyin current. According to a longtime HADAS member, "Here in Kuwait, you can distinguish the pro-Iranian Shi'a from the nationalist [Shi'a]. The Salafis and the tribes don't do this."[4]

Yet, for many Salafis, such distinctions fell flat. Longtime observer of Sunni Islamist politics in the Gulf Muhanna Hubayl has argued that the electoral decline of HADAS and like-minded Muslim Brotherhood groups on the peninsula was due to their being on the wrong side of public sentiment with regard to the Shi'a and Iran. This was nowhere as apparent as the Egyptian Muslim Brotherhood's support for Hizballah during the summer 2006 Lebanon War, which carried over to Gulf Brotherhood affiliates, regardless of whether their views approximated those of the Cairo-based organization. Hubayl wrote in 2008: "Islamic public opinion in the Gulf was surprised to see that the Muslim Brotherhood's support for Hizballah in Lebanon was several times stronger than its support for HAMAS. We are particularly referring to certain statements by Muslim Brotherhood officials, including statements by General Guide Muhammad Mahdi Akif who openly supported Hizballah's incursion into Beirut and the subsequent political agreement among the Lebanese parties. This showed that the brotherhood supported Hizballah's political stance and not merely its summer war against the Zionist enemy."[5]

The Salafis

In contrast to the Brotherhood-inspired HADAS, the Salafi current in Kuwait took a harder line toward the Shiʿa. Much of it was due to Salafism's doctrinal intolerance of other sects and currents within Islam. More important, however, were the local socioeconomic disparities, which increasingly pitted the Salafi tribal opposition against the regime and its Shiʿa allies.

The Salafi movement in Kuwait first took formal shape with the Scientific Salafi Movement (Harakat Salafiyya ʿAlmiya) formed in 1997, headed by Hamid al-ʿAli from 1997 to 2000.[6] Hamid al-ʿAli's resonance extended well beyond his former tenure as the secretary-general of this organization, and it is worth considering his background and writings. Born in Kuwait in 1962, al-ʿAli received his clerical education in Saudi Arabia and then served as a professor of Islamic culture at the College of Islamic Education at Kuwait University and a mosque imam in Kuwait City.[7] In the aftermath of the 2003 invasion of Iraq, al-ʿAli's writings and fatwa adopted an increasingly hostile and militant tone, attaining widespread notoriety among the virtual jihadi community as well as among actual militants fighting in Iraq and Afghanistan. His writings, sermons, and interviews on pan-Arab media such as al-Jazeera have canvassed a broad swathe of topics: the legitimacy of volunteering for jihad in the Iraq War, suicide operations, globalization, personal jihadi ethics, and the illegitimacy of elections.[8] Unsurprisingly, these writings attracted the ire of the Kuwait security forces. In 2003, he received a two-year suspended prison sentence for publicly opposing Kuwait's stance on the Iraq War and was released in November 2005. At times, his intellectual grist for the jihadist enterprise crossed the line into operational and material support for Kuwait's Salafi jihadists.[9] In 2005, he was accused but later acquitted of the charge of conspiracy against the regime.[10]

It is on Shi'ism, however, where al-'Ali has been the most prolific and vitriolic.[11] Many Shi'a activists and politicians in Kuwait have cited him as having the most noxious influence on anti-Shi'a tendencies within the Salafi current.[12] Like the Saudi clerics with whom he shares doctrinal affinity, al-'Ali resurrects in his writings the timeworn trope of the Shi'a as internal saboteurs of Muslim unity and cohesion.[13] To this, he has added the specter of Iranian meddling in the Gulf's internal affairs—a theme that achieved particular resonance in the wake of the Mughniyah crisis of 2008.[14]

From 2000 onward, the Salafi movement fell under the leadership of another cleric, Hakim al-Mutayri, who hailed from a prominent tribe. In 2005, al-Mutayri announced the establishment of a formal Salafi society, the Society of the Islamic Community (Hizb al-Ummah), which adopted markedly more conservative views than the majority of Kuwait's Salafis. Indeed, many of the society's goals were aligned with the militants that at the time were conducting a campaign of violence on Kuwaiti soil: the eviction of foreign troops from Iraq and the Gulf, the establishment of a more just social order, and greater morality on family matters and social practice.[15] In the context of Kuwait's ongoing counterterrorism campaign and the Hizb al-Ummah's questionable legality, al-Mutayri was subjected to several hours of questioning in Jahra (a predominately tribal town to the west of Kuwait City, where Salafism has attracted a strong following). Moreover, at least fifteen society members were banned from travel.[16]

A more moderate wing of Salafis demurred on joining the Hizb al-Ummah and formed their own parliamentary block—the ISA.[17] The informal head of this group is Khalid al-Sultan, who hails from a notable Sunni *hadhar* merchant family. Another key member is Walid al-Tabtaba'i, from the outer districts, whose tribal background typified the profile of those joining the Salafis' ranks after 2005.[18]

The Tribal Defection to Salafism, 2005–2006

To fully understand the way Kuwait's participatory structures fell prey to sectarianism, it is important to explore how shifting demographics impacted relations between the royalty, the urban elite, and rural tribes.

Nowhere is this more applicable than in understanding how the *badu* influx to Salafism helped turn it from pro-regime force into an opposition that, by default, became increasingly anti-Shiʿa in its outlook. Throughout the 1960s and 1970s, the *badu* were successfully cultivated as regime allies to the urban merchant class of *hadhar*. In tandem, the ruling family saw Islamists as useful bulwarks against the rising tide of Nasserism and pan-Arabism. According to Kuwait scholar Mary Ann Tétreault, "Kuwait's rulers were attracted by Islamists preaching the virtues of a hierarchical ethical order that included loyalty to Kuwait's ruling autocracy."[19] Yet by 2005 the scales had shifted. From 2005 onward, it was the tribes rather than the liberals that dominated the opposition.[20]

Much of this change had to do with shifts in the social and economic policies of the new prime minister, Nasser Muhammad al-Ahmed Al Sabah, who took office in 2006. In contrast to his predecessor, Nasser Al Sabah initially pursued more moderate policies on social matters, women's rights, and media freedom. In addition, he launched a concerted drive for privatization and economic liberalization.[21] All of these shifts proved threatening to the *badu* tribes, who were typically more conservative on family and social matters and who depended on state subsidies and employment in the bloated public sector. The new prime minister's policies appeared to undermine directly the tribes' historically privileged position while implicitly favoring the merchant *hadhar* class. As one tribal member interviewed in 2009 noted, "In Jahra [Kuwait's third largest city and a tribal stronghold], we have only one bilingual school and one hospital. They try to isolate us. We want to be treated like them [the *hadhar*]. We want equal access to jobs, services, and housing. We are Kuwaitis like everyone else. There is no difference."[22]

These socioeconomic tensions increasingly took on a religious hue. The disaffected *badu* gravitated toward Salafism as a mobilizing force. This "defection" to Salafism was likely driven by several factors.[23] The first was the longstanding links between these tribes and Saudi Arabia. Throughout the 1990s, the Saudi government and semiofficial charities had dispensed financial assistance to a variety of Kuwaiti Salafi networks, hospitals, and mosques in the country's outer districts as both leverage against the Al Sabah and as a counterweight to Kuwaiti liberals.[24] Second, Salafism's tenets aligned well with the tribes' socially conservative outlook. Third,

Salafism's doctrinaire, antihierarchical worldview has typically appealed to those societal segments attempting to challenge political or economic power disparities.[25] In this respect, the tribes gravitated toward Salafism as a sort of de facto alternative to the other Islamist current in the country, HADAS, which had been a longtime stronghold of the wealthier, urban *hadhar*.

Faced with this opposition, the government increasingly relied upon the urban Shiʿa as allies. As one informed observer noted, "The Sunni *badu* tell the *hadhar*, 'Watch out for the Shiʿa.' The Shiʿa tell the *hadhar*, 'Watch out for the *badu*.' Politics here is really a contest to win over the *hadhar*."[26]

SECTARIANISM AND PARLIAMENTARY CRISES

The post-2005 period saw the growing confluence of internal and external crises that exacerbated sectarianism and threatened the nascent parliament. Specifically, Shiʿa MPs' attendance at a eulogy for slain Hizballah commander ʿImad Mughniyah, the victory of Salafi Islamists in the 2008 parliamentary election, and continued provocations by the exiled Shiʿa cleric Yasser al-Habib contributed to an increasingly contentious domestic climate. Mounting fears in the Gulf about Iran's nuclear program and support to pro-Iranian proxies heightened these tensions.

In many cases, however, the Sunni opposition used this alarm as a political weapon against liberal factions in the royalty. Salafi MPs condemned the prime minister for being too cozy toward the Shiʿa and encouraging pro-Iranian influence in the emirate. At first glance, this mudslinging may seem inconsequential—the normal "static" of parliamentary politics. By 2010, however, the pressure had increased to the point where the government had become dysfunctional, and the Ministry of Interior took the momentous step of banning public gatherings and clamping down on media freedom.

The Earthquake of the Mughniyah Eulogy

The tribal Salafi bloc's escalating sectarian challenge to the government reached its pinnacle on February 17, 2008, when members of the pro-

Iranian INA—including two sitting MPs, Ahmed Lari and ʿAdnan ʿAbd al-Samad—attended a highly publicized commemoration for slain Lebanese Hizballah field commander ʿImad Mughniyah, held at the al-Husayn Shiʿa mosque in the Shiʿa suburb of Salmiya in Kuwait City. Several former Shiʿa MPs were also found to be in attendance—ʿAbd al-Muhsin Jamal, Nasser Sarkhu, and the cleric Husayn al-Maʿtuk, who served as the INA secretary-general.[27]

By itself, the incident was sufficiently inflammatory to cause a media uproar. Aside from being an affront to Sunni Arabs, the laudatory remarks, poetry, and pro-Lebanese Hizballah banners that festooned the event stirred Kuwait's collective memory—Mughniyah, after all, was the mastermind behind the spate of Shiʿa terrorist attacks that had afflicted Kuwait in the 1980s, including a 1985 assassination attempt on the emir.[28] Yet the real provocation came the following day, when ʿAbd al-Samad gave an interview with the Arabic newspaper al-Elaph denying that Mughniyah had been behind the 1985 assassination plot against the emir and a subsequent hijacking of a Kuwaiti airliner in 1988 in which two Kuwaitis were killed. Instead, he accused Sunni hard-liners of trying to inflate the event to stir up sectarianism. These "parasites"—as he called them—were trying to divide Kuwait society and were unable to understand that supporting Mughniyah as a "resistance" icon against Israel was not fundamentally incompatible with Kuwaiti nationalism.[29] "When a Hizballah flag is raised," he argued, "it does not mean that one is against his country, but only that he sympathizes with Hizballah."[30]

The Sunni Counterreaction to the Mughniyah Episode

The regime and Sunni reaction to the eulogy was swift. In early March, the two former MPs, Muhsin and Jamal, were arrested, along with the cleric Husayn al-Maʿtuk (the latter's detention sparked a Shiʿa protest outside the prison where he was held). Sunni MPs demanded that parliamentary immunity for ʿAdnan ʿAbd al-Samad and Ahmad Lari be lifted to pave the way for prosecution.[31] A tribal Salafi deputy, Muhammad Hayif al-Mutayri, went further, exhorting the government to strip ʿAbd al-Samad of his Kuwaiti citizenship and ban the INA as an organization on the grounds that it was effectively a front for Kuwaiti Hizballah.[32] Al-Mutayri went on to call for the Ministry of Interior to investigate the presence of purported training camps run by Lebanese Hizballah in the Kuwaiti desert.[33] Many of the tribal MPs unsurprisingly shifted the attack to the government itself, arguing that it knew about the eulogy in advance and had anticipated the Sunni backlash but allowed it to proceed anyway.[34]

In response, the INA, through its online news source *al-Dar*, denied the presence of any Hizballah sleeper cells, pointing out the irony that the greatest, proven threat of sleeper cells in Kuwait had emerged from among the Sunnis, not the Shiʿa—from Salafi militants who had tried to blow up the Shuʿaybah oil refinery, the State Security Building, and Arifijan camp.[35] For their part, ʿAbd al-Samad and Lari issued a response to the outcry, but it fell short of a formal apology and offered only a general condemnation of the terrorism that had taken place in Kuwait in the 1980s without specifying the perpetrators.[36]

The Government Response: Prevarication and Crackdown

For their part, the royals prevaricated in responding to the Mughniyah issue. According to one source, much of the delay was because the Ministry of Interior had initially sanctioned the eulogy, whose organizers had sought permission in advance. It was only in the face of the concerted and unexpected Sunni opposition that it retreated. In the weeks that followed, a split emerged between the foreign minister, who adopted a hard line, and the prime minister, who attempted to defuse the situation by saying there was no evidence that Mughniyah was involved in the 1988 hijacking.[37]

Among the key roles played by Parliament Speaker Jasim al-Khurafi was that of mediator. In response to Sunni demands, he argued that any decision to lift the two deputies' immunity would have to be made through formal Ministry of Justice channels.[38] He did, however, appeal for calm, saying, "I call on Kuwaiti society to be solidly united and stay away from these tensions which are against our national interest. Our country cannot bear this . . . we should remember what happened to us when our country was occupied."[39]

In the end, the emir dissolved the Parliament, which effectively stripped the two MPs of their parliamentary immunity. The Popular Action Bloc (Kutlat al-ʿAmal al-Shaʿbi), a cross-sectarian parliamentary bloc that focused on welfare issues such as housing and subsidies, expelled them.[40] The government's ultimate charge against the MPs was not related to the eulogy but rather to their belonging to a banned group, the Kuwaiti Hizballah—a tactic that was obviously intended as sort of a compromise to defuse tension.[41] But the accusation exacerbated tensions by effectively discrediting the INA as a legitimate political society. Even more worrisome, the government also banned the *diwaniya*, reinstating a law that outlawed public gatherings.[42] In an effort to limit the sectarian fallout of the incident, it had effectively set back Kuwaiti democracy.

Based on lawsuits prepared by the Ministries of Interior, Religious Endowments, and Justice, the authorities detained and questioned a total of eight current or former MPs and the cleric Husayn al-Maʿtuk before releasing them on bail. In a marked escalation of the crackdown, the minister of public works and municipalities, a Shiʿa, was detained briefly in March over suspected links to the Kuwaiti Hizballah.[43] In April, a total of seven Shiʿa—the four Shiʿa MPs, the cleric al-Maʿtuk, and two others— were formally charged with "spreading false news about the country" and "weakening the situation of the state abroad."[44] In October 2008, a court acquitted the seven defendants, arguing that attending the eulogy itself was not grounds for criminal punishment.[45]

Implications of the Mughniyah Crisis

The implications of the crisis were far-reaching with respect to national unity and the position of the Kuwaiti Shiʿa.[46] Commentators inside and outside Kuwait lamented the country's steady descent into polarization, remarking that before the incident sectarianism had been confined to "pockets," whereas now it was widespread. As in previous cases discussed in this study, moderate voices were forced to "take sides" in an increasingly polarized political landscape. "The Mughniyah episode split our society," noted a moderate Sunni parliamentarian. "It was very dangerous; the Shiʿa were increasingly being treated as non-Kuwaitis."[47] The incident and the resulting Sunni outrage forced the average Shiʿa into daily protestations of their national loyalty—an increasingly impossible litmus test, given the paranoid political climate. "If you're a Shiʿite in Kuwait, you have to swear five times a day after each prayer that you hate Iran and love Israel in order to prove your loyalty," quipped the columnist ʿAbd al-Hamid al-Dashti in the Kuwaiti daily *al-Nahar*.[48]

The tension quickly escalated to outside the region. In response to the Kuwaiti government's refusal to acknowledge Mughniyah as a martyr, the Kuwaiti embassy in Beirut received a number of death threats. Hizballah's parliamentary bloc in Lebanon sent a cable to the Kuwaiti parliamentary Speaker, Jasim al-Khurafi, saying that the fourteen-member bloc was "offended" by the statements of legislators, ministers, and media toward a "great commander" of the Islamic resistance.[49] Muhammad Husayn Fadlallah, the revered Shiʿa cleric, semiofficial guide to Hizballah, and *marjaʿ* to countless Gulf Shiʿa, levied similar criticism.[50] Such statements only fueled Sunni suspicion that Iran had encouraged the Kuwaiti Shiʿa's provocations. Still others resurrected the timeworn trope that the United States had orchestrated the crisis as part of its strategy of sowing "creative chaos" (*al-fawda al-khalaqa*) in the region—that is, its master plan for inciting ethnic and sectarian particularism inside Arab societies to increase U.S. leverage and control in the Middle East.[51]

For many, it seemed as if Kuwait had returned to the dark days of the 1980s. "The issue has snowballed from an action against the Mughniyah rally into a major crackdown on a political grouping known for its bold national positions," noted the chairman of the Kuwaiti Society for the Advancement of Democracy (al-Jamʿiyya al-Kuwaytiyya li-Tanmiyat al-Dimuqratiyya).[52] Echoing its policies in this period, the government threatened to deport foreign Shiʿa who participated in the eulogy.[53] "There is regression on every level," noted one journalist. "It is obvious that Kuwait was rapidly influenced by the tense climate surrounding it in the region."[54] The greatest impact, however, was on the upcoming parliamentary elections.

The 2008 Elections

In the run-up to the elections, the government's handling of the incident had inadvertently hardened sectarian sympathies. It allowed itself to be pressured by Salafi hard-liners, creating further Shiʿa entrenchment and prompting the INA and the Shiraziyyin to bridge their differences in support of the two parliamentarians. The result was an election that was fractured along sectarian lines and tribal lines. "I think that sectarian polarization in this election is much higher than during the 2006 polls," noted one Shiʿa candidate.[55]

Much of this fracturing along sectarian lines had to do with how the redistricting had shifted the demographic distribution of Kuwaiti voters. In the past, there were two deputies for each electoral district, and the Shiʿa were a majority in only two constituencies. Under the new system, each district would elect ten deputies; Shiʿa constitute more than half the voters in the first district, covering Bayan and Rumaythia, and a sizeable number in the remaining four.[56] Another key feature of the 2008 elections that resulted in further polarization was the so-called tribal primaries—preelection voting forums where tribes hammered out a consensus about which of their shaykhs (tribal chiefs) to support. These primaries were technically illegal, although they had long been tolerated at the informal level. In 2008, the government took the unprecedented step of trying to shut them down, leading to several scuffles with police and the detention of key tribal figures.[57] The result was that tribes retreated further into the ranks of hard-line Salafi candidates.

In the final tally, the biggest loser was the Muslim Brotherhood-inspired HADAS, which had acted as a bridge between Sunnis and Shiʿa and which was counting on Shiʿa votes in the mixed Shiʿa–Sunni third district. Indeed, even the Shiʿa had hoped before the Mughniyah episode that under the five-district scheme their votes would elect moderate HADAS candidates to offset the Salafis.[58] Yet in the new Parliament HADAS saw its seats decreased from six to three, while Salafi candidates from the ISA or backed by the ISA won ten of the fifty available seats, effectively doubling their number. Another eight seats went to independent Sunni Islamists with strong Salafi and tribal leanings.[59] For their part, the Shiʿa Islamists gained five seats.

As in the case of Bahrain, the 2008 Kuwait Parliament became a hotly contested institution in which Salafi leaders opposed the cabinet on virtually every issue and frequently "played the Shiʿa card" to discredit the prime minister and undermine moderates in HADAS. All of this mudslinging was ultimately at the expense of one of the Parliament's core functions: holding the government accountable on real, substantive issues.

The Salafi Assault on the Prime Minister

In the new Parliament, the Salafi tribal deputies mounted a concerted campaign to bring down the prime minister, which they perceived as being hostile or unsympathetic to Sunni tribal interests, particularly with regard to subsidies and employment. As noted earlier, Sunni Islamist pressure began shortly after the U.S. invasion of Iraq, when Salafis perceived the government to be excessively deferential to the Shiʿa by establishing a Jaʿfari court and supporting the building of new Shiʿa mosques and a school to teach Shiʿa theology. The Shiʿa were stymied in their effort to maintain a presence on the cabinet, however, after the minister of information (a Shiʿa) was forced to resign in 2004.

In 2006, the ascension of the new prime minister, Nasser Muhammad al-Ahmed Al Sabah, further rankled the Salafis and polarized the Kuwaiti political field.[60] As noted earlier, the prime minister evinced a markedly more liberal outlook than his predecessor, and his policies of privatization increasingly threatened the tribes' dependence on the state sector. Compounding this approach, he was seen as excessively deferential to the Shiʿa. He had served in Iran as Kuwait's ambassador, spoke Persian, and had led several parliamentary delegations to Iran that, unsurprisingly, included Shiʿa MPs.[61] As one Sunni interlocutor noted, "Our prime minister is acting like a foreign minister, and our foreign minister has no power."[62] Others saw him as too involved in the day-to-day affairs of state, which undermined his grasp of the emirate's larger issues. "Our foreign minister is a *muwadhdhaf* [employee] rather than a *sahib qarar* [decision maker]," noted another MP.[63]

In November 2008, shortly after the installment of the polarized Parliament, these tensions came to a head. Three Salafi deputies from tribal districts—Walid al-Tabtabaʾi, Muhammad al-Mutayr, and Muhammad Hayif al-Mutayri[64]—filed a motion to interpellate the prime minister and, they hoped, ultimately force his resignation. The charge was, predictably, excessive coziness with the Shiʿa. The prime minister's office, they alleged, had allowed an Iranian Shiʿa cleric, Muhammad Baqir al-Fali, to enter Kuwait despite his having been placed earlier on a no-travel list.[65]

In response, Shiʿa MPs lambasted the interpellation as a "political blunder" that risked inflaming sectarianism in Kuwait, especially in light of the ongoing strife in neighboring Iraq.[66] Outside of Kuwait, commentators noted that although the Salafi deputies were within their constitutional right to grill the prime minister, they had effectively fallen into a "sectarian trap." The editor of *al-Sharq al-Awsat* argued: "The al-Fali crisis signals a dangerous sectarian escalation in Kuwait. Questioning the prime minister is a constitutional and democratic right but should not to be used for scoring political points and obstructing the interests of the country."[67]

The fractious Parliament attracted criticism from the Gulf, lending grist to the mills of rulers who saw Kuwait's burgeoning democratic institutions as a threat to their own authoritarian power. On the sidelines of a United Nations meeting, GCC leaders reportedly cautioned the Kuwaiti emir about the emirate's "democratic chaos," questioning why an institution that was supposed to promote dialogue and consensus (the Parliament) was instead sowing discord and division.[68]

In mid-2010, sectarian tensions worsened with the disclosure on May 1 that Kuwaiti authorities had disrupted a ten-person spy ring—consisting of six Kuwaitis, two stateless *bidun,* and two unspecified individuals—that was surveying U.S. and Kuwaiti military facilities on behalf of Iran's Revolutionary Guards. The Kuwaiti prosecutor general implemented a complete media ban on reporting on the spy ring, which worsened the general climate of paranoia about a fifth column lurking among the country's Shiʿa.[69] In late 2010, the country's political field was shaken by its third sectarian crisis—one that would result in a significant curtailment of civic freedoms and media openness.

THE ROW OVER YASSER AL-HABIB

As noted in the previous chapter, the cleric Yasser al-Habib had long existed as the radical right wing of Kuwait's Shiʿa community, launching provocative attacks on the regime and deploying pan-Shiʿa rhetoric. In hiding in London since December 2004, he resurfaced as a lightning rod for sectarian tensions in September 2010. This time the catalyst was a sermon (broadcast on his satellite station and widely disseminated on the Internet) in which he slandered Aisha, Muhammad's wife, as an "enemy of God."[70] The provocation followed a long history of his denigrating the Sunni branch of Islam. But in the context of regional tensions with Iran and an increasingly polarized Parliament, this latest statement crossed a red line in Kuwait. The reaction from Sunni Islamists and the government was swift. Sunni MPs called for the revocation of his citizenship and his extradition from the United Kingdom. As in the case of the Mughniyah episode, the Yasser al-Habib affair effectively undermined the moderate Sunnis who had served as bridges to the Shiʿa. As a HADAS parliamentarian noted, "Yasser al-Habib made the Sunnis think that he represented all Shiʿa. . . . [W]e were backed into a corner."[71]

The Shiʿa reaction was to dismiss al-Habib as a marginal figure. Other Shiʿa figures made counteraccusations that it was the Sunnis who were actually responsible for firing the first salvo in the sectarian strife. Saleh al-Ashur, the Shiʿa parliamentarian, noted that "there is, as well, an insult to the Jaʿfari school of thought by well-known figures in the country and by some university professors, preachers, officials, journalists on well-known satellite TV stations."[72] Other Shiʿa argued for the prosecution of prominent Salafi preachers in Kuwait who had slandered and attacked the Shiʿa, such as ʿOthman al-Khamis.[73] With regard to the Salafi response, many Shiʿa argued that the incident had given hard-line Salafis the pretext they had always desired to pressure the government toward anti-Shiʿa reforms.[74]

The Government Crackdown on Civil Liberties

The government's response to the increasingly volatile situation was twofold: to accede to Sunni Islamist demands and, more worrisomely, to crack down on civil liberties and media freedom in an effort to staunch sectarian strife. On September 16, 2010, the cabinet chaired a special session aimed at curtailing media clashes over the Yasser al-Habib affair.[75] On September 19, the government took the extraordinary step of banning public gatherings. "This is a [sectarian] rift, and it must be stopped," a Ministry of Interior representative told a press conference. The edict went on to prohibit any public gathering, procession, or demonstration without prior approval from the government. Violators would face a two-year prison term.[76]

This response was ironically due not to any agitation on the part of the Shiʿa in defense of al-Habib, but rather to Sunni gatherings. The edict came on the eve of several threats from prominent Islamist tribal deputies to interpellate the prime minister over his failure to act against Yasser al-Habib. Sunni pressure on the government continued to mount in the wake of the crisis. The independent tribal MP Musallam al-Barrak accused the cabinet of helping to spread sectarianism by opting not to punish media outlets that published or broadcast material that damaged national unity.[77] The ISA and HADAS had also announced several "seminars" or rallies to condemn Yasser al-Habib. In this context, the government's ban on rallies can be seen as a move against tribal opposition rather than a measure aimed at containing sectarianism.[78]

In late 2010, this ban brought the government into direct physical confrontation with parliamentarians when security forces scuffled with attendees at the *diwaniya* of a Sunni tribal deputy. The prominent Salafi MP Walid al-Tabtabaʾi (ironically the chair of the Parliament's Human Rights Committee) suffered a broken arm, and ten other attendees were hospitalized.[79] The entire incident and its aftermath saw the country divided along sectarian lines. Whereas Sunnis opposed the minister of interior's actions as unconstitutional, Shiʿa figures such as the Khat al-Imam cleric Husayn Qallaf and Muhammad Baqir al-Muhri urged the citizenry to support the government in its enforcement of the ban.[80] Compounding this tension, the government withdrew the credentials of al-Jazeera's Kuwait bureau and evicted its staff from Kuwait for broadcasting graphic video footage of the security forces' melee with the *diwaniya* attendees.[81]

Regional Implications of the Yasser al-Habib Crisis

Aside from its toxic effects on Kuwait's domestic politics, the Yasser al-Habib incident had a far-reaching impact outside the emirate. The row was incorrectly but frequently linked to Iranian meddling; al-Habib him-self adopted a dismissive and frequently contemptuous attitude toward the Islamic Republic, even going so far as to criticize Supreme Leader Khamenei's clerical credential. Other respected *maraji*' such as Muham-mad Husayn Fadlallah were also targets of his ire; al-Habib lambasted the late Lebanese cleric as a misguided "innovator" (*mubtadi*').[82] In response to these outrages, Supreme Leader Khamenei issued a fatwa forbidding any Shi'a cleric from insulting the companions of the Prophet or otherwise denigrating the Sunni tradition.[83]

Elsewhere in the Gulf, the incident attracted increased attention from official and nonofficial voices. On October 30, 2010, a group of sixty Saudi and Gulf Arab clerics and intellectuals submitted a statement urging Kuwait's parliamentarians to desist from sectarian rhetoric and for the government of Kuwait to rescind its repressive media law.[84] From Saudi Arabia, the editor in chief of *al-Sharq al-Awsat* warned that the incident risked dragging the entire Gulf into conflict.[85]

Kuwait's participatory institutions—the Parliament and the *diwaniya*—proved to be both assets and liabilities for the regime. On the one hand, these forums provided a pressure release for sectarian tensions to be aired and for criticism to be deflected away from the ruling family. The coun-try's practice of consultation and parliamentary debate, despite its frac-tious nature, effectively "nationalized" the opposition and reduced its proclivity to turn to outside patronage or support. As one Kuwaiti aca-demic noted, "The regime realizes that components of Kuwaiti society have external relations—the Shi'a with Iran and the Salafis with Saudi Arabia. It has tried to temper this with institutions for dialogue, such as the *diwaniya*."[86]

On the other hand, the Parliament and the *diwaniya* became vehicles for the Salafi tribal opposition to attack the Shi'a and the prime minis-ter. This was particularly evident after the 2008 parliamentary elections, which handed a victory to tribal and Salafi candidates while dealing a setback to more moderate Islamists such as HADAS and to liberals. In the new Parliament, politics became increasingly fractious, conservative, and personalized. The tribal and Salafi deputies mounted a concerted offensive against the prime minister, using a variety of attacks ranging from criticism of the appointment of women cabinet members to accusations of corruption and partiality to the Shiʿa. On sectarian issues, the friction was especially severe, in part because of missteps by the Shiʿa and worsening regional tensions.

The tension and resulting gridlock in the Parliament was ultimately, however, not so much the result in any escalation or shift in strategy by the Shiʿa or their susceptibility to transnational influences but rooted in local power dynamics unique to Kuwait—the struggle between the *badu* and the *hadhar* as well as between the emergent Salafi opposition and the prime minister. Sectarianism was deployed as the vocabulary in this struggle but was not its immediate cause. This dynamic became all the more evident in the wake of the 2011 Arab uprisings.

ELEVEN

A BALANCING ACT GOES AWRY

Sectarianism and Kuwait's Mass Protests

By late 2010, Kuwait's Parliament had become increasingly rife with tension, and its much-heralded civic and media freedoms greatly curtailed. Old fissures reappeared in even sharper contrast; *hadhar* and *badu* vitriol had reached new levels, and conservative Islamists were seeking to implement more conservative social legislation. In response, the regime implemented a far-reaching set of media restrictions intended to temper and mitigate sectarian tensions.

When the Arab uprisings in 2011 finally crashed over Kuwait, these preexisting fissures widened. A youthful protest movement within Kuwait gained steam. Sectarian tensions increased as parliamentarians and citizens took increasingly partisan positions toward the uprising in Bahrain. The country was hit by labor strikes, anticorruption demonstrations, and outrage over proposals to change the voting districts—a move that many suspected was a unilateral plot to elect a Parliament that was friendly to the ruling family. In the protests that rocked Kuwait in late 2012, sectarianism seemed to be subsumed by cross-sectarian class and youth affiliations.

Yet sectarianism flared nevertheless, and the ruling family exploited it to counter a widespread boycott by Sunni Islamist societies of the December 2012 parliamentary elections. In the final tally, the Shiʿa won a staggering seventeen seats in a pro-regime Parliament that faced an aggrieved

Sunni majority that had opted out of politics. At the end of 2012, the political situation of Kuwait was a mirror image of Bahrain's sectarian impasse—with both regimes having resorted to the same dangerous tactics.

SECTARIAN DEBATE OVER THE GCC PENINSULA SHIELD INTERVENTION

The most visible, immediate aftershock of the Arab uprisings on Kuwait was the polarizing debate over the deployment of the GCC's Peninsula Shield force in Bahrain and the question of whether and to what degree Kuwait should support the intervention. On streets and in Parliament, this watershed event divided Kuwaiti society—most commonly along Sunni–Shi'a lines. On March 18, 2011, hundreds of Kuwaiti citizens and some MPs gathered in Kuwait City to support the Pearl Roundabout protestors in Manama, Bahrain, and oppose the entry of Peninsula Shield forces.

The clearest expression of dissent by the Kuwaiti Shi'a came during the mid-March parliamentary debate about intervention. Shi'a lawmakers from across the ideological spectrum protested the GCC deployment and objected to any Kuwaiti support to the Bahraini regime, either unilaterally or as part of the Peninsula Shield forces. Adnan 'Abd-al-Samad described the deployment as a "flagrant intervention in the internal affairs of Bahrain and an attempt to curb the legitimate demands of the Bahraini people for reforms," and Rola Dashti said that troops should be sent "to defend Bahrain against any external aggression, but sending our soldiers there for the possibility of more killings is totally rejected." On March 15, Saleh 'Ashur threatened to interpellate the prime minister if he committed Kuwait troops to the GCC intervention.[1] Still others highlighted the potential contradiction of the Kuwaiti government's attempts to mediate the crisis even while it was participating in an operation to suppress the dissent.[2] "While His Highness the Amir Sheikh Al Sahah al-Ahmad Al Sahah is exerting reconciliation efforts in Bahrain, some media outfits and lawmakers are doing the opposite by engaging in destructive activities," argued the Shi'a MP Dr. Aseel al-'Awadhi.[3] Other Shi'a figures organized sit-ins and marches in solidarity with the Bahraini protestors.[4]

From the Sunni side, parliamentarians—particularly from the Salafi blocs—argued that it was incumbent upon Kuwait to support the Bahraini government as a signal of GCC fraternity and a gesture of reciprocity for Bahrain's aid to Kuwait during the 1990–1991 Iraqi occupation. Many of these figures cited the Bahrain unrest as yet another front in Iran's ongoing war against the Gulf states, with some advocating Gulf support to ethnic Arab dissidents in Iran's restive Khuzestan Province as a form of retribution.[5] Others went so far as to appear on Bahraini state television in vocal defense of the Al Khalifa. Even more ominously for Kuwait's domestic stability, the Salafi parliamentarians hinted that they would file yet another interpellation against the prime minister if Kuwait abstained from providing forces.[6]

Faced with this domestic opposition and fearful that the Bahrain crisis would exacerbate the deepening sectarian tensions in Parliament and lead to the dissolution of the cabinet, the prime minister's office prevaricated and delayed a decision about sending troops. When it finally acted, its contribution was limited to medical aid convoys and, later, naval forces—a sort of face-saving middle ground that was probably calculated to placate both Shi'a and Sunnis. Ironically, however, Bahraini authorities turned back Kuwait's medical convoys, with press reports speculating that the Bahraini government suspected them of belonging to "Kuwaiti Hizballah."[7] By late March, the Sahah al-Ahmad Al-Sabah were voicing vocal support for the Peninsula Shield operation, and the Kuwaiti defense minister stated that "if Bahrain asks us for more troops, we will be more than willing to oblige them."[8]

The debate over the GCC intervention in Bahrain and the resulting sectarian fissures also affected the country's already-eroded press freedoms. In late February 2012, the regime shut down the Shi'a newspaper *al-Dar* for using the term *invasion* to report on the Saudi troop deployment in Bahrain. Its editor in chief was briefly incarcerated. Criticism of the move was widespread, especially among Shi'a MPs.[9] As summer unfolded, the newspaper endured an onslaught of legal action. On May 20, it announced that it was back in print, but with limited coverage of Shi'a affairs in Bahrain and Saudi Arabia.[10] By July, however, this brief reprieve had ended; the government shuttered the newspaper for another three months.[11]

What the Peninsula Shield debate showed is that attempts to enforce monarchical, pan-Arab solidarity exposed the fragility of nation-state identity in a divided society such as Kuwait's. Despite its limited powers, Kuwait's Parliament acted as a check against the government's pursuing a one-sided sectarian foreign policy. But the government's final position on the Shield's intervention was not without domestic cost.

MORE ESCALATION BY SUNNI ISLAMISTS

In the latter half of 2011, the royal family's attempts to find a middle ground in the Peninsula Shield debate failed to placate the Salafi opposition. Powerful MPs used the regime's prevarication as evidence of its dereliction. On March 20, Muhammad Hayif al-Mutayri and Walid al-Tabtaba'i had announced their intention to interpellate the prime minister, citing his failure to uphold Article 3 of the GCC charter, which called for the organization to extend assistance to any member nation under attack.[12] The motion was deferred, but in late May the delegates launched another attack to bring down the prime minister, citing his cozy relationship with Iran and his recent hosting of the Iranian foreign minister just at a time when Kuwait had uncovered a spy ring allegedly working for Iran's Revolutionary Guards.[13]

In 2011, Kuwait witnessed a dramatic upsurge in anti-Iranian, anti-Shiʿa rhetoric by Sunni politicians and the media. On April 2, the Kuwaiti daily *al-Seyassah* posted the results of a poll of responses to the question "Do you support deporting expatriate Shiʿa linked to Hizballah and the Islamic Revolutionary Guards Corps from GCC countries?" The results indicate the poll surveyed 3,450 respondents: 90 percent were in favor of deporting the Shiʿa in question; 9 percent did not agree; and 1 percent was uncertain.[14]

The crescendo of anti-Shiʿism peaked on April 20, when prominent figures from the Salafi current held a conference in Kuwait City entitled "Kuwait and the Iranian Threat." A succession of speakers mounted the stage with accusations that the country was falling into Iran's orbit and that Kuwaiti Shiʿa were Iran's fifth column. The Salafi MP Khalid al-Sultan announced that seven Iranian spy cells had already been captured in Kuwait.

A few speakers went so far as to call for supporting the protests by Arabs in Iran's Khuzestan as a form of retaliation for Iran's alleged meddling in Kuwaiti affairs.[15]

In May, these tensions erupted with full force in the Parliament, with much of the ire directed at one figure in particular, the independent Shiʿa MP Husayn al-Qallaf. This pro-Khamenei politician had already received death threats for his vocal support of Bahraini protests and the Allawite-led regime in Syria.[16] Then, during a parliamentary session, he referred to the Kuwaiti Sunni detainees at the U.S. military prison at Guantanamo Bay, Cuba, as "al-Qaʿida," triggering a physical assault upon him by Salafi MPs. A vicious fistfight ensued, showcasing just how far the Kuwaiti Parliament had descended into sectarian bickering.[17]

MASS PROTESTS AND THE FEBRUARY 2012 PARLIAMENT

Many of the early protests in Kuwait directly inspired by the 2011 Arab uprisings were economically driven, demanding better wages and an end to privatization. In late October and early November 2011, massive anticorruption protests wracked the country. Roughly fifteen MPs, many drawn from tribal backgrounds, were suspected of taking bribes and money laundering. At the center of the storm was the despised prime minister, Nasser Al Sabah. By mid-November, there were sustained sit-ins outside the Parliament, and growing crowds chanted for his resignation. In a shocking move, more than fifteen thousand protestors stormed the Parliament on November 16, wounding several security personnel.[18] Dubbed "Black Wednesday," the occupation of the Parliament proved a watershed—and a stark reminder of the frustration felt by Kuwait's increasingly restive youth. By November 28, the pressure had reached a tipping point; the prime minister tendered his resignation. He had long been an object of opposition ire, particularly from the Sunni *badu*, so his departure should have lessened the opposition's pressure on the royal family.

It did not. Buoyed by this watershed change of office, the Sunni Islamist opposition rallied. A key turning point in their ascendancy occurred on

December 16, 2011, when, in a remarkable act, the emir dissolved the Parliament elected in 2009 and called for new elections in February 2012. In the polling, a diverse constellation of Sunni Islamists (from both HADAS and the Salafi societies), tribal candidates, leftists, and nationalists landed a resounding victory, largely on the basis of an anticorruption platform. A crucial attribute of the new Parliament was its tribal composition—thirty-four of the fifty winning candidates hailed from an Islamist, tribal background, leading some observers to label the February 2012 elections a *"badu* revolution" against the *hadhar*.[19] The al-Mutayr, who had long spearheaded the opposition to privatization and cuts in state subsidies, were at the forefront of this push. The independent al-Mutayri MP Musallam al-Barrak secured the highest number of parliamentary seats in Kuwait's electoral history. Yet even the tribal bloc was not monolithic. Among Kuwait's leading tribal luminaries, several had been implicated in the anticorruption platform.

For liberals, Shiʿa, and women, the election was a blow. Of the twenty-three women candidates in the election, none was elected. Self-declared liberals saw their seats decrease from eight to five, and the Shiʿa bloc went from nine to seven.

SECTARIAN DEBATES OVER SYRIA

The new Parliament proved to be short-lived. Even worse, many sessions were preoccupied with debating Kuwait's position on the worsening civil war in Syria rather than with legislation. Sectarianism invariably reared its head in these debates; as in Bahrain, the issue of whether and how Kuwait should support the Syrian opposition polarized and paralyzed the Parliament.

On February 28, a Sunni-sponsored proposal in the Kuwaiti National Assembly to recognize the Syrian National Council as the legitimate representative of the Syrian people spurred significant clashes along sectarian lines. Forty-four MPs, including all cabinet ministers in the session, backed the proposal, five voted against it, one abstained, and three refused to vote.[20]

Most of those who opposed the motion were Shiʿa MPs, leading to heated debate and accusations of disloyalty to the state.[21] "The Syrian people are resisting the Iranians, Hizballah and the Iraqi militias," argued the Salafi MP Muhammad Hayif al-Mutayri, "yet the agents sitting among us in the National Assembly remain silent about this matter."[22] The clash forced Deputy Speaker Khalid al-Sultan to adjourn the session for fifteen minutes.[23]

TWITTER WARS: SOCIAL MEDIA AND SECTARIAN TENSIONS

In the aftermath of the Arab uprisings, Kuwait's social media scene quickly captivated both the country's citizens and outside observers. In a political culture already infused with open, transparent discussions of political and social topics, Twitter seemed tailor made.[24] As of April 2012, there were more than one million Twitter accounts in Kuwait out of a population of 3.6 million—according to one data-compilation firm, this number represented an astounding twofold increase in the course of one year.[25] "[Twitter] has replaced the *diwaniya*," noted one longtime social activist.[26] Still other observers noted that in periods when the Parliament was dissolved, more Kuwaitis opened Twitter accounts, as if to compensate for the lack of a participatory political forum.[27]

The question then arises: Did the explosion of content on social media, especially Twitter, contribute to worsening sectarian tensions in the wake of the Arab uprisings? For some, the answer is obvious. As discussed previously, Kuwait's tolerant and open media had already been accused of stoking sectarian tensions, especially during sensitive periods of regional tumult, such as the Iraq War and the assassination of 'Imad Mughniyah.[28] Twitter continued, however, and intensified this trend. By effectively democratizing media access, Twitter revolutionized Kuwait's social and political life. But the results were mixed. It empowered the massive, anticorruption protests against the prime minister, Nasser Muhammad Al Sahah, but it also created an echo chamber for amplifying the regional sectarian shocks from Bahrain, eastern Saudi Arabia, Iran, and Syria.[29]

Other observers argued that Kuwait's open media and Parliament were crucial in mediating and tempering the contagion effect of the Arab uprisings—acting, in effect, as a release valve for political pressures that, if kept suppressed and obstructed, would explode in a manner similar to the outcome in Bahrain. As one seasoned Kuwaiti analyst noted, "Kuwait is accustomed to [sectarian] tension, but it has channels through which people can vent their grievances; particularly the media. Secrecy is what causes things to deteriorate. Here everything is out in the open."[30]

In the wake of the Arab uprisings, elements of both narratives were present. Social media did not create sectarianism in Kuwait, nor did they politicize it. But the proliferation of Twitter did confront the Kuwaiti government with significant dilemmas about whether longstanding laws against insulting religions or religious figures applied to the raucous and unregulated realm of the microblog. Twitter was increasingly the scene of vicious Shiʿa–Sunni infighting and, although less frequently, mudslinging between the *badu* and *hadhar*.[31] As noted, there were numerous instances of Sunni figures attacking the Shiʿa in both traditional and social media, which sparked demands by Shiʿa lawmakers that the government take stronger action. For instance, in early February the Shiʿa MP Faysal al-Duwaysan proposed an antihatred bill that called for stiff jail terms for those who incite religious, social, racial, and gender hatred. The move stipulated a jail term of between one and three years and a fine of up to $72,000; repeat offenders would get seven years and a penalty of $180,000.[32]

Any attempt by the regime to curtail the excessive vitriol stirred suspicions by prominent Sunni Islamists that the ruling family was using press laws to mount a concerted campaign against the country's Sunni opposition and its supporters. For instance, on May 8, 2011, Mubarak al-Bathali, a longtime opponent of the Shiʿa, was arrested for anti-Shiʿa tweets. A Kuwaiti court sentenced him to three years in prison, which was subsequently shortened to six months, for threatening national unity and insulting a religious sect.[33] Later, on February 2, 2012, an employee of the Ministry of Islamic Affairs and widower with four children, Muhammad al-Mulayfi, was arrested for insulting the Shiʿa on Twitter, sentenced to seven years' imprisonment, and given a hefty fine.[34] On May 31, however, a Kuwaiti court of appeals reduced the sentence to six months.

As if to balance this crackdown, the regime also targeted Shiʿa transgressions on Twitter. Importantly, most of the arrests and prosecution cited insults to the Bahraini and Saudi rulers or undue sympathy with the Bahraini Shi'a. The Kuwaiti government was clearly enforcing a transnational sectarian solidarity in the social media sphere as a way to insulate itself from mounting domestic pressure from Sunni Islamists. This remarkable turn of events demonstrates just how far the Arab uprisings had been "sectarianized" by mid-2012.

Nowhere was this more evident than in the case of Nasser Abul, a Shi'a tweeter who had long criticized Sunni doctrine and lambasted the Saudi and Bahraini regimes for their stance against the Bahraini protests. The prominent Salafi MP and oppositionist Walid al-Tabtaba'i was the first to demand Abul's arrest in May 2012, posting snapshots of his tweets on Facebook and other social media. During Abul's arraignment, he was charged with "insulting a religious sect and insulting neighboring regimes"—a clear reference to Bahrain and Saudi Arabia. On September 27, 2011, a Kuwaiti court found Abul guilty and sentenced him to three months in jail—time that he had already served. He was immediately freed. All along, Abul denied writing the problematic tweets, arguing that his account had been hacked. When asked about the Bahraini flag on his avatar, he stated unapologetically that he was a Kuwaiti protesting in support of the Bahraini uprising.[35]

The Twitter war ratcheted up in early 2012, sparking new levels of vitriol and, most worrisomely, a push toward even more draconian anti-blasphemy legislation by the country's Sunni-dominated Parliament. On March 27, Hamad al-Naqi, a Shi'a tweeter with more than four thousand followers, posted a tweet stating that the Prophet Muhammad feared one of his Companions more than God and, even more grotesquely, that the Prophet had made an indecent videotape with his wife. He was swiftly arrested amidst a chorus of condemnations by Kuwait's Sunnis, with several MPs calling for his execution. Protests soon flared in the streets and in front of the State Security headquarters.

The vitriol expanded to encompass Kuwait's Shi'a population writ large. Despite the fact that al-Naqi's tweet was nonsectarian in nature, the backlash erupted along sectarian lines. On March 28, protestors converged on Irada Square; several burned the Iranian flag.[36] The action elicited a strong rebuke from the Kuwait Foreign Ministry, which was eager to maintain good relations with Tehran.[37] Kuwait's main newspapers were quick to condemn al-Naqi, but a few voices wondered why the outrage over a puerile attack on all Muslims had worsened the country's Sunni–Shiʿa polarization. Writing in *al-Raʾy* newspaper, the columnist Muhammad al-Sabti pondered: "I do not understand why the entire Shiʿa community was targeted for a single error committed by one Shiʿa citizen." Echoing this view, Husayn al-Qallaf, one of the seven Shiʿa MPs remaining in Kuwait's Parliament, lamented, "Some are provoking Sunnis to fight with Shiʿites and Shiʿites to fight with Sunnis. This is also happening on Twitter and Facebook now."[38]

Even more worrisome, the outcry expanded to the legislative realm, with Sunni MPs demanding that the country's penal code be amended to allow the execution of the twenty-two-year-old tweeter al-Naqi. In May 2012, voting fifty-two to forty-six, Kuwaiti lawmakers approved an amendment applying the death penalty for anyone who is found guilty of mocking God, the Prophet Muhammad, Muslim prophets, or Muhammad's wives.[39] Unsurprisingly, the seven Shiʿa MPs rejected the law, arguing that the measure should also include penalties for insulting the Twelve Imams of Shiʿism.[40] In the face of such tumult, the government tried to steer a middle course. On June 4, a Kuwaiti court sentenced al-Naqi to ten years in prison for the crime of insulting Islam and the rulers of Saudi Arabia and Bahrain; his lawyer stated that capital punishment could not be applied because his alleged crime took place before the amendment had been enacted. At any rate, on June 5 the emir struck down the measure as unconstitutional.[41] Yet in August the government once again moved in the direction of criminalizing hate speech.

The entire episode prompted widespread concern and alarm among liberal observers both in Kuwait and in the West. Many wondered if the country's relatively open media culture had fallen victim to sectarianism. More directly, the al-Naqi affair demonstrated that trying to regulate sectarianism through hate speech can be a Faustian bargain, leading to excessive politicization if the judiciary is not entirely independent from the executive branch.

DIGNITY AND SECTARIANISM:
THE MASS PROTESTS OF 2012

On October 21, 2012, an estimated one hundred thousand people gathered in Kuwait City's Irada (Willpower) Square. It was reportedly the largest gathering in Kuwait's history. Drawn from a diverse coalition of youth, Islamists, and tribes, the protestors festooned their gatherings with orange ribbons—an explicit reference to Ukraine's famed Orange Revolution. Unlike other Arab uprisings, the crowds did not demand the overthrow of the royal family. That said, the brazenness and tone of the protests were unprecedented—unlike previous criticism, they targeted the very legitimacy of the ruling family. On October 15, Musallam al-Barrak leveled a direct salvo at the character of the emir himself, stating: "We will not allow you, your highness, to take Kuwait into the abyss of autocracy." The subsequent arrest of this enormously popular oppositionist only enraged the protestors even more. By the end of the month, protests demanding his release had grown to ten thousand, with several banners proclaiming him the "conscience of the nation."[42]

The roots of these protests extend back to June 2012, when the Constitutional Court dissolved the February 2012 Parliament. Faced with a wave of cabinet resignations in the face of the Parliament's efforts to censure royally appointed ministers, the Court decreed that the procedure the emir had used to dissolve the Parliament in November 2011 was unconstitutional. The more pliable 2009 Parliament was reinstated, but it never convened. On October 7, 2012, the emir decided to dissolve the 2009 Parliament for a second time. Meanwhile, an interim cabinet—which was entirely appointed—began drafting emergency laws that the opposition suspected were designed to ensure the selection of a more pliable Parliament in the next election, to be held, by law, no later than sixty days from the dissolution. Chief among these laws was a measure to reduce the number of votes each citizen can cast—from four to one. In the ensuing weeks, Kuwaiti MPs were bitterly divided over the move; pro-government deputies supported the reduction, whereas the opposition unsurprisingly demanded that the elections be held on the basis of the current law, which, they pointed out, the Constitutional Court had upheld on September 25.[43]

Generation Versus Sect

What role did sectarian identity play in the protests? On the surface, it seemed to be subsumed by an array of other affiliations—the most salient being age. If there was one important fissure that defined the protests, it was a generational one. Many of the opposition movement's young leaders made a concerted effort to move past sectarianism and include both Shi'a and Sunni youth in order to increase their numbers and overall impact. One youth group tweeted, "Defending the oppressed does not stop at religion or class. It is our duty to help the people who have been hit, arrested, or had the security forces enter their homes to be victorious tomorrow."[44] Echoing this, another member of the youth movement argued that Kuwait was moving past tribal and sectarian identities. "In the past, candidates to the parliament would traditionally be supported by a tribe, a family or a sect, keeping young people in the shadows. Today, however, a quantum leap has taken place and the proof is that former MPs have complied with the wishes and aspirations of the youth. Those who have led and are currently leading the political movement are loyal young Kuwaitis who are directly linked to Kuwait."[45]

Despite such wishful thinking, sectarianism did persist. At times, the government itself appeared to be playing up these divisions. For instance, on March 24 they canceled the Youth Awakening Forum (Multaqa al-Nahda), which was meant to bring together liberals and Islamists, Shi'a and Sunni, from across the Arab world to debate religion and politics. Some participants said that Salafis had pressured the Interior Ministry to stop the forum.

But the ultimate litmus test for the cross-sectarian cohesion of the protests took shape in the boycott of the December 2012 parliamentary elections.

A Sectarian Boycott

In the run-up to the December 1 parliamentary elections, many oppositionists threatened a boycott. On October 28, 2012, the major opposition blocs made good on this threat. The Popular Action Bloc, the Development and Reform Bloc (Kutlat al-Tanmiya wa al-Islah), the National Democratic Alliance (al-Tahaluf al-Watani al-Dimuqrati), the al-ʿAwazim tribe—the largest Kuwaiti tribe—and other groups announced their decision to boycott the upcoming elections due to the emir's decree of changes in voting law, which he finally announced on October 19.[46]

For the Shiʿa, the decision whether to participate or boycott set them at odds with the broader protest movement. The overwhelming majority decided to participate: the INA, the National Islamic Accord, the Justice and Peace Assembly (Tajammuʿ al-ʿAdala wa al-Salam), and the National Pact Assembly.[47] "Your participation in the elections is a bullet in the chest of those who boycott. . . . [D]on't let the country become a mob," tweeted the cleric Husayn al-Qallaf on November 28.[48]

The participation of Shiʿa candidates was facilitated by adroit government moves. At the eleventh hour, on November 27, the Kuwaiti judiciary overturned its previous ban against key Shiʿa MPs' running in the election. Chief among them was Saleh al-ʿAshur of the Assembly for Justice and Peace and ʿAbd al-Hamid al-Dashti, an independent.[49] "Thank God and thank our just judges who chose to cancel the decision," al-Dashti tweeted on November 28.[50] In the final polling results, voter turnout was said to be a little more than 50 percent. Others claimed a much more modest figure of 26 percent. "The Kuwaiti people have succeeded in bringing down [this] election by not taking part," the oppositionist Musallam al-Barrak tweeted. Regardless, the most important effect was that the Shiʿa won an unprecedented seventeen seats in the country's fifty-member Parliament—a doubling of their number from the previous Parliament.[51] The Sunni Islamists, represented by HADAS, independents, and Salafi societies, boycotted the election en masse. The result was that the Sunni Islamists' share of the seats dropped from twenty-three to four. Meanwhile, none of Kuwait's three major tribal groupings—the al-Mutayr, the Ajman, and the Awazim—secured seats. In its sectarian and tribal makeup, the new Parliament was nearly a mirror image of the previous one.

Like other regimes in the region, the Kuwaiti government proved adept at playing the sectarian card to neutralize what were essentially mass protests led by Sunni Islamists, tribes, and youth. Shiʿa gains in the new Kuwaiti Parliament sent sectarian shivers across the Gulf. From Bahrain, the state-owned press lambasted the new deputies as proxies of Iran.[52] Yet the ultimate victim in this sectarian strategy was the country's fragile, quasi-democratic experiment.

CONCLUSION

Like any social or political fissure, sectarianism is not an immutable feature of the Gulf landscape. Neither is it a manufactured construct, as some have alleged. In times of uncertainty and upheaval, political and media elites have manipulated and exploited it, and ordinary citizens have latched on to it as a safety net. Sectarianism's ripples across national boundaries are most acute in conditions of political inequality and institutional weakness, among marginalized social groups and embattled elites. The Iranian Revolution, the Iraqi civil war, the Hizballah–Israel war in Lebanon, and, most recently, the Syrian civil war have echoed throughout the Gulf, exciting sectarian passions and stirring expressions of partisanship. But the ultimate roots of Sunni–Shiʿa tensions lie in the domestic context rather than in regional events.

The so-called rise of the Shiʿa in the wake of Saddam Husayn's fall did not create sectarianism in the Gulf. Although the Gulf Shiʿa took a degree of inspiration from the actions of their coreligionists in Iraq, Iran, and Lebanon, they ultimately strove for greater rights in a nonsectarian, nationalist framework, cooperating with Sunni Islamists and liberals. What is qualitatively different about the post-2003 period is the intensity of threat perception by Gulf regimes and Sunni elites. It was this perception that fueled regime attempts to stifle meaningful political change through cosmetic reforms and by stoking sectarianism—a bankrupt strategy that left a younger generation of Shiʿa increasingly embittered and sparked the protests of early 2011, which have yet to fully abate.

SHIʿA ACTORS: PUSHING FOR CROSS-SECTARIAN REFORMS

The cross-border affinities of the Gulf Shiʿa affect sectarian mobilization, but not in the way previously assumed. True, the Shiʿa have frequently turned outside the Gulf for empowering, revolutionary ideologies to challenge the status quo. Much of this diffusion has been enabled by familial and clerical relationships that link the Gulf Shiʿa to their coreligionists in Lebanon, Iraq, and Iran.

But in the wake of the 2003 Iraq War, Shiʿa political actors actually redoubled their efforts to "nationalize" their political strategies within existing domestic institutions rather than, as was commonly suspected, to seek external guidance and support from their ascendant coreligionists elsewhere in the region. In a few instances, Shiʿa clerical figures, usually on the fringes of the Shiʿa mainstream, appealed to Iran, Lebanese Hizballah, or Iraqi Shiʿa authorities. But these expressions of transnational solidarity should be seen for what they are: tactics in an intra-Shiʿa contest for power or means to pressure regimes into greater concessions and not as evidence of a broad shift in Gulf Shiʿa proclivity to foreign influences.

In Bahrain, the decision by the main Shiʿa political grouping, al-Wifaq, to end its four-year electoral boycott was legitimated by the emergence of independent Shiʿa religious authorities in Najaf, Iraq. It is inaccurate, however, to say that Grand Ayatollah al-Sistani directly influenced the society's decision making. The Iraqi cleric and his local Bahraini interlocutors—ʿIsa al-Qasim and Husayn Najati—continually emphasized that it was not the place for foreign-based *marajiʿ* to interfere in local politics. The trend of local actors attempting to appropriate al-Sistani's authority for leverage is not unique to Bahrain but is rather found throughout the region—so much so that Sistani's office has issued statements decrying the use of his imprimatur for political agendas. That said, the al-Wifaq leadership did try to draw broad parallels between the electoral success of the Shiʿa in neighboring Iraq and the situation of the Bahraini Shiʿa as a means to bolster popular support for its decision to participate in the 2006 parliamentary elections.

The rising profile of Lebanese Hizballah and its war with Israel similarly provided a useful model for the militant Haq movement to legitimate its own decision to boycott the elections and to contrast its rejectionist outlook with al-Wifaq's more accommodating one. Yet there was little concrete evidence of Hizballah's involvement in the Bahraini political scene, either rhetorically or materially. If it did intervene, it was to emphasize that Bahraini politics was the autonomous preserve of the Bahrainis themselves and not for a Lebanese entity to influence or determine. In the aftermath of the Arab uprisings, however, this restraint shifted, with Hizballah and Iranian authorities adopting a much more vocal and partisan policy.

In some cases, nonsectarian events that were unconnected to the rise of Iran or the ascendancy of Shiʿa power in Iraq had an equally strong demonstration effect on Bahrain Shiʿa sensitivities. Protests in Sitra and Manama in May 2005 were inspired more by Lebanon's Cedar Revolution and Ukraine's Orange Revolution than by any incitement from Iran or exhortation from Najaf-based authorities. In particular, these national-based demonstrations appear to have resulted in a "rebranding" of Shiʿa protest symbols—that is, a discarding of Iranian and Hizballah flags in favor of the Bahraini flag, emblazoned with the slogan "Constitutional Reform First."

In the wake of the Arab uprisings of 2011, these dynamics became even more apparent. The contagion effect of the revolts in Tunis, Cairo, and Benghazi on Bahraini Shiʿa embodied a nonsectarian blend of populism, youthful frustration, and class. But early attempts to portray the Pearl Roundabout demonstrations as cross-sectarian expressions for democratic change ultimately foundered due to the regime's media countermobilization, the security crackdown, tactical missteps by al-Wifaq, and growing divisions within the opposition. Most ominous, the institutionalized opposition represented by al-Wifaq has found itself under pressure by the street protests of the February 14 Youth Movement.

The trend of unmet expectations and generational conflict among the Shiʿa is mirrored in Saudi Arabia. Here, Eastern Province Shiʿa have long looked outside the kingdom for guidance, inspiration, and support, given the intense pressures of religious discrimination and political exclusion. Yet in the wake of the Iraq War, Saudi Shiʿa reformists actually intensified their efforts to ground their activism in the domestic context rather than to seek support from reemergent centers of Shiʿa power in Iraq or an increasingly assertive Iran. Led by Hassan al-Saffar, clerics, intellectuals, and activists from the Islahiyyin pursued a number of strategies: voicing their demands for change through the longstanding practice of the petition; de-emphasizing the transnational authority of the *marjaʿiyya*; engaging in cross-sectarian outreach with Sunni liberals and Islamists; and participating in regime-sponsored reform initiatives, such as the National Dialogue and the municipal council elections. This institutionalization of these former oppositionists extended across diverse ideological currents. Even the staunchest Shiʿa defenders of *velayet-e faqih*, such as the former Hizballah al-Hijaz leader Hassan al-Nimr, argued for a more nationalist interpretation of the concept, which would allay Sunni anxieties in the kingdom.

Yet this approach came under increasing pressure due to a number of regional and domestic factors. Mounting sectarian strife in Iraq and tensions with Iran, the failure of cosmetic institutional reforms to deliver real material change, and the regime's security crackdown in response to the 2009 Medina riots gradually shifted the dynamics of power in the Eastern Province. Bolder, more rejectionist voices secured an ever wider following. The most charismatic figure in this new trend was the firebrand cleric Nimr al-Nimr, who drew support from the long-marginalized town of al-ʿAwamiya. In his wildly popular sermons, al-Nimr made provocative calls for supporting Iran, secession, and the ouster of the Al Saʿud. Yet his most captivating appeal was a simple demand for dignity.

In the wake of Tunis and Tahrir Square, the paralysis of reform in Saudi Arabia would stoke the embers of unrest among an increasingly frustrated cadre of Shiʿa youth. Disenchanted with their elders' conciliatory approach, these younger activists demanded more sweeping changes that, among some quarters, included the downfall of the monarchy. For their part, the older clerics found their authority increasingly challenged by this newer, "postideological" cohort who have attempted to build bridges with like-minded youth across the country.

Like their counterparts in Saudi Arabia, the Kuwaiti Shiʿa saw the invasion of Iraq as an opening to push for greater concessions in the cultural and religious sphere, while at the same emphasizing their continued loyalty to the monarchy. As in the case of both Bahrain and Saudi Arabia, there were instances in Kuwait where local Shiʿa clerics deliberately inflated their access to foreign *marajiʿ* or advanced radical claims of secession in an effort to boost their authority and popularity. Key examples include Muhammad Baqir al-Muhri, who frequently claimed to speak on behalf of Grand Ayatollah al-Sistani, and the radical cleric Yasser al-Habib, who called for an independent Shiʿa state comprising the Eastern Province, Kuwait, Bahrain, and Basra. At the same time, the post-2003 period witnessed increased factionalism among the Kuwaiti Shiʿa as a result of outside actors. Encouraged by the reemergence of Grand Ayatollah al-Sistani in Najaf, the Shiraziyyin in Kuwait attempted to marginalize their rivals in the pro-Iranian INA.

In the wake of the Arab uprisings of 2011, Kuwaiti Shiʿa parliamentarians found their nationalist bona fides once again under fire in debates about whether to support the Peninsula Shield in Bahrain and the Syrian opposition. In many cases, polarizing statements by a few Shiʿa figures about supporting Iran or Syria elicited vitriolic attacks against the community writ large. The advent of mass protests in late 2012 posed yet another challenge to cross-sectarian cooperation: Shiʿa candidates found themselves at odds with independent, tribal, and Islamist Sunnis over whether to boycott the December parliamentary elections.

REGIMES AND SUNNI ELITES: SECTARIANISM AS POLITICAL STRATEGY

This study has argued that sectarian primacy has historically not been one of the central pillars of official governance in the GCC. At the ideational level, Gulf regimes have historically deployed ecumenical forms of Islam and Arabism to buttress their standing at home. That said, what is distinctive about the post-2003 environment is that the norms of Arabism and

Islam in the Gulf became increasingly conflated with Sunnism by a variety of official and semiofficial actors. In the wake of the Arab uprisings of 2011 this dynamic has intensified. In all three countries—but especially in Saudi Arabia and Bahrain—this conflation was largely a defensive reaction to the perceived rise of Iranian and Shi'a power and, after 2011, to the contagion of revolutionary upheaval from Tunis and Cairo.

Among regimes and their allies in the Sunni elite, sectarianism has been used instrumentally for a wide array of purposes: to deflect criticism over failures in governance, to induce divisions among the opposition, and to rally domestic audiences against the external threat from Iran. For certain Sunni actors, such as the Salafi clerical establishment in Saudi Arabia, sectarianism provides real material benefits. It ensures their continued and exclusive access to political power. Any formal recognition of Shi'a identity—whether in the political, legal, or cultural spheres—would effectively undermine this primacy. In Kuwait, the situation is reversed: Sunni Islamists in opposition deployed sectarianism as a critique in their assault on the prime minister.

In contrast to this majority trend, a smaller current of Sunni liberals and Islamists avoided sectarian exclusivity and tried to build bridges with Shi'a reformists. Partly as a result of worsening tensions in the region, these figures faced mounting pressure to "pick sides" and were frequently derided as "traitors" to their sect. In addition, Gulf regimes sought to regulate cross-sectarian contacts through initiatives such as "national dialogues," ensuring that reform-minded Sunnis faced considerable difficulty in building real, sustainable links with Shi'a activists. That said, the communication persists, often enabled by social media channels that are beyond the purview of regime control.

It is in Bahrain where the use of sectarianism as a political strategy has been the most evident. The collapse of the Saddam regime in Iraq left Bahrain the one country in the Arab world where a Sunni minority rules over a Shi'a majority. With Iraq's quick descent into civil war, the Bahraini Parliament became a sort of political theater where sectarian partisanship frequently carried the day at the expense of more substantive discussions. The ultimate winner in this wrangling were the Al Khalifa family, who portrayed themselves as an indispensable arbiter over a fractious and divided citizenry. Bahrain's two main Sunni Islamist societies, al-Minbar and al-Asala, proved to be critical bulwarks in the royal family's strategy of sectarian balancing.

In the wake of the Arab uprisings of 2011, Sunni dynamics in Bahrain shifted toward fractionalization and entrenchment. Specifically, the emergence of a more vocal Sunni opposition that embodied the grievances of lower-class Sunnis toward the corruption and economic mismanagement of the Al-Khalifa presented al-Wifaq with a potential opportunity for cross-sectarian coordination. But whatever potential existed was undone by the combination of pressure and co-option by hard-line factions in the Al Khalifa, missteps by al-Wifaq, the military intervention of the GCC in Bahrain, and growing fissures among the Sunnis themselves. Specifically, the post-2011 period saw the consolidation of a hard-line faction in the Al Khalifa—the Al Khawalid branch of the royal family—who co-opted and subsidized more hard-line Sunni actors such as the Sahwat al Fatih (Awakening of Fatih) to counter the Shiʿa-led protests.

In Saudi Arabia, the U.S. invasion of Iraq raised the specter of Shiʿa mobilization to a degree that was not found in Bahrain and Kuwait. In the run-up to the war, there was growing fear in Saudi officialdom that the Eastern Province Shiʿa, inspired by Shiʿa empowerment in Iraq or encouraged by Iran (or even by the United States), might move toward secession. In addition, the Iraq War, the 2006 Lebanon War, and the Zaydi rebellion in neighboring Yemen created a domestic backlash among the Salafi clerical establishment, prompting increased vitriol against the Shiʿa. Many of these figures, holding powerful positions in education, censorship, and social affairs, were doctrinally opposed to Shiʿism and saw any formalization of Shiʿa rights as a threat to their power. At the height of the Iraq War, several popular Salafi clerics agitated for a greater government role in defending Iraq's Sunnis from Iranian-backed Shiʿa militias.

To close ranks with these figures, the Al Saʿud monarchy tacitly permitted the proliferation of anti-Shiʿa tracts, sermons, and Internet statements, many of them recycled from the kingdom's ideological counteroffensive against the Islamic Revolution of 1979. Anti-Shiʿism became a useful normative weapon for the monarchy—a means to silence potential critics in the Salafi establishment and deflect popular sentiment away from the regime's failings. As the regime faced a growing threat from al-Qaʿida, this tactic grew in importance. Salafi clerics became useful interlocutors and allies for the regime in the ideological struggle to turn young Saudis away from al-Qaʿida, and the "price" of this cooperation was increased regime tolerance of the clerics' anti-Shiʿa outlook.

In the wake of the Arab uprisings of 2011, the regime responded with timeworn strategies of attempting to placate dissent with subsidies, co-opting more quietist Shiʿa clerics to dampen the anger of the youth, and framing the Eastern Province protests as inspired by Iran. Of these policies, playing the sectarian card to contain the spread of the unrest has had the most profound effect on the kingdom's social fabric. "The 2005 to 2007 days of Shiʿa–Sunni reconciliation are gone," lamented one Shiʿa activist in al-Ahsa in early 2013. "Now, many of the Salafi clerics who did the outreach have done a 180 degree reversal."[1]

Most significant, the regime's response took a decidedly violent turn in late 2011 and again in mid-2012, with the shooting and arrest of Nimr al-Nimr. These repressive spikes ironically bolstered the popularity of the very figure the government was trying to marginalize, resulting in widespread expressions of solidarity with the imprisoned cleric. They also deepened the divide between the older generation of clerics and the youthful activists.

In Kuwait, Sunni oppositionists played an especially deleterious role in stoking sectarian tensions, starting in 2005. During this period, the Sunni tribes effectively withdrew from their previous alliance with the royal family, supplanting the liberals as the Al Sahah's main adversary. For these oppositionists—many of them *badu* drawn from the environs outside Kuwait City—anti-Shiʿism became a "card" to discredit the royals, specifically the prime minister, and a tactic to win over the *hadhar* Sunnis by enforcing a sort of sectarian solidarity. Mounting regional tensions over Iran, Iraq, and the Lebanese Hizballah enabled this tactic. Specifically, the Sunni tribal opposition repeatedly charged that the prime minister was not doing enough to assist Sunnis in Iraq and was being too partial to Iran's interests.

In the wake of the Arab uprisings, Sunni deputies continued their assault. The parliamentary debate over GCC's Peninsula Shield intervention in Bahrain proved to be a lightening rod for sectarian tensions. Sunni Islamists demanded that Kuwait support the Shield as an expression of fraternity with a fellow Gulf state, whereas Shiʿa representatives opposed it, arguing that it was not appropriate for Kuwaiti foreign policy to interfere in Bahrain's domestic affairs. With the escalation of Syria's civil war, Kuwait's Sunnis continued to play the sectarian card in a debate about Kuwaiti support to the Syrian opposition. Outside of Parliament, a vitriolic war in social media contributed further to sectarianism.

In late 2012, mass protests erupted over the dissolution of the February 2012 Parliament, which had been dominated by Sunni tribal members. Many of the movement's leaders made a concerted effort to move past sectarianism: a diverse coalition of youth activists, Muslim Brothers, Salafis, and liberals joined the demonstrations. Yet Shiʿa politicians remained on the sidelines or stayed allied with the Al Sahah. Moreover, the youth activists allied themselves with Sunni tribal former parliamentarians who had long been the most vociferous critics of the Shiʿa and supported the Saudi intervention in Bahrain. Among activists in Bahrain and the Eastern Province, there were uncomfortable debates about whether to support the mass movement in Kuwait, given the prominence of anti-Shiʿa figures in its ranks. In a further split, Sunni Islamist candidates boycotted the October 2012 parliamentary elections, resulting in Shiʿa candidates winning the highest number of seats in the Parliament's history. The overall outcome was a sectarian split between the country's quasi-democratic institution and its political opposition—and a mirror image of the landscape in Bahrain.

SECTARIAN INSTITUTIONS

In each country, domestic institutions—parliaments, consultative councils, *diwaniya*, clerical establishments, labor unions, government ministries, and especially the media—had a determinant effect on sectarianism. They acted as filters for regional contagion, mediating the tensions that rippled across the Gulf from Iraq, Lebanon, Tunis, and Cairo. In many cases, these institutions inflamed sectarianism by excluding key societal groups or by lacking real authority to make meaningful progress on reform. In others, they were instruments for entrenched elites to regulate and stifle demands for reform. Social media in particular proved to be a double-edge sword. On the one hand, Twitter and Facebook amplified the most polarizing voices on both sides of the Sunni–Shiʿa divide, creating a cycle of escalation that provided a pretext for regimes to enact sweeping restrictions on freedom of expression. At the same time, social media gave Shiʿa and Sunni reform activists channels to engage in cross-sectarian communication outside of the regime-sponsored forums.

In Bahrain, a dysfunctional Parliament and institutional discrimination played a central rule in fueling sectarianism. The 2006 parliamentary elections at least initially created a climate of hope for positive change that acted as a pressure release. The mainstream Shiʿa opposition society, al-Wifaq, was brought into the country's political experiment, temporarily sidelining more rejectionist voices. Yet in the years following the elections, parliamentary life became increasingly rife with sectarian wrangling. The Salafi groups sponsored by hard-line elements in the monarchy became more entrenched and publicly hostile toward the Shiʿa. The legislative and oversight limitations of the Parliament meant that al-Wifaq's participation produced few tangible results for lower-class Shiʿa. A turning point was the regime's 2010 crackdown in response to burgeoning cross-sectarian cooperation in Parliament on the investigation of royal corruption. It was this repression, along with the structural weaknesses of the Parliament, that stoked mounting resentment among the country's Shiʿa youth—and led to the Pearl Roundabout uprising.

In the wake of this uprising, sectarian tensions infected the country's institutions. Virtually every corner of public life was affected: media, schools, ministries, and labor unions became increasingly divided along Sunni–Shiʿa lines. The government undertook widespread purges of Shiʿa from municipalities as well as from ministries such as Education and Health. In the wake of the BICI (Bassiouni) report, there has been only token progress by the government in reversing these trends; many of its recently created institutions are hollow and devoid of real authority. Key sectors of governance remain bastions of sectarian discrimination. Nowhere is this more apparent than in the security realm, where Shiʿa exclusion from the military and police forces continues to be a major driver of dissent.

Social media in Bahrain has developed into an especially contested field, with parliamentarians, officials, and commentators on both sides resorting to increasingly vicious attacks. Yet much of the blame for sectarian vitriol on Twitter and Facebook falls squarely on the shoulders of the regime, which made use of these platforms to delegitimize demands for reform, while at the same time, ironically, warning the country's youth to avoid excessive reliance on them.

In Saudi Arabia, sectarianism has been formalized in a wide array of institutions, ranging from the Senior Ulema Council, the judiciary, schools, and the media. As a result of worsening tensions in the region, sectarian partisanship in these fields escalated. Nowhere was this more apparent than in the clerical establishment and the array of websites and satellite TV channels associated with prominent Salafi figures. Even the mainstream media adopted a sectarian discourse, particularly during periods of heightened Saudi–Iranian confrontation and during episodes of unrest in the East, such as the aftermath of the Medina riots and the shooting and arrest of Nimr al-Nimr. The net effect of this "static" was highly toxic, undermining the royal family's claims of reform and sowing distrust in the Eastern Province. At the same time, however, Eastern Province youth have used Twitter to engage with Sunni youth across the country, demonstrating how social media can also bridge the sectarian divide.

Much of the frustration that fueled the unrest of 2011 in the Eastern Province can be traced to the failure of institutional reforms to live up to their promise. In 2009, for example, a cabinet reshuffle created unmet expectations about Shiʿa representation in the Senior Ulema Council. By nearly any account—from Shiʿa youth to clerics to intellectuals—King ʿAbdallah's reform initiatives, such as the National Dialogue and the National Society for Human Rights, proved to be fundamentally cosmetic. The municipal council elections similarly raised hopes about improvements to local administration in the East, but they, too, proved to be a disappointment, with ultimate power remaining in the hands of the governor of the Eastern Province and in the Ministry of Interior.

What distinguishes Kuwait from Bahrain and Saudi Arabia are the cooptive and accommodative resources available to the ruling family. Most important, the Al Sabah's legitimacy has long rested on a symbiotic relationship with powerful societal segments, especially the Shiʿa merchant sector. In the post-2003 era, the greatest threat to Kuwaiti stability and a major enabler of sectarianism came not from Shiʿa political or economic marginalization, but from Kuwaiti tribes and Salafis, who felt excluded from the urban "center" and grew increasingly resentful of the alliance between the Al Sahah and the Shiʿa merchant class.

Kuwait's quasi-democratic structures and media freedom proved to be a mixed blessing in the midst of this tension. On the one hand, they provided a pressure release for sectarian passions and a buffer against the ripple effects of the Iraq War and growing alarm over Iran. On the other hand, this very openness seemed to encourage and harden sectarian identities in the emirate—a paradox that frequently occupied Kuwaiti commentators in the press. This Janus-face quality was particularly evident in the social media realm, where Twitter had arguably eclipsed the *diwaniya* as a political and social forum. In the wake of the Arab uprisings of 2011, Twitter content seemed to be inflaming sectarian tensions, with the government playing the heavy-handed role of arbiter by criminalizing insults to either sect (as well as to the ruling family).

Parliamentary dynamics in Kuwait became increasingly rife with sectarian tensions after the 2008 elections, which saw a campaign by tribal Salafis to bring down the government of the prime minister, whom it accused of neglecting Kuwait's rural *badu*. The resulting gridlock in the Parliament was not so much the result of any shift in strategy by the Shiʿa or their susceptibility to transnational influences. Rather, it was rooted in local power dynamics unique to Kuwait—the struggle between the *badu* and the *hadhar* as well as between the emergent Salafi opposition and the prime minister. Sectarianism was deployed as the vocabulary in this struggle but was not its immediate cause.

This dynamic became even more evident in the 2011 Arab uprisings' manifestation in Kuwait—a markedly nonsectarian, external event that some domestic actors nonetheless interpreted through a sectarian lens. The fact that the Kuwaiti prime minister adopted a somewhat neutral stance toward the intervention of the Peninsula Shield forces in Bahrain, sending only a token amount of Kuwaiti assistance (and no ground troops), provides an important illustration of how domestic sectarian tensions constrain foreign-policy choices. The decision also exposed him to even fiercer attacks by the Salafi parliamentary opposition.

By the end of 2012, the Kuwaiti regime, like other regimes, had played the sectarian card, co-opting Shiʿa candidates to counter the parliamentary boycott of the mostly Sunni-led opposition.

Sectarianism, this study has demonstrated, is not an inescapable facet of political life in the Gulf—or, for that matter, the rest of the Middle East. Rather, it arises from a combination of exclusionary policies at home and regional shocks from abroad, both of which have been highly damaging to the Gulf's social fabric and to Gulf regimes' long-term stability. In many respects, the persistence of Sunni–Shiʻa tensions is ultimately a bellwether for the deeply entrenched problems of governance in the Gulf: the legitimacy deficit of ruling families, feeble participatory institutions, and the uneven distribution of political and economic capital. It is these deficiencies—rather than the Shiʻa's national loyalty, doctrinal differences between Islamic sects, or the influence of outside actors such as Iran—that should properly guide the efforts of those who seek to move the region forward.

NOTES

INTRODUCTION

1. "Al-Sira' al-ta'ifi fi al-'Iraq wa al-mintaqa" (The Sectarian Conflict in Iraq and the Region), al-Jazeera, *Bila hudud* (Without Borders) program, aired January 20, 2007, http://www.aljazeera.net/NR/exeres/0CC386B3-DF0D -42B3-8F80-C26148784DE8. See also 'Abd al-Rahman al-Rashid, "Li-hadhihi al-asbab, nakhsha Iran" (For These Reasons, We Fear Iran), *al-Sharq al-Awsat*, April 18, 2006; Mishari al-Dhaydi, "Uhadhir 'an taqdi 'alihi al-'ama'im" (I Warn Against the Religious Establishment), *al-Sharq al-Awsat*, July 19, 2007. For a Shi'a counterperspective, see Hamza Hassan, "'Alaqa Shi'a al-Saudiyya al-kharijiyya madhhabiyyan wa siyasiyyan" (The Political and Sectarian Foreign Relations of the Saudi Shi'a), al-Jazeera, October 3, 2004, http://www .aljazeera.net/NR/exeres/F79762CF-6D0D-471A-AA57-6BD052C9240A.htm; and 'Abd al-Aziz al-Tuwayjri, "Iran wa al-siyasat al-ta'ifiyya" (Iran and Sectarian Policies), *al-Hayat*, August 29, 2012.

2. Bayna al-Malham, "Mufa'il Iran fi al-Khalij: Man ash'al al-fatil?" (Iran's Reactor in the Gulf . . . Who Lit the Fuse?), al-'Arabiya website, July 15, 2012, http://www.alarabiya.net/views/2012/07/15/226385.html.

3. Muhammad bin 'Abd al-Latif al-Shaykh, "Lajm al-ta'ifiyya darrura mulihha" (Curbing Sectarianism Is an Urgent Necessity), al-'Arabiya television

website, August 5, 2012, http://www.alarabiya.net/views/2012/08/05/230540.html.

4. Muhammad Gamal Arafa, "Al-ʿIraq . . . al-harb al-taʾifiyya didd al-Sunna badaʾat rasmiyyan!" (Iraq: The Sectarian War Against the Sunnis Has Officially Begun!), al-Muslim website, January 2006, http://www.almoslim.net/node/85786.

5. ʿAbd al-Aziz al-Tuwayjri, "Tawatuʾ bayn al-quwa al-mutasarʾa" (Collusion Between the Rival Forces), *al-Hayat*, August 9, 2012.

6. Halima Muzaffar, "Shuyukh 'Twitter' am shuyukh 'tawattur'?" (Twitter Shaykhs or Tension Shaykhs?), al-ʿArabiya television website, September 26, 2012; Hamud Hamud, "Al-tawtalitariyya am al-taʾifiyya" (Totalitarianism or Sectarianism), *al-Hayat*, May 20, 2012.

7. Mishari al-Dhaydi, "Al-taʾifiyya wa al-tuyuf al-siyasiyya" (Sectarianism and the Political Spectrum), *al-Sharq al-Awsat*, January 9, 2007. See also Majid Kayali, "Fi ma yukhass al-masaʾla al-taʾifiyya" (Regarding the Issue of Sectarianism), *al-Hayat*, July 13, 2012.

8. Vali Nasr, *The Shiʿa Revival: How Conflicts Within Islam Will Shape the Future* (London: Norton, 2007).

9. This line of thinking is reflected in Yitzhak Nakash, "The Shiʿites and the Future of Iraq," *Foreign Affairs* 82, no. 4 (July–August 2003): 17–26.

10. The most notorious example of this view is the twenty-four-slide Powerpoint briefing to a Pentagon advisory panel by French-born defense analyst Laurent Murawiec, which argued for the effective partition of Saudi Arabia and the creation of a separate state in the Eastern Province. Thomas E. Ricks, "Briefing Depicted Saudis as Enemies," *Washington Post*, August 6, 2002.

11. As Francis Fukuyama notes, "The problem with the current Middle East debate is it's completely stuck. Nobody knows what to do. Vali Nasr offers a plausible alternative that may gain traction." Quoted in Peter Waldman, "Rising Academic Sees Sectarian Split Inflaming Middle East," *Wall Street Journal*, August 8, 2006.

12. Vali Nasr, "The Dangers Lurking in the Arab Spring," *New York Times*, August 27, 2011. See also Edward Luttwak, "Revenge of the Sunnis," *Foreign Policy*, December 7, 2011. For the argument that Iran is poised to exploit the Arab revolts, see Michael Scott Doran, "The Heirs of Nasser: Who Will Benefit from the Second Arab Revolution?" *Foreign Affairs* 90, no. 3 (2011): 17–25.

13. See Neil McFarquhar, "U.S. Sees Sunni Gains as Way to Isolate Iran," *New York Times*, November 28, 2012.

14. Author's interview with a Saudi reformist, Riyadh, Saudi Arabia, February 13, 2013.

1. GOVERNANCE, SOCIETY, AND IDENTITY IN THE GULF

1. For explanations of Gulf regimes' longevity, see Michael Herb, *All in the Family: Absolutism, Revolution, and Democracy in the Middle Eastern Monarchies* (New York: New York University Press, 1999); Gerd Nonneman, "Security and Inclusion: Regime Responses to Domestic Challenges in the Gulf," in Sean McKnight, Niel Partrick, and Francis Toase, eds., *Gulf Security: Opportunities and Challenges for the New Generation* (London: Royal United Services Institute, September 2000), 107–117; Anoushirvan Ehteshami, "Reform from Above: The Politics of Participation in the Oil Monarchies," *International Affairs* 79, no. 1 (2003): 53–75.

2. Kristian Coates Ulrichsen, "Internal and External Security in the Gulf," *Middle East Policy* 16, no. 2 (2009): 39–58.

3. F. Gregory Gause III, *The International Relations of the Persian Gulf* (New York: Cambridge University Press, 2010), 6–7. Gulf Arab authors themselves have echoed this paradigm, albeit with a more realist, balance-of-power approach. For an example, see ʿAbd al-Jalil Zaid al-Marhun, *Al-amn al-khaliji baʿd al-harb fi al-ʿIraq* (Gulf Security After the Iraq War) (Riyadh: Institute for Diplomatic Studies, 2005); and Gamil Matar and ʿAli al-Din al-Hilal Dessouki, *Al-nidham al-iqlimi al-ʿArabi* (The Arab Regional Order) (Beirut: Dar al-Mustaqbal al-ʿArabi, 1983).

4. F. Gregory Gause III makes this argument in "Threats and Threat Perception in the Gulf," *Middle East Policy* 14, no. 2 (2007), 123, and in "Saudi Arabia: Iraq, Iran, the Regional Power Balance, and the Sectarian Question," *Strategic Insights* 6, no. 2 (2007), http://www.isn.ethz.ch/isn/Digital-Library/Publications/Detail/?ots591=0c54e3b3-1e9c-be1e-2c24-a6a8c7060233&lng=en&id=30985.

5. Morten Valbjørn and André Bank, "Signs of a New Arab Cold War: The 2006 Lebanon War and the Sunni–Shiʿi Divide," *Middle East Report* 242 (Spring 2007), 7.

6. Gerd Nonneman notes the demonstration of effect of political liberalization in the Gulf context in "Political Reform in the Gulf Monarchies: From Liberalization to Democratization? A Comparative Perspective," in Anoushiravan Ehteshami and Steven Wright, eds., *Reform in the Middle East Oil Monarchies* (New York: Ithaca Press, 2008), 26. He writes, "The regional environment is important in a number of ways. The effects can either enhance or inhibit the prospects for political reform; they can do so either by affecting elites' perceptions or calculations or by influencing popular perceptions and aspirations; and they can arise from, and affect, both material facts/interests and ideas."

7. This is particularly the case in Bahrain, where much of the Shiʿa opposition has been class based.

8. Ulrichsen, "Internal and External Security in the Gulf," 44.

9. Hassan al-Saffar, *Al-madhhab wa al-watan* (Sect and Homeland) (Beirut: al-Muʾassasa al-ʿArabiyya lil-Dirasat wa al-Nashr, 2006), 85. The term *madhhab* refers to the four traditional schools of Islamic jurisprudence: Hanbali, Shafiʿi, Maliki, and Hanafi—each exhibiting distinctive legal interpretations of the canonical Islamic sources. In other instances, it is used to denote a specific sect or current within Islam—that is, Shiʿa or Sufi.

10. Author's interview with a Shiʿa activist, Qatif, Saudi Arabia, March 5, 2007. The "Partners in One Nation" document ("Al-shurakaʾ fi al-watan al-wahid"), April 30, 2003, was an important cross-sectarian petition submitted to the Saudi king by Shiʿa and Sunni oppositionists, intended to preempt any accusations of disloyalty in light of the impending U.S. invasion of Iraq.

11. For more on this question in the Gulf context, see Faisal al-Salem, "The Issue of Identity in Selected Arab Gulf States," *Journal of South Asian and Middle Eastern Studies* 4 (Summer 1981): 21–32; and Ghassan Salamé, "Perceived Threats and Perceived Loyalties," in B. R. Pridham, ed., *The Arab Gulf and the Arab World* (London: Croom Helm, 1988), 235–250.

12. The exception is Oman, which is ruled over by the Ibadis, a sect that is doctrinally distinct from both Sunnism and Shiʿism.

13. Michael Herb, "Subordinate Communities and the Utility of Ethnic Ties to a Neighboring Regime: Iran and the Shiʿa of the Arab States of the Gulf," in Leonard Binder, ed., *Ethnic Conflict and International Politics of the Middle East* (Gainesville: University Press of Florida Press, 1999), 159.

14. For a provocative exploration of these efforts, see Christopher M. Davidson, *After the Sheikhs: The Coming Collapse of the Gulf Monarchies* (London: Hurst, 2012).

15. Neil Partrick, *Nationalism in the Gulf States* (London: Kuwait Programme on Development, Governance, and Globalisation in the Gulf States, London School of Economics, October 2009).

16. Paul Aarts, *The Internal and the External: The House of Saud's Resilience Explained*, Mediterranean Programme Series Working Paper no. 2004/332004 (Montecatini, Italy: Robert Schuman Centre for Advanced Studies, European University Institute, 2004).

17. For an example, see the interview with Shi'a cleric Hassan al-Nimr, al-Rasid, August 16, 2006, http://www.rasid.com/artc.php?id=12371. This information also comes from author's interviews with various individuals in Manama, Bahrain, and Riyadh, Saudi Arabia, November 2006 and March 2007, respectively.

18. Author's interviews with officials in Manama, Bahrain, November 2006, and Riyadh, Saudi Arabia, March 2007. For representative examples from the local media, see 'Abdallah al-Askar, "Al-ta'ifiyya fi al-Khalij" (Sectarianism in the Gulf), *al-Riyadh*, June 20, 2007; Karim 'Abed, "Khalfiyat wa ahdaf al-tadakhkhul al-Irani fi al-'Iraq" (The Background and Objectives of the Iranian Interference in Iraq), *al-Hayat*, May 20, 2007; 'Abd al-Rahman al-Rashid, "Li-hadhihi al-asbab naksha Iran" (For These Reasons We Fear Iran), *al-Sharq al-Awsat*, April 18, 2006; Ghassan Charbel, "Iran al-kha'ifa . . . wa al-mukhifa" (Iran: Fearful and Feared), *al-Hayat*, January 17, 2008, http://www.daralhayat.com/opinion/editorials/01-2008/Item-20080116-84559eef-c0a8-10ed-01ae-81ab20e27512/story.html.

19. Saud Sirhan, "Nahwa marja'iya Shi'a mustaqlila fi al-Khalij" (Toward an Independent Shi'a Source of Emulation in the Gulf), *al-Sharq al-Awsat*, February 24, 2003; Hassan al-Saffar, "La wa lan naqbil aya' marja'an takfiriyan wa narfud tadakhkhul aya' marja' fi al-shu'un al-siyasi al-dakhili li-biladina" (We Do Not and Will Not Welcome Any *Marja'* That Promotes Excommunication and We Oppose the Interference of Any *Marja'* in the Internal Political Affairs of Our Country), *al-Risalah*, February 16, 2007.

20. This argument is developed in F. Gregory Gause III, "Revolutionary Fevers and Regional Contagion: Domestic Structures and the 'Export' of Revolution

in the Middle East," *Journal of South Asian and Middle Eastern Studies* 14, no. 3 (1991): 1–23.

21. A member of the appointed Consultative Council conveyed this view in an interview by the author in Manana, Bahrain, November 12, 2006. This individual noted that the "king is above sectarian passions" and that the Consultative Council is a "buffer" against sectarianism. See also Frederic Wehrey, "Bahrain: Elections and Managing Sectarianism," *Arab Reform Bulletin* (Carnegie Endowment for International Peace), December 2006, http://www .carnegieendowment.org/files/wehrey.pdf; Abdulhadi Khalaf, "Contentious Politics in Bahrain: From Ethnic to National and Vice Versa," paper presented at the Fourth Nordic Conference on Middle Eastern Studies, "The Middle East in a Globalizing World," Oslo, August 13–16, 1998, http://www.smi.uib.no/ pao/khalaf.html (as of June 10, 2007).

22. Khalaf, "Contentious Politics in Bahrain." See also Munira Fakhro, "The Uprising in Bahrain: An Assessment," in Gary Sick and Lawrence Potter, eds., *The Persian Gulf at the Millennium: Essays in Politics, Economy, Security, and Religion* (New York: Palgrave Macmillan, 1997), 168–188; Fred H. Lawson, "Repertoires of Contention in Contemporary Bahrain," in Quintan Wiktorowicz, ed., *Islamic Activism: A Social Movement Theory Approach* (Bloomington: Indiana University Press, 2003), 89–111; Graham Fuller and Rend Rahim Francke, *The Arab Shiʿa: The Forgotten Muslims* (New York: Palgrave Macmillian, 1999), 121–154. On the continued importance of the 1973 Constitution, see Herb, *All in the Family*, 173–177. This sentiment was also borne out during the author's discussions with Shiʿite and liberal activists in Bahrain on the eve of the November 2006 parliamentary elections.

23. Khalaf, "Contentious Politics in Bahrain."

24. Katja Niethammer, *Voices in Parliament, Debates in Majalis, and Banners on Streets: Avenues of Political Participation in Bahrain*, Mediterranean Programme Series no. 27 (Montecatini, Italy: Robert Schuman Center for Advanced Studies, European University Institute, September 2006), 2.

25. ʿAbd al-Nabi al-Ekri, "Bahrain: Reform Project: Prospect and Limitations," paper presented at the Sixth Mediterranean Social and Political Research Meeting, Robert Schuman Centre for Advanced Studies, European University Institute, Montecatini, Italy, March 16–20, 2005.

26. Author's interview with a Bahraini sociologist, Manama, Bahrain, November 11, 2006.

27. International Crisis Group (ICG), *Bahrain's Sectarian Challenge*, ICG Middle East Report no. 40 (Brussels: ICG, May 6, 2005), 7.

28. Niethammer, *Voices in Parliament*, 5. According to one activist, the Parliament cannot formally introduce legislation but rather "propose a wish" (*iqtarah raghba*) to the Consultative Council. Author's interview with a Shiʿa activist, Manama, Bahrain, November 8, 2006.

29. Pew Forum on Religion and Public Life, "The Future of the Global Muslim Population," January 17, 2011, http://pewforum.org/future-of-the-global -muslim-population-sunni-and-shia.aspx. Bahrain does not account for sectarian affiliation in its official census.

30. J. E. Peterson, "Bahrain: Reform—Promise and Reality," in Joshua Teitelbaum, ed., *Political Liberalization in the Persian Gulf* (New York: Columbia University Press, 2009), 180.

31. Yitzhak Nakash, *Reaching for Power: The Shiʿa in the Modern Arab World* (Princeton, N.J.: Princeton University Press, 2006), 54–71.

32. Author's interview with a Bahraini activist, Manama, Bahrain, February 25, 2012. See also Fuad I. Khuri, *Tribe and State in Bahrain: The Transformation of Social and Political Authority in an Arab State* (Chicago: University of Chicago Press, 1980), 4–11. Among Bahraini Sunnis, there are important distinctions as well—between tribal Arabs of the Najd, nontribal Arabs, and the *hawala*. The Arab tribes from the peninsula are linked by marriage to the ruling Al Khalifa and accompanied the Al Khalifa to Bahrain in 1783. It is no surprise that this class occupies key posts in the government, military, business, and bureaucracy. They tend to be vigorous opponents of concessions to the Shiʿa. The nontribal Arabs from the Najd are those Sunni Arabs who, although not enjoying tribal pedigree and not linked to the Al Khalifa, still enjoy preferential status. The Najdi, nontribal Arabs, constitute the bulk of Bahrain's Salafi movement and are also involved in banking and business. The so-called *hawala* (derived from the Arabic verb for "to revert back") are composed of Sunni Arabs who migrated to western Iran and then returned to Bahrain. The *hawala* tend to be prominent businesspeople who coexist with the Shiʿa in mixed neighborhoods such as Muharraq and evince a more accommodating attitude toward the Shiʿa than the tribal and Najdi Sunni Arabs. Membership in the Bahraini Muslim Brotherhood is drawn overwhelmingly from the *hawala*.

33. Uzi Rabi and Joseph Kostiner, "The Shiʿis in Bahrain: Class and Religious Protest," in Ofra Bengio and Gabriel Ben-Dor, eds., *Minorities and the State in the*

Arab World (Boulder, Colo.: Lynne Rienner, 1999), 184. For more on the economic roots of Shiʿa dissent in Bahrain, see Louay Bahry, "The Socioeconomic
Foundations of the Shiʿite Opposition in Bahrain," *Mediterranean Quarterly*
11, no. 3 (2000): 129–143.

34. For accounts of the uprising, see, Munira Fakhro, "The Uprising in Bahrain:
An Assessment," in Sick and Potter, eds., *The Persian Gulf at the Millennium*,
167–188; Lawson, "Repertoires of Contention in Contemporary Bahrain";
Fuller and Francke, *The Arab Shiʿa*, 121–154.

35. Fred Lawson's study of "repertoires of contention" in Bahrain attaches primacy to these economic drivers, and downplays perceptions of a democracy
defecit, sectarian motives or views of regime illegitimacy. Lawson, "Repertoires of Contention in Contemporary Bahrain," 91–94.

36. Ibid., 105.

37. Author's interview with a Shiʿa activist, Sitra, Bahrain, November 14, 2006.

38. For more on Salafism and its manifestation in the Saudi context, see Hamid
Algar, *Wahhabism: A Critical Essay* (North Haledon, N.J.: Islamic Publications
International, 2002), 31–36; Khalid Abou El-Fadl, *The Great Theft* (San Francisco: Harper Collins, 2005), 45–94; Oliver Roy, *Globalized Islam: The Search
for a New Ummah* (New York: Columbia University Press, 2004), 232–289;
Mansur al-Nuqaydan, "Al-kharita al-Islamiyya fi al-Saʿudiyya wa qadiyat al-
takfir" (The Islamist Map in Saudi Arabia and the Question of Excommunication), *al-Wasat* (Bahrain), February 28, 2003.

39. Saʿud al-Qahtani, "Al-Sahwa al-Islamiyya" (The Islamic Awakening), *Gulf
Issues*, December 23, 2003, http://www.gulfissues.net/mpage/gulfarticles/
article53-1.htm; Toby Craig Jones, "The Clerics, the *Sahwa*, and the Saudi State,"
Strategic Insights 4, no. 3 (2005), http://www.ccc.nps.navy.mil/si/2005/Mar/
jonesMar05.asp; Stéphane Lacroix, *Awakening Islam: The Politics of Religious
Dissent in Saudi Arabia* (Cambridge, Mass.: Harvard University Press, 2011).

40. David Commins, *The Wahhabi Mission and Saudi Arabia* (New York: Tauris,
2006), 181–183. The first petition was signed by more than four hundred religious scholars.

41. It is important not to overcharacterize these early demands as democratic in
nature. As Michael Herb notes, "The writers of the *mudhakirat* (memoranda)
did not call for elections and little in their program can be described as liberal." Herb, *All in the Family*, 171.

42. Gwenn Okruhlik, "Networks of Dissent: Islamism and Reform in Saudi Arabia," *Current History*, January 2002, 26.

43. Author's discussion with noted Salafi reformer, Riyadh, Saudi Arabia, March 13, 2007.

44. Thomas Hegghammer and Stéphane Lacroix note that, "[i]deologically, bin Ladin was at heart a *Sahwist*, whose views were shaped by (Safar) al-Hawali." ICG, *Saudi Arabia Backgrounder: Who Are the Islamists?* ICG Middle East Report no. 31 (Brussels: ICG, 2004), 6.

45. The membership currently stands at 140.

46. Author's discussion with Jedda-based reformist and political science professor, Jedda, Saudi Arabia, March 6, 2007, and with an Eastern Province activist, Saudi Arabia, March 15, 2007.

47. Pew Forum on Religion and Public Life, "The Future of the Global Muslim Population," January 17, 2011, http://pewforum.org/future-of-the-global -muslim-population-sunni-and-shia.aspx.

48. Author's interviews with Shi'a activists, Eastern Province, Saudi Arabia, March 2007. See also Madawi al-Rasheed, "The Shi'a of Saudi Arabia: A Minority in Search of Cultural Authenticity," *British Journal of Middle Eastern Studies* 25, no. 1 (1998): 121–138.

49. Human Rights Watch, *Denied Dignity: Systematic Discrimination and Hostility Toward Saudi Shi'a Citizens* (New York: Human Rights Watch, September 2009); Toby Craig Jones, "Saudi Arabia's Not So New Anti-Shi'ism," *Middle East Report* 242 (Spring 2007): 29–32; and the "Human Rights Reports" issued by the Saudi Shi'a newspaper *al-Rasid*, December 2005 and April 2007.

50. Fouad Ibrahim, *The Shi'is of Saudi Arabia* (London: Saqi Books, 2006), 140–177.

51. Al-Rasheed, "The Shi'a of Saudi Arabia," 130–134.

52. Some of these disagreements stem from longstanding tensions among the major Shi'a families and notables of the Eastern Province.

53. For an overview, see Frederic Wehrey, "Eastern Promises: Will Change Come to Saudi Arabia's Shia Minority?" *Sada* (Carnegie Endowment for International Peace), February 12, 2013, http://carnegieendowment.org/sada/2013/02/12/ eastern-promises/ffnh.

54. Mary Ann Tétreault has noted that "sectarianism remains an important mobilizing force for Sunni Kuwaitis." Mary Ann Tétreault, *Stories of Democracy*:

Politics and Society in Contemporary Kuwait (New York: Columbia University Press, 2000), 119. Echoing this point, Jill Crystal notes that "one of the most important divisions in Kuwait is the sectarian division between Sunni and Shi'a." Jill Crystal, *Kuwait: The Transformation of an Oil State* (Boulder, Colo.: Westview Press, 1992), 76.

55. As Lori Plotkin Boghardt notes, "Regional events have inspired particular communities in Kuwait to challenge Kuwaiti rulers' policies, practices and legitimacy." Laurie Plotkin Boghardt, *Kuwait Amid War, Peace, and Revolution: 1979–1991 and New Challenges* (London: St. Antony's College and Palgrave MacMillan, 2007), 11.

56. For example, in its first week of independence in 1991 the tiny emirate was faced with the threat of annexation from Iraq. See 'Abdul-Reda Assiri, *Kuwait's Foreign Policy: A City-State in World Politics* (Boulder, Colo.: Westview Press, 1990), 7.

57. The process of Kuwait's steps toward reform is covered in Paul Salem, *Kuwait: Politics in a Participatory Emirate* (Washington, D.C.: Carnegie Endowment for International Peace, July 2007).

58. Michael Herb, "Kuwait: The Obstacle of Parliamentary Politics," in Teitelbaum, ed., *Political Liberalization in the Persian Gulf*, 133.

59. Mary Ann Tétreault, "Kuwait: Slouching Toward Democracy?" in Teitelbaum, ed., *Political Liberalization in the Persian Gulf*, 127.

60. Anh Nga Longva, "Nationalism in Pre-modern Guise: The Discourse on *Hadhar* and *Badu* in Kuwait," *International Journal of Middle East Studies* 38 (2006): 171–187. The *hadhar* are also known as *ahl al-sur*, or "people of the wall," whereas the *badu* are called *kharij al-sur*, "beyond the wall."

61. Author's interview with Shi'a human rights activist, Kuwait City, Kuwait, February 2006. See also Fuller and Francke, *The Arab Shi'a*, 159.

2. THE LONG SHADOW OF THE IRANIAN REVOLUTION

1. Examples include Radhi al-Musawi, "Thalathun 'aman ba'd al-Thawra al-Iraniya" (Thirty Years After the Iranian Revolution), *al-Waqt*, February 5, 2009; and Muhammed Alush, "Taftit al-'Iraq wa matamih Iran fi al-Khalij" (The Fragmentation of Iraq and Iran's Ambitions in the Gulf), *Majallat al-'Asr*, November 5, 2006.

2. Abd al-Rahman al-Rashid, "Escalating Sectarian Conflicts," *al-Sharq al-Awsat* (English ed.), October 3, 2010; Muammar Fawzi Khalil, "Mustaqbal al-Shiʿa fi al-Khalij" (The Future of the Shiʿa in the Gulf), al-Muslim website, June 2, 2003, http://albainah.net/index.aspx?function=Item&id=1236&lang=. A representative example includes a rich media debate over the Iraq War's impact on the Gulf: "Al-sira' al-taʾifi fi al-Iraq wa al-mintaqa" (The Sectarian Conflict in Iraq and the Region), *Bila Hudud* (Without Borders), al-Jazeera television, January 20, 2007, http://www.aljazeera.net/NR/exeres/0CC386B3-DF0D-42B3-8F80-C26148784DE8; Abed al-Ilah Bilqaziz, "Al-ʿArab wa Iran: Min al-ummah ila al-madhhab" (The Arabs and Iran: From the *Umma* to the Sect), National Justice Movement (Harakat al-ʿAdalah al-Watanya), February 20, 2007, http://www.3dala.org/print.php?id=1313&PHPSESSID=abaf5e a087b1cf63bfbe02d8776a2db0; "Al-nufudh al-Irani fi al-mintaqa al-ʿArabiya" (The Iranian Influence in the Arab Region), *Al-Ittijah al Muʿakis* (Opposite Direction), al-Jazeera, February 4, 2007, http://www.aljazeera.net/NR/exeres/7CD25C46-A887-424E-AB08-BCCA7EF0FD25; ʿAbdallah al-ʿAskar, "Al-taʾifiya fi al-Khalij lam wa lan taʿarif al-harb al-taʾifiya fi al-Khalij" (Sectarianism in the Gulf Does Not Mean a Sectarian War in the Gulf), *al-Riyadh*, July 20, 2007.

3. Abdulhadi Khalaf, "Contentious Politics in Bahrain: From Ethnic to National and Vice Versa," paper presented at the Fourth Nordic Conference on Middle Eastern Studies, "The Middle East in a Globalizing World," Oslo, August 13–16, 1998, http://www.smi.uib.no/pao/khalaf.html, accessed June 10, 2007.

4. The state security law was presented as a measure against communism, and a strong appeal was made to solicit the support of conservative Islamists on the grounds that communism was "heretical." Another important tactic used by the regime was its reliance on a constitutional stipulation that all fourteen ministers be ex officio full members of the Parliament. See Khalaf, "Contentious Politics in Bahrain."

5. Fuad Khuri, *Tribe and State in Bahrain: The Transformation of Social and Political Authority in an Arab State* (Chicago: University of Chicago Press, 1980), 231–233; Uzi Rabi and Joseph Kostiner, "The Shiʿis in Bahrain: Class and Religious Protest," in Ofra Bengio and Gabriel Ben-Dor, eds., *Minorities and the State in the Arab World* (Boulder, Colo.: Lynne Rienner, 1999), 180–187.

6. Author's interviews with an official of Haq and an al-Wifaq activist, Manama, Bahrain, November 15–16, 2006.

7. Toby Craig Jones, "Rebellion on the Saudi Periphery: Modernity, Marginalization, and the Shiʿa Uprising of 1979," *International Journal of Middle East Studies* 38 (2006), 217–222.

8. Najib al-Khunayzi, "Tanshit siyasi al-Shiʿa fi al-Saʿudiyya" (Political Activism of the Saudi Shiʿa), *al-Jazirah*, June 2, 2002.

9. Jones, "Rebellion on the Saudi Periphery," 218, citing a pamphlet by the OIR.

10. Hassan al-Saffar, *Al-madhhab wa al-watan* (Sect and Homeland) (Beirut: al-Muʾassasa al-ʿArabiyya lil-Dirasat wa al-Nashr, 2006), 122, 166.

11. Madawi al-Rasheed, "The Shiʿa of Saudi Arabia: A Minority in Search of Cultural Authenticity," *British Journal of Middle Eastern Studies* 25, no. 1 (1998), 122. Many of the Saudi Shiʿa ARAMCO workers developed labor activism skills through contact with Bahraini oil workers who sought work in Saudi Arabia after the decline of Bahraini oil reserves. Ibrahim al-Hatlani, *Al-Shiʿa al-Saʿudiyyun: Qiraʿa tarikhiya wa siyasiya li-namadhij matlabiya* (The Shiʿa of Saudi Arabia: A Historical and Political Inquiry Into Patterns of Activism) (Beirut: Dar Riyad al-Rayyis, 2009), 141–150.

12. Author's interview with Saudi Shiʿa dissident, United States, May 24, 2011.

13. Jones, "Rebellion on the Saudi Periphery," 217.

14. Moojan Momen, *An Introduction to Shiʿi Islam: The History and Doctrines of Twelver Shiʿism* (New Haven, Conn.: Yale University Press, 1987), 127.

15. Author's interview with Saudi Shiʿa activist, United States, June 2011.

16. Lori Plotkin Boghardt, *Kuwait Amid War, Peace, and Revolution, 1979–1991 and New Challenges* (London: St. Antony's College and Palgrave Macmillan, 2007), 32; Abdul-Reda Assiri, *Kuwait's Foreign Policy: City-State in World Politics* (Boulder, Colo.: Westview Press, 1990), 66.

17. Boghardt, *Kuwait Amid War, Peace, and Revolution*, 32.

18. Author's interviews with a Kuwaiti academic, Kuwait City, Kuwait, December 12, 2010, and a Shiʿa MP, Kuwait City, Kuwait, December 8, 2010. Even worse from the Shiʿa perspective, in the fall of 1979 the royal family outlawed *diwaniya* gatherings that exceeded twenty people. Although not explicitly anti-Shiʿa in nature, the measure nonetheless deprived the Shiʿa of an important civil society venue.

19. As F. Gregory Gause III notes, "[The] trend of increasing state capacities to control society paid off for regimes during the 1980s as they scrambled to meet the threats posed by the Iranian Revolution as ideology and the

revolutionary state." F. Gregory Gause III, "Revolutionary Fevers and Regional Contagion: Domestic Structures and the 'Export' of Revolution in the Middle East," *Journal of South Asian and Middle Eastern Studies* 14, no. 3 (1991), 17.

20. R. K. Ramazani, "Iran's Export of the Revolution: Politics, Ends, and Means," in John L. Esposito, ed., *The Iranian Revolution: Its Global Impact*, 40–62 (Miami: Florida International University Press, 1990).

21. Joseph Kostiner, "Shiʿi Unrest in the Gulf," in Martin Kramer, ed., *Shiʿism, Resistance, and Revolution* (Boulder, Colo.: Westview Press, 1987), 178.

22. Laurence Louër, *Transnational Shiʿa Politics: Religious and Political Networks in the Gulf* (London: Hurst, 2008), 179.

23. Tobias Matthiesen, "Hizbullah al-Hijaz: A History of the Most Radical Saudi Shiʿa Opposition Group," *Middle East Journal* 64, no. 2 (2010), 182.

24. Pars News Agency, "Interview with Arabian Peninsula Organization Member," *BBC Summary of World News Broadcast*, August 7, 1980.

25. Matthiesen, "Hizbullah al-Hijaz," 184. According to a former member of the OIR, Iran wanted to use the OIR to conduct a retaliatory attack against the Saudi government following the deaths of Iranian pilgrims during hajj riots in 1987. Al-Saffar refused, thus chilling relations with Tehran. Author's interview with a Saudi Shiʿa dissident, United States, May 24, 2011.

26. For an illustration of the importance that the Islamic Republic attached to transnational media, see the Arabic tract by Ayatollah ʿAli Khamenei, *Daur wasaʾil al-aʿlam fi al-siraʿ al-siyasi wa al-thaqafi* (The Role of Media in Political and Cultural Conflict), ed. Shaykh ʿAli Dhahir (Beirut: Dar al-Hadi, 2006), 39–59. The book praises the effects of radio, TV, and other media in cultivating Islamic ideals after the revolution and deflecting Western misrepresentations of the Islamic Republic.

27. Joseph Kostiner and Toby Craig Jones point to the indigenous, communal, and populist nature of the dissent (see Kostiner, "Shiʿi Unrest in the Gulf," and Jones, "Rebellion on the Saudi Periphery"), whereas Jacob Goldberg argues that the revolution "seems to have produced a new consciousness among the Shiʿis in Hasa (al-Ahsa) and served as a model for their future conduct." Jacob Golberg, "The Shiʿi Minority in Saudi Arabia," in Juan R. I. Cole and Nikki R. Keddie, eds., *Shiʿism and Social Protest* (New Haven, Conn.: Yale University Press, 1986), 239.

28. Falah ʿAbdallah al-Mdeires, "Shiʿism and Political Protest in Bahrain," *Digest of Middle East Studies* 11, no. 1 (2002), 21–23.

29. Ibid., 30.

30. Author's interview with a Bahraini academic, Manama, Bahrain, March 3, 2012.

31. Falah ʿAbdallah al-Mdeires, *Dirasat hawl al-harakat al-Islamiyya fi al-Bahrayn, 1938–2001* (Study of Islamic Movements in Bahrain, 1938–2001) (Beirut: Dar al-Kunuz al-Adabiyya, 2004).

32. Al-Mdeires, "Shiʿism and Political Protest in Bahrain," 30.

33. See the book published by the IFLB, *Tajribat 73 sajinan fi sujun al-Bahrayn* (The Experience of the 73 Prisoners in Bahraini Prison) (n.p.: n.p., 1996), http://www.shaheed-bh.com/forumdisplay.php?f=169. For a more recent treatment, see Hasan Tariq al-Hasan, "The Role of Iran in the Failed Coup of 1981: The IFLB in Bahrain," *Middle East Journal* 65, no. 4 (2011): 603–617.

34. Munira Fakhro, "The Uprising in Bahrain: An Assessment," in Gary G. Sick and Lawrence G. Potter, eds., *The Persian Gulf at the Millennium: Essays in Politics, Economy, Security, and Religion* (New York: Palgrave Macmillan, 1997), 179–180. By the mid-1990s, the IFLB enjoyed a rebirth under the leadership of a Bahraini cleric affiliated with the Shirazi current, Shaykh Muhammad Mahfouz. Although the IFLB called for the overthrow of the Al Khalifa during the mid-1990s uprising, it subsequently adopted political participation as its strategy as part of the general amnesty offered by the new emir, Hamad, in 2002, changing its name to "Islamic Action Society" and later to "Islamic Action Movement."

35. Author's interview with Bahraini government official, Manama, Bahrain, November 10, 2006.

36. Mansur al-Jamri, "Baʿd min sanawat al-haraka al-Islamiyya al-Shiʿiya fi al-Bahrayn" (Some Years of the Shiʿa Islamist Movement in Bahrain), *al-Wasat*, August 5, 2005.

37. Author's interview with a leader of al-Wifaq, Manama, Bahrain, November 21, 2006.

38. Mansoor al-Jamri, "The Shia and the State in Bahrain: Integration and Tension," *Alternative Politics*, special issue (November 2010): 1–24.

39. Muhammad ʿIzz al-ʿArab, "Al-nukhba wa al-islah al-siyasi fi al-Bahrain" (The Elite and Choice of Political Reform in Bahrain), *Arab Journal of Democracy*,

January 1, 2010, http://democracy.ahram.org.eg/News/147/%D8%A7%D9%
84%D9%86%D8%AE%D8%A8%D8%A9-%D9%88%D8%A7%D9%84%D8%
A7%D8%B5%D9%84%D8%A7%D8%AD-%D8%A7%D9%84%D8%B3%D9%
8A%D8%A7%D8%B3%D9%8A-%D9%81%D9%8A-%D8%A7%D9%84%D8
%A8%D8%AD%D8%B1%D9%8A%D9%86.aspx. These measures did little to
alleviate the class-based grievances that fueled the uprising of 1994–1998.

40. Jones, "Rebellion on the Saudi Periphery," 216–17.

41. Author's interview with a Saudi Shiʿa activist, Qatif, Saudi Arabia, March 15,
2007. See also al-Saffar, *Al-madhhab wa al-watan*, 166–167. For the Saudi regime, this act of defiance carried particular significance, coming just days after the Juhayman al-Utayba uprising in Mecca. It also followed disturbances
in Bahrain in early September, which the Saudi regime publicly accused Iran
of inciting.

42. Jones, "Rebellion on the Saudi Periphery," 227–29.

43. Ibid., 220–21.

44. Fouad Ibrahim, *The Shiʿis of Saudi Arabia* (London: Saqi Books, 2006), 122.

45. Louër, *Transnational Shiʿa Politics*, 167.

46. Author's interview with a Saudi Shi'a activist, Qatif, Saudi Arabia, March 11,
2007.

47. Author's interview with a Shi'a cleric, Qatif, Saudi Arabia, March 15, 2007.

48. The amnesty offer included members of Hizballah al-Hijaz. Ibrahim, *The
Shiʿis of Saudi Arabia*, 178.

49. Louër, *Transnational Shiʿa Politics*, 249.

50. Ibrahim, *The Shiʿis of Saudi Arabia*, 195–196; Matthiesen, "Hizbullah al-Hijaz,"
183–185.

51. Matthiesen, "Hizbullah al-Hijaz," 188–189. A typical table of contents in *Ri-
salat al-Haramayn* included articles on U.S. policy in the Gulf, attacks on the
"Wahhabis" and the Al Saʿud, Shiʿa rituals, and Arabic poetry. The journal
featured commentary by Saudis as well as by Iraqi Shiʿa and members of
Lebanese Hizballah—apparently aimed at fostering a transnational sense of
Shiʿa political identity.

52. Today, Hizballah al-Hijaz's principal website is www.hrmain.com.

53. Author's interview with a Shi'a cleric from the Khat al-Imam, Dammam,
Saudi Arabia, March 17, 2007.

54. Louër, *Transnational Shiʿa Politics*, 166.

55. Author's interview with a senior Shi'a activist, Qatif, Saudi Arabia, March 15, 2007.

56. Author's interview with a Shi'a intellectual and writer, Qatif, Saudi Arabia, March 15, 2007.

57. As noted previously, the Parliament had been suspended since 1976.

58. Louër, *Transnational Shi'a Politics*, 173.

59. Ibid., 169–170.

60. Falah 'Abdallah al-Mdeires, *Al-haraka al-Shi'iyya fi al-Kuwait* (The Shi'a Movement in Kuwait) (Kuwait City: Dar Qurtas lil-Nashr, 1999), 156.

61. Kuwait News Agency, September 27, 1979.

62. Al-Mdeires, *Al-haraka al-Shi'iyya fi al-Kuwait*, 173.

63. Boghardt, *Kuwait Amid War, Peace, and Revolution*, 30.

64. According to Boghardt, the Kuwait government increased its deportations of Iranians from 100 in September 1979 to 421 in January 1980. Ibid., 38.

65. Al-Mdeires, *Al-haraka al-Shi'iyya fi al-Kuwait*, 175–178.

66. Ibid., 179.

67. Boghardt, *Kuwait Amid War, Peace, and Revolution*, 47.

68. Kostiner, "Shi'i Unrest in the Gulf," 181.

69. Louër, *Transnational Shi'a Politics*, 171–172.

70. Boghardt, *Kuwait Amid War, Peace, and Revolution*, 121–122.

3. DEBATING PARTICIPATION: THE BAHRAINI SHI'A AND REGIONAL INFLUENCES

1. Built in 944 C.E., the mosque is a major religious site for Shi'a, housing the remains of the revered tenth and eleventh Imams. Its golden dome was destroyed in a bombing by Sunni militants in February 2006, and the minarets were demolished in another attack in July 2007. The February 2006 bombing sparked a wave of sectarian violence in Iraq.

2. Rosemary Said Zahlan, *The Making of the Modern Gulf States* (London: Ithaca Press, 1988), 53.

3. These dissidents included Shaykh 'Isa al-Qasim, Shaykh 'Ali Salman, Sayyid Haydar al-Sitri, and Mansur al-Jamri. J. E. Peterson, "Bahrain's First Reforms Under Emir Hamad," *Asian Affairs* (London) 33, part 2 (June 2002), 222.

4. Katja Niethammer, *Voices in Parliament, Debates in Majalis, and Banners on Streets: Avenues of Political Participation in Bahrain*, Mediterranean Pro-

gramme Series no. 27 (Montecatini, Italy: Robert Schuman Center for Advanced Studies, European University Institute, September 2006).

5. Both compete for the *baharna*. A third bloc comprises Shiʿa of Persian descent, the so-called al-Ikhaʾ society. International Crisis Group (ICG), *Bahrain's Sectarian Challenge*, ICG Middle East Report no. 40 (Brussels: ICG, May 6, 2005).

6. Interview with an al-Wifaq activist, Washington, D.C., March 11, 2013. Katja Niethammer also gives this figure, citing an interview with al-Wifaq chairman ʿAli Salman. See Niethammer, *Voices in Parliament*, 17.

7. Author's interview with a senior leader in al-Wifaq, Manama, Bahrain, November 6, 2006. See also Niethammer, *Voices in Parliament*, 6.

8. For example, its leaflets and manifestos frequently refer to the "State of Bahrain" rather than to the "Kingdom of Bahrain."

9. Interlocutors in Bahrain identified three factions within al-Wifaq. The "Jamri" faction is represented by two brothers-in-law, Hadi Musawi and ʿAbd al-Jalil Khali, and is regarded as the most liberal and moderate. Their wives are daughters of the late ʿAbd al-Amir al-Jamri (1937–2006), the spiritual leader of the Bahraini Shiʿa and key luminary during the 1990s intifada. In the middle are the "Effendis," led by ʿAli Salman, Khalil Marzuq, and Mattar Ibrahim Mattar. Both of these factions are reportedly composed of *baharna*. Finally, the "Fayruz" faction consists of Jawad Fayruz and his brother, Jalal Fayruz. Both are *ʿajam* and believed to be more hard-line and closer to Iran. Author's interviews in Bahrain, February and September 2012.

10. Fred H. Lawson, "Repertoires of Contention in Contemporary Bahrain," in Quintan Wiktorowicz, ed., *Islamic Activism: A Social Movement Theory Approach* (Bloomington: Indiana University Press, 2003), 89.

11. Al-Qasim set up this council in 2005. Although in theory the council has its own board and is run by consensus, al-Qasim exerts a preponderance of influence over it. The council as a whole looks to Najaf for guidance, although al-Qasim follows Khamenei as his *marjaʿ*. For a discussion about Qasim's ambiguous views of the *marjaʿiyya*, see Sajjad H. Rizvi, "Shiʿism in Bahrain: *Marjaʿiyya* and Politics," *Orient* 4 (2009): 16–24.

12. Author's interview with an al-Wifaq activist, Manama, Bahrain, November 14, 2006.

13. In an interview, a senior al-Wifaq official noted, "The Upper House now has the upper hand. Under the 1973 Constitution, the king had three duties; now

he has twelve. The royalty sit on top of the judiciary council and the head of the council that oversees finance—these roles should properly be with the Parliament." Author's interview with ʿa senior leader of al-Wifaq, Manama, Bahrain, November 6, 2006.

14. Author's interview with a senior leader of al-Wifaq, Manama, Bahrain, November 6, 2006.

15. Author's interview with a senior leader of al-ʿAmal, Manama, Bahrain, November 12, 2006.

16. Habib Toumi, "Bahrain Shiʿite Body Accused of Bias," *Gulf News*, November 14, 2006.

17. Laurence Louër, *Transnational Shiʿa Politics: Religious and Political Networks in the Gulf* (London: Hurst, 2008), 285.

18. Mahdi Rabiʿ, "Al-Bahrayn: Al-tahaluf al-rubaʿi yashtarit ʿal-taʿdilat al-mujziya' l-khud al-intikhabat" (Bahrain: The Four-Way Alliance Requires "Reward Amendments" to Enter the Elections), *al-Hayat*, February 2, 2005.

19. Mahdi Rabi, "Bahrayn: Bawadir ishtiqaq fi al-tiyar al-Islami al-Shiʿi" (Bahrain: Signs of a Split in the Shiʿite Islamic Current), *al-Hayat*, August 24, 2004, http://international.daralhayat.com/archivearticle/53482.

20. Ibid.

21. Muhammad al-ʿAli, "Al-Wefaq to Vote on Political Societies Law Today," *Gulf Daily News*, October 6, 2005.

22. See United Nations Development Program (UNDP), *Program on Governance in the Arab World* (Paris: UNDP, May 2008), http://www.pogar.org/countries/ civil.asp?cid=2. Al-Wifaq, al-ʿAmal, and al-Waʿd also organized sit-ins to protest the new law. Muhammad al-ʿAli, "Hundreds Rally Over New Law," *Gulf Daily News*, July 30, 2005. The law also stipulated that societies could not be formed with a sectarian or religious bias, and it raised the age of participation to twenty-one. Many Shiʿa saw these stipulations as efforts to co-opt and effectively dismantle the Shiʿa opposition.

23. Edward Burke, *Bahrain: Reaching a Threshold*, Working Paper no. 61 (Madrid: Fundación para las Relaciones Internacionales y el Diálogo Exterior, June 2008), 9, 14.

24. Author's interview with an al-Waʿd official, Manama, Bahrain, November 8, 2006.

25. Ibid.

26. Walid Noueihed, "Al-ʿIraq ʿam al-ʿIraqat" (Iraq or "Iraqs"), *al-Wasat*, December 17, 2005, http://www.alwasatnews.com/1198/news/read/507263/1/%D8%A7%D8%AD%D8%AA%D9%84%D8%A7%D9%84.html. *Al-Wasat* is a centrist, semi-independent Bahraini newspaper founded in 2002 by Mansur al-Jamri, a Shiʿa activist, the son of the revered Shiʿa cleric ʿAbd al-Amir al-Jamri. Laurence Louër has noted: "The idea was to not only obtain a communiqué from the *marjaʿ* enjoining Bahrainis to participate but, more broadly, to create a process of emulation between the Bahraini and Iraqi situations that would lead Bahrainis to identify their situation with that of Iraq, where Shiʿas went in large numbers to the polls in December 2005." Louër, *Transnational Shiʿa Politics*, 289.

27. Noueihed, "Al-ʿIraq 'um al-ʿIraqat.' "

28. *Khaleej Times*, "Bahraini Shiʿites Answer Sistani Call to Protest Bombing," February 23, 2006.

29. Louër, *Transnational Shiʿa Politics*, 290.

30. Ibid., 291.

31. Haq's early founders also included prominent leftist activists such as ʿAli Rabiʿa.

32. According to one Haq member, "Al-Wifaq used fatwas in the 2006 elections because they cannot compete against us." Author's interview with a Haq official, November 9, 2006.

33. Author's interview with a Haq member, Manama, Bahrain, November 11, 2006.

34. The full report is available at http://www.bahrainrights.org/files/albandar.pdf, accessed April 18, 2011.

35. Author's interview with a Haq official, Manama, Bahrain, November 9, 2006.

36. Aside from al-Sistani's influence, Haq must compete with local clerics affiliated with al-Wifaq. Field interviews in Manama, Bahrain, on November 12, 2006, suggested that al-Wifaq-affiliated cleric ʿIsa al-Qasim visited Sitra in early April that year asking people to vote.

37. Author's interview with an Haq official, Manama, Bahrain, November 9, 2006.

38. ʿAli Rabiʿa quit Haq in mid-2009.

39. Author's interviews with Haq official, Manama, Bahrain, November 9, 2006.

40. Louër, *Transnational Shiʿa Politics*, 257.

41. Author's interview with a senior Haq member, Manama, Bahrain, November 11, 2006.

42. Louër, *Transnational Shiʿa Politics*, 257.

43. Ibid.

44. Author's interview with an al-Waʿd official, Manama, Bahrain, November 8, 2006.

45. ICG, *Bahrain's Sectarian Challenge*, 14; Niethammer, *Voices in Parliament*, 20.

46. ICG, *Bahrain's Sectarian Challenge*.

47. Author's interviews with Shiʿa activists in Manama, Bahrain, November 15–17, 2006.

48. Author's interview with a Salafi cleric and politician, Manama, Bahrain, November 10, 2006.

49. Author's interviews in Manama, Bahrain, November 15–17, 2006.

50. Author's interview with newspaper publisher, Manama, Bahrain, November 9, 2006.

51. Quoted in Salman Dossari, "Bahrayn: ʿIqaf Sheikh Salafi ʿn al-khajaba bʾd ghadba lil Shiʿa" (Bahrain: Stop the Salafi Sheikh from Using Angry Rhetoric in Response to Shiʿa Anger), *al-Sharq al-Awsat*, June 21, 2008, http://www.aawsat.com/details.asp?issueno=10626&article=475729#.UTjLGtY3v_o. The accusation subsequently fueled rioting by outraged Shiʿa in Manama in July 2008.

52. Louër, *Transnational Shiʿa Politics*, 28.

53. Author's interviews with various individuals in Sitra and Manama, Bahrain, November 2006. See also Louër, *Transnational Shiʿa Politics*, 287–288.

54. Author's interview with a senior al-Wifaq official, Manama, Bahrain, November 6, 2006.

55. Author's interview with a Shiʿa cleric, Manama, Bahrain, November 11, 2006.

56. *Gulf News*, "Bahraini Shiʿites Want a Secular Iraq," January 27, 2005.

57. Salman al-Dawsiri, "Interview with ʿAli Salman," *al-Sharq al-Awsat*, May 22, 2007. Al-Wifaq's Facebook page on March 21, 2011, also contained a refutation of the accusation of Iranian influence. Al-Wifaq's detractors would argue that ʿAli Salman's protestations are an example of the Shiʿa practice of *taqqiya* (religiously sanctioned dissimulation or obfuscation of one's true intention or loyalty).

58. *Gulf States Newsletter*, "Interview with 'Ali Salman," 30, no. 795 (2006), 2.

59. Sayed Abdul Qadir, "Iqtirah wazir al-dakhiliya bi tashdid al-'aqubat 'ala jira'm al-shaghab" (The Interior Minister Suggests Strengthening Punishments for the Crime of Rioting), *Akhbar al-Khalij*, December 22, 2008, http:// www.akhbar-alkhaleej.com/11231/article/284254.html.

60. Niethammer, *Voices in Parliament*, 18.

4. SECTARIAN BALANCING: THE BAHRAINI SUNNIS AND A POLARIZED PARLIAMENT

1. Baquer al-Najjar, *Al-harakat al-diniyya fi al-Khalij al-'Arabi* (Religious Movements of the Gulf) (Beirut: Dar al-Saqi, 2007), 30–45. Al-Islah's website is at http://www.eslahhwf.org.

2. Author's interview with al-Minbar member, Muharraq, Bahrain, November 14, 2006.

3. Ikhwanonline, "Interview with Saleh 'Ali," November 7, 2006, http://ikhwan online.com/Article.aspx?ArtID=24297&SecID=270.

4. Author's interview with al-Minbar member, Manama, Bahrain, November 14, 2006.

5. *Al-Sharq al-Awsat*, "Al-Bahrain: Bayan idanat al-hajum 'ala Al-Faluja yata-hawwal li-munawashat bayn al-nawab wa rafa' da'awa didd 3 suhuf" (Bahrain: A Statement Condemning the Attack on Fallujah Turns Into Skirmishes Between the House of Representatives and Suing 3 Newspapers), November 16, 2004, http://www.aawsat.com/details.asp?section=4&article=26596 4&issueno=9485#.UVxDl6I3v_o.

6. Author's interview with al-Minbar member, Muharraq, Bahrain, November 14, 2006.

7. The Islamic Education Society's background can be found on its website at http://www.alasalah-bh.org/main/index.php?option=com_content&view= article&id=1&Itemid=2, accessed April 18, 2011.

8. Muhammad 'Uthman al-Muharraq, "Al-faruq al-Salafiyya fi al-Bahrayn" (Salafi Groups in Bahrain)," *al-Wasat*, June 29, 2005.

9. The case of the former secretary-general 'Adil al-Ma'awada is instructive in this regard. He began his political involvement as a young man as part of the Jama'iyyat al-Tabligh, then became a Sufi, then a member of the Muslim

Brotherhood, and finally a Salafi, which he noted offered a set of principles that was authentic and fundamental. Author's interview with ʿAdil al-
Maʿawada, Manama, Bahrain, November 6, 2006.

10. Hamdi ʿAbd al-Aziz, "Al-ʿunf fi al-Bahrayn: Tahlil mawaqif al-Islamiyyin" (Violence in Bahrain: An Analysis of the Islamists' Positions), al-Quds al-ʿArabi,
March 4, 2004.

11. Author's interview with a nonaligned MP, Manama, Bahrain, November 7,
2006.

12. Author's interview with ʿAdil al-Maʿawada, Manama, Bahrain, November 10,
2006. Saudi clerical influence is evident in the society's rallies and material;
at a 2006 rally attended by the author, a prominent Saudi cleric was featured
as the guest speaker.

13. Author's interview with Bahraini activist, Manama, Bahrain, November 6,
2006; Muhammad ʿUthman al-Muharraq, "Al-furuq al-Salafiyya fi al-Bahrayn"
(Salafi Groups in Bahrain), al-Wasat, June 29, 2005.

14. Author's interviews with Bahraini Shiʿa in Sitra, Bahrain, November 2006.

15. Niethammer, "Stubborn Salafis and Moderate Shiʿites."

16. Author's interview with al-Minbar member, Manama, Bahrain, November 14,
2006.

17. Author's interview with ʿAdil al-Maʿawada, Manama, Bahrain, November 6,
2006.

18. Al-Muharraq, "Al-furuq al-Salafiyya fi al-Bahrayn."

19. Author's interview with a Bahraini academic, Manama, Bahrain, November 6, 2006.

20. Author's interview with a nonaligned MP, Manama, Bahrain, November 6,
2006.

21. In subsequent interviews, al-Bandar, whom Bahraini authorities quickly deported to the United Kingdom, emphasized that the king and the prime minister were not implicated in the report, only Shaykh Atiyatallah in his capacity as
the head of the Central Informatics Office—Bahrain's version of the CIA or MI6.
The full report is available at http://www.bahrainrights.org/files/albandar
.pdf, accessed April 18, 2011. As of early 2012, Atiyatallah held the position of
minister of the royal court for follow-up affairs.

22. Author's interview with an activist, ʿIsa Town, Bahrain, November 2006.

23. Habib Trabelsi, "Bahrain's Shiʿite Muslims Cry Foul Over Dual Nationality
Plan," Khaleej Times, June 16, 2002. See also the report aired on al-ʿArabiya

TV, "Maʿ haqiqat qadiya al-tajnis fi al-Bahrayn" (The Truth About the Issue of Naturalization in Bahrain), *Panorama TV*, February 9, 2009.

24. Author's interview with a Shiʿa activist, Sitra, Bahrain, November 12, 2006.

25. Mansur al-Jamri, "State and Civil Society in Bahrain," *Society for Gulf Arab Studies Newsletter* 9, no. 1 (2000), http://bahrain.wikia.com/wiki/State_and _Civil_Society_in_Bahrain. The naturalization of foreign Sunnis was widely believed to have impacted the outcome of the 2006 parliamentary elections. Yet ʿAli Salman denied this in a 2006 interview, arguing that "[al-Wifaq's] districts were not affected by naturalization or the military's participation. But we are against participation of [the] newly naturalized because the law stipulates that ten years should pass after their naturalization before they are allowed to vote. Article 6 in the 1963 law that organizes naturalization states that people cannot vote until ten years after naturalization." *Al-Elaph*, interview with ʿAli Salman, November 29, 2006.

26. Niethammer, "Stubborn Salafis and Moderate Shiʿites."

27. Author's interview with an official of the Ministry of Foreign Affairs, Manama, Bahrain, November 13, 2006.

28. Author's interview with a Bahraini academic, Manama, Bahrain, November 6, 2006.

29. Author's interview with an al-Waʿd official, Manama, Bahrain, November 8, 2006.

30. Author's interviews with various individuals in Muharraq, Bahrain, November 2006.

31. Habib Toumi, "Bahrain King Appoints a Liberal Upper Council to Offset Islamists," *Gulf News*, December 7, 2006. The former secretary-general of al-Asala, ʿAdil al-Maʿawada, argued that an appointed Consultative Council "is an ordinary thing, especially at the beginning of the democratic process." *Al-Sharq al-Awsat*, interview with ʿAdil al-Maʿawada, July 22, 2005. An official in the Ministry of Foreign Affairs noted, "The parliamentary structure was devised so it couldn't be hijacked by extremists. We don't want a forty-member House composed of religious clerics who will ban alcohol, ban women from driving, take Bahrain backwards, and drive away the foreigners who enjoy our liberal society." Author's interview, Manama, Bahrain, November 13, 2006.

32. Author's interviews with Haq officials, Manama, Bahrain, November 11, 2006.

33. Author's discussions with Shiʿa in Sitra, ʿIsa Town, Bilad al-Qadim, Muharraq, and Sanabis, Bahrain, November 2006. See also Michael Herb, "Emirs and Parliaments in the Gulf," *Journal of Democracy* 13, no. 4 (2002): 41–47.

34. Author's interview with an organizer of the Muntadyat, Manama, Bahrain, November 13, 2006.

35. This observation was buttressed by an al-Minbar member's comments noting that the "Sunnis are disorganized. They have civil society leaders; but no *marjaʿ* like the Shiʿa. The morale of Sunnis is low." Author's interview, Manama, Bahrain, November 14, 2006.

36. Salman al-Dossari, "Roundup: Bahrain Elections, 2006," *al-Sharq al-Awsat* (English ed.), November 28, 2006. See also F. Gregory Gause III, "Bahrain Parliamentary Election Results: 25 November and 2 December 2006," *International Journal of Middle East Studies* 39 (May 2007), 170–171.

37. A women's rights campaigner noted tacit cooperation between Salafis and al-Wifaq over morality issues and social matters, such as inheritance and divorce laws. An al-Haq figure also accused al-Wifaq of "flirting" with the Salafis. Author's interviews with a women's rights campaigner and an Haq official, Manama, Bahrain, November 13 and 5, 2006, respectively.

38. Author's interview with a senior al-Wifaq official, Manama, Bahrain, November 6, 2006.

39. Author's interview with a senior al-Wifaq official, Manama, Bahrain, February 12, 2013.

40. Ibid.

41. *Al-Waqt*, "Al-hakuma tuhil qanun al-jinsiyya ila Majlis al-Nuwwab al-dawr al-muqbil" (The Government Refers the Citizenship Law to Parliament for the Next Session), October 15, 2008.

42. Ibid.

43. Al-Wifaq needed twenty-one votes for a proposed constitutional amendment.

44. Said Shehabi, "Abʿad mahalliyya wa iqlimiyya lil-tawattur fi al-Bahrayn" (Local and Regional Dimensions of Tensions in Bahrain), *al-Quds al-ʿArabi*, February 17, 2004.

45. Shakyh ʿAbdallah al-ʿAli quoted in Salman al-Dawsiri, "Argument Over 'Early Signs' of Sectarian Sedition in Bahrain: When Parliament Becomes a Stage for Sunni–Shiʿite Friction," *al-Sharq al-Awsat* (English ed.), July 6, 2006.

46. One telling example of these tensions is popular perceptions of the Bahraini media. A Bahraini activist noted that different transnational media outlets

in Bahrain are believed to have a decidedly sectarian bias: many Bahrainis regard al-Jazeera as a "Sunni channel," whereas it is said that the Lebanese Hizballah's popular TV station al-Manar helps promote Shiʿa identity. Al-ʿArabiya television appears to be the most balanced in its sectarian orientation. More locally, the newspaper *al-Watan*—dominated by a Salafi board of advisers—serves as a counterweight to the Shiʿa-dominated *al-Wasat*. *Al-Watan* is heavily influenced by Saudi Arabia and, the activist asserted, has frequently tried to inflame Sunni opinion. One example of this newspaper's purported indifference to Shiʿa concerns was its failure to mention the February 2006 al-ʿAskari Mosque bombing in Iraq. Author's interview with a Bahraini activist, Manama, Bahrain, May 10, 2006.

47. Mahdi Rabiʾ, "Al-ab al-ruhi lil-ikhwan yara fi al-khilaf al-madhhabi sahabat sayf al-Bahrayn: al-dimuqratiyyun wa al-salaf yatabannun mithaq sharaf li-nabdh al-firqa" (The Spiritual Father of the Brotherhood Sees Sectarian Divisions as a Summer Cloud Over Bahrain: Democrats and Salafis Adopt a Code of Honor to Shun Discord), *al-Hayat*, November 26, 2004.

48. "Yanqusuhum Muqtada Sadr Bahrayni Faqat!" (They Only Lack a Bahraini Muqtada Sadar), *al-Watan*, June 19, 2008.

49. Author's interview with a Saudi Shiʿa activist, United States, May 24, 2011.

50. Author's interview with a member of Haq, Manama, Bahrain, November 12, 2006.

51. *Al-Sharq al-Awsat*, "Jamiʿya mahalliyya Shiʿa tuwajjihu bayanan lil-marja-ʿiyyat al-Shiʿiyya ʿAbr safaratay al-baladayn" (A Local Shiʿa Group Sends a Message to Shiʿa *Marajiʿ* by Way of Both Countries' Embassies), September 21, 2008. See also *al-Aafaq*, "Jamiʿya al-tahdid al-Bahrayniya: Khitabna al-marajiʿa al-fiqhiya fi al-Iyran al-ʿIraq li dafaʿ al-durur ʿn al-watan" (BCR: We Talked to Religious Authorities in Iran, Iraq, to Avoid Problems in the Country,) September 22, 2008.

52. *Al-Aafaq*, "Nabil Rajab li *Aafaq*: Al-Tabqa al-hakima bil Bahrayn tumaris al-tathir did al-Shiʿa" (Nabil Rajab to *Aafaq*: Bahrain's Ruling Class Practices Apartheid Against Shiʿites), October 26, 2008.

53. Al-Jazeera, August 27, 2009. The northern rebellion by followers of Zaydi cleric Husayn al-Huthi (d. September 2004) was reportedly triggered in late 2004 by Zaydi alarm that the government was playing "sectarian politics"—that is, co-opting radical Salafi factions against the marginalized northern Zaydi tribes. The conflict, however, is not merely a sectarian one but rather

is rooted in longstanding center–periphery tensions that afflict Yemen as a whole.

54. *Oxford Analytica Daily Brief*, "Bahrain: Yemen's Rebellion Adds to Sectarian Tensions," January 12, 2010, http://www.oxan.com/display.aspx?ItemID= DB156920.

55. *The Peninsula*, "Bahrainis Protest Against Iran Province Claim," July 14, 2007.

56. *Gulf News*, "Bahraini Shi'ite Group Flays Iran Rhetoric," February 8, 2009.

57. Author's interview with member of the Ministry of Foreign Affairs, Manama, Bahrain, November 13, 2006.

58. Author's interview with al-Minbar member, Manama, Bahrain, November 14, 2006.

59. Author's interview with senior Haq member, Manama, Bahrain, November 10, 2006.

60. Author's interview with senior Saudi diplomat, Manama, Bahrain, November 12, 2006.

61. International Crisis Group (ICG), *Bahrain's Sectarian Challenge*, Middle East Report no. 40 (Brussels: ICG, May 6, 2005), http://www.crisisgroup.org/~/ media/Files/Middle%20East%20North%20Africa/Iran%20Gulf/Bahrain/ Bahrains%20Sectarian%20Challenge.pdf.

62. Author's interview with al-Wa'd activist, Manama, Bahrain, November 13, 2006.

5. INTO THE ABYSS: THE PEARL ROUNDABOUT UPRISING AND ITS AFTERMATH

1. Habib Tumi, "Bahrain Pledges Zero Tolerance, Arrests Opposition Figure," *Gulf News*, August 14, 2010.

2. Personal interview with Bahraini academic, Manama, Bahrain, February 24, 2012.

3. Personal interview with Bahraini activist, Manama, Bahrain, February 26, 2012.

4. Habib Tumi, "Bahrain's Candidates Hone Their Speeches," *Gulf News*, October 22, 2010.

5. *Gulf Daily News*, "The Use of Cutting-Edge Technology to Undermine International Relations Is a Dangerous Phenomenon," December 7, 2010.

6. As of January 2011, Bahrain was second among Arab countries for Facebook usage as a percentage of population (34.27 percent). Dubai School of Government, *Arab Social Media Report*, vol. 1, no. 1 (Dubai: Dubai School of Government, January 2011), available http://www.dsg.ae/portals/0/ASMR%20Final%20May%208%20high.pdf.

7. Author's interview with a member of the February 14 Youth Coalition, Manama, Bahrain, February 25, 2012.

8. *Al-Sharq al-Awsat*, "Ra'is kutlat al-Wifaq al-mu'arada al-Barlamaniya fi al-Bahrayn: Nabhath 'an wasata Khalijiya ma' al-hukuma" (The Head of the al-Wifaq Opposition Parliamentary Bloc: We Are Searching for Gulf Mediation with the Government), March 26, 2011, http://www.aawsat.com/details.asp?section=4&article=614309&issueno=11806.

9. Author's interview with al-Wifaq official, Manama, Bahrain, February 25, 2012.

10. International Crisis Group (ICG), *Popular Protests in North Africa and the Middle East: Bahrain's Rocky Road to Reform*, Middle East/North Africa Report no. 111 (Brussels: ICG, July 28, 2011), 1–2.

11. ICG, *Popular Protests in North Africa and the Middle East: The Bahrain Revolt*, Middle East/North Africa Report no. 105 (Brussels: ICG, April 6, 2011), 15.

12. Author's interview with al-Wifaq official, Manama, Bahrain, February 22, 2012.

13. Bahraini Independent Commission of Inquiry (BICI, al-Lajna al-Bahrayniyya al-Mustaqila li-Taqassi al-Haqa'iq), *Bahrain Independent Commission Report*, (November 23, 2011), 219, http://www.bici.org.bh/BICIreportEN.pdf; hereafter *BICI Report*.

14. Ibid.

15. Reuters, " 'Bahrain Pulled Back from "Sectarian Abyss" ' — Foreign Minister," February 17 2011.

16. The alliance's statement of its position was posted to various websites in mid-April 2012 — for instance, http://www.fajrbh.net/vb/showthread.php?t=18614. Its Facebook page is at http://www.facebook.com/Republic Alliance.

17. Tahaluf min Ajl al-Jumhuriya, "Bayan al-mawaqif" (Statement of Principles), April 15, 2011, http://www.fajrbh.net/vb/showthread.php?t=18614.

18. ICG, *Popular Protests in North Africa and the Middle East: Bahrain's Rocky Road to Reform*, 12.

19. Ibid., 2.

20. Ibid., 13.

21. Author's interview with Bahraini activist, Manama, Bahrain, February 23, 2012.

22. *BICI Report*, 165–166.

23. Author's interview with NUG secretary-general 'Abd al-Latif Mahmud, Muharraq, Bahrain, September 22, 2012.

24. Author's interview with senior al-Wifaq official, Manama, Bahrain, September 18, 2012.

25. See Justin Gengler, *Bahrain's Sunni Awakening*, Middle East Research and Information Project (MERIP) report (Washington, D.C.: MERIP, January 17, 2012); Andrew Hammond, "Sunnis Seek Their Own Voice in Bahrain's Turmoil," *Daily Star*, April 7, 2012.

26. Most famously, NUG secretary-general 'Abd al-Latif Mahmud gave an interview with the *Washington Times* calling for the ouster of the prime minister. His office later retreated from this statement. Ben Birbaum, "Top Sunni: PM Should Mull Quitting After Crisis," *Washington Times*, August 18, 2011.

27. Author's interview with liberal Sunni oppositionist, Manama, Bahrain, September 20, 2012.

28. *BICI Report*, 86–87.

29. From 2006 to 2010, al-Minbar and al-Asala held a total of fifteen seats; in the 2010 elections, they secured five.

30. Author's interview with NUG members, Muharraq, Bahrain, September 22, 2012.

31. Author's interview with NUG secretary-general 'Abd al-Latif al-Mahmud, Muharraq, Bahrain, September 22, 2012.

32. *Al-Sharq al-Awsat*, "Ra'is al-Wahda al-Wataniya bi-al-Bahrayn: Za'im al-mu'arada haddad bi-al-istinjad bi-Iran idha dakhalat quwat 'Dira' al-Khalij'" (Head of the National Unity Gathering in Bahrain: Leader of the Opposition Threatened to Ask for Iran's Help if the "Peninsula Shield" Entered), March 20, 2011, http://www.aawsat.com/details.asp?section=4&article=613 363&issueno=11800.

33. *Gulf Daily News*, "'Stop Meddling' Call to Tehran," March 31, 2011.

34. *Al-Akhbar*, interview with Hassan Mushayma, February 28, 2011.

35. Frederic Wehrey, "Uprisings Jolt the Saudi–Iranian Rivalry," *Current History* 110 (December 2011), 353–354.

36. Fars News Agency, "Iran's FM Voices Concern about Bahrain in Letters to UN, OIC, Arab League" (in English), March 17, 2011.

37. *Mehr News* (in English), "Learn Lesson from Saddam's Fate: Ahmadinejad," March 16, 2011.

38. For a good discussion of Iran's rhetorical attacks, see Joshua Teitelbaum, "Saudi Arabia Faces a Changing Middle East," *Middle East Review of International Affairs* 15, no. 3 (2011), http://www.gloria-center.org/2011/10/saudi-arabia-faces-a-changing-middle-east/.

39. *Mehr News*, "Uprising in Bahrain Has Nothing to Do with Shiism or Sunnism: Leader," March 22, 2011, http://mehrnews.com.

40. Moussa Mahmoud al-Jamal and Sonia Farid, "Is Iran 'Sectarianizing' Bahrain Conflict?" al-ʿArabiya TV website, April 20, 2011, http://english.alarabiya.net/articles/2011/04/20/146144.html.

41. Tariq al-Humayd, "Iran taʾifi . . . wa al-Diraʿ al-Khaliji la" (Iran Is Sectarian . . . but the Peninsula Shield Is Not), *al-Sharq al-Awsat*, March 15, 2011.

42. Mohamad al-Araba, "Qaradawi Says Bahrain's Revolution Sectarian," al-ʿArabiya TV website, March 19, 2011, http://www.alarabiya.net/articles/2011/03/19/142205.html.

43. *JafriaNews*, "Grand Ayatollah Sistani Condemns the Saudi and Bahrain's [sic] Crackdown on Bahrain's Shiʿa While Kuwait Refuses to Send Troops" (in English), March 17, 2011, http://jafrianews.com/2011/03/17/grand-ayatollah-sistani-condemns-the-saudi-and-bahrains-force-crackdown-on-bahrains-shia-while-kuwait-refuses-to-send-troops.

44. *World Bulletin*, "Iraq's Sadr Calls for Protest Against Bahrain Deaths," March 16, 2011, http://www.worldbulletin.net/?aType=haber&ArticleID=71168; al-Amarah News Network, "Iraq's Zealous Sons March in Support of Downtrodden Bahraini People" (in English), March 16, 2011, http://al3marh.net/news (al-Amarah News Network is affiliated with al-Sadr).

45. Agence France Presse and *NOW Lebanon*, "Thousands Across Iraq Protest Bahrain Crackdown," March 18, 2011.

46. Anne Hagood, "The Narrative of Resistance: Bahrain and Iraq," *Arab Media and Society*, no. 13 (Summer 2011), http://www.arabmediasociety.com/?article=774.

47. Ibid.

48. Muhammad al-Ahmad, "The Democratic Alliance Secedes from al-Wifaq Perceiving Sectarian Danger," *al-Ayyam*, April 4, 2011.

49. *Bahrain Online*, "Al-Mu'arada taluhh bil-insihab min al-hiwar al-watany" (Opposition Insists on Withdrawing from National Dialogue), July 3, 2011, http://bahrainonline.org/showthread.php?t=273184.

50. *The National*, "Bahrain Moves to Dissolve Main Opposition Group, al-Wefaq," April 15, 2011.

51. Quoted in Ben Birbaum, "Pro-government Cleric to Start Own Party," *Washington Times*, August 10, 2011; Sandeep Singh Grewal, "Pullout by al-Wifaq 'Selfish' Says Cleric," *Gulf Daily News*, July 22, 2011.

52. *Gulf Daily News*, "New Shock: Wikileaks Revelations," May 24, 2011.

53. Quoted in ibid.

54. Muhammad al-'Ali, "Two Civic Councils Face Dissolution," *Gulf Daily News*, May 1, 2011.

55. Bahrain News Agency, "Security and Stability Top Priorities Now, Foreign Minister Says," March 29, 2011.

56. Jay Solomon, "Bahrain Sees Hezbollah Plot in Protests," *Wall Street Journal*, April 25, 2011.

57. Sawsan al-Sha'er, "Hizballah: Min al-rahim al-Lubnani ila al-hadana al-Bahrayniya" (Hizballah: From the Lebanese Womb to the Bahraini Incubator), *al-Watan*, September 20, 2011, http://www.alwatannews.net/writer-read.aspx?id=0gueSqr1n1HmokSkA9wmzJRPggQS+FyZEEUoX8tV29U=.

58. *BICI Report*, 69–70.

59. ICG, *Popular Protests in North Africa and the Middle East: Bahrain's Rocky Road to Reform*, 3.

60. Ibid., 6.

61. In March 2011, the government restricted access to Press TV's Internet site.

62. Human Rights Watch, "Drop Charges Against Editor of Independent Daily," April 11, 2011, http://www.hrw.org/news/2011/04/11/bahrain-drop-charges-against-editor-independent-daily.

63. Ibid.

64. Ibid.

65. Much of the opposition's use of social media outlets was under the framework of Bahrain's National Dialogue Media Center, which established accounts on YouTube, Twitter, and Facebook to maintain effective communication with the Bahraini public. Bahrain News Agency, "The National Dialogue's Media Centre Launches Its Official Website and Accounts on Social Media Channels," June 22, 2011, http://www.bna.bh/portal/en/news/461965.

66. Quoted in *Gulf Daily News*, "'Refrain from Using Social Networking Sites' Appeal," February 20, 2011, http://www.gulf-daily-news.com/ArchiveNews Details.aspx?date=02/20/2011&storyid=300029.

67. Bahrain News Agency, "Bahrain Youths' Role in Social Media," April 14, 2011.

68. Bahrain News Agency, "The National Dialogue's Media Centre Launches Its Official Website."

69. Bahrain News Agency, March 24, 2011.

70. See http://twitter.com/khalidalkhalifa.

71. Al-Jazeera website (English ed.), "Bahrain National Dialogue Begins," July 2, 2011, http://www.aljazeera.com/news/middleeast/2011/07/20117214754858684 .html.

72. ICG, *Popular Protests in North Africa and the Middle East: Bahrain's Rocky Road to Reform*, 18–19.

73. Reuters, "Proposal to Expand Powers of Bahrain Parliament 'Lies': Shiite Group," July 26, 2011.

74. ICG, *Popular Protests in North Africa and the Middle East: Bahrain's Rocky Road to Reform*, 19.

75. Author's interview with activist in the February 14 Youth Coalition, Sitra, Bahrain, February 28, 2012.

76. C. More, "It's Now Time to Show Maturity," *Gulf Daily News*, July 18, 2011, http://www.gulf-daily-news.com/NewsDetails.aspx?storyid=310043.

77. Quoted in Sadeep Singh Grewal, "Former Intelligence Officer Eagerly Awaits Beginning of Negotiations," *Gulf Daily News*, June 29, 2011.

78. Sandeep Singh Grewal, "Dialogue Drama," *Gulf Daily News*, July 13, 2011.

79. Al-Wifaq, "Fariq al-hiwar ra'a anna al-hiwar lan yuntij hallan siyassiyan li-al-azma fi al-Bahrayn" (The Negotiating Team Believes That Dialogue Will Not Produce a Political Solution to the Crisis in Bahrain), Facebook posting, July 17, 2011, http://www.facebook.com/photo.php?fbid=101503182463030 72&set=pu.203200448071&type=. See also Agence France Presse, "Bahrain Shiite Opposition Pulls Out of Talks," July 17, 2011.

80. "Istimrar al-hiwar fi al-Bahrain bil-rughm min al-mʿavada al-Shiʿa" (The National Dialogue Continues Despite the Withdrawal of the Shiʿa Opposition), *Elaph*, July 18, 2011, http://www.elaph.com/Web/news/2011/7/669791.html.

81. Author's interview with senior al-Wifaq official, Manama, Bahrain, September 22, 2012.

82. Quoted in Reuters, "Proposal to Expand Powers of Bahraini Parliament 'Lies.'"

83. Quoted in *Gulf Daily News*, "Al-Wifaq Pulled Out on Orders from Abroad," July 19, 2011.

84. *BBC Monitoring International Reports Middle East* and al-ʿArabiya TV, "Politician Accuses Opposition Party of Planning Islamic Republic in Bahrain," July 14, 2011.

85. Frederik Richter, "Kuwait to Mediate in Bahrain Crisis," Reuters, March 27, 2011.

86. Glen Carey, "Kuwait Isn't Involved in Bahrain Mediation," *Bloomberg*, March 28, 2011.

87. Quoted in Salim al-Wawan and Raʾid Yusuf, "Kuwait Hosts Today a Dialogue for Bahrain with the Participation of al-Wifaq Society in Order to Outline the Initiative," *al-Seyassah*, March 27, 2011. Bahrain's state press also reported that al-Khurafi refused to involve the Kuwaiti emir unless the Bahraini opposition dropped its demands for a constitutional monarchy and the prime minister's resignation. This assertion could not be independently corroborated, and, given Bahrain's state press's proclivity for distortion, it should be treated with suspicion. Habib Toumi, "Kuwaiti Speaker Wants Bahrain Opposition Request for Mediation," *Gulf Daily News*, March 26, 2011.

88. Bahrain TV, October 4, 2011.

89. *BICI Report*, 416.

90. Ibid.

91. Ibid., 411–415.

92. These measures included installing closed-circuit television in Bahraini police stations and interrogation rooms, promulgating a code of conduct for Bahraini police, and eliminating the National Security Agency's arrest power. These steps are detailed in a statement by the Bahraini ambassador to the United States to the Tom Lantos Human Rights Commission on August 1, 2012, http://houdanonoo.wordpress.com/2012/07/31/my-statement-to-the -tom-lantos-human-rights-commission/.

93. Author's interview with Western diplomat based in Manama, Bahrain, September 20, 2012.

94. *Bahrain Mirror*, "Wali al-ʿahd tukhris Flayfil wa li-wazir al-dakhaliya: Qamaʾkum yandhakar bas ma yunʿad" (The Crown Prince Silences Flay-

fil and Tells Minister of Interior: May Your Oppression Be Remembered but Not Repeated), December 5, 2011, http://bhmirror.no-ip.org/article .php?id=2460&cid=73; "Al-Dakhaliya: I'tirad al-mawakib al-husayniya ghayr qanuni" (The Ministry of Interior: Intercepting Ashura Convoys Is Illegal), al-Wasat, December 4, 2011, http://www.alwasatnews.com/3375/news/read/612663/1.html.

95. As summarized later in U.S. State Department, "Senior Administration Officials on Bahrain," May 11, 2012, http://www.state.gov/r/pa/prs/ps/2012/05/189810.htm.

96. Reuters, "US Resumes Bahrain Arms Sales Despite Rights Concerns," May 11, 2012.

97. See also Frederic Wehrey, "The March of Bahrain's Hardliners" (Carnegie Endowment for International Peace), May 31, 2012, http://carnegieendowment .org/2012/05/31/march-of-bahrain-s-hardliners/b0zr.

98. Author's interview with al-Wifaq official, Manama, Bahrain, September 18, 2012.

99. Ibid.

100. Ironically, Samira Rajab is a Shi'a. For an overview of her background, see Dan Murphy, "After Formula One Scrutiny, Bahrain Hires a Fan of Saddam Hussein to Improve Its Image," Christian Science Monitor, April 25, 2012.

101. "Group is Dissolved" Gulf Daily News, July 10, 2012, http://www.gulf-daily -news.com/source/XXXV/112/pdf/PAGE01.pdf.

102. Human Rights Watch, "Testimony of Tom Malinowski Before the Tom Lantos Human Rights Commission on the Implementation of the Bahrain Independent Commission of Inquiry Report," August 1, 2012, http://tlhrc.house.gov/docs/transcripts/2012_08_01_Bahrain/08_01_12_Bahrain.pdf.

103. Author's interview with member of the February 14 Youth Coalition, Manama, Bahrain, February 28, 2012.

104. Laurence Louër, "Houses Divided: The Splintering of Bahrain's Political Camps," Sada (Carnegie Endowment for International Peace), April 4, 2012, http://carnegieendowment.org/sada/2012/04/04/houses-divided-splintering -of-bahrain-s-political-camps/a6ej.

105. According to several Shi'a interlocutors interviewed in February 2012, al-Wifaq's only success during its parliamentary tenure was investigating government corruption.

106. Author's telephone interview with a Bahraini youth activist, October 26, 2012.

107. Author's interview with ʿAli Salman, Manama Bahrain, September 22, 2012.

108. Ibid.

109. Author's interview with Western diplomat, Manama, Bahrain, September 22, 2012.

110. See the photos of protestors from July 10, 2012, at Bahraini Online, http://www.bahrainonline.org.

111. An example of this exclusive focus on clerical authority is Ali Alfoneh, *Between Reform and Revolution: Sheikh Qassim, the Bahraini Shiʿa, and Iran* (Washington, D.C.: American Enterprise Institute, July 15, 2012).

112. Author's interview with a February 14 Youth Coalition activist, Manama, Bahrain, February 28, 2012.

113. Author's interview with al-Wifaq official, Manama, Bahrain, February 28, 2012.

114. Ibid.

115. Ibid.

116. A coalition among these groups included two Sunni Islamist parliamentary groups—the Muslim Brotherhood–affiliated al-Minbar society and the Salafi al-Asala society—as well as one nonparliamentary group, the Shura Islamic Society (Jamaʿiyat al-Shura al-Islamiyya); the Arab Nationalists; and the so-called "Azharis"—graduates of al-Azhar University in Cairo who adhere to the Muslim Brotherhood line but are not formerly part of al-Minbar.

117. In mid-2012, the NUG announced the formation of a rival labor union to counter the General Federation of Bahrain Trade Unions, which it argued was penetrated and controlled by al-Wifaq.

118. A Bahraini academic argued that the "NUG has no program other than opposing the opposition." Author's interview, Manama, Bahrain, February 27, 2012.

119. Author's interviews with Bahraini academics and NUG members, Manama and Muharraq, Bahrain, September 2012.

120. This charge was echoed by a Sunni liberal interlocutor between the NUG and al-Wifaq, who noted that "Muharraq [NUG] is getting softer toward Manama [al-Wifaq]." Author's interview, Manama, Bahrain, September 20, 2012.

121. In March 2012, signs outside the al-Asala headquarters in Muharraq bore images of al-Wifaq leaders with nooses around their necks. Author's observation, Muharraq, Bahrain, March 2012.

122. These politicians included MP ʿAbd al-Halim Murad, the secretary-general of al-Asala; ʿAdil al-Muʿawda, the second Deputy Speaker of the Parliament; former MP Hamad al-Muhannadi; and a Salafi cleric, Faysal al-Ghariri.

123. "Bahraini Group Denies Flouting Rules to Aid Syria Rebels," *Gulf News*, August 12, 2012, http://gulfnews.com/news/gulf/bahrain/bahraini-group-denies -flouting-rules-to-aid-syria-rebels-1.1061012.

124. See, for example, Sawsan al-Shaʾir, "Premeditated Bigotry," *al-Watan*, August 13, 2012.

125. Author's interview with a senior member of the Bahraini Foreign Ministry, Manama, Bahrain, February 29, 2012.

126. ShiaPost, "Linking the Crisis in Bahrain to the Outside Is Baseless and Chaotic," August 25, 2012, http://en.shiapost.com/2012/08/26/alwefaq-confutes -walid-maaloufs-pro-dictatorship-allegations/.

127. *BICI Report*, 51.

128. Husayn al-Harbi, "Al-Mushir Khalifa bin Ahmed Al Khalifa li-*al-Raʾy*: Naʿam hunaka muʾamara li-qalb nidham al-hukm . . . wa laysa li-muʿarada sila bi-al-Rabiʿ al-ʿArabi" (Field Marshal Khalifa bin Ahmed al-Khalifa to *al-Raʾy*: Yes, There Is a Conspiracy to Overthrow the Ruling System . . . and There Is No Connection Between the Opposition and the Arab Spring), *al-Raʾy*, March 11, 2011.

129. "HM King Hamad Issues Amended Law Decree," Bahrain News Agency, August 15, 2012, http://bna.bh/portal/en/news/521000.

130. Quoted in al-Harbi, "Al-Mushir Khalifa bin Ahmed al-Khalifa li-*al-Raʾy*."

131. Agence France Presse, "Bahrain PM for Gulf Union, Opposition Wants Referendum," May 13, 2012.

132. Author's interview with a Bahraini academic, Manama, Bahrain, February 28, 2012.

133. In the wake of calls for Saudi–Bahraini union, Iranian officials and press resurrected a timeworn Iranian claim to Bahrain. Most notably, in May 2012 the conservative newspaper *Kayhan*, supervised by the Office of the Supreme Leader, called for the annexation of Bahrain. "Iran's Khamenei-Run Newspaper Calls for Bahrain Annexation After GCC Union Talks," *al-ʿArabiya News* (in English), May 16, 2012.

134. Author's interview with a Sunni member of al-Waʿd, Manama, Bahrain, September 22, 2012.

135. Ibid.

136. See Frederic M. Wehrey, "The Securitization of the Shiʿa Issue in the Gulf," paper presented at the New York University Abu Dhabi conference "The U.S., Iran, and the Gulf: Regional Context and Transnational Currents," December 15–16, 2010.

137. Author's interview with al-Wifaq official, Manama, Bahrain, February 22, 2012.

6. LOYALTIES UNDER FIRE: THE SAUDI SHIʿA IN THE SHADOW OF IRAQ

1. Pew Forum on Religion and Public Life, "The Future of the Global Muslim Population," January 17, 2011, http://pewforum.org/future-of-the-global -muslim-population-sunni-and-shia.aspx. Some estimates put the figure as low as 5 percent and as high as 20 percent. See U.S. Department of State, *Saudi Arabia: Report on International Religious Freedom* (Washington, D.C.: U.S. Department of State, 2010), http://www.state.gov/g/drl/rls/irf/2010/148843 .htm.

2. Madawi al-Rashid, "Shiʿat al-Saudiyya: Bayn ighraʾ al-hakim wa fatawa al-mashayikh" (Saudi Shiʿa: Between the Ruler's Enticement and the Clerics' Fatwas), *al-Quds al-Arabi*, January 15, 2007; al-Rasid, "Al-taqrir al-thani li-huquq al-insan" (The Second Human Rights Report), December 21, 2005, http://www .rasid.com, http://www.alquds.co.uk/index.asp?fname=data\2007\01\01-17\14 a32.htm; Stéphane Lacroix, *Awakening Islam: The Politics of Religious Dissent in Saudi Arabia* (Cambridge, Mass.: Harvard University Press, 2011), 223–224.

3. Lacroix, *Awakening Islam*, 224.

4. Author's interviews with Sunni reformists in Jeddah and Riyadh, Saudi Arabia, March 2007. See also Stéphane Lacroix, "Saudi Arabia's New 'Islamo-Liberal' Reformers," *Middle East Journal* 58, no. 3 (2004), 360.

5. Al-Aafaq website, interview with Fouad Ibrahim, available at the al-Rasid website, December 23, 2007, https://www.rasid.com/index.php?act=artc& id=14564.

6. Mai Yamani, "The Rise of Shiʿa Petrolistan," Project Syndicate, March 3, 2004, http://www.project-syndicate.org/commentary/the-rise-of-shia-petrolistan.

7. Interview on al-ʿArabiya television, July 19, 2004.

8. Laurence Louër writes, "The rumour culminated in the weeks preceding the American invasion of Iraq and was cleverly used by the Shiraziyyin to show

the rulers that improving the lot of their Shi'a citizens was not only a matter of justice but a strategic choice for the kingdom's security." Laurence Louër, *Transnational Shi'a Politics: Religious and Political Networks in the Gulf* (London: Hurst, 2008), 246.

9. Hamza Hassan, "'Alaqat shi'at al-Sa'udiyya al-kharijiya li-Shi'at madhhabiyyan wa siyasiyyan" (The Foreign Political and Sectarian Relations of the Saudi Shi'a), al-Jazeera website, October 3, 2004, http://www.aljazeera.net/NR/exeres/F79762CF-6D0D-471A-AA57-6BD052C9240A.htm.

10. Lacroix, "Saudi Arabia's New 'Islamo-Liberal' Reformers," 360. For the petition, see "Ru'iya li-hadir al-watan wa mustaqbalihi" (Vision for the Present and the Future of the Homeland), *al-Quds al-'Arabi*, January 30, 2003.

11. Ibid. Importantly, Hassan al-Saffar did not sign the petition.

12. Author's interviews with various individuals in the Eastern Province, Saudi Arabia, March 2007.

13. The Arabic document is available at the al-Jazeera website, http://www.aljazeera.net/NR/exeres/D06168A6-DA8B-4339-9FB7-82A66AE12A3C.htm, accessed January 10, 2013. A full translation in English can be found in Fouad Ibrahim, *The Shi'is of Saudi Arabia* (London: Saqi Books, 2006), 257–262.

14. Ibrahim, *The Shi'is of Saudi Arabia*, 215.

15. Ibid.

16. Quoted in Hassan M. Fattah and Rasheed Abou Samh, "Saudi Shi'a Fear Gains Could Be Lost," *New York Times*, February 5, 2007.

17. *Al-Elaph*, interview with Hassan al-Saffar, June 25, 2007.

18. For more on the constitutional movement, see Abdalhadi Khalaf and Giacomo Luciani, eds., *Constitutional Reform and Political Participation in the Gulf* (Dubai: Gulf Research Center, 2006).

19. Quoted in al-Rasid, "Al-taqrir al-thani li-huquq al-insan."

20. Author's interview with a Sunni clerical reformist, Riyadh, Saudi Arabia, March 13, 2007.

21. 'Abdallah's speech is available at http://www.saudinf.com/display_news.php?id=859, accessed April 2011.

22. Naeem Tamim al-Hakeem, "Tribal, Regional Identity Under Dialogue Center Spotlight," *Saudi Gazette* (in English), December 28, 2010.

23. Toby Matthiesen, "Hizbullah al-Hijaz: A History of the Most Radical Saudi Shi'a Opposition Group," *Middle East Journal* 64, no. 2 (2010), 195–196.

24. Saudi Press Agency, June 4, 2008.

25. Exact numbers are murky and hard to verify, but the issue of Sunni-to-Shiʿa conversion (*tashaʾyu*) was closely linked to popular acclaim for the Lebanese Hizballah after 2006 and the sense that Shiʿism was now the "winning sect." Iran was typically described as orchestrating these conversions.

26. Author's interviews with various individuals in the Eastern Province, Saudi Arabia, March 2007.

27. According to one interlocutor, Hassan al-Saffar had originated the idea of Sunni and Shiʿa dialogue in 2002 with a planned meeting at his *husayniya* in Qatif. The minister of interior canceled the meeting, and the government subsequently announced its own dialogue sessions in 2003. Author's interview with Saudi Shiʿa activist, United States, May 24, 2011.

28. Author's interview with a Sunni human rights activist, Riyadh, Saudi Arabia, March 12, 2007.

29. Nur al-Islam website, May 30, 2008, http://nuralislam.com.

30. Author's observations in Qatif, March 2007 and January 2013.

31. E-mail correspondence to the author from members of the Tuesday Salon 2008–2011.

32. Lacroix, "Saudi Arabia's New 'Islamo-Liberal' Reformers," 358.

33. Al-Rasid, interview with Hassan al-Nimr by Iman Qahtani, August 8, 2006, http://www.rasid.com/index.php?act=artc&id=12371&hl=%D8%AD%D8%B3%D9%86%20%D8%A7%D9%84%D9%86%D9%85%D8%B1.

34. Muhammad Mahfouz, ed., *Al-hiwar al-madhhabi fi al-Mamlaka al-ʿArabiyya al-Saʿudiyya* (Sectarian Dialogue in the Kingdom of Saudi Arabia) (Qatif, Saudi Arabia: Atyaf lil-Nashr wa al-Tawziʿ, 2007).

35. Author's interview with Sunni human rights activist, Riyadh, Saudi Arabia, March 12, 2007.

36. Author's interview with Hassan al-Saffar, Qatif, Saudi Arabia, March 15, 2007.

37. "Al-Shaykh Saʿd al-Barayk yadʿ al-Saffar ti muajiha haquq imam al-jamiyʿ" (Shaykh Saʿd al-Barayk Confronts al-Saffar in Front of Everyone), *al-Madina*, February 2, 2007. http://www.almadinapress.com/index.a...ticleid=203170 (original link no longer works, so see http://www.qassimy.com/vb/show thread.php?t=109700 for complete text).

38. Hassan al-Saffar, "La wa lan naqbil ayaʾ marjaʿan takfiriyan wa narfud tadakhkhul ayaʾ marjaʿ fi al-shuʾun al-siyasi al-dakhili li-biladina" (We Do Not and Will Not Welcome Any *Marjaʿ* Who Promotes Excommunication, and We Oppose the Interference of Any *Marjaʿ* in the Internal Political Affairs of Our Country), *al-Risalah*, February 16, 2007.

39. Al-ʿArabiya TV, interview with Hassan al-Saffar, September 19, 2004.

40. Author's interview with Saudi Shiʿa cleric, Dammam, Saudi Arabia, March 17, 2007.

41. Author's interviews with Saudi Shiʿa reformists, Eastern Province, Saudi Arabia, March 2007.

42. Author's interview with Muhammad Mahfouz, Qatif, Saudi Arabia, March 15, 2007.

43. Author's interviews with Shiʿa reformists, Qatif, Saudi Arabia, March 2007. Saud Sirhan, "Nahwa marjaʿiyya Shiʿa mustaqlila fi al-Khalij" (Toward an Independent Shiʿa Source of Emulation in the Gulf), al-Sharq al-Awsat, February 24, 2003.

44. Author's interview with Muhammad Mahfouz, Qatif, Saudi Arabia, March 15, 2007.

45. Matthiesen, "Hizbullah al-Hijaz," 196.

46. Author's interview with Saudi Shiʿa cleric, Qatif, Saudi Arabia, March 15, 2007.

47. Al-Elaph, interview with Hassan al-Saffar, June 25, 2007.

48. Author's interview with Saudi Shiʿa activist and intellectual, Tarut Island, Saudi Arabia, March 15, 2007; see also Tawfiq al-Sayf, Nadhriyat al-sulta fi fiqh al-Shiʿi (Theories of Political Power in Shiʿa Jurisprudence) (Casablanca: Markaz al-Thaqafi al-ʿArabi, 2002).

49. Al-Hurra TV, interview with Tawfiq al-Sayf, December 10, 2007, http://www.saudishia.com/?act=artc&id=82.

50. Based in Najaf, Ayatollah Muhammad Husayn Naʾini taught Grand Ayatollah Abu al-Qassim al-Khoei, who was the mentor of Grand Ayatollah ʿAli al-Sistani. For more on him, see Abdul Hadi Haʾiri, Shiʿism and Constitutionalism in Iran (Leiden: Brill, 1977), 165–220; see also Muhammad Hussayn Naʾini, Tanbih al-ummah wa-tanzih al-milla (Warning the Community of Believers and Cleansing the Sect) (publication information unknown).

51. Quoted in al-Rasid, "Makarem Shirazi li ʿahali al-Asha wa al-Qatif: Tajanabu ifstifzaz ʿahl al-Suna" (Makarem Shirazi to the People of Ahsa and Qatif: Avoid Provoking Sunnis), June 13, 2007, https://rasid.com/writers.php?pid=&id=1&t=1&p=1385 (original link not working, republished at http://www.ebaa.net/khaber/2007/06/14/khaber008.htm).

52. According to one Shiʿa interlocutor, even Hizballah's television station al-Manar was not popular among Saudi Shiʿa because it consistently adopted a tone that was critical of Iraqi Shiʿa parties, such as Supreme Council for the

Islamic Revolution in Iraq (al-Majlis al-aʿala lil thawra al-Islamiya fi al-ʿIraq), later the Supreme Iraqi Islamic Council (al-Majlis al-aʿala al-Islami al-ʿIraqi), toward whom the Saudi Shiʿa felt a strong affinity. It was not until the 2006 Lebanon War that al-Manar's resonance increased, largely due to its compelling battlefield footage. Author's interview with Shiʿa activist, Eastern Province, Saudi Arabia, March 18, 2007.

53.   Hassan al-Saffar, "Khatab al-Muqawama," July 24, 2006, at al-Saffar's personal website, http://www.saffar.org/?act=artc&id=1020.

54.   Many of al-Nimr's supporters also hail from al-ʿAwamiya. Populated entirely by Shiʿa and isolated by a forest of palm trees, the town suffers from high unemployment, crime, and school dropout rates. It had long existed as an enclave of political activism; many of the second- and third-tier leaders of the OIR were born here. Author's interviews in al-ʿAwamiya, Saudi Arabia, January, 2013.

55.   See the biography of al-Nimr at http://www.alnemer.ws/?act=artc&id=90.

56.   Author's interview with activists in al-ʿAwamiya, Saudi Arabia, January 2013. The correspondence between al-Mudarrisi and al-Nimr appears in the Bahrain Online Forum, January 2002, http://bahrainonline.org/showthread.php?t=26493.

57.   Al-Rasid, "Sheikh Hassan al-Saffar wa al-rihan al-khasr!" (Sheikh Hassan al-Saffar and the Lost Bet!), November 22, 2009, http://www.rasid.com/index.php?act=artc&id=26&hl=%25D8%25A7%25D9%2584%25D8%25B7%25D8%25A7%25D8%25BA%25D9%2588%25D8%25AA%20%25D9%2586%25D9%2585%25D8%25B1%20%25D8%25A7%25D9%2584%25D9%2586%25D9%2585%25D8%25B1.

58.   Al-Rasid, "Al-ʿAwamiya: Al-Shaykh al-Nimr yadʿu li tashkil jabha maʿrada diniya jadida fi al-Saʿudiyya" (Al-ʿAwamiya: Sheikh al-Nimr Calls for the Formation of a Religious Opposition Front in Saudi Arabia), January 20, 2008, http://www.rasid.com/index.php?act=artc&id=20226&hl=%D8%AC%D8%A8%D9%87%D8%A9%20%D8%A7%D9%84%D9%85%D8%B9%D8%A7%D8%B1%D8%B6%D8%A9%20%D8%A7%D9%84%D8%B1%D8%B4%D9%8A%D8%AF%D8%A9.

59.   "Rajal al-Din al-Shiʿa al-Saudi: Nahnu maʾ al-Iran wa laha al-haq fi Darab Masalih Amrika wa Tadmir Israʾyil" (Saudi Shiʿa Cleric: We Are with Iran, and It Has the Right to Strike America and Destroy Israel), al-Aafaq, July 17, 2008, http://aafaq.org/reports.aspx?id_rep=778.

60. The IslamOnline interview of al-Nimr was conducted on July 22, 2008, and is available at http://www.sharqeyah.us/vb/showthread.php?t=39040.

61. *Al-Ukhdud*, "Al-Shaykh Nimr: Lam idagh li-istiquwa' al-Shi'a fi al-Sa'udiy bi al-quwwa al-kharijiya" (Shaykh al-Nimr: I Did Not Call for the Bolstering of the Saudi Shi'a by Foreign Forces), July 26, 2008, okhdood.com/?act= artc&id=2569.

62. Author's interview with a Shi'a activist, al-'Awamiya, Saudi Arabia, January 22, 2013.

63. Al-Rasid, "Al-Sulta al-Sa'udiya tatlaq sarah rajal al-din al-ma'rada al-Shaykh Nimr al-Nimr" (The Saudi Government Releases the Opposition Cleric Shaykh Nimr al-Nimr), August 24, 2008, http://www.rasid.com/print.php?id=23875.

64. Habib Trabelsi, "Heightened Shi'ite–Sunni Tension in Medina," *Middle East Online*, February 24, 2009, http://www.middle-east-online.com/english/? id=30601.

65. Human Rights Watch, *Denied Dignity: Systematic Discrimination and Hostility Toward Saudi Shi'a Citizens* (New York: Human Rights Watch, September 2009), 16.

66. Quoted in Caryle Murphy, "Shi'ite Bias Claim Laid Bare After Showdown," *The National*, April 26, 2009.

67. Al-Rasid, "Al-Saffar yuhajim al-mu'assasa al-diniya wa yada' li-rafa' al-tamiz wa al-ta'asub al-dini fi al-mamlaka" (Al Saffar Criticizes the Religious Establishment and Calls for Rejecting Discrimination and Fanaticism in the Kingdom), originally published in al-Rasid on March 15, 2009, but now at http:// hajrnet.net/hajrvb/showthread.php?t=402972621.

68. Al-Rasid, "Itlaq al-mahtajazin 'ala khalfiat ahdath al-Baqi' yu'aqib laqa' juma' 'Abdallah bil-wafd al-Shi'a" (Release of Detainees in the Wake of the Baqi' Events Followed a Meeting Between King Abdullah and a Shiite Delegation), March 3, 2009, http://www.rasid.com/?act=artc&id=27287.

69. Author's interviews with Kuwaiti Shi'a activists, Kuwait City, Kuwait, November 2010.

70. Author's interview with youth activists in al-'Awamiya, Saudi Arabia, January 2013.

71. Al-Rasid, "Dafa'aa 'an al-Shaykh al-Nimr . . . awqafu al-tamiz al-ta'ifi" (In Shaykh Nimr's Defense . . . Stop Sectarian Discrimination), March 16, 2009. https://www.rasid.com/?act=artc&id=27619; author's interview with activists in al-'Awamiya and Qatif, Saudi Arabia, January 2013.

72. Al-Rasid, " ʿItisam hashid fi al-ʿAwamiya tadammunan ma al-Shaykh al-Nimr al-mutarad min al-sulalat" (Protest Rally in al-ʿAwamiya in Solidarity with Shaykh Nimr, a Fugitive from the Authorities), March 19, 2009, https://www.rasid.com/?act=artc&id=27679.

73. Al-Rasid, "Rijal din wa muthaqifun Shiʿa fi al-Saʿudiya yurfidun ʿal-tahdid wahda al-watan'" (Shiʿite Clerics and Intellectuals in Saudi Arabia Reject "Threats to the Unity of the Homeland"), April 6, 2009, http://hajrnet.net/hajrvb/showthread.php?t=402974154.

74. Haramayn Website, "Alan taʾssis Harakat Khalas fi aal-Jazira al-Arabiya" (Announcement of the Formation of the Salvation Movement on the Arabian Peninsula), March 5, 2009, http://www.alhramain.com/hiic/index.php?sec=V1...A13C61B13CE7A5FB}&id=12860&act=show&Sectyp=163.

7. UNDER SIEGE: THE SALAFI AND REGIME COUNTERMOBILIZATION

1. For a representative editorial, see ʿAbd al-Rahman al-Rashid, "Li-hadhihi al-asbab, nakhsha Iran" (For These Reasons, We Fear Iran), al-Sharq al-Awsat, April 18, 2006, http://www.asharqalawsat.com/leader.asp?section=3&issue=10003&article=358858&search=إيران&state=true. See also Mamoun Fandy, "Al-ʿIraq: Jaʾizat al-ʿArab al-kubra" (Iraq: The Great Arab Prize), al-Sharq al-Awsat, June 9, 2008, http://www.asharqalawsat.com/leader.asp?section=3&issueno=10786&article=474218. Fandy writes that "a nonnuclear Iran uses Iraq as a platform for its influence and dominance in Lebanon, Gaza, Yemen, Bahrain, Kuwait, and other Gulf countries."

2. Joost Hiltermann has noted, "[Iran] wants to have the greatest influence possible, and it can only do that if it is not a sectarian actor. . . . It can be more effective if it does not play the Shiʿite card." Quoted in Scott Peterson, "Saudi Arabia, Iran Target Mideast's Sectarian Discord," Christian Science Monitor, March 5, 2007. ʿAbd al-Rahman al-Rashid, the director of al-ʿArabiya television and a frequent contributor to al-Sharq al-Awsat, noted this same thing in an op-ed piece. See ʿAbd al-Rahman al-Rashid, "Nijad yilʿab fi al-saff al-ʿArabi" (Ahmadinejad Plays in the Arab Ranks), al-Sharq al-Awsat, January 7, 2007.

3. Author's interview with a Consultative Council member, Riyadh, Saudi Arabia, March 12, 2007.

4. Toby Craig Jones, "Saudi Arabia's Not so New Anti-Shiʿism," *Middle East Report* 242 (Spring 2007): 29–32. For a broader exploration of Salafism's intellectual tradition of anti-Shiʿism, see Guido Steinberg, "Jihadi Salafism and the Shiʿis: Remarks About the Intellectual Roots of Anti-Shiʿism," in Roel Meijer, ed., *Global Salafism: Islam's New Religious Movement* (New York: Columbia University Press, 2009), 117–125.

5. Mansur al-Nuqaydan, "Al-kharita al-Islamiyya fi al-Saʿudiyya wa qadiyat al-takfir" (The Islamist Map in Saudi Arabia and the Question of Excommunication), *al-Wasat*, February 28, 2003.

6. The seminal works condoning *takfir* against the Al Saʿud and attacking the official clerical establishment for tolerating their excesses include Abu Muhammad al-Maqdisi, *Al-kawashif al-jaliyya fi kufr al-dawla al-Saʿudiyya* (Clear Evidence on the Infidel Nature of the Saudi State) (n.p.: n.p., 1990 or 1991[?]), http://www.tawhed.ws; and Safar al-Hawali, "Dhahirat al-ʿirja" (The Phenomenon of Prevarication), Ph.D. diss., Umm al-Qura University, Mecca, 1985, http://www.tawhed.ws. This argument can also be found in an article by noted Saudi cleric ʿAli Bin Khudayr al-Khudayr, "Man aledhi yamluk huq al-takfir?" (Who Has the Right to Excommunication?), http://www.tawhed.ws, accessed December 12, 2005.

7. Several Shiʿa activists in the Eastern Province portrayed King ʿAbdallah as constrained by his reliance on the Salafi clerical establishment. Author's interviews with various activists in Qatif, Ahsa, and al-Dammam, March 10–11, 2007. In contrast, two scholars of the kingdom take a more instrumental approach. Toby Craig Jones has written, "Unlike in the 1980s, when Saudi Arabia met the ideological threat posed by Khomeini head-on, the kingdom's rulers have not consistently manipulated sectarian hostility." Yet he later concludes that "managing and strategically deploying anti-Shiism is nevertheless an important part of [King ʿAbdallah's] government's political calculus." Jones, "Saudi Arabia's Not So New Anti-Shiism," 29. Gregory Gause has argued for a similar ambivalence in Saudi policy, noting that "the Saudi government itself has not played the sectarian card in recent crises," but he still frames sectarianism as a form of "cynical manipulation" and likens it to "playing with fire." F. Gregory Gause III, "Saudi Arabia: Iraq, Iran, the Regional Power Balance, and the Sectarian Question," *Strategic Insights* 6, no. 2 (2007), http://www.isn.ethz.ch/isn/Digital-Library/Publications/Detail/?ots591=0c54e3b3

-1e9c-be1e-2c24-a6a8c7060233&lng=en&id=30985. See also al-Nuqaydan, "Al-kharita al-Islamiyya fi al-Saʿudiyya wa qadiyat al-takfir."

8. Stéphane Lacroix has written that the Saudi regime "played the card of the Shirazi Shiʿite opposition." The first goal was to relieve pressure on the Saudi regime, but also to prevent the Sahwa from developing contacts with the Shirazi opposition in exile. Stéphane Lacroix, *Awakening Islam: The Politics of Religious Dissent in Saudi Arabia* (Cambridge, Mass.: Harvard University Press, 2011), 223–224.

9. The fatwa was originally posted on Islam Today, the website of the Saudi Salafi cleric Salman al-Awda. For the signatories of the so-called jihad fatwa on Iraq, see this website at http://www.islamtoday.net/articles/show_articles_content.cfm?id=72&catid=76&artid=4436. For an English translation, see http://www.pbs.org/wgbh/pages/frontline/shows/saud/etc/fatwa.html, accessed July 24, 2011.

10. Toby Craig Jones, "The Iraq Effect in Saudi Arabia," *Middle East Report* 237 (Winter 2005): 20–25.

11. The text of the fatwa "Nidaʾ li-ahl al-Sunna fi al-ʿIraq wa ma yajib ʿala al-umma min nasrathim" (An Appeal to the Sunnis of Iraq and What Is Necessary for the Community of Believers to Do for Them to Be Victorious) is available at Saudi cleric Nasr al-Umar's website, al-Muslim, http://www.almoslim.net, accessed April 14, 2008.

12. "Shaykh Salman al-ʿAwda Warns of Sectarian War in Iraq; Holds the U.S. Responsible," OSC Document, GMP20061107866002, November 5, 2006, mentioned in a 2007 Congressional Research Service report, *Iraq: Regional Perspectives and U.S. Policy* (Washington, D.C.: Congressional Research Service, January 12, 2007), http://www.policyarchive.org/handle/10207/bitstreams/3064_Previous_Version_2007-01-12.pdf.

13. "Fi al-Saʿudiyya tadʿu fatawa ila hadm darih Imam Husayn wa Sayida Zaynab" (In Saudi Arabia, Fatwas Call for the Complete Destruction of the Imam Husayn and Sayida Zaynab Shrines), Nahrain website, July 19, 2007, http://www.nahrainnet.net/news/52/ARTICLE/10075/2007-07-19.html.

14. Many Sunni Arab audiences interpreted the execution through a sectarian lens because of its timing (December 30, 2006, the first day of the Muslim holiday of Eid al-Adha) and the disclosure (via cellphone video recording) that the Shiʿa guards were shouting "Muqtada al-Sadr!" as Saddam was executed. Both of these features of the execution contributed to the perception

that the death of Saddam was a blow to Sunnism by the ascendant Shiʿas in Baghdad. Donna Abu-Nasr, "Sectarianism Casts Shadow Over Mideast," Associated Press, January 29, 2007.

15. See, for instance, Muhammad Surur Zayn al-ʿAbidin, *Wa jaʾa dawr al-Majus* (And Then Came the Turn of the Magi), http://www.tawhed.ws/a?i=402, accessed October 19, 2007.

16. The list of such anti-Shiʿa websites includes al-Bainah, http://www.albainah.net (November 2003); D-Sunnah, http://www.d-sunnah.net (May 2002); al-Wylish, http://www.wylsh.com (October 2004); and Khomainy, http://www.khomainy.com (March 2004).

17. Al-Rasid, "Masirat hashida tunadi 'mawt lil Israʾyl'" (Al-Qatif: Tumultuous Marches with Shouts "Death to Israel"), August 2, 2006, http://www.rasid.net; original link no longer working, so see the full text at https://bahrainforums.com/vb/%C7%E1%DA%D1%C8-%E6%C7%E1%DA%C7%E1%E3/142071.htm.

18. Faris Bin-Hizam, "Khilafat dakhil al-tiyar al-Salafi fi mawqif harb Lubnan" (Disagreements Within the Salafi Trend in the Stand on Lebanon War), *al-Hayat*, August 25, 2006, http://www.alwakad.net/go/news.php?action=view&id=135.

19. Faraj Ismaʿil, "Bin Jibrin yuʾkid ʿn fatwahu lam tukun an Hizballah" (Bin Jibrin Confirms That His Fatwa Doesn't Apply to Hizballah), al-ʿArabiya television website, August 8, 2006, http://www.alarabiya.net.

20. Fouad Ibrahim, *The Shiʿis of Saudi Arabia* (London: Saqi Books, 2006), 197. For the full fatwa in Arabic, see http://www.islamway.com/?iw_s=Article&iw_a=view&article_id=1876, accessed September 18, 2006.

21. Ismaʿil, "Bin Jibrin yuʾkid ʿn fatwahu lam tukun an Hizballah."

22. "Saudi Cleric Issues Anti-Hezbollah Edict," Associated Press, August 6, 2006.

23. Ismail, "Bin Jibrin yuʾkid ʿn fatwahu lam tukun an Hizballah."

24. Quoted in "Al-Awda: Nakhtalif ma Hizb Allah wa lakin narafid adwan Israel" (Al-Awda: We Differ with Hizballah, but We Reject Israeli Aggression), *Islam Today*, July 22, 2006, http://islamtoday.net/salman/artshow-78-7650.htm.

25. Born in Jizan in 1931, al-Madkhali studied under the Ethiopian-born cleric Muhammad Amin Jamii at the Islamic University of Medina and later taught hadith there. In the early 1990s, he emerged as the most prominent figure of what was known as the "Jamii" or "Medina Salafi" clerical school. Key tenets of this current were its opposition to Sayyid Qutb's ideas and Muslim

Brotherhood thought, unquestioning loyalty to the Saudi regime, and, most important, criticism of Sahwa clerics such as Safar al-Hawali and Salman al-ʿAwda. For opposing the Sahwa, al-Madkhali was reported to have received extensive support from the Saudi government through the Ministry of Interior. In Saudi clerical discourse, the term *Madkhali* is used derisively to refer to an obsequious, careerist, and excessively quietist brand of Salafism. ʿAbd al-Muhsin al-ʿUbaykan was born in 1952, studied at the Faculty of Shariʿa in Riyadh, and later became a judge. An early member of the Sahwa, he later moved into the Saudi regime's camp, becoming the vice minister of justice and a strong proponent of dissuading Saudi youth from volunteering for jihad in Iraq. Lacroix, *Awakening Islam*, 212; al-Nuqaydan, "Al-kharita al-Islamiyya fi al-Saʿudiyya wa qadiyat al-takfir."

26. On ʿAbd al-Muhsin al-ʿUbaykan's statement, see "Saudi Shura Council Member Sheikh al-ʿObikan: According to Shariʿa Hizbullah Operations Are Illegitimate; a Temporary Peaceful Settlement with Jews Is Needed," Middle East Media Research Institute (MEMRI), Special Dispatch no. 1222, August 1, 2006, http://www.memri.org.

27. Al-Rasid, "Al-suljaj al-amaniya tustʿdy al-katib al-Alaq li-intiqadhu fatwa takfiriya" (Security Authorities Summon Writer ʿAllaq for Critcizing Excommunication Fatwa), October 4, 2006, https://www.rasid.com/?act=artc&id=12955.

28. Al-Hramain website, "Bayan Hizballah al-Hijaz " (Statement by Hizballah al-Hijaz Follows the Heroic Odysseys in Lebanon and the Treacherous Statement by the Sons of Saʿud), http://www.alhramain.com/hiic/index.php?sec=V1d4 a1IySm5QVDA9&sub=V1cweFYwMHlUak5RVkRBOQ==&r={000CF6F/000 054374BAA23D3F3233/000000062626352BEC262309/000054374BAA23D3 F3233/0000000B19B02A924BE1CBAF}&Sectyp=190, accessed July 23, 2011.

29. Abu Majid (pseudonym), "Libnan bayn al-Waʿd al-Sadiq wa al-Mawqif al-Mutakhathil" (Lebanon Between the True Promise and the Defeatist Position) (editorial), al-Rasid, July 15, 2006, http://www.rasid.net/artc.php?id=11963.

30. In reality, however, the sectarian factor played a relatively minor role; the insurgency is rooted in complex center–periphery, tribal, and class tensions that afflict Yemen as a whole. For more on the Huthi conflict, see Barak Salmoni, Byrce Loidolt, and Madeleine Wells, *Regime and Periphery in Northern Yemen: The Huthi Phenomenon* (Santa Monica, Calif.: RAND Corporation, 2010).

31. *Al-Sharq al-Awsat*, "Al-tamarud al-Huthi harb Iyraniya ʿala al ʿArab" (The Houthi Rebellion Is an Iranian War on the Arabs), November 3, 2009, http://www.aawsat.com/leader.asp?section=3&article=546949&issueno=11328#.UTuEQdY9-So.

32. *Al-Watan*, "Al-Saudiya: Nahdhar al-Houthiyun ʿumlaʾ al-tawsiʿa al-Iraniya" (Saudi Arabia: Warns That the Houthis Are Agents of Iranian Expansion), November 5, 2009, http://www.aljazeera-online.net/index.php?t=1&id=78&s=1&tab=3.

33. Nasir al-ʿUmar, "Bayan al-ʿulema hawl ʿadwan al-Huthyiyyin al-rafidha" (The Declaration of the Ulema Regarding the Aggression of the Huthi Rejectionists), al-Muslim website, November 12, 2009, http://www.almoslim.net.

34. Hassan al-Saffar, "Al-Saffar yadin ʿadwan al-mutasalalin wa yuaʾkid al-waquf maʿ al-watan" (Saffar Condemns Aggression and Confirms That He Stands with the Homeland), *al-Riyadh*, November 10, 2009, http://www.alriyadh.com/2009/11/10/article473178.html.

35. Turki al-Hamad, "Al-maskut ʿanhu fi masaʾlat al-Huthiyyin wa masaʾil ukhra" (That Which Is Not Discussed on the Huthi Dilemma and Other Dilemmas), *al-Sharq al-Awsat*, November 19, 2009.

36. Hamza al-Muzayni, "Majahil al muwaqiʿin" (Unknown Signatories), *al-Elaph*, November 19, 2009.

37. Author's interviews in the Eastern Province, Saudi Arabia, March 12–13, 2007. See also the unattributed interview with Saudi Shiʿa activist-researcher Fouad Ibrahim in al-Rasid, January 23, 2007, http://www.rasid.net.

38. The statement was originally posted to the Nur al-Islam website on May 30, 2008, and can be found at http://www.alqadisiyya3.com/q3/index.php?option=com_content&view=article&id=128:----&catid=34&Itemid=215.

39. The document is signed by major figures across the spectrum, such as ʿAbd al-Karim al-Hubayl, Munir al-Khabbaz, and Hassan al-Saffar. See al-Tawafuq website, "Al-Shiʿa bi al-mamlaka yasdarun bayan radan ʿala Bayan li-22" (The Shiʿa of the Kingdom Issue a Statement Responding to the Statement of the 22), July 1, 2008, http://www.altwafoq.net/v2/print.php?rpt=7599.

40. Munir al-Nimr, "Al-Saffar Yantaqid al-Tatarruf wa Yadʿau li-Tʿaziz al-Hiwar al-Dakhili" (Al-saffar criticizes extremism and calls for the implementation of internal dialogue), *al-Riyadh*, June 15, 2008, http://www.alriyadh.com/2008/06/15/article350968.html.

41. Ahmed al-Masari, "Ulema al-Shiʿa yadʾaun li-ʿiqala imam al-haram" (Shiite Religious Scholars Call for Dismissal of Mecca Mosque Imam), *al-Quds al-Arabi*, May 11, 2009, http://81.144.208.20:9090/pdf/2009/05/05-10/qfi.pdf.

42. Author's interview with Saudi Shiʿa cleric, Dammam, Saudi Arabia, March 17, 2007.

43. Author's interview with Saudi Shiʿa activist, United States, May 25, 2011.

44. Author's interview with Saudi Shiʿa reformist Jaber al-Ahmad al-Jaber Al Sahah, al-Qatif, Saudi Arabia, March 15, 2007.

45. Author's interview with member of the Consultative Council, Riyadh, Saudi Arabia, March 12, 2007.

46. Joe Avacena, "EP Vote May Reflect Split Electorate," *Saudi Gazette*, March 2, 2005.

47. P. K. ʿAbdul Ghafour, "Prominent Figures Win EP Elections," *Arab News*, March 5, 2005.

48. Paul Melly, "Religious Rights and Political Enfranchisement Provide the Basis of a New Compact with the Shiʿa," *Gulf States Newsletter* 27, no. 23 (2005): 8–9.

49. Ibtihal Mubarak, "Islamic Scholars See New Era of Unity, Openness," *Arab News*, August 7, 2005.

50. Author's interview with a Sunni reformist based in Dammam, Saudi Arabia, March 8, 2007.

51. Ibid.

52. Ibid.

53. Habib Mahmud, "An-nas yakhtalif maʿ al-hukam—Wayn al-mushkila?" (People Differ with the Rulers—Where Is the Problem?), al-Rasid, October 25, 2006, http://www.rasid.net.

54. Human Rights Watch, *Dignity Denied: Systematic Discrimination and Hostility Toward Saudi Shiʿa Citizens* (New York: Human Rights Watch, September 2009).

55. Author interview with a Shiʿa intellectual in al-Qatif on March 12, 2007. This figure also argued that there is "some [Shiʿa] cooperation with the Salafis, but many are afraid of pressure from the extremists. There is an exchange of email and ideas, but there is no institutionalized framework for reform cooperation." Author's interview with Shiʿa cleric, Qatif, Saudi Arabic, March 12, 2007.

56. Author's interview with a Shiʿa activist, al-Ahsa, Saudi Arabia, March 15, 2007.

57. Author's interview with Shiʿa activists, Eastern Province, Saudi Arabia, March 2007.

58. Author's interview with a former member of the Saudi security services assigned to the Eastern Province, undisclosed location, July 15, 2011.

8. WAVING ʿUTHMAN'S SHIRT: SAUDI ARABIA'S SECTARIAN SPRING

1. Hani al-Dhahiri, "ʿDarajat al-Basij' fi al-ʿAwamiya!" ("Basij Motorcycles" in al-ʿAwamiya!), *al-Hayat*, October 11, 2011.

2. Author's interview with Saudi Shiʿa oppositionist, London, October 28. 2011.

3. The petition is located here: http://www.metransparent.com/spip.php?article13117&lang=ar&id_forum=19643. A second petition, *Nahwa dawlat al-huquq wa al-muʾassasat* (Toward a State of Rights and Institutions), was signed by twenty-two figures, most of them Islamists, including Salman al-Awda, http://www.ahewar.org/debat/show.art.asp?aid=247642. See also Madawi al-Rasheed, "Saudi Arabia: Local and Regional Challenges," *Contemporary Arab Affairs* 6, no. 1 (2013), 29.

4. Facebook page of the Free Youth Coalition, http://ar-ar.facebook.com/ksa1Freedom1day, accessed December 18, 2011.

5. Author's interview with Saudi Shiʿa activists, al-ʿAwamiya, Saudi Arabia, January 20, 2013.

6. Facebook, "Statement by the Free Youth Coalition," March 1, 2011, http://www.facebook.com/ksa1Freedom1day.

7. Facebook, "Thawrat Mintaqat al-Sharqiya" (The Eastern Region Revolution), http://www.facebook.com/Revolution.East, accessed December 2011. As of October 2011, the site had more than fifteen thousand followers.

8. Ibid.

9. Ibid. See also al-Rasid, "Al-tadhahirat fi al-Ahsa lil afraj an al-Sheikh Tawfiq al-ʿAmir" (Protests in al-Ahsa Calling for the Release of Sheikh Tawfiq al-ʿAmir), March 4, 2011, https://www.rasid.com/?act=artc&id=43190.

10. Facebook page of the Free Youth Coalition, http://ar-ar.facebook.com/ksa1Freedom1day, accessed December 18, 2011.

11. *Al-Boraq Islamic Forum*, "Movement Confirms Truth About the Hunayn Revolution in Response to Rumors and False Reports," March 6, 2011.

12. Reuters, "Shiʿites Stage Small Protest in Saudi Oil Province," March 3, 2011.

13. Markaz al-Haramayn lil-ʿAlam al-Islami (Hizballah al-Hijaz website), "Yawm al-ghadab fi al-Ahsa ihtijajan ʿala iʿtiqal al-Shaykh al-ʿAmar" (Day of Rage in al-Ahsa Protesting Against the Detention of Shaykh al-ʿAmar), March 3, 2011, cited in al-Rasid, https://www.rasid.com/?act=artc&id=43169.

14. *Human Rights Watch*, "Saudi Arabia: Stop Stifling Peaceful Dissent," March 8, 2011.

15. Associated Press, "Saudi Police Open Fire During Protest," March 11, 2011.

16. Markaz al-Haramayn lil-ʿAlam al-Islami (Hizballah al-Hijaz website), "Al-sultat al-Saʿudiyya tutliq sirah daʿiat huquq al-insan al-Shaykh Tawfiq al-ʿAmir" (Saudi Authorities Release Human Rights Activist Shaykh Tawfiq al-ʿAmir from Prison), March 7, 2011, http://www.taghribnews.com/vdcjhaex .uqevazf3fu.html. See also Ian Black, "Middle East Crisis: Saudi Arabia: Expectations High Before 'Day of Rage' with Modest Aims," *The Guardian*, March 10, 2011; al-Rasid, "Al-tadhahirat fi al-Ahsa lil afraj an al-Sheikh Tawfiq al-ʿAmir."

17. Al-Rasid, "Al-Sayyid Nimr yastankar muwajhat al-taʾbir al-silmi bi-itlaq al-rasas" (Sayyid Nimr Denounces Confronting Peaceful Expressions by Firing Bullets), March 12, 2011.

18. Al-Rasid, "Silsilat maysirat fi al-mintaqa al-sharqiya tutalib bi-islahat wa itlaq sujanaʾ" (Eastern Region Demonstrations Demand Reforms and the Freeing of Prisoners), March 12, 2011.

19. Al-Rasid, "Al-maysirat tajtah mudun wa baldat Qatif tadamunan maʿ al-shaʿb al-Bahrayni" (Demonstrations Spread Across the Cities and Villages of Qatif in Solidarity with the Bahraini People), March 18, 2011.

20. Quoted in Reuters, "Shiites Protest Peacefully in Eastern Saudi Arabia," March 18, 2011.

21. Hassan al-Saffar, "Nadaʾ min al-Shaykh Hassan al-Saffar hawl al-ahdath al-alima fi al-Bahrayn" (Appeal from Shaykh Hassan al-Saffar on the Painful Events in Bahrain), al-Saffar website, March 11, 2011, http://www.saffar.org/ ?act=artc&id=2632.

22. Author interviews in Qatif, Saudi Arabia, January 2013.

23. *Jafrianews*, "Saudi Monarchy Bows to Pressure, Order Release of Detained Shia Activists" (in English), March 9, 2011, http://jafrianews.com/2011/03/ 09/saudi-monarchy-bows-to-pressure-order-release-of-detained-shia -activists/.

24. Al-Rasid, "Wafd shabab al-Qatif yaltaqi naʾib ʿamir al-mintaqa al-sharqiya" (Qatif Youth Delegation Meets with the Deputy Governor of the Eastern Region), March 31, 2011.

25. Al-Rasid, "Rijal al-din fi al-Qatif yadʿun li waqf al-tadhahurat al-ihtijajiyya" (Religious Scholars in Qatif Call for an End to Protests), April 21, 2011, http://www.rasid.com/artc.php?id=44029.

26. See, for example, the interview with a member of the Eastern Province Revolution in Rosie Bsheer, "Saudi Revolutionaries: An Interview," *Jadaliyya*, June 21, 2012; see also Muhammad Qabasi, "Taʿliqan ʿala bayan al-makhzi lil-Shaykh al-Khunayzi" (Commentary on the Despicable Announcement from Shaykh al-Khunayzi), *al-Watan*, July 17, 2013, http://www.elwatandz.com/watanarabi/5717.html; and the comments of the "Ahrar Awamiya" movement at https://www.facebook.com/Rasadnews.net/posts/2478278752 57847?utm_medium=twitter&utm_source=twitterfeed.

27. Assad Abboud, "Riot-Hit Saudi Town 'Calm' After Iran Fears," Agence France Presse, October 5, 2011.

28. Patrick Cockburn, "Saudi Police 'Open Fire on Civilians' as Protests Gain Momentum," *The Independent,* October 5, 2011.

29. Ministry of Interior website, http://www.moi.gov.sa; see also *Arab News*, "Foreign Elements Blamed for Qatif Riots," October 5, 2011.

30. Mshari al-Dhaydi, "Al-ʿAwamiya: Al-qisa laysat taʾifiya" (Al-ʿAwamiya: The Story Is Not a Sectarian One), *al-Sharq al-Awsat*, October 11, 2011.

31. Announcement on the Ministry of Interior website, http://www.moi.sa.gov, accessed December 17, 2011.

32. *Saudi Gazette*, "Saudi Grand Mufti: Nation's 'Foes Use Protests to Create Sedition,'" March 10, 2011.

33. Muhammad al-Habadan, "Limadha lam tanjah al-mudhahirat fi al-Saʿ-udiyya?" (Why Did the Demonstrations Not Succeed in Saudi Arabia?), Nur al-Islam website, March 9, 2011, https://www.islamlight.net/index.php?option=content&task=view&id=21576&Itemid=23.

34. Muhammad al-Sulami, "Calls Mount for Prosecution of 'Day of Rage' Dissidents," *Arab News*, March 15, 2011.

35. Facebook page of the Free Youth Coalition, http://ar-ar.facebook.com/ksa1Freedom1day, March 7, 2011.

36. Author's interview with Sunni activist, Riyadh, Saudi Arabia, January 18, 2013.

37. Abeer Allam, "Online Law Curbs Saudi Freedom of Expression," *Financial Times*, April 6, 2011.

38. Al-Sulami, "Calls Mount for Prosecution of 'Day of Rage' Dissidents."

39. An example of one such banned channel is Revolution2East, http://www .youtube.com/user/Revolution2East?ob=0&feature=results_main. See Leila [pseud.], "Saudi Arabia: The Shiʿa of al-Sharqiyya" (in English), *Muftah*, April 20, 2012.

40. "Shurta al-Sharqiyya tatalqa balaghatha ala Faysbuk" (Police of al-Sharqiyya Receive Their Communications on Facebook), *al-Yaum*, November 2, 2011, http://www.alyaum.com/News/art/35133.html.

41. Facebook, "Samud min ʿajal al-hadood" (Steadfastness for the Borders of Qatif), http://ar-ar.facebook.com/qatifterritory. A similar Facebook page is "Al-Ahsa yurid taghir al-amir" (Al-Ahsa Wants to Change Its Emir), http://www .facebook.com/home.php?sk=group_138668152864845.

42. For a good earlier overview of this benefits package, see Robert Danin, "Is Saudi Arabia Next?" *Atlantic Monthly*, December 4, 2011.

43. ʿAbid al-Suhaymi, "Al-Saudiya talan bidaʾ al-mawsam al-intikhaby lil majlis al-baladi 22 abril al-muqbil" (Saudi Arabia Announces the Beginning of the Municipal Elections Season Will Be April 22), *al-Sharq al-Awsat*, March 23, 2011, http:// aawsat.com/details.asp?section=43&article=613770&issueno=11803#.UTub gNY9-.

44. Walaa Hawari, "Women Launch Facebook Campaign to Participate in Municipal Elections," *Arab News*, February 7, 2011.

45. Tariq al-Humayd, "Saudi Arabia: The Day of the Silent Bayaa," *al-Sharq al-Awsat* (English ed.), March 12, 2011, http://www.asharq-e.com/print.asp? artid=id24478.

46. Free Youth Coalition, "Limadha fashalat al-daʿwa li-al-tadhahur yawm 11 Maris?" (Why Did the Call for Protest on March 11 Fail?), April 19, 2011, http://www.saudiwave.com/ar/2010-11-09-15-55-47/706———11—.html.

47. Author's interview with a Sunni activist, Riyadh, Saudi Arabia, January 18, 2013. In October 2011, the writer Hamad al-Majid implored Saudi Shiʿa not to make blanket accusations against the country's Sunnis and to reject acts of violence by members of their community. Hamad al-Majid, "The Saudi Shiites and the al-ʿAwamiya Riots," *al-Sharq al-Awsat* (English), October 18, 2011.

48. Quoted in Patrick Cockburn, "Saudi Arabia: Four Men Killed as Shia Protests Against the State Intensify," *The Independent*, November 25, 2011.

49. Quoted in *BBC World News*, "New Clashes in Saudi Arabia Leave 'Protester' Dead," February 11, 2012, http://www.bbc.co.uk/news/world-middle-east -16995286.

50. Bsheer, "Saudi Revolutionaries."

51. Author's interview with a Saudi Shiʿa activist, al-ʿAwamiya, Saudi Arabia, January 20, 2013.

52. Al-Saffar's July 21, 2012, sermon can be found on his website at http://www .saffar.org/?act=artc&id=3007. See also the interview with Tawfiq al-Sayf, who echoes this point. "The youth said to the leaders: 'You stop. You haven't delivered what you have promised. Now we will do our best.'" Quoted in *Kuwait Times*, "Saudi Shiite Protests Show Rise of Radical Generation— Authorities Accuse Iran of Stirring Unrest," July 21, 2012.

53. Author's interview with a Shiʿa youth activist, al-ʿAwamiya, Saudi Arabia, January 20, 2013.

54. Author's interview with Shiʿa youth activist, Safwa, Saudi Arabia, January 24, 2013.

55. Author's interview with a Shiʿa youth activist, Tarut, Saudi Arabia, January 24, 2013.

56. Facebook page of the Free Youth Coalition, http://ar-ar.facebook.com/ ksa1Freedom1day.

57. Facebook page of Missionary Youth Movement, http://www.facebook.com/ pages/%D8%B4%D8%A8%D8%A7%D8%A8-%D8%A7%D9%84%D8%AD% D8%B1%D8%A7%D9%83-%D8%A7%D9%84%D8%B1%D8%B3%D8%A7%D 9%84%D9%8A/175097632543743.

58. Facebook page of the Solidarity Group, http://www.facebook.com/pages/ %D8%AA%D8%B6%D8%A7%D9%85%D9%86-%D8%A3 %D9%87%D8%A7%D9%84%D9%8A-%D8%A7%D9%84%D9%82%D8% B7%D9%8A%D9%81-%D9%85%D8%B9-%D8%A7%D9%84%D9%85%D8% B9%D8%AA%D9%82%D9%84%D9%8A%D9%86-%D8%A7%D9%84%D9% 85%D9%86%D8%B3%D9%8A%D9%8A%D9%86/209682735724698.

59. Facebook page of the Free Men of Sayhat, http://www.facebook.com/asad .sahat.

60. Facebook page of the Free Men of Tarut, https://www.facebook.com/groups /248466898563448/?ref=ts&fref=ts.

61. Facebook page of the Supporters of Qatif, https://www.facebook.com/ qateefioona.

62. Facebook page of the Women Supporters of the Zaynab School in Qatif, https://www.facebook.com/Qatifiyat?fref=ts. "Zaynab" refers to Zaynab bint ʿAli, the daughter of ʿAli.

63. Facebook, "The Eastern Region Revolution," https://www.facebook.com/rev .east?ref=ts&fref=ts.

64. Author's interview with a Saudi Shiʿa activist, Tarut, Saudi Arabia, January 24, 2013.

65. See the FJC's Facebook page at https://www.facebook.com/cofaj. Also, author's email correspondence with an FJC member, February 12, 2013, and interviews with Eastern Province youth, Saudi Arabia, January 2013.

66. Author's e-mail correspondence with an FJC member, February 12, 2013.

67. Author's interview with a Saudi Shiʿa cleric, Tarut, Saudi Arabia, January 24, 2013.

68. Author's interview with a Saudi Shiʿa intellectual, Qatif, Saudi Arabia, January 20, 2013.

69. Al-Rasid (in English), "Sheikh Saffar Refuses Exploiting Awamiya Events to Attack Shiites," October 13, 2011, http://www.rasid.com/english/index .php?act=artc&id=364&hl=Saffar%20exploit.

70. For this sermon, see al-Saffar's website, "Hadath al-ʿAwamiya wa al-Taʿbiʾa al-Taʿifiya" (The Events of Awamiya and Sectarian Mobilization), February 10, 2012, http://www.saffar.org/index.php?act=artc&id=2801&hl=%D8%A7% D9%84%D8%B9%D9%88%D8%A7%D9%85%D9%8A%D8%A9.

71. Saudi Press Agency, February 20, 2012, http://www.spa.gov.sa/English/ details.php?id=972172.

72. For example, the al-Hayat article calling for the "liquidation" of Shiʿa dissidents: al-Dhahiri, " ʿDarajat al-Basij' fi al-ʿAwamiya!"

73. The video of al-Nimr's speech is available at http://www.youtube.com/ watch?v=4x358ZGNgeA.

74. Al-Akhbar (English ed.), "Saudi Minister Says Shiʿa Cleric 'Mentally Ill,'" July 30, 2012, http://english.al-akhbar.com/content/saudi-minister-says-shia -cleric-mentally-ill.

75. On May 11, for example, ʿAbdallah dismissed ʿAbd al-Muhsin al-ʿUbaykan, an ultraconservative adviser to the royal court, for publicly criticizing the king's reform agenda on a local radio station. Al-ʿUbaykan had long been a source of embarrassment to the royals; his polarizing remarks on gender relations in

2010 were a key impetus for ʿAbdallah's subsequent ban on nonofficial fatwas. Al-ʿUbaykan's ouster followed the king's dismissal of the head of the *mutawaʿin* (morality police) because of similarly hard-line views on gender relations. The escalating civil war in Syria prompted a further curtailment of Sunni clerical power. The Syria crisis long animated Salafi clerical sympathies in the kingdom. In most cases, clerical statements adhered closely to the official Saudi line on Syria, providing helpful theological top cover to Saudi foreign policy. In Friday sermons, tweets, and Facebook posts, the clerics demonized the Assad regime and the Alawites, expressed solidarity with civilian suffering, and pushed for greater Gulf involvement, to include arming the Syrian opposition. Yet there were also more militant calls for jihad and humanitarian aid to the Syrian citizenry. On May 26, a group calling itself the "Ulema Committee to Support Syria" (Lajnat al-ʿUlamaʾ li-daʿm Suriya), announced its existence on Facebook, posting its bank account numbers for prospective donors and organizing a fund-raising drive on May 28 at the Bawardi Mosque in Riyadh. On May 29, Arabic press indicated that King ʿAbdallah of Saudi Arabia had summoned twenty prominent Salafi clerics to Riyadh to ban them from soliciting donations for Syria's embattled citizenry. In the following days, a number of these clerics announced on their social media platforms that they had been contacted by authorities and ordered to desist from collecting funds for Syria. See Frederic Wehrey, *Saudi Arabia Reins in Its Clerics on Syria* (Washington, D.C.: Carnegie Endowment for International Peace, June 14, 2012).

76. This argument was put forward by the provocative and immensely popular tweeter "@Mujtahidd" in posts during the summer. See, for instance, Twitter, @Mujtahidd, July 9, 2012, https://twitter.com/mujtahidd.

77. *Al-Watan*, "Hurriyat al-raʾy la ta ʿni al-tahrid ʿala al-fitna" (Freedom of Expression Does Not Mean Incitement of Chaos), July 10, 2012.

78. Author's interview with a Shiʿa cleric, Safwa, Saudi Arabia, January 24, 2013.

79. Facebook, "The Eastern Region Revolution," July 12, 2012, http://www.facebook.com/Revolution.East.

80. The statement is found on the al-Jazira al-ʿArabiya website, July 12, 2012, http://shmsaljazereh.blogspot.com/2012/07/5.html.

81. Al-Jazeera television website (in English), "Shia Cleric Arrested in Saudi After Shootout," July 18, 2012, http://www.aljazeera.com/news/middleeast/2012/07/20127819561763436.html.

82. ShiaPost, "Saudi Wahhabi Security Forces Demolished Imam Hussein Mosque in al-ʿAwamiyah," September 16, 2012, http://en.shiapost.com/?p=6543.

83. ShiaPost, "Saudi Police Arrest Shiʿa Cleric for Participating in Anti-US Demo," September 26, 2012, http://en.shiapost.com/?p=6719.

84. The letter can be found at http://www.qatifnews.com/media/files/13421 35485.pdf.

85. The letter can be found at http://www.aleqt.com/2012/08/20/article_684737. html; see also the al-ʿArabiya television website (in English), "Saudi Shiʿite Clerics Condemn Violence in Restive Qatif," August 21, 2012, http://english. alarabiya.net/articles/2012/08/21/233432.html. Echoing this view, an August 31 sermon by Hasan al-Saffar warned that social networks could be used for spreading untrue rumors that "break down the bridges of trust between people and cause sedition and problems." Quoted in al-Rasid, "As-Shaykh al-Saffar yuhdhar min fawda istikhdam mawaqiʿ al-tawasul al-ijtamaʿi" (Shaykh Saffar Warns of Chaos from Using Social Networking Sites), September 3, 2012, http://www.rasid.com/artc.php?id=50472.

86. Author's interview with Saudi Shiʿa youth activists, al-ʿAwamiya, Saudi Arabia, January 20, 2013.

87. Author's interview with a Saudi Shiʿa cleric, Sayhat, Saudi Arabia, January 24, 2013.

88. Author's interview with a Saudi Shiʿa cleric, Tarut, Saudi Arabia, January 24, 2013.

89. Author's interview with a Saudi Shiʿa youth activist in al-Awamiya, Saudi Arabia, January 20, 2013.

90. On July 24, 2012, Saudi protesters took to the streets in the central province of al-Qassim to show their support for political prisoners held in the kingdom's prisons. The protest broke out in the city of Buraydah on Monday night, where demonstrators shouted slogans against the Al Saʿud regime and called for an immediate release of prisoners. "The nation wants the release of prisoners," they chanted. For two days, on September 23–24, hundreds of protesters gathered outside of a prison in al-Qassim demanding the release of prisoners, and dozens of relatives of prisoners staged a sit-in. On October 23, Saudi youths staged a rally in the kingdom's eastern city of Khobar, calling for the release of political prisoners held in jails in al-Qassim, Jeddah, and the capital Riyadh.

91. See the program's Twitter account, https://twitter.com/tawasul_qatif.

92. Author's interview with a Saudi Shiʿa activist, Qatif, Saudi Arabia, January 19, 2013.

93. For background on the Islahiyya's dialogue efforts, see Tawfiq al-Sayf, "An takun Shiʿiyyan fi al-Saʿudiyya: Ishkalat al-muwatana wa al-huwiya fi mujtamaʿ taqlidi" (To Be a Shiʿa in Saudi Arabia: Questions of Citizenship and Identity in a Traditional Society), January 2013, http://talsaif.blogspot.com/2012/12/view-to-be-shia-in-saudi-arabia-on_25.html.

94. An illustrative example of al-ʿAwda's views on democracy can be found at https://twitter.com/salman_alodah/status/280321067069865984.

95. Author's interview with a Saudi Shiʿa activist, Qatif, Saudi Arabia, January 20, 2013.

96. Al-Mokhtsar, "Mandub Suriya yaqtarah irsal biladihi quwat li-himayat sukan al-Qatif" (Syrian Delegate Suggests His Country Send Troops to Protect the Population of Qatif), May 3, 2012, http://www.almokhtsar.com/node/39904.

97. Author's interview with Saudi Shiʿa writer, Qatif, Saudi Arabia, January 22, 2013.

98. Author's interviews with Saudi Shiʿa activists in Qatif, Saudi Arabia, January 2013..

99. ʿAbd al-Rahman Muhammad ʿAmr al-ʿAqil, Ahdath al-ʿAwamiya wa al-Qatif (The Events of ʿAwamiya and Qatif) (Riyadh, Saudi Arabia: King Faysal Center for Research and Islamic Studies, February 10, 2012); the full report is at http://t.co/wltovJtn.

100. Author's interview with a Saudi Shiʿa cleric, Safwa, Saudi Arabia, January 24, 2013.

9. RENEGOTIATING A RULING BARGAIN: THE KUWAITI SHIʿA

1. Laurence Louër, Transnational Shiʿa Politics: Religious and Political Networks in the Gulf (London: Hurst, 2008), 252.

2. Author's interview with a Shiʿa cleric, Kuwait City, Kuwait, November 19, 2010. This sentiment was increasingly echoed by other figures. "It is time for the government to recognize Ashura as a day off in the country," the parliamentarian Saleh al-ʿAshur told al-Hayat in 2004. Quoted in Vincent Vulin, "After Saddam, Shiʿites in Kuwait Becoming Vocal About Rights," Gulf News, March 12, 2004.

3. Agence France Press, "Kuwait's Shi'ite Muslims Press for Religious Education," September 21, 2004; Hamad al-Jasir, "Deputies, Former Ministers Hold
Protest Meeting: Kuwaiti Shi'is Express Reservations Over Their 'Exclusion'
from Posts," al-Hayat, June 11, 2005, as reported on BBC Monitoring Middle
East, June 13, 2005.

4. A common refrain from Sunni opponents was that Shi'as in Kuwait enjoyed
far better rights than Sunnis in Iran. An editorialist in Kuwait opposing concessions to the Shi'a pointed to a purported comment by Ayatollah Khomeini
when asked about building mosques for Sunnis in Iran: "Why don't they pray
in the mosques of their Shi'ite brothers?" "Kuwait: What do Kuwaiti Shi'ites
Actually Want?" Right Vision News, April 1, 2010.

5. Ibid. The next time a Shi'a was appointed to the cabinet, it was Dr. Mas-
suma Mubarak, a female professor of political science, to the Ministry of
Planning.

6. Author's interview with a Shi'a cleric, Kuwait City, Kuwait, November 19,
2010. As currently configured, Shi'a financial transactions had to be vetted
and were subject to veto by the Ministry of Religious Endowments' leadership, which was dominated by conservative Sunni Islamists.

7. Rawafidh (rejectionists; sing. rafidha) is a derogatory term used by opponents
of Shi'ism to denigrate the sect by portraying them as having strayed from Islamic orthodoxy. Takfir (the act of pronouncing a Muslim or a non-Muslim an
unbeliever or kafir) is a theological precept rooted in early Islamic tradition.
Islamic scholars and jurists are divided over the term's scope and applicability and over who can use it. Doctrinaire Salafis believe it is incumbent on
all practicing Muslims to denounce as unbelievers those they witness trans-
gressing Islamic norms. More liberal writers argue that the term can be used
only by qualified scholars after a lengthy juridical process. For Shi'a, the term
takfir is especially abhorrent; opponents of Shi'ism frequently deploy it to
denigrate and delegitimize the sect. B. Izzak, "Cancel 'Sectarian' Education:
Shatti," Kuwait Times, May 9, 2008; author's interview with a Shi'a cleric,
Kuwait City, Kuwait, November 19, 2010.

8. Author's interview with a Shi'a MP, Kuwait City, Kuwait, December 8, 2010.

9. Agence France Presse, "Kuwait's Shi'ite Muslims Press for Religious Education," September 21, 2004; see also U.S. Department of State, International Religious Freedom Report: Kuwait (Washington, D.C.: U.S. Department of State,
2010), http://www.state.gov/g/drl/rls/irf/2010/148828.htm.

10. Ibid.; see also Louër, *Transnational Shiʿa Politics*, 250.

11. Agence France Presse, "Government Move to Monitor Shiʿite Mosques Stirs Row in Kuwait," March 15, 2005.

12. *Kuwaiti Times*, "Sectarian Controversy Over Abdalli Border Incident," April 5, 2010.

13. Hamza Hendawi, "Worsening Shiʿite–Sunni Tensions Seen Even in Affluent, Tolerant Kuwait," Associated Press, November 1, 2006.

14. Reported on al-Jazeera, April 11, 2004.

15. Author's interview with a Sunni government official, Kuwait City, Kuwait, November 21, 2010.

16. Author's interview with a nongovernment organization head, Kuwait City, Kuwait, November 24, 2010.

17. Quoted in Omar Hassan, "Gulf Arab Shiʿites Want Non-sectarian Rule in Iraq," Agence France Presse, January 26, 2005.

18. Louër, *Transnational Shiʿa Politics*, 252.

19. Quoted in Hamid Jasr, "Mutalibat Shiʿa fi al-Kuwayt bi-idkhal al-fiqh al-Jaʿfari fi al-manahij" (Shiʿa of Kuwait Demand the Inclusion of Jaʿfari Jurisprudence in the Curriculum), *al-Hayat*, September 22, 2004. Al-Muhri specifically mentioned the U.S. State Department's annual *Human Rights Report on Kuwait* to buttress his demands.

20. Quoted in Hassan, "Gulf Arab Shiʿites Want Non-sectarian Rule in Iraq."

21. Ibid. See also Jasr, "Mutalibat Shiʿa fi al-Kuwayt bi-idkhal al-fiqh al-Jaʿfari fi al-manahij."

22. Quoted in *Al-Hayat*, "Al-Shaykh Al Sahah yarfud idkhal al-fiqh al-Jaʿfari ila al-manahij wa yahdhir min al-tasrihat al-taʾifiyya" (Shaykh Al Sahah Rejects the Inclusion of Jaʿfari Jurisprudence Into the Curriculum and Warns Against 'Sectarian Statements'), September 24, 2004.

23. Ibid.

24. *Al-Elaph*, "Kuwait: Youths Attack Shiʿite Mosque, Creating Fear of Sedition," as reported on *BBC World Monitoring*, October 10, 2005.

25. Quoted in ibid.

26. Ibid.

27. *Kuwait Times*, "Jahra Mosque Attack Sparks Security Fears: Al-Zarqawi Influence Growing?" October 16, 2005.

28. Agence France Presse, "Kuwaiti Emir Warns of Lessons of Iraq," January 29, 2007.

29. The cleric Muhammad Baqir al-Muhri argued that the Shiʿa should use every means possible to defend themselves against Salafi critics and press for their rights, including satellite TV and Internet. Hassan, "Gulf Arab Shiʿites Want Non-sectarian Rule in Iraq."

30. Author's interview with a Shiʿa MP, Kuwait City, Kuwait, December 8, 2010.

31. The channel broadcasts mainly from Washington, D.C., and has offices in Kuwait, Syria, Bahrain, Lebanon, and Isfahan. Author's interview with a Shiʿa activist, Kuwait City, Kuwait, December 8, 2010.

32. Al-Anwar TV website, http://www.alanwartv.com, accessed September 7, 2011.

33. Al-Zahra television website, June 20, 2006, http://www.alzahra.tv.

34. Al-Jazeera website, "NILESAT Suspends Another Religious Satellite Channel Amid Conflicting Reasons," October 17, 2010, reported on *BBC Monitoring Middle East*, October 19, 2010.

35. Omar Hassan, "Kuwait: Shiʿite Marriage TV Drama Hits Sectarian Nerve," Agence France Presse, September 16, 2007

36. Author's interview with Shiʿa parliamentarian, Kuwait City, Kuwait, November 20, 2010.

37. Quoted in Agence France Presse, "Kuwait Sunni Group, MP Blast Shiʿite Leader," January 30, 2007.

38. Agence France Presse, "Kuwaiti Emir Pardons Shiʿite Activist Who Abused Muslim Caliphs," February 26, 2004.

39. For Yasser al-Habib's views, see his website al-Qatrah (The Drop) at http://www.alqatrah.net, accessed September 13, 2011.

40. A. Saleh, "Habib Sees Kuwait as Part of Shiʿite Nation," *Kuwait Times*, March 8, 2009.

41. *Al-Elaph*, "Al-Habib yarudd ala ʿisqat jinsiyathu al-Kuwaitiya bi fadiʾya Fadak" (Al-Habib Responds to Losing His Kuwaiti Nationality with the Satellite Channel Fadak), September 20, 2010, http://www.elaph.com/Web/news/2010/9/597933.html?entry=articleRelatedArticle.

42. Ibid.

43. Salah al-Ghazali, *Al-jamaʿat al-siyasiya al-Kuwaytiya fi qurn* (Political Parties in Kuwait Throughout the Century) (Kuwait City: Jamiʿyyat al-Haquq Mahfudha, 2007).

44. Author's interview with Shiʿa parliamentarian, Kuwait City, Kuwait, November 25, 2010. See also J. E. Peterson, "Political Activism Among the Shiʿa of Kuwait," Arabian Peninsula Background Note no. APBN-008, July 2009, http://www.JEPeterson.net.

45. Al-Ghazali, *Al-jamaʿat al-siyasiya al-Kuwaytiya fi qurn*, 398.

46. Ibid., 400.

47. Author's interviews with Shiʿa Islamists in Kuwait City, Kuwait, December 2010.

48. For background on ʿAbd al-Wahhab al-Wazzan, see his memoir *Hajis al-watan wa al-dawla* (The Concept of the Nation and the State) (Kuwait City: Jamiya al-Haquq Mahfudha lil-Majmuʿa, 2007).

49. Al-Ghazali, *Al-jamaʿat al-siyasiya al-Kuwaytiya fi qurn*, 394.

50. Ibid., 391.

51. Louër, *Transnational Shiʿa Politics*, 253.

52. Quoted in al-Ghazali, *Al-jamaʿat al-siyasiya al-Kuwaytiya fi qurn*, 392.

53. Samih Shams al-Din, "Jabha Shiʿiyya jadida li-muharabat Hizballah" (A New Shiʿa Front to Fight Hizballah), *al-Seyassah*, December 30, 2004.

54. Fawzi ʿUways, "The National Groupings Coalition: We Are Prepared to Include Any Sunni Forces," *al-Seyassah*, October 22, 2005.

55. Al-Ghazali, *Al-jamaʿat al-siyasiya al-Kuwaytiya fi qurn*, 401; Louër, *Transnational Shiʿa Politics*, 251.

56. Xinhua General News Service, "Kuwaiti PM Says Iran Not a Rival," May 15, 2004.

57. As Nathan Brown has argued, the redistricting measure was supposed to "recast Kuwaiti elections from neighborhood contests fought over hundreds of votes to more ideological competitions favoring groups with clear programs." Nathan Brown, "Kuwait's 2008 Parliamentary Elections: A Setback for Democratic Islamism," web commentary, Carnegie Endowment for International Peace, May 2008, http://www.carnegieendowment.org/files/brown_kuwait2.pdf.

58. Mary Ann Tétreault, "Kuwait's Annus Mirabilis," *Middle East Report Online*, September 7, 2006, http://www.fpif.org/articles/frankensteins_lament_in_kuwait.

59. Democracy Reporting International and Kuwait Transparency Society, *Kuwait: Assessment of the Electoral Framework: Final Report* (Berlin: Democracy Reporting International; Kuwait City: Kuwait Transparency Society, November 2008).

60. Mamduh al-Muhayni, "Al-Kuwayt: Man huwwa li-aghlaq al-sanduq Bandura aladhi futiha qabla nahwa shahr?" (Kuwait: Who Is to Close the Pandora's Box That Was Opened About a Month Ago?), *al-Elaph*, March 17, 2008.

10. TILTING TOWARD REPRESSION: THE SUNNI OPPOSITION AND THE KUWAITI REGIME

1. For background on the *hadhar–badu* divide, see chapter 1. See also Anh Nga Longva, "Nationalism in Pre-modern Guise: The Discourse on *Hadhar* and *Badu* in Kuwait," *International Journal of Middle East Studies* 38 (2006): 171–187.

2. Lori Plotkin Boghardt notes, "[K]ey grievances of both today's Kuwaiti Sunni militants and yesterday's Kuwaiti Shi'ite militants relate significantly to Al Sahah policy positions, the former to the support for the United States in Iraq, and the latter to support for Iraq in the Iran–Iraq War." Lori Plotkin Boghardt, *Kuwait Amid War, Peace, and Revolution: 1979–1991 and New Challenges* (New York: St. Antony's College and Palgrave Macmillan, 2007), 177.

3. Falah 'Abdallah al-Mdeires, *Jam'iyyat al-Ikhwan al-Muslimin fi al-Kuwayt* (Muslim Brotherhood Groups in Kuwait) (Kuwait City: Dar Qurtas lil-Nashr, 1999). Brotherhood-inspired movements had existed in Kuwait since the 1960s and 1970s, particularly on university campuses and student unions.

4. Author's interview with HADAS member, Kuwait City, Kuwait, November 22, 2010.

5. Muhanna Hubayl, "Halat al-ikhwan fi al-Khalij: Ruwaya naqdiya" (The State of the Brotherhood in the Gulf: A Critical View), IslamOnline, June 3, 2008, http://www.islamonline.com.

6. As noted in previous chapters, formal political parties are banned in Kuwait; only "societies" are allowed. Salah al-Ghazali, *Al-jama'at al-siyasiya al-Kuwaytiya fi qurn* (Political Parties in Kuwait Throughout the Century) (Kuwait City: Jami'yyat al-Haquq Mahfudha, 2007), 264.

7. Ibid., 261.

8. Norwegian scholar of transnational jihadism Thomas Hegghammer has identified Hamid al-'Ali as "the most important mufti for jihadist groups operating in Iraq." Thomas Hegghammer, "Global Jihadism After the Iraq War," *Middle East Journal* 11, no. 60 (2006), 20.

9. The exact number of armed Salafi jihadists in Kuwait is unknown. However, Kuwaitis were captured or killed fighting alongside al-Qaʿida in Iraq and Afghanistan. In addition, Kuwait security forces have disrupted plots against U.S. military bases and Kuwaiti government facilities. According to Kuwaiti government sources, Hamid al-ʿAli played a key role in recruiting and inspiring the plotters in several instances. For background, see William F. McCants, *Militant Ideology Atlas* (West Point, N.Y.: Combatting Terrorism Center, November 2006), http://www.ctc.usma.edu/wp-content/uploads/2010/06/Atlas-ResearchCompendium1.pdf.

10. Al-ʿAli's biography can be found at http://www.islamway.com/?iw_s=Scholar&iw_a=info&scholar_id=500, accessed August 9, 2006.

11. Al-ʿAli's writings frequently appear on the Islamist chatrooms al-Meer, http://www.almeer.net; al-Sakifah, http://www.alsakifah.org; and Islamway, http://www.islamway.com.

12. Author's interviews with a Shiʿa cleric, December 12, 2010, and a Kuwaiti journalist, November 21, 2010, Kuwait City, Kuwait.

13. For the intellectual origins of anti-Shiʿism in Salafism, see Guido Steinberg, "Jihadi Salafism and the Shiʿis: Remarks About the Intellectual Roots of anti-Shiʿism," in Roel Meijer, ed., *Global Salafism: Islam's New Religious Movement* (New York: Columbia University Press, 2009), 107–125.

14. Al-Jazeera, "Interview with Hamid al-ʿAli," March 27, 2007, reported on *BBC Monitoring Middle East*, April 7, 2007.

15. Al-Ghazali, *Al-jamaʿat al-siyasiya al-Kuwaytiya fi qurn*, 265–266.

16. *Arab Reform Bulletin* (Carnegie Endowment for International Peace), "Kuwait Ummah Party Formed," March 26, 2005, http://carnegieendowment.org/2008/08/26/kuwait-umma-party-formed/6dsp.

17. Democracy Reporting International and Kuwait Transparency Society, *Kuwait: Assessment of the Electoral Framework: Final Report* (Berlin: Democracy Reporting International; Kuwait City: Kuwait Transparency Society, November 2008). See also Dahim al-Qahtain, "Reading the Structure of the Members of the 2008 National Assembly: Political Belonging, Tendency, Tribe and Sect," *al-Raʾy*, June 17, 2008.

18. Al-Ghazali, *Al-jamaʿat al-siyasiya al-Kuwaytiya fi qurn*, 261. See also Falah ʿAbdallah al-Mdeires, *Al-jamiʿyat al-Salafiyya fi al-Kuwayt* (Salafi Groups in Kuwait) (Kuwait City: Dar Qurtas lil-Nashr, 1999).

19. Mary Ann Tétreault, "Frankenstein's Lament in Kuwait," *Foreign Policy in Focus*, November 29, 2001, 1, http://www.fpif.org/articles/frankensteins _lament_in_kuwait.

20. Jamie Etheridge, "Kuwaiti Tribes Turn Parliament to Own Advantage," *Financial Times*, February 2, 2009.

21. Paul Salem, *Kuwait: Politics in a Participatory Emirate* (Washington, D.C.: Carnegie Endowment for International Peace, July 2006), 1.

22. Quoted in Etheridge, "Kuwaiti Tribes Turn Parliament to Own Advantage."

23. A Gulf scholar used the term *mutiny* to describe this shift. Author's interview, Manama, Bahrain, March 16, 2008.

24. Al-Mdeires, *Al-jami'yat al-Salafiyya fi al-Kuwayt*, 30–50.

25. Olivier Roy, *Globalized Islam: The Search for a New Ummah* (New York: Columbia University Press, 2004), 232–289; Meijer, ed., *Global Salafism*. An important exploration of Salafism as vehicle for social mobility in hierarchical societies is found in Alexander Knysh, "Contextualizing the Salafi—Sufi Conflict (from the Northern Caucasus to Hadramawt)," *Middle Eastern Studies* 43, no. 4 (2007), 524.

26. Author's interview with a nongovernmental organization head, Kuwait City, Kuwait, November 25, 2010.

27. Associated Press, "Seven Kuwaiti Shi'ites to Face Trial Over Eulogy of Slain Hezbollah Militant," April 15, 2008.

28. *Al-Elaph*, "Hizballah yakhtaf al-Kuwayt . . . mujaddan!" (Hizballah Holds Kuwait Hostage . . . Again!), August 15, 2008.

29. *Al-Elaph*, " 'Abd al-Samad li-*Elaph*: Al-tufiliyat tasma 'Imad Mughniyah irhabiyan!" ('Abd al-Samad to *Elaph*: Parasites Call Mughniyah a Terrorist!), February 17, 2008.

30. Quoted in Diana Elias, "Kuwait Questions Two Members of Dissolved Parliament Over Eulogizing Hezbollah Militant," Associated Press, March 25, 2008.

31. Associated Press, "Seven Kuwaiti Shi'ites to Face Trial"; *Kuwait Times*, " 'Abd al-Samad, Lari Face Rising Anger," February 21, 2008.

32. The al-Mutayr are a historically powerful *badu* tribe, with members concentrated in the outlying Fourth and Fifth districts. Aside from Muhammad Hayif al-Mutayri, other significant Salafi politicians hail from the tribe—the most important being the MP Musallam al-Barrak and Hakim al-Mutayri, who followed Hamid al-'Ali as the secretary-general of the Kuwaiti Scientific Salafi

Movement in 2000. *Al-Hayat*, "Al-Kuwayt: Da'wat ila ihtwa' azmat ta'bin Mughniyah wa tark amrha ila al-qada'" (Kuwait: Calls to Contain the Crisis of Mughniyah's Commemoration and Leave the Matter to the Judiciary), March 3, 2008.

33. *Al-Seyassah*, "Muhammad Hayif: Mu'askarat li-tadrib Hizballah al-Kuwayti fi al-Wifara wa al-'Abdli" (Muhammad Hayif: Hizballah Kuwait Training Camps Are in al-Wifara and al-'Abdli), February 19, 2008.

34. Ahmad al-Khalid, "Erase Dissolution of the Parliament: Al-Muslim," *Kuwait Times*, May 6, 2008.

35. *Al-Dar*, "Al-thawabit al-Shi'iyya: La wajud li-Hizballah al-Kuwayti wa la khalaya Shi'iyya na'ima aw mastayqidha" (The Shi'a Bloc: There Is No Kuwaiti Hizballah and No Sleeping or Active Shi'a Cells), October 11, 2009, http://www.aldaronline.com/Dar/Detail2.cfm?ArticleID=74089&CFID=10804983&CFTOKEN=17850428.

36. *Kuwait Times*, " 'Abd al-Samad, Lari Face Rising Anger," February 21, 2008.

37. Author's interviews with HADAS member, Kuwait City, Kuwait, November 22, 2010, and with a Shi'a cleric, Kuwait City, Kuwait, December 12, 2010.

38. *Al-Watan*, " 'Abd al-Samad wa Lari yu taliban min al-Kharafi al-tahdi'a wa i'adat 'alaqatihima ma' muntqadihima min al-nuwwab: Ra'is al-Majlis: Lan asmah munaqishat ta'biin Mughniyah fi al-jalsa ghadan wa la yumkin al-mutaliba bisahb jinsiyat al-na'ibayn" ('Abd al-Samad and Lari Request Calm from al-Kharafi and the Restoration of Their Relationships with Their Deputy Critics: Parliament Speaker: I Will Not Permit Discussion of Mughniyah's Commemoration at the Session Tomorrow and the Stripping of the Two Deputies' Nationality Cannot Be Demanded), March 3, 2008.

39. Quoted in Omar Hassan, "Shi'ite Crackdown Fuels Sectarian Tensions in Kuwait," Agence France Presse, March 13, 2008. See also Mona Kareem, "Shi'aphobia Hits Kuwait," *Jadaliyya*, May 17, 2011.

40. The Popular Action Bloc was composed of seven members prior to 2008. Headed by former Speaker of Parliament Ahmad Sadoun, it included prominent Salafi MPs such as Musallam al-Barrak.

41. Diana Elias, "Government Criticizes Shi'ites Who Eulogized Mughniyah, Warns of Civil Strife," Associated Press, February 18, 2008.

42. Ibid.

43. Kenneth Katzman, *Kuwait: Security, Reform, and U.S. Policy* (Washington, D.C.: Congressional Research Service, December 9, 2009), 3.

44. Elias, "Kuwait Questions Two Members of Dissolved Parliament"; Associated Press, "Seven Kuwaiti Shi'ites to Face Trial."
45. Diana Elias, "Kuwaiti Court Acquits Shi'ites of Militant Eulogy," Associated Press, October 22, 2008.
46. Mamduh al-Muhayni, "Al-Kuwayt: Man huwwa li-aghlaq al-sanduq Bandura aladhi futiha qabla nahwa shahr?" (Kuwait: Who Is to Close the Pandora's Box That Was Opened About a Month Ago?), al-Elaph, March 17, 2008.
47. Author's interview with a Sunni Islamist, Kuwait City, Kuwait, November 29, 2010.
48. Quoted in Hassan, "Shi'ite Crackdown Fuels Sectarian Tensions in Kuwait."
49. Al-Nahar, "Hizbullah Complains to Kuwait Against Mughniyah Critics" (in English), February 22, 2008, http://old.naharnet.com/domino/tn/NewsDesk.nsf/0/D526A6CD1A8A3DEAC22573F700613802?OpenDocument.
50. Ibid.
51. Hassan, "Shi'ite Crackdown Fuels Sectarian Tensions in Kuwait."
52. Quoted in ibid.
53. United Press International, "Kuwait to Deport Foreigners Who Mourned Hezbollah Chief," March 2, 2008.
54. Al-Muhayni, "Al-Kuwayt."
55. Quoted in Omar Hassan, "Kuwait's Shi'ites Seek Election Boost Amid Sectarian Tensions," Agence France Presse, May 15, 2008.
56. Ibid.
57. Jamie Etheridge, "Kuwaiti Tribes Turn Parliament to Own Advantage," Financial Times, February 2, 2009.
58. Lamia Radi, "Sunni–Shi'ite Battle for Kuwait Parliamentary Seats," Middle East Online, June 28, 2006, http://www.middle-east-online.com/english/?id=16851.
59. Reported on BBC Monitoring Middle East, May 19, 2008, and al-'Arabiya TV, Panorama, May 18, 2008.
60. Part of the concerted parliamentary opposition to the new prime minister can be explained by a law enacted by Emir Jabr al-Ahmed Jabar Al Sahah in 2003, before his death in 2006. The law effectively separated the roles of crown prince and prime minister; before 2003, the Parliament had been unable to interpellate the prime minister because he was in line to become emir, and the emir, by constitution, was off limits from questioning. Even so, the next prime minister, Sahah al-Ahmed (2003–2006), was not subjected

to questioning because many Kuwaitis believed (correctly) that he would be the next emir. These reservations were not present during the tenure of Nasser al-Muhammad, who was subjected to questioning soon after taking office. See Mona Kareem, "Kuwait's Prime Ministerial Dilemma and the Prospects for Constitutional Monarchy," *Arab Reform Bulletin* (Carnegie Endowment for International Peace), June 22, 2011, http://carnegieendowment .org/2011/06/22/kuwait-s-prime-ministerial-dilemma-and-prospects-for -constitutional-monarchy/6b7n.

61. Al-Jazeera online (in English), "Kuwait Prime Minister Survives Confidence Vote," January 5, 2011, http://english.aljazeera.net/news/middleeast/2011/ 01/20111581427365727.html.

62. Author's interview with a Kuwaiti academic, Kuwait City, Kuwait, December 2, 2008.

63. Author's interview with a Shiʿa MP, Kuwait City, Kuwait, December 8, 2010.

64. Muhammad al-Mutayr and Muhammad Hayef al-Mutayri hail from the same tribe but are not directly related.

65. Agence France Presse, "Kuwait Islamist MPs to Quiz Premier Over Iran Cleric," November 16, 2008; Duraid Al Baik, "Kuwait MPs May Question PM on Iranian Cleric Visit," *Gulf News*, November 16, 2008.

66. Mahmud Baʿlabaki, "Lari wa Jawhar wa ʿAbd al-Samad: Hathari min al-fitna al-taʾifiya" (Lari, Jawhar, and Abd al-Samad: Beware of Sectarian Sedition), *al-Dar*, December 26, 2008, http://www.dar-al-seyassah.com/news_details .asp?nid=36354&snapt=first%20page.

67. Tariq al-Humayd, "Irani fi al-Kuwayt" (An Iranian in Kuwait), *al-Sharq al-Awsat*, November 17, 2008.

68. Khalid al-Hajiri, "Ihtijaj khaliji ʿalin ʿala fawda al-dimoqratiya fi al-Kuwayt" (Loud Protest in the Gulf Against the Chaos of Democracy in Kuwait), *al-Seyassah*, November 21, 2008, http://www.elaph.com/Web/NewsPapers/ 2008/11/384538.htm.

69. Reporters sans Frontieres, "Kuwaiti Media Forbidden from Covering Dismantling of Spy Ring," May 10, 2010.

70. The sermon and statement are available on Yasser al-Habib's English-language website The Drop (al-Qatrah), http://www.the-drop.net/en/edara/ index.php?id=108, accessed September 9, 2011.

71. Author's interview with a HADAS member, Kuwait City, Kuwait, November 22, 2010.

72. Al-Jazeera, September 8, 2010.

73. Habib Toumi, "Kuwait Government Calls for Restraint by Politicians," *Gulf News*, September 15, 2010, http://gulfnews.com/news/gulf/kuwait/kuwait -government-calls-for-restraint-by-politicians-1.682375.

74. Author's interviews in Kuwait City, Kuwait, November 2010.

75. Kuwait News Agency, "Cabinet Session Targets Recent Media Tensions in Kuwait" (in English), September 16, 2010, http://www.kuna.net.kw/Article Details.aspx?language=en&id=2111467.

76. *Kuwait Arab Times*, "Ban on Public Gatherings to Contain Rift," September 20, 2010, http://www.arabtimesonline.com/NewsDetails/tabid/96/smid/414/ ArticleID/159721/reftab/63/t/KUWAIT-ACTS-TO-CURB-SHIITE-SUNNI -TENSIONS/Default.aspx.

77. *Kuwait Times*, "Barrak Demands Government Action on Sectarianism," September 13, 2010; *Arab Times*, "MPs Criticize Government's 'Handling' of Habeeb Crisis as Weak, Inefficient," September 18, 2010, http://www.arab timesonline.com/Portals/0/PDF_Files/pdf10/sep/19/02.pdf.

78. *Arab Times*, "Ban on Public Gatherings to Contain Rift," September 20, 2010.

79. Amnesty International, "Kuwait Urged to Investigate Police Raid on MPs Gathering," December 10, 2010, http://www.amnesty.org/en/library/info/ MDE17/007/2010/en.

80. B. Izzak, "MoI [Ministry of Interior] Cracks Down on Public Rallies," *Kuwait Times*, October 12, 2010.

81. *The Guardian*, "Kuwait Shuts Down al-Jazeera for Covering Opposition Protest Meeting," December 13, 2010, http://www.guardian.co.uk/world/2010/ dec/13/kuwait-shuts-aljazeera-opposition-meeting.

82. Al-Qatra website, "Shaykh al-Habib Hails Our Great Scholars' Refusal to Pay Tribute to Fadlullah," July 7, 2010, http://alqatrah.net/en/edara/index .php?id=102.

83. *Tehran Times*, "Sunni World Welcomes Leader's Fatwa," October 5, 2010, http://old.tehrantimes.com/Index_view.asp?code=227879.

84. Ahmad al-Misri, "Al-muthaqifun al-Saʿudiyyun wa al-Khalijiyyun yadaʿun ila tasuddi lil-siyasiyat al-taʾifiyya al-rasmiyya" (Saudi, Gulf Intellectuals Call for Confronting Official Sectarian Policies), *al-Quds al-ʿArabi*, November 1, 2010.

85. Tariq al-Humayd, "The Sunnis and Shiʿites: The Knife Has Cut to the Bone," *al-Sharq al-Awsat* (English ed.), September 21, 2010.

86. Author's interview with a Kuwaiti academic, Kuwait City, Kuwait, December 12, 2010.

11. A BALANCING ACT GOES AWRY: SECTARIANISM AND KUWAIT'S MASS PROTESTS

1. All quoted in ʿAbd al-Nasr Ibrahim, "Daʿu ʾila ʿitimad al-hiwar li-haqn dam al-shaʿb wa tahqiq al-istiqrar" (They Called for the Adoption of Dialogue to Immunize the People and Achieve Stability), *al-Seyassah*, March 18, 2011, http://www.al-seyassah.com/AtricleView/tabid/59/smid/438/ArticleID/131320/Default.aspx.

2. B. Izzat, "MPs Divided Over Troops in Bahrain," *Kuwait Times*, March 16, 2011.

3. Quoted in *Arab Times*, "MPs, Media Hype Hiking Sectarian Tension Locally; Government Silence Draws Criticism," March 27, 2011.

4. Ibrahim, "Daʿu ʾila ʿitimad al-hiwar li-haqn dam al-shaʿb wa tahqiq al-istiqrar."

5. Muhammad Nazal, "Al-Salafi yuhadhdhir fi al-Rumaythiya min ʿUm al-Qura al-Iraniyaʾ: Al-Khatar al-Safawi qaʾim wa la yuhaddiduna bi-alʿab nariyya" (Salafis Warn in Rumaythiya of an "Iranian Um al-Qura": The Safavid Threat Is Coming and Is Not Threatening Us with Fireworks!), *al-Raʾy*, March 20, 2011, http://www.alraimedia.com/Alrai/Article.aspx?id=270321.

6. Ibid.

7. Marwa al-Bahrawi, "Try Again: Aid Convoy," *Arab Times*, March 22, 2011.

8. Quoted in *Arab Times*, "MPs, Media Hype Hiking Sectarian Tension Locally; Government Silence Draws Criticism," March 27, 2011.

9. *Al-Dar*, "ʾAwsaʿ istinkar li-iqfal *al-Dar*" (Wide Condemnation Over the Closure of *al-Dar*), February 1, 2012.

10. Reuters, "Kuwait Daily Cautious After Sectarian Ban Lifted," May 20, 2012.

11. *Al-Qabas*, "ʾIghlaq *al-Dar* 3 ashhur" (*Al-Dar* Shut Down for 3 Months), July 6, 2012.

12. Abu-Bakar A. Ibrahim and Nihal Sharaf, "Sunni and Shiʿa MPs Lock Horns Over Shield Troops," *Arab Times*, March 20, 2011.

13. Habib Toumi, "Kuwait's Parliament Wading Deeper Into Controversy," *Gulf News*, May 24, 2011.

14. *Al-Seyassah*, "Hal tuʾyid ʿibad al-wafadin al-Shiʿi al-murtabin bi ʿHizb Allaʾ wa al-Haras al-Thawri al-Irani min duwal Majlis al-ʿArabi al-khaliji" (Do You

Support Deporting Expatriate Shiʿa Linked to "Hizballah" and the Islamic Revolutionary Guards Corps from GCC Countries?), public-opinion poll, April 2, 2011.

15. Nazal, "Al-Salafi yuhadhdhir fi al-Rumaythiya min ʿUm al-Qura al-Iraniya.'"

16. *Al-Dar*, "Istihdaf al-Shiʿa . . . yabdaʾ bi-tahdid al-Qallaf" (Targeting the Shiʿa Starts with Threatening al-Qallaf), May 1, 2011.

17. B. Izzak, "Disgraceful," *Kuwait Times*, May 19, 2011; *Media Line*, "Kuwaiti Parliament Scuffle Reveals Sectarian Cleavages," May 19, 2011.

18. *BBC News*, November 16, 2011.

19. Tribal forces led the electoral battle in the fourth and fifth constituencies—namely, al-Rashaida tribe in the Fourth District and al-Awazim and al-ʿAjman tribes in the Fifth District. In the elections, the opposition won eighteen out of twenty seats in the two tribal electoral districts.

20. *Kuwait Times*, "Sparks Fly as Kuwaiti MPs Vote to Recognise Syrian Council," February 29, 2012, http://www.bridgingthegulf.org/en/news/news/Sparks_fly_as_Kuwaiti_MPs_vote_to_recognise_Syrian_council__.html?id=239.

21. Hailing from the First District, al-Dashti has also called for Kuwait to adopt closer relations with Iran and Iraq. Abubakar A. Ibrahim, "Dashti Criticizes Difficulties Faced by Kuwaiti Shiʿites," *Arab Times*, June 17, 2012.

22. Quoted in Muhyi Amir and Hasan al-Muhanna, "Jalsa Suriyya . . . Taʾifiya" (A Sectarian Session on Syria), *al-Jaridah*, March 2, 2012.

23. Badrya Darwish, "Before It Is Too Late," *Kuwait Times*, May 23, 2012, http://www.gulfinthemedia.com/index.php?m=opinions&id=602477&lim=30&lang=en&tblpost=2012_05.

24. Mona Kareem, "Twitter Revolutionises Kuwaiti Political Sphere," *Gulf News*, June 29, 2012.

25. Cited in Sylvia Westall, "Kuwaitis Worry Twitter Cases Stir Sectarian Tensions," Reuters, May 2, 2012.

26. Author's email exchange with a Kuwait political activist, October 31, 2012.

27. Nawara Fattahova, "NA [National Assembly] Dissolution Inspires Many to Create Twitter Accounts," *Kuwait Times*, December 7, 2011.

28. Lindsey Stephenson, "Ahistorical Kuwaiti Sectarianism," *Foreign Policy*, Middle East Channel, April 29, 2011, http://mideast.foreignpolicy.com/posts/2011/04/29/ahistorical_kuwaiti_sectarianism.

29. Ibid.

30. Quoted in *The Media Line*, "Kuwaiti Parliament Scuffle Reveals Sectarian Cleavages."

31. An example is the *hadhar* MP Mohammad al-Juwayhil, who was arrested on July 31, 2012, for attacking the Mutayr tribe and other *badu* personalities as well as Kuwait's stateless communities (the *bidun*) on Twitter. The government charged him with trying to "compromise the social fabric and instigate tribal and sectarian divides." Reuters, "Kuwaiti Royal Detained Over Tweets: Rights Group," July 31, 2010, http://mobile.reuters.com/article/worldNews/idUSBRE86U0TI20120731?irpc=932.

32. *NOW Lebanon*, "Kuwaiti Shiʿa MP Proposes Bill on Hate Crimes," February 23, 2012.

33. Global Voices Advocacy, "Kuwait: Three Netizens Detained," September 28, 2011.

34. *Al-Akhbar*, "Kuwaiti Writer Gets Seven Years for Anti-Shia Tweets," April 10, 2012, http://english.al-akhbar.com/node/6043.

35. *NOW Lebanon*, "Kuwaiti Shiʿa Tweeter Denies Insulting Prophet, Lawyer Says," May 21, 2012.

36. *Al-Watan*, "Haraq al-ʿalam al-Irani fi tajamʿu li nusra al-Rasul bil Irada" (Burning the Iranian Flag in Irada Square), March 28, 2012, http://alwatan.kuwait.tt/articledetails.aspx?Id=182788.

37. *NOW Lebanon*, "Kuwait Condemns Sunnis for Burning Iran Flag," March 29, 2012.

38. Quoted in Westall, "Kuwaitis Worry Twitter Cases Stir Sectarian Tensions."

39. According to the Kuwait state news agency, the death penalty applies only if the offender acknowledges the crime and refuses to repent or if the person declares himself or herself to be a prophet. For non-Muslims, the jail sentence is not to exceed ten years.

40. The Shiʿa MPs Husayn al-Qallaf, Saleh al-ʿAshur, ʿAbd al-Hamid al-Dashti, and Adnan al-Mutawwa voted against the amendments, but Ahmed Lari and ʿAdnan ʿAbd al-Samad abstained. Nihal Sharaf, "Minority MPs Urge Caution . . . Cite Case of Non-Muslims," *Arab Times*, April 12, 2012.

41. Agence France Presse, "Kuwait Ruler Rejects Death Penalty for Religious Crimes," June 6, 2012, http://www.google.com/hostednews/afp/article/ALeqM5gangkcNpzQsVw4LfjTn8wfnZCJjg?docId=CNG.97688a235ae0de3b620d965c3080aab9.a41.

42. Omar Hassan, "Detention of Leading Opponent Sparks Violence in Kuwait," Agence France Presse, October 31, 2012.

43. *Kuwait Times*, "Election Looms Amir Dissolves Parliament Sixth Dissolution Since 2006," October 7, 2012, http://news.kuwaittimes.net/2012/10/07/election-looms-amir-dissolves-parliament-sixth-dissolution-since-2006/.

44. Kafi_Q8 Twitter post, December 22, 2011, https://twitter.com/Kafi_Q8.

45. Quoted in Rima al-Baghdadi, "Kuwaiti Youth Emerge as Force in Protests Against the State," *al-Hayat*, October 22, 2012, translated by al-Monitor, October 23, 2012.

46. "Shiite Political Group Says Will Boycott Polls," Arab *Times*, October 28, 2012, http://www.arabtimesonline.com/NewsDetails/tabid/96/smid/414/ArticleID/189370/reftab/96/t/Shiite-political-group-says-will-boycott-polls/Default.aspx.

47. *Al-Nahar*, November 28, 2012, and Agence France Presse, "Al-Intikhabat fi al-Kuwayt fi dhil maqat'a wa ihtizaz al-istiqrar" (The Elections in Kuwait in the Shadow of the Boycott and Instability), November 29, 2012.

48. *Dera News* (Twitter), November 28, 2012.

49. See Saleh al-'Ashur's website for November 28, 2012, http://www.saleh ashoor.com/news.php?action=show&id=206.

50. 'Abd al-Hamid al-Dashti, Twitter post, November 28, 2012, https://twitter .com/JoIn_Q8/status/273785511682920448/photo/1.

51. Al-Jazeera, December 2, 2012. The INA garnered the most seats, with five across all five districts. In second place was the Assembly for Justice and Peace, with two, in the First and Second districts. The Humanitarian Message Assembly (Tajammu' al-Risala al-Insaniyya, electing 'Adnan al-Mutawwa') and the National Pact Assembly (electing Yusuf al-Zilzila) won in the Second and First districts, respectively. The other eight winners were independents, including 'Abd al-Hamid al-Dashti, Husayn Qallaf, and Masuma al-Mubarak.

52. *Gulf Daily News*, "New Kuwait MPs Have Terror Links," December 2, 2012.

CONCLUSION

1. Author's interview with a Shi'a activist, al-Ahsa, Saudi Arabia, January 23, 2013.

BIBLIOGRAPHY

BOOKS AND CHAPTERS IN BOOKS

Algar, Hamid. *Wahhabism: A Critical Essay*. North Haledon, N.J.: Islamic Publications International, 2002.

Assiri, ʿAbdul-Reda. *Kuwait's Foreign Policy: A City-State in World Politics*. Boulder, Colo.: Westview Press, 1990.

Boghardt, Laurie Plotkin. *Kuwait Amid War, Peace, and Revolution: 1979–1991 and New Challenges*. London: St. Antony's College and Palgrave MacMillan, 2007.

Commins, David. *The Wahhabi Mission and Saudi Arabia*. New York: Tauris, 2006.

Crystal, Jill. *Kuwait: The Transformation of an Oil State*. Boulder, Colo.: Westview Press, 1992.

Davidson, Christopher. *After the Sheikhs: The Coming Collapse of the Gulf Monarchies*. London: Hurst, 2012.

Democracy Reporting International and Kuwait Transparency Society. *Kuwait: Assessment of the Electoral Framework: Final Report*. Berlin: Democracy Reporting International; Kuwait City: Kuwait Transparency Society, November 2008.

Esposito, John, ed. *The Iranian Revolution: Its Global Impact*. Miami: Florida International University Press, 1990.

El-Fadl, Khalid Abou. *The Great Theft*. San Francisco: Harper Collins, 2005.

Fakhro, Munira. "The Uprising in Bahrain: An Assessment." In Gary G. Sick and Lawrence G. Potter, eds., *The Persian Gulf at the Millennium: Essays in Politics, Economy, Security, and Religion*, 168–188. New York: Palgrave Macmillian, 1997.

Fuller, Graham, and Rend Rahim Francke. *The Arab Shiʿa: The Forgotten Muslims.* New York: Palgrave Macmillian, 1999.

Gause, F. Gregory, III. *The International Relations of the Persian Gulf.* New York: Cambridge University Press, 2010.

Al-Ghazali, Salah. *Al-jamaʿat al-siyasiya al-Kuwaytiya fi qurn* (Political Parties in Kuwait Throughout the Century). Kuwait City: Jamiʿyyat al-Haquq Mahfudha, 2007.

Golberg, Jacob. "The Shiʿi Minority in Saudi Arabia." In Juan R. I. Cole and Nikki R. Keddie, eds., *Shiʿism and Social Protest*, 230–246. New Haven, Conn.: Yale University Press, 1986.

Haʾiri, Abdul Hadi. *Shiʿism and Constitutionalism in Iran.* Leiden: Brill, 1977.

Al-Hatlani, Ibrahim. *Al-Shiʿa al-Saʿudiyyun: Qiraʿa tarikhiyya wa siyasiya li-namadhij matlabiya* (The Shiʿa of Saudi Arabia: A Historical and Political Inquiry Into Patterns of Activism). Beirut: Riad al-Rayyes Books, 2009.

Herb, Michael. *All in the Family: Absolutism, Revolution, and Democracy in the Middle Eastern Monarchies.* New York: New York University Press, 1999.

———. "Kuwait: The Obstacle of Parliamentary Politics." In Joshua Teitelbaum, ed., *Political Liberalization in the Persian Gulf*, 133–156. New York: Columbia University Press, 2009.

———. "Subordinate Communities and the Utility of Ethnic Ties to a Neighboring Regime: Iran and the Shiʿa of the Arab States of the Gulf." In Leonard Binder, ed., *Ethnic Conflict and International Politics of the Middle East*, 155–180. Gainsville: University Press of Florida Press, 1999.

Ibrahim, Fouad. *The Shiʿis of Saudi Arabia.* London: Saqi Books, 2006.

Islamic Front for the Liberation of Bahrain (IFLB). *Tajribat 73 sajinan fi sujun al-Bahrayn* (The Experience of the 73 Prisoners in Bahraini Prison). N.p.: n.p., 1996. http://www.shaheed-bh.com/forumdisplay.php?f=169.

Khalaf, Abdalhadi, and Giacomo Luciani, eds. *Constitutional Reform and Political Participation in the Gulf.* Dubai: Gulf Research Center, 2006.

Khamenei, Ayatollah ʿAli. *Dawr wasaʾil al-aʿlam fi al-siraʿ al-siyasi wa al-thaqafi* (The Role of Media in Political and Cultural Conflict). Ed. Shaykh ʿAli Dhahir. Beirut: Dar al-Hadi, 2006.

Khuri, Fuad. *Tribe and State in Bahrain: The Transformation of Social and Political Authority in an Arab State.* Chicago: University of Chicago Press, 1980.

Kostiner, Joseph. "Shiʿi Unrest in the Gulf." In Martin Kramer, ed., *Shiʿism, Resistance, and Revolution*, 173–188. Boulder, Colo.: Westview Press, 1987.

Lacroix, Stéphane. *Awakening Islam: The Politics of Religious Dissent in Saudi Arabia.* Cambridge, Mass.: Harvard University Press, 2011.

Lawson, Fred H. "Repertoires of Contention in Contemporary Bahrain." In Quintan Wiktorowicz, ed., *Islamic Activism: A Social Movement Theory Approach*, 89–111. Bloomington: Indiana University Press, 2003.

Louër, Laurence. *Transnational Shi'a Politics: Religious and Political Networks in the Gulf.* London: Hurst, 2008.

Mahfouz, Muhammad, ed. *Al-hiwar al-madhhabi fi al-Mamlaka al-'Arabiyya al-Sa'udiyya* (Sectarian Dialogue in the Kingdom of Saudi Arabia). Qatif, Saudi Arabia: Atyaf lil-Nashr wa al-Tawzi', 2007.

Al-Maqdisi, Abu Muhammad. *Al-kawashif al-jaliyya fi kufr al-dawla al-Sa'udiyya* (Clear Evidence on the Infidel Nature of the Saudi State). 1991. http://www.tawhed.ws.

Al-Marhun, 'Abd al-Jalil Zaid. *Al-amn al-khaliji ba'd al-harb fi al-'Iraq* (Gulf Security After the Iraq War). Riyadh: Institute for Diplomatic Studies, 2005.

Matar, Gamil, and 'Ali al-Din al-Hilal Dessouki. *Al-nidham al-iqlimi al-'Arabi* (The Arab Regional Order). Beirut: Dar al-Mustaqbal al-'Arabi, 1983.

Al-Mdeires, Falah 'Abdallah. *Dirasat hawl al-harakat al-Islamiyya fi al-Bahrayn, 1938–2001* (Study of Islamic Movements in Bahrain, 1938–2001). Beirut: Dar al-Kunuz al-Adabiyya, 2004.

———. *Al-haraka al-Shi'iyya fi al-Kuwait* (The Shi'a Movement in Kuwait). Kuwait City: Dar Qurtas lil-Nashr, 1999.

———. *Jam'iyyat al-Ikhwan al-Muslimin fi al-Kuwayt* (Muslim Brotherhood Groups in Kuwait). Kuwait City: Dar Qurtas lil-Nashr, 1999.

———. *Al-jam'iyyat al-Salafiyya fi al-Kuwayt* (Salafi Groups in Kuwait). Kuwait City: Dar Qurtas lil-Nashr, 1999.

Meijer, Roel, ed. *Global Salafism: Islam's New Religious Movement.* New York: Columbia University Press, 2009.

Momen, Moojan. *An Introduction to Shi'i Islam: The History and Doctrines of Twelver Shi'ism.* New Haven, Conn.: Yale University Press, 1987.

Al-Najjar, Baquer. *Al-harakat al-diniyya fi al-Khalij al-'Arabi* (Religious Movements of the Arabian Gulf). Beirut: Dar al-Saqi, 2007.

Nakash, Yitzhak. *Reaching for Power: The Shi'a in the Modern Arab World.* Princeton, N.J.: Princeton University Press, 2006.

Nasir, Muhammad Shahatah. *Siyasat al-andhima al-hakima fi al-Bahrayn, wa al-Kuwayt, wa al-'Arabiyya al-Sa'udiyya fi al-ta'amul ma' al-matalib al-Shi'iyya (2003–2008): Dirasa muqarna* (The Policies of the Ruling Regimes in Bahrain, Kuwait, and Saudi Arabia in Dealing with Shi'a Demands [2003–2008]: A Comparative Study). Beirut: Markaz Dirasat al-Wahda al-'Arabiyya, 2011.

Nasr, Vali. *The Shi'a Revival: How Conflicts Within Islam Will Shape the Future.* London: Norton, 2007.

Niethammer, Katja. *Voices in Parliament, Debates in Majalis, and Banners on Streets: Avenues of Political Participation in Bahrain.* Mediterranean Programme Series no. 27. Montecatini, Italy: Robert Schuman Center for Advanced Studies, European University Institute, September 2006.

Nonneman, Gerd. "Analyzing the Foreign Policies of the Middle East and North Africa: A Conceptual Framework." In Gerd Nonneman, ed., *Analyzing Middle East Foreign Policies and the Relationship with Europe*, 6–18. New York: Routledge, 2005.

———. "Political Reform in the Gulf Monarchies: From Liberalization to Democratization? A Comparative Perspective." In Anoushiravan Ehteshami and Steven Wright, eds., *Reform in the Middle East Oil Monarchies*, 3–46. New York: Ithaca Press, 2008.

———. "Security and Inclusion: Regime Responses to Domestic Challenges in the Gulf." In Sean McKnight, Niel Partrick, and Francis Toase, eds., *Gulf Security: Opportunities and Challenges for the New Generation*, 107–117. London: Royal United Services Institute, September 2000.

Partrick, Neil. *Nationalism in the Gulf States*. London: Kuwait Programme on Development, Governance, and Globalisation in the Gulf States, London School of Economics, October 2009.

Peterson, J. E. "Bahrain: Reform, Promise, and Reality." In Joshua Teitelbaum, ed., *Political Liberalization in the Persian Gulf*, 157–186. New York: Columbia University Press, 2009.

Rabi, Uzi, and Joseph Kostiner. "The Shiʿis in Bahrain: Class and Religious Protest." In Ofra Bengio and Gabriel Ben-Dor, eds., *Minorities and the State in the Arab World*, 171–190. Boulder, Colo.: Lynne Rienner, 1999.

Ramazani, R. K. "Iran's Export of the Revolution: Politics, Ends, and Means." In John L. Esposito, ed., *The Iranian Revolution: Its Global Impact*, 40–62. Miami: Florida International University Press, 1990.

Roy, Olivier. *Globalized Islam: The Search for a New Ummah*. New York: Columbia University Press, 2004.

Al-Saffar, Hassan. *Al-madhhab wa al-watan* (Sect and Homeland). Beirut: al-Muʾassasa al-ʿArabiyya lil-Dirasat wa al-Nashr, 2006.

Saghiyah, Hazim. *Nawasib wa Rawafidh: Munazaʿat al-Sunna wa al-Shiʿa fi al-ʿalam al-Islami al-yawm* (Nawasib and Rawafidh: The Sunni-Shiʿa Confrontation in the Islamic World Today). Beirut: Dar al-Saqi, 2009.

Salamé, Ghassan. "Perceived Threats and Perceived Loyalties." In B. R. Pridham, ed., *The Arab Gulf and the Arab World*, 235–250. London: Croom Helm, 1988.

Salem, Paul. *Kuwait: Politics in a Participatory Emirate*. Washington, D.C.: Carnegie Endowment for International Peace, July 2007.

Salmoni, Barak, Bryce Loidolt, and Madeleine Wells. *Regime and Periphery in Northern Yemen: The Huthi Phenomenon*. Santa Monica, Calif.: RAND Corporation, 2010.

Al-Sayf, Tawfiq. *Nadhriyat al-Sulta fi Fiqh al-Shiʿi* (Theories of Political Power in Shiʿa Jurisprudence). Casablanca: Markaz al-Thaqafi al-ʿArabi, 2002.

Steinberg, Guido. "Jihadi Salafism and the Shi'is: Remarks About the Intellectual Roots of Anti-Shi'ism." In Roel Meijer, ed., *Global Salafism: Islam's New Religious Movement*, 107–125. New York: Columbia University Press, 2009.

——. "The Wahhabi Ulama and the Saudi State." In Paul Aarts and Gerd Nonneman, eds., *Saudi Arabia in the Balance: Political Economy, Society, and Foreign Affairs*, 11–34. New York: New York University Press, 2006.

Tétreault, Mary Ann. "Kuwait: Slouching Toward Democracy?" In Joshua Teitelbaum, ed., *Political Liberalization in the Persian Gulf*, 107–132. New York: Columbia University Press, 2009.

——. *Stories of Democracy: Politics and Society in Contemporary Kuwait*. New York: Columbia University Press, 2000.

Al-Wazzan, 'Abd al-Wahhab. *Hajis al-watan wa al-dawla* (The Concept of the Nation and the State). Kuwait City: Jamiya al-Haquq Mahfudha lil-Majmu'a, 2007.

Zahlan, Rosemary Said. *The Making of the Modern Gulf States*. London: Ithaca Press, 1988.

JOURNAL ARTICLES AND REPORTS

Aarts, Paul. *The Internal and the External: The House of Saud's Resilience Explained*. Working Paper no. 2004/332004. Montecatini, Italy: Robert Schuman Centre for Advanced Studies, European University Institute, 2004.

Aggestam, Lisbeth. *Role Conceptions and the Politics of Identity in Foreign Policy*. ARENA Working Papers. Oslo: Center for European Studies, April 28, 1999. http://www.sv.uio.no/arena/english/research/publications/arena-publications/workingpapers/working-papers1999/wp99_8.htm.

Alfoneh, Ali. *Between Reform and Revolution: Sheikh Qassim, the Bahraini Shi'a, and Iran*. Washington, D.C.: American Enterprise Institute, July 15, 2012.

Al-'Arab, Muhammad 'Izz. "Al-nukhba wa al-islah al-siyasi fi al-Bahrain" (The Elite and Choice of Political Reform in Bahrain). *Arab Journal of Democracy*, January 1, 2010, http://democracy.ahram.org.eg/News/147/%D8%A7%D9%84%D9%86%D8%AE%D8%A8%D8%A9-%D9%88%D8%A7%D9%84%D8%A7%D8%B5%D9%84%D8%A7%D8%AD-%D8%A7%D9%84%D8%B3%D9%8A%D8%A7%D8%B3%D9%8A-%D9%81%D9%8A-D8%A7%D9%84%D8%A8%D8%AD%D8%B1%D9%8A%D9%86.aspx.

Arab Reform Bulletin (Carnegie Endowment for International Peace). "Kuwait Ummah Party Formed," March 26, 2005, http://carnegieendowment.org/2008/08/26/kuwait-umma-party-formed/6dsp.

Bahry, Louay. "The Socioeconomic Foundations of the Shi'ite Opposition in Bahrain." *Mediterranean Quarterly* 11, no. 3 (2000): 129–143.

Burke, Edward. *Bahrain: Reaching a Threshold*. Working Paper no. 61. Madrid: Fundación para las Relaciones Internacionales y el Diálogo Exterior, June 2008.

Congressional Research Service. *Iraq: Regional Perspectives and U.S. Policy*. Washington, D.C.: Congressional Research Service, January 12, 2007. http://www.policyarchive.org/handle/10207/bitstreams/3064_Previous_Version_2007-01-12.pdf.

Democracy Reporting International and Kuwait Transparency Society. *Kuwait: Assessment of the Electoral Framework*. Berlin: Democracy Reporting International; Kuwait City: Kuwait Transparency Society, November 2008.

Doran, Michael Scott. "The Heirs of Nasser: Who Will Benefit from the Second Arab Revolution?" *Foreign Affairs* 90, no. 3 (2011): 17–25.

Dubai School of Government. *Arab Social Media Report*. Vol. 1, no.1. Dubai: Dubai School of Government, January 2011. http://www.dsg.ae/portals/0/ASMR%20Final%20May%208%20high.pdf.

Ehteshami, Anoushirvan. "Reform from Above: The Politics of Participation in the Oil Monarchies." *International Affairs* 79, no. 1 (2003): 53–75.

Gause, F. Gregory, III. "Bahrain Parliamentary Election Results: 25 November and 2 December 2006." *International Journal of Middle East Studies* 39 (May 2007): 170–171.

———. "Revolutionary Fevers and Regional Contagion: Domestic Structures and the 'Export' of Revolution in the Middle East." *Journal of South Asian and Middle Eastern Studies* 14, no. 3 (Spring 1991): 1–23.

———. "Saudi Arabia: Iraq, Iran, the Regional Power Balance, and the Sectarian Question." *Strategic Insights* 6, no. 2 (2007), http://www.isn.ethz.ch/isn/Digital-Library/Publications/Detail/?ots591=0c54e3b3-1e9c-be1e-2c24-a6a8c7060233&lng=en&id=30985.

———. "Threats and Threat Perception in the Gulf." *Middle East Policy* 14, no. 2 (2007): 119–124.

Gengler, Justin. *Bahrain's Sunni Awakening*. Middle East Research and Information Project (MERIP) report. Washington, D.C.: MERIP, January 17, 2012.

Gulf States Newsletter. "Interview with ʿAli Salman." 30, no. 795 (2006): 2.

Hagood, Anne. "The Narrative of Resistance: Bahrain and Iraq." *Arab Media and Society*, no. 13 (Summer 2011), http://www.arabmediasociety.com/?article=774.

Al-Hawali, Safar. "Dhahirat al-ʿirja" (The Phenomenon of Prevarication). Ph.D. diss., Umm al-Qura University, Mecca, 1985, http://www.tawhed.ws.

Hegghammer, Thomas. "Global Jihadism After the Iraq War." *Middle East Journal* 11, no. 60 (2006): 11–32.

Herb, Michael. "Emirs and Parliaments in the Gulf." *Journal of Democracy* 13, no. 4 (October 2002): 41–47.

Human Rights Watch. *Denied Dignity: Systematic Discrimination and Hostility Toward Saudi Shiʿa Citizens*. New York: Human Rights Watch, September 2009.

———. "Testimony of Tom Malinowski Before the Tom Lantos Human Rights Commission on the Implementation of the *Bahrain Independent Commission of Inquiry Report*." August 1, 2012, http://tlhrc.house.gov/docs/transcripts/2012_08_01_Bahrain/08_01_12_Bahrain.pdf.

International Crisis Group (ICG). *Bahrain's Sectarian Challenge*. ICG Middle East Report no. 40. Brussels: ICG, May 6, 2005. http://www.crisisgroup.org/~/media/Files/Middle%20East%20North%20Africa/Iran%20Gulf/Bahrain/Bahrains%20Sectarian%20Challenge.pdf.

———. *Popular Protests in North Africa and the Middle East: The Bahrain Revolt*. Middle East/North Africa Report no. 105. Brussels: ICG, April 6, 2011.

———. *Popular Protests in North Africa and the Middle East: Bahrain's Rocky Road to Reform*. Middle East/North Africa Report no. 111. Brussels: ICG, July 28, 2011.

———. *Saudi Arabia Backgrounder: Who Are the Islamists?* ICG Middle East Report no. 31. Brussels: ICG, 2004.

Al-Jamri, Mansoor. "The Shiʿa and the State in Bahrain: Integration and Tension." *Alternative Politics*, special issue (November 2010): 1–24.

———. "State and Civil Society in Bahrain." *Society for Gulf Arab Studies Newsletter* 9, no. 1 (2000), http://bahrain.wikia.com/wiki/State_and_Civil_Society_in_Bahrain.

Jones, Toby Craig. "The Clerics, the *Sahwa*, and the Saudi State." *Strategic Insights* 4, no. 3 (2005), http://www.ccc.nps.navy.mil/si/2005/Mar/jonesMar05.asp.

———. "The Iraq Effect in Saudi Arabia." *Middle East Report* 237 (Winter 2005): 20–25.

———. "Rebellion on the Saudi Periphery: Modernity, Marginalization, and the Shiʿa Uprising of 1979." *International Journal of Middle East Studies* 38 (2006): 213–233.

———. "Saudi Arabia's Not So New Anti-Shiʿism." *Middle East Report* 242 (Spring 2007): 29–32.

Kareem, Mona. "Kuwait's Prime Ministerial Dilemma and the Prospects for Constitutional Monarchy." *Arab Reform Bulletin* (Carnegie Endowment for International Peace), June 22, 2011. http://carnegieendowment.org/2011/06/22/kuwait-s-prime-ministerial-dilemma-and-prospects-for-constitutional-monarchy/6b7n.

Katzman, Kenneth. *Kuwait: Security, Reform, and U.S. Policy*. Washington, D.C.: Congressional Research Service, December 9, 2009.

Knysh, Alexander. "Contextualizing the Salafi–Sufi Conflict (from the Northern Caucasus to Hadramawt)." *Middle Eastern Studies* 43, no. 4 (2007): 503–530.

Lacroix, Stéphane. "Saudi Arabia's New 'Islamo-Liberal' Reformers." *Middle East Journal* 58, no. 3 (2004): 345–365.

Longva, Anh Nga. "Nationalism in Pre-modern Guise: The Discourse on *Hadhar* and *Badu* in Kuwait." *International Journal of Middle East Studies* 38 (2006): 171–187.

Matthiesen, Tobias. "Hizbullah al-Hijaz: A History of the Most Radical Saudi Shiʿa Opposition Group." *Middle East Journal* 64, no. 2 (2010): 179–197.

———. "The Shiʿa of Saudi Arabia at the Crossroads," *Middle East Report Online*, May 6, 2009, http://www.merip.org/mero/mero050609.

McCants, William F. *Militant Ideology Atlas*. West Point, N.Y.: Combatting Terrorism Center, November 2006. http://www.ctc.usma.edu/wp-content/uploads/2010/06/Atlas-ResearchCompendium1.pdf.

Al-Mdeires, Falah ʿAbdallah. "Shiʿism and Political Protest in Bahrain." *Digest of Middle East Studies* 11, no. 1 (2002): 20–44.

Melly, Paul. "Religious Rights and Political Enfranchisement Provide the Basis of a New Compact with the Shiʿa." 27, no. 23 (2005): 8–9.

Nakash, Yitzhak. "The Shiʿites and the Future of Iraq." *Foreign Affairs* 82, no. 4 (2003): 17–26.

Okruhlik, Gwenn. "Networks of Dissent: Islamism and Reform in Saudi Arabia." *Current History*, January 2002: 22–28.

Oxford Analytica Brief. "Bahrain: Yemen's Rebellion Adds to Sectarian Tensions." January 12, 2010, http://www.oxan.com/display.aspx?ItemID=DB156920.

Peterson, J. E. "Bahrain's First Steps Toward Reform Under Emir Hamad." *Asian Affairs* (London) 33, part 2 (June 2002): 216–227.

Al-Qahtani, Saʿud. "Al-Sahwa al-Islamiyya" (The Islamic Awakening). *Gulf Issues*, December 23, 2003, http://www.gulfissues.net/mpage/gulfarticles/article53-1.htm.

Al-Rasheed, Madawi. "The Shiʿa of Saudi Arabia: A Minority in Search of Cultural Authenticity." *British Journal of Middle Eastern Studies* 25, no. 1 (May 1998): 121–138.

Rizvi, Sajjad H. "Shiʿism in Bahrain: Marjaʿiyya and Politics." *Orient* 4 (2009): 16–24.

Al-Salem, Faisal. "The Issue of Identity in Selected Arab Gulf States." *Journal of South Asian and Middle Eastern Studies* 4 (Summer 1981): 21–32.

Tariq al-Hasan, Hasan. "The Role of Iran in the Failed Coup of 1981: The IFLB in Bahrain." *Middle East Journal* 65, no. 4 (2011): 603–617.

Teitelbaum, Joshua. "Saudi Arabia Faces a Changing Middle East." *Middle East Review of International Affairs* 15, no. 3 (2011), http://www.gloria-center.org/2011/10/saudi-arabia-faces-a-changing-middle-east/.

Tétreault, Mary Ann. "Frankenstein's Lament in Kuwait." *Foreign Policy in Focus*, November 29, 2001, http://www.fpif.org/articles/frankensteins_lament_in_kuwait.

———. "Kuwait's Annus Mirabilis." *Middle East Report Online*, September 7, 2006, http://www.fpif.org/articles/frankensteins_lament_in_kuwait.

Al-Ubaykan, ʿAbd al-Muhsin. "Saudi Shura Council Member Sheikh al-ʿObikan: According to Shariʿa Hizbullah Operations Are Illegitimate; a Temporary Peaceful Settlement with Jews Is Needed." Middle East Media Research Institute (MEMRI), Special Dispatch no. 1222, August 1, 2006, http://www.memri.org.

Ulrichsen, Kristian Coates. "Internal and External Security in the Gulf." *Middle East Policy* 16, no. 2 (2009): 39–58.

United Nations Development Program (UNDP). *Program on Governance in the Arab World*. Paris: UNDP, May 2008. http://www.pogar.org/countries/civil.asp ?cid=2.

U.S. Department of State. *International Religious Freedom Report: Kuwait*. Washington, D.C.: U.S. Department of State, 2010. http://www.state.gov/g/drl/rls/ irf/2010/148828.htm.

———. *Saudi Arabia: Report on International Religious Freedom*. Washington, D.C.: U.S. Department of State, 2010. http://www.state.gov/g/drl/rls/irf/2010/ 148843.htm.

Valbjørn, Morten, and André Bank. "Signs of a New Arab Cold War: The 2006 Lebanon War and the Sunni–Shiʿi Divide." *Middle East Report* 242 (Spring 2007): 6–11.

Wehrey, Frederic. "Bahrain: Elections and Managing Sectarianism." *Arab Reform Bulletin* (Carnegie Endowment for International Peace), December 2006, http:// www.carnegieendowment.org/files/wehrey.pdf.

———. "The March of Bahrain's Hardliners." Carnegie Endowment for International Peace, May 31, 2012, http://carnegieendowment.org/2012/05/31/ march-of-bahrain-s-hardliners/bozr.

———. "The Precarious Ally: Bahrain's Impasse and U.S. Policy." Carnegie Endowment for International Peace, February 2013, http://www.carnegieendowment .org/2013/02/06/precarious-ally-bahrain-s-impasse-and-u.s.-policy/fayg.

———. *Saudi Arabia Reins in Its Clerics on Syria*. Washington, D.C.: Carnegie Endowment for International Peace, June 14, 2012.

———. "Uprisings Jolt the Saudi–Iranian Rivalry." *Current History* 110 (December 2011): 352–357.

Yamani, Mai. "The Rise of Shiʿa Petrolistan." Project Syndicate, March 3, 2004, http://www.project-syndicate.org/commentary/the-rise-of-shia-petrolistan.

CONFERENCE PROCEEDINGS

Al-Ekri, ʿAbd al-Nabi. "Bahrain: Reform Project: Prospect and Limitations." Paper presented at the Sixth Mediterranean Social and Political Research Meeting, Robert Schuman Centre for Advanced Studies, European University Institute, Montecatini, Italy, March 16–20, 2005.

Khalaf, Abdulhadi. "Contentious Politics in Bahrain: From Ethnic to National and Vice Versa." Paper presented at the Fourth Nordic Conference on Middle Eastern Studies, "The Middle East in a Globalizing World," Oslo, August 13–16, 1998, http://www.smi.uib.no/pao/khalaf.html.

Niethammer, Katja. "Stubborn Salafis and Moderate Shiʿa: Islamic Political Parties in Bahrain." Paper presented at the International Studies Association Forty-eighth Annual Convention, Chicago, February 28, 2007.

NEWSPAPERS AND OTHER MEDIA

Al-Aafaq (United States)
Agence France Presse
Al-Ahram Weekly (Egypt)
Al-Akhbar (Lebanon)
Akhbar al-Khalij (Bahrain)
Al-Anbaʾ Online (Kuwait)
Al-ʿArabiya (television) (Saudi Arabia)
Arab News (Saudi Arabia)
Arab Times (Kuwait)
Associated Press
Atlantic Monthly
Al-Ayyam (Bahrain)
Bahrain Mirror
Bahrain News Agency
BBC Monitoring Middle East
BBC News
BBC World Monitoring
BBC World News
Bloomberg
Al-Boraq Islamic Forum
Christian Science Monitor
Daily Star (Lebanon)
Al-Dar (Kuwait)
Dera News (Twitter)
Al-Elaph (London based, Saudi owned)
Financial Times
Foreign Affairs
Foreign Policy
The Guardian
Gulf Daily News (Bahrain)
Gulf News (United Arab Emirates)
Al-Hayat (London, Saudi owned)
Al-Hurra (television) (U.S. based)

The Independent
Jadaliyya (Arab Studies Institute)
Al-Jaridah (Kuwait)
Al-Jazeera (television, Qatar)
Al-Jazirah (Saudi Arabia)
Khaleej Times (United Arab Emirates)
Kuwait News Agency
Kuwait Times
Al-Madina (Saudi Arabia)
Majallat al-ʿAsr
Al-Manar (television) (Lebanon)
The Media Line
Middle East Online
Al-Mokhtsar (Saudi Arabia)
Muftah
Al-Nahar (Kuwait)
New York Times
NOW Lebanon
Al-Qabas (Kuwait)
Al-Quds al-ʿArabi (U.K.-based Arabic paper)
The Peninsula (Qatar)
Al-Rasid (news service, Saudia Arabia)
Al-Raʾy (Kuwait)
Reuters
Reporters sans Frontieres (Paris)
Right Vision News
Al-Risalah (Saudi-funded Islamic TV)
Al-Riyadh (Saudi Arabia)
Sada (Carnegie Endowment Middle East Program, formerly *Arab Reform Bulletin*)
Saudi Gazette
Saudi Press Agency
Al-Seyassah (Kuwait)
Al-Sharq al-Awsat (Saudi Arabia)
Tehran Times
al-Ukhdud (Saudi Arabia)
United Press International
Wall Street Journal
Al-Waqt (Bahrain)
Al-Wasat (Bahrain)
Washington Post
Washington Times

Al-Watan (Bahrain)
World Bulletin
Xinhua General News Service
Al-Yaum (Saudi Arabia)

WEBSITES

Al-Amarah News Network, http://www.al3marh.net/news
Al-Anwar television, http://www.alanwartv.com
Al-Bainah, http://www.albainah.net
D-Sunnah, http://www.d-sunnah.net
Facebook, http://www.facebook.com
Al-Hramain, http://www.alhramain.com
Ikhwanonline, http://www.ikhwanonline.com
IslamOnline, http://www.islamonline.com
Islam Today, http://www.islamtoday.net
Islamway, http://www.islamway.com
Al-Jazira al-ʿArabiya, http://www.aljazeeraalarabianews.com
Khomainy, http://www.khomainy.com
Markaz al-Haramayn lil-ʿAlam al-Islami, http://www.alhramain.com/hrmin/
    index.php
Al-Meer, http://www.almeer.net
Al-Multaqa, http://www.multaqa.org
Al-Muslim, http://www.almoslim.net
Nahrain, http://www.nahrain.com/ar/ or http://www.nahrainnet.net
Nur al-Islam, http://nuralislam.com
Al-Qatrah, http://www.alqatrah.net; the English version of this site is the Drop,
    http://www.the-drop.net
Saudi Ministry of Interior, http://www.moi.gov.sa
Al-Saffar, http://www.al-saffar.org
Al-Sakifah, http://www.alsakifah.org
ShiaPost, http://en.shiapost.com
Shiavoice, http://www.shiavoice.com
Al-Tawafuq, http://www.walfajr.net/?act=writers&id=159&t=1
Twitter, http://www.twitter.com
Al-Wifaq, http://www.alwefaq.net
Al-Wylish, http://www.wylsh.com
Al-Zahra television, http://www.alzahra.tv

INDEX

seminary (*hawza* initiative), 114; relationships with external *maraji'* inflated by local clerics, 55, 163, 166–67, 211; and Saudi Qatifis, 24; and Saudi Shi'a, 106, 112–15; transnational authority as obstacle to Shi'a integration, xv, 8, 17

al-Marzuq, Khalil, 46, 97

al-Matruk, 'Ali, 163–64

al-Ma'tuk, Husayn, 168, 171, 181, 183

media, x, xiv. *See also* newspapers; social media; television stations; *and following headings*

media (Bahrain), 245–46n46; crackdown on, 11, 75, 85–87; media campaigns against opposition, 73, 85–87; newspapers, 70, 86, 144, 239n26, 245–46n46; television stations, 86. *See also* social media (Bahrain)

media (Iran), 25, 26, 86

media (Kuwait), 37; crackdown on, 167, 173, 188–89, 192, 194; liberal nature of, 19, 161; as mixed blessing, 218; newspapers, 194, 195; sectarian media wars, 165–66; television stations, 165–66

media (Lebanon), 86, 245–46n46, 259–60n52

media (Saudi Arabia): crackdown on, 145; media campaigns against protestors, 144–45; newspapers, 144; television stations, 85–86, 245–46n46

Medina riots of 2009, 119–21, 210, 217

al-Mhayshi, Nasser, 147

al-Milad, Zaki, 108

al-Minbar, 53, 59, 212–13; and al-Asala, 62–63; and debate forums (Muntadayat), 66–67; and fracturing of Sunni opposition, 97–98; leadership, 59–60; membership, 59, 62; and negotiations of 2011, 89; and NUG, 79; platform, 59–60; and siege of Fallujah, 69

Montazeri, Muhammad, 26, 32

mourning houses, 29, 36

Movement of Vanguards' Missionaries (MVM), 26, 32

Mubarak, Hosni, 82

al-Mubarak, Masuma, 292n51

al-Mudarrisi, Hadi, 26, 29, 30, 94, 117, 118

al-Mudarrisi, Muhammad Taqi, 32, 37, 166

Mughniyah, 'Imad, 37, 173, 175, 180–84

al-Muhammad, Nasser (former prime minister of Kuwait), 287n60

Muhammad bin Abi Bakr Mosque, 164

al-Muhri, 'Abbas, 26, 35, 36

al-Muhri, Muhammad Baqir, 160–61, 163, 164, 280n29; and ban on *diwaniya*, 189; and fracturing of Shi'a community, 170; and al-Sistani, 161, 163, 167, 211

al-Mulayfi, Muhammad, 200

Muntadayat (debate forums; Bahrain), 66–67

al-Musawi, Hadi, 90, 237n9

Mushayma, Hassan, 45, 46, 49, 70, 81, 96

Muslim Brotherhood, xi, 176; and Bahrain, 59, 227n32 (*see also* al-Minbar); and Kuwait, 175–77 (*see also* HADAS); and Saudi Arabia, 14, 124 (*see also* Sahwa)

mut'a (temporary marriage), 166

al-Mutawa', 'Adnan, 162

al-Mutayr (tribe), 197, 205, 284n32, 291n31

al-Mutayr, Muhammad, 186

al-Mutayri, Hakim, 178, 284n32